Topic review

Wesentliche Fakten werden zur Wiederholung, Erweiterung und Prüfungsvorbereitung dargelegt.

Topic project

Erworbene Kompetenzen werden in einer komplexen Lernaufgabe angewendet.

Exam practice

Musterprüfungen dienen dem Training zentraler Prüfungsformate.

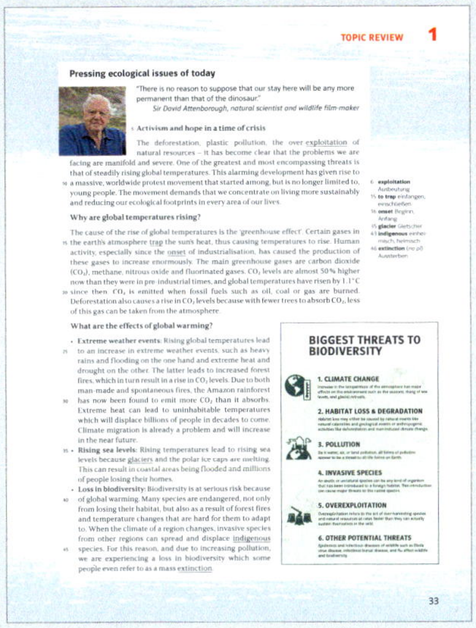
TOPIC REVIEW 1

Pressing ecological issues of today

"There is no reason to suppose that our stay here will be any more permanent than that of the dinosaur."
Sir David Attenborough, natural scientist and wildlife film-maker

Why are global temperatures rising?

What are the effects of global warming?

BIGGEST THREATS TO BIODIVERSITY

1. CLIMATE CHANGE
2. HABITAT LOSS & DEGRADATION
3. POLLUTION
4. INVASIVE SPECIES
5. OVEREXPLOITATION
6. OTHER POTENTIAL THREATS

33

1 TOPIC PROJECT

Sustainable Europe: A film project

32

EXAM PRACTICE 1

1 Lesen und Schreiben

Prince Charles's speech at the World Economic Forum 2020 in Davos, Switzerland

35

Anhang

Mediation workshops:
Gezieltes Training von Sprachmittlung

Helping hand:
Hilfestellungen zu Aufgaben in den Topics

Skills files:
Alle wichtigen Kompetenzen im Überblick

Grammar files:
Kompaktgrammatik zum Nachschlagen und Lernen

Vocabulary:
Chronologische Vokabellisten zu den Topics

Symbole

○ Differenzierung: leichter Text

→ ○ Verweis auf Helping hand im Anhang

● Differenzierung: schwieriger Text bzw. schwierige Aufgabe

Partnerarbeit

Gruppenarbeit

MK Hinweis zur Medienkompetenz

→ S 3 Verweis auf die *Skills files*

→ G 4 Verweis auf die *Grammar files*

→ WB p. 1 Verweis auf das Workbook Challenge, Jahrgangstufen 1 und 2

A Audio

V Video

I interaktiv

D Dokument

Alle Audios, Videos, interaktive Übungen und Dokumente zum Schulbuch finden Sie in den Medien zum Schulbuch und im eBook.

INHALTSVERZEICHNIS

	Themen	Kompetenzschwerpunkte	
	Abiturvorbereitung – Ihr Weg zum Abitur		10
TOPIC 1	**Ecological issues**		12
Getting started	Talking about resources	Working with an infographic • Listening • Discussion • Writing an email	13
Text workshop	**A How to feed the world** Going vegan: can switching to a plant-based diet really save the planet? (newspaper article)	Working with a picture • Working with a diagram • Reading for gist • Reading for detail • Words matter • Discussion • Listening • Writing a personal letter	14
Skills workshop	Writing a speech		18
Text workshop	**B Facing climate change** What a Dutch court ruling means for Shell and Big Oil (online article)	Reading for gist • Reading for detail • Focus on analysis • Writing a speech • Working with a diagram • Giving a presentation • Creating a flyer	20
Grammar workshop	Talking about ability, permission, necessity	Modal auxiliaries	24
Text workshop	**C The blue planet** A 52-year-old man is swimming through the Pacific Garbage Patch. (online article)	Working with an infographic • Scanning • Reading for detail • Words matter • Focus on grammar • Writing a comment • Working with a video • Creating an informative handout	25
Text workshop	**D Water shortage** Dry *by Neil and Jarrod Shusterman* (extract from a novel)	Conducting a survey • Reading for gist • Reading for detail • Focus on analysis • Writing a diary entry • Discussion • Project	29
Topic project	Sustainable Europe: a film project	Making a film	32
Topic review	Pressing ecological issues of today		33
Exam practice	Prince Charles's speech at the World Economic Forum 2020 in Davos, Switzerland (extract from a speech)	Lesen und Schreiben Hörverstehen Kommunikation	35
TOPIC 2	**Science and technology**		38
Getting started	Talking about technology	Working with pictures • Discussion • Listening	39
Text workshop	**A A smarter world** Data for the people: How to make our post-privacy economy work for you, *by Andreas Weigend* (extract from a non-fiction book)	Reading for gist • Reading for detail • Focus on analysis • Writing an email • Working with a video • Project	40
Text workshop	**B Benefits of innovative technologies** Revolutionary technologies will drive African prosperity – this is why (online article)	Reading for gist • Reading for detail • Words matter • Focus on analysis • Writing a comment • Working with a diagram • Role play • Listening • Working with a cartoon • Project	43

Grammar workshop	Talking about processes	The Passive	47
Skills workshop	Analysing the structure of a non-fictional text		48
Text workshop	**C Genetic engineering** Gene editing will let us control our very evolution. Will we use it wisely? (newspaper article)	Reading for gist • Reading for detail • Focus on analysis • Writing a blog post • Focus on grammar • Online research • Words matter • Working with a cartoon • Listening • Working with a diagram	50
Text workshop	**D Surveillance and state control** Inversion *by Colin Neville* (extract from a short story)	Reading for gist • Reading for detail • Words matter • Focus on analysis • Writing a letter • Working with a chart • Project	54
Topic project	Analysing a film / series about the future	Working with a video • Analysing and presenting a film/series • Writing a review	58
Topic review	Opportunities and challenges of modern technologies and interconnected societies		59
Exam practice	Helsinki's huge VR gig hints at the potential of virtual tourism (newspaper article)	Lesen und Schreiben Hörverstehen	61

TOPIC 3 Consumerism 64

Getting started	Talking about shopping habits	Working with pictures • Listening • Discussion	65
Text workshop	**A Shopping addiction** Confessions of a 20-something man who found solace in online shopping (addiction) & overcame it (magazine article)	Reading for gist • Reading for detail • Replying to readers' reactions • Project • Working with a cartoon	66
Text workshop	**B Sustainable consumption** A guide to the language of sustainable fashion (newspaper article)	Reading for gist • Reading for detail • Words matter • Listening • Online research • Project • Writing an email	70
Text workshop	**C Working in advertising** Copygirl *by Anna Mitchael and Michelle Sassa* (extract from a novel)	Reading for gist • Reading for detail • Words matter • Focus on analysis • Writing a diary entry • Working with a cartoon • Listening • Working with a video	73
Skills workshop	Working with advertisements		76
Text workshop	**D Brands with purpose** The power of purpose: How taking a stand helps brands to win customers' hearts (online article)	Reading for gist • Reading for detail • Words matter • Focus on analysis • Listening	78
Topic project	Creating a marketing campaign	Create a campaign • Discussion	81

Topic review	The birth of modern consumerism Consumerism today		82
Exam practice	When too much stuff gets in the way of all the good stuff (online article)	Lesen und Schreiben Hörverstehen Kommunikation	84
TOPIC 4	**Land of dreams?**		88
Getting started	Talking about the USA in the past and present	Working with pictures • Listening • Working with a video • Giving a talk	89
Text workshop	**A Shaping the USA** 'Hamilton', the musical now in Canada, tells the story of America's founding passions (online article)	Reading for gist • Words matter • Reading for detail • Focus on analysis • Writing a comment • Listening • Creating a timeline	90
Text workshop	**B Dreaming the American Dream** Call me American *by Abdi Nor Iftin* (extract from a novel)	Reading for gist • Reading detail • Focus on analysis • Working with a graphic novel • Writing a dialogue • Listening	94
Skills workshop	Analysing style, tone and register		98
Text workshop	**C Space and innovation** The space race is back on – but who will win? (newspaper article)	Reading for gist • Reading for detail • Focus on analysis • Writing a letter • Working with diagrams	99
Text workshop	**D The USA and the world** Remarks by President Biden on America's Place in the World (extract from a speech)	Words matter • Reading for gist • Reading for detail • Focus on analysis • Listening	102
Topic project	The USA seen from abroad – Creating a podcast	Plan and record a podcast • Conducting a survey • Writing a script	106
Topic review	The promised land?		107
Exam practice	Americans reflect on a divided nation: "This doesn't feel like America" (online article)	Lesen und Schreiben Hörverstehen	110
TOPIC 5	**The UK and its people**		112
Getting started	Talking about the UK	Working with pictures • Listening • Working with a cartoon • Discussion	113
Text workshop	**A English and its regional varieties** If you can't embrace regional dialect, you can kiss my chuddies (newspaper article)	Reading for gist • Words matter • Reading for detail • Focus on analysis • Writing a letter to the editor • Working with a graph • Discussion	114

	Themen	Kompetenzschwerpunkte	
Text workshop	B **National identity** 'The Great British Bake Off' can win any culture war (online article)	Scanning • Reading for detail • Words matter • Working with videos • Writing a blog post	117
Skills workshop	Working with maps		121
Text workshop	C **History from another perspective** Blonde Roots *by Bernadine Evaristo* (extract from a novel)	Scanning • Reading for detail • Words matter • Focus on analysis • Working with a map • Discussion	123
Text workshop	D **Food poverty in the UK** 'Protect the vulnerable': Marcus Rashford's emotional letter to MPs (extract from a letter)	Reading for gist • Reading for detail • Words matter • Focus on analysis • Writing an informative handout • Working with a video • Working with a cartoon	127
Topic project	Staging a talk show	Preparing, staging and reflecting a talk show	131
Topic review	A brief history of the British Empire The influence of the past on today's Britain		132
Exam practice	Ethnic diversity makes Britain's culture great. It would be a disaster if we lost it (newspaper article)	Lesen und Schreiben Hörverstehen	134

TOPIC 6	**Diverse identities**		136
Getting started	Talking about diverse identities	Working with pictures • Listening • Discussion	137
Text workshop	A **Challenging identities** The Vanishinhg Half *by Brit Bennett* (extract from a novel)	Reading for gist • Reading for detail • Words matter • Focus on analysis • Writing a comment • Discussion • Working with a video	138
Text workshop	B **Diversity in gender** Changing more than pronouns: a non-binary teen fights education laws (newspaper article)	Reading for gist • Reading for detail • Words matter • Focus on analysis • Writing a personal letter • Working with a video • Online research	142
Grammar workshop	Talking about conditions	If-clauses	145
Text workshop	C **Two worlds?** The Big Sick (extract from a screenplay)	Reading for gist • Reading for detail • Focus on grammar • Focus on analysis • Writing a comment • Working with pictures • Project	146
Text workshop	D **Invisible identity?** My employer made me feel my depression was invalid (blog post)	Reading for gist • Reading for detail • Words matter • Focus on analysis • Writing a letter • Project • Working with a cartoon	150
Topic project	Talking about stereotypes	Create a poster about stereotypes	154

INHALTSVERZEICHNIS

	Themen	Kompetenzschwerpunkte	
Topic review	All men are created equal?		155
Exam practice	Shared skin colour doesn't equal connection (online article)	Lesen und Schreiben Hörverstehen	157

TOPIC 7	**Issues of globalisation**		160
Getting started	Talking about globalisation	Working with pictures • Listening • Working with quotes	161
Text workshop	**A Global work** Transmission by *Hari Kunzru* (extract from a novel)	Reading for gist • Reading for detail • Focus on analysis • Writing a personal email • Listening • Giving a presentation • Writing an argumentative essay	162
Skills workshop	**Writing a blog post**		165
Text workshop	**B Working across cultures** Working across countries and cultures: collaboration tips and tricks (blog post)	Reading for gist • Words matter • Reading for detail • Focus on analysis • Writing a blog post • Working with pictures • Project	167
Text workshop	**C Global trade** Today's global economy runs on standardized shipping containers, as the Ever Given fiasco illustrates (online article)	Reading for gist • Reading for detail • Words matter • Focus on analysis • Working with a video • Role play	171
Text workshop	**D Global economy?** "Doughnut economic" model arrives in California (online article)	Reading for gist • Reading for detail • Words matter • Focus on analysis • Giving a recommendation	175
Topic project	A survey on English as a company language	Conducting and presenting a survey • Writing a formal email	179
Topic review	Different faces of globalisation		180
Exam practice	Experienced planner with talent for improvisation (online article)	Lesen und Schreiben Hörverstehen Kommunikation	182

TOPIC 8	**The world of work**		186
Getting started	Talking about the world of work	Working with pictures • Listening • Working with a chart	187
Text workshop	**A Why do we work?** How much is enough? *by Robert Skidelsky and Edward Skideslky* (extract from a non-fiction book)	Reading for gist • Reading for detail • Words matter • Focus on analysis • Writing an email • Listening	188

Text workshop	**B A fair wage** One wage by Rosalyn Kelly (extract from a short story)	Reading for gist • Reading for detail • Words matter • Focus on analysis • Writing a personal letter • Listening	191
Grammar workshop	Talking about likes and dislikes	Gerund	194
Text workshop	**C Inequality at work** Gender pay gap begins for students straight after university (newspaper article)	Reading for gist • Reading for detail • Words matter • Focus on analysis • Working with an infographic • Writing an email • Online research • Focus on grammar • Listening • Working with a cartoon	195
Text workshop	**D Workforce of the future** What the world can learn from Japan's robots (online article)	Reading for gist • Reading for detail • Words matter • Focus on analysis • Writing an argumentative essay • Giving a presentation • Discussion • Working with a video	199
Topic project	Designing a social media job advert		203
Topic review	The world of work now and then		204
Exam practice	Forget stereotypes … how to recruit talented, neurodiverse employees (newspaper article)	Lesen und Schreiben Hörverstehen Kommunikation	206

Anhang

Mediation workshops	210
Operatoren	216
Helping hand	217
Skills files	235
Grammar files	280
Vocabulary	298
Irregular verbs	341
Map UK	344
Map USA	345

Ihr Weg zum Abitur

Hörverstehen:

Die Abiturprüfung umfasst Aufgaben zur Überprüfung des Hörverstehens.
– Aufgabenformate: z.B. Mehrfachwahl-, Zuordnungsaufgaben, Kurzantworten

In *Challenge* finden Sie Aufgaben zum Training des Hörverstehens an verschiedenen Stellen der Topics. Zusätzlich zum Schulbuch finden Sie auch im Workbook viele *Listening*-Aufgaben.

Leseverstehen:

Im Abitur bearbeiten Sie auf Grundlage eines Textes die folgenden Schwerpunkte:

- **Integrierte Aufgabe zum Leseverstehen**
  - Wiedergabe relevanter inhaltlicher Aspekte gemäß Aufgabenstellung
  - Operatoren: z.B. outline, describe, summarise, state, illustrate

- **Textanalyse**
  - Schreiben einer kohärenten und strukturierten Analyse (z.B. das Herausarbeiten der rhetorischen Mittel und deren Wirkung)
  - Operatoren: z.B. analyse, examine

- **Erörterung/Stellungnahme**
  - Zur Auswahl stehen eine argumentierende/bewertende oder eine kreative Schreibaufgabe (z.B. ein Kommentar, ein Blogeintrag oder eine Rede)
  - Operatoren: z.B. comment on, evaluate, discuss, compare … to, write)

In *Challenge* finden Sie Aufgaben zu diesen Bereichen unter „Reading for detail/gist", „Focus on analysis" und „Writing …". Zusätzlich gibt es im Schulbuch neben diesen Aufgaben Verweise *(Self-check)* auf digitale Selbsteinschätzungstests und interaktive Übungen.

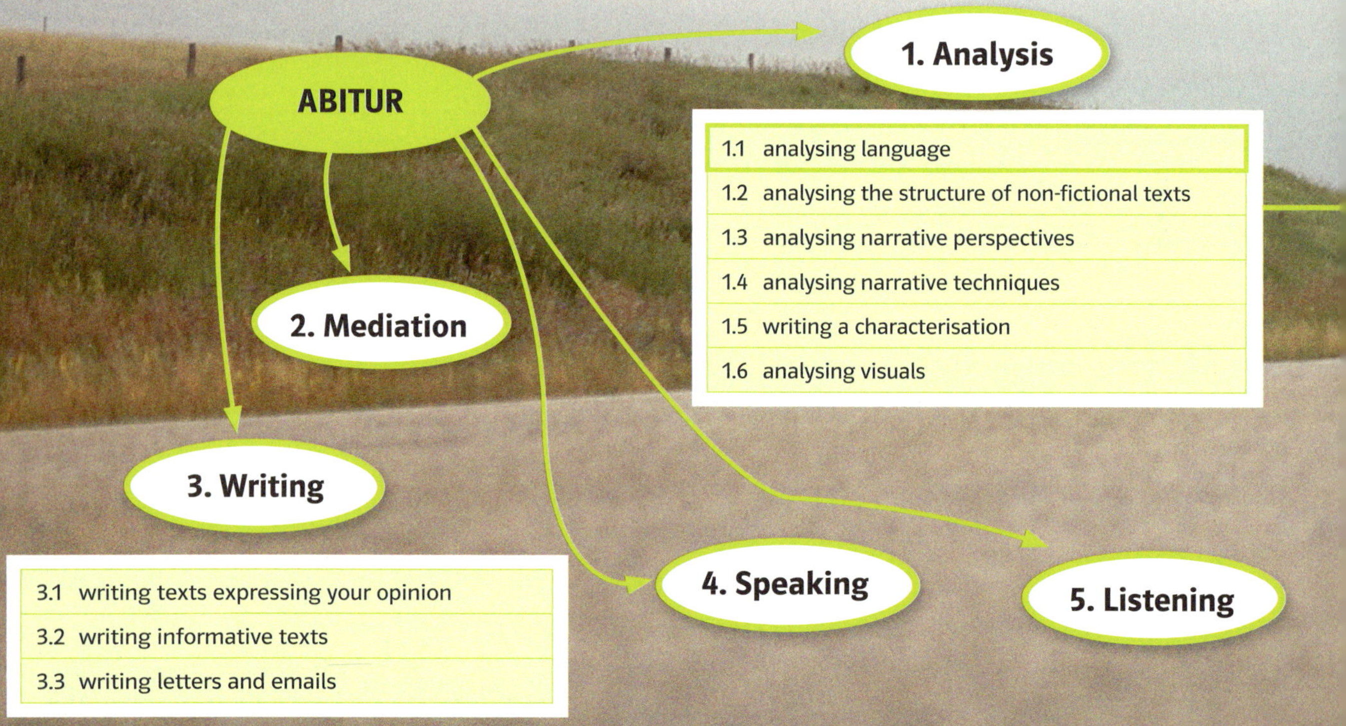

Kommunikation:

Zudem werden Sie in der Abiturprüfung an einer Kommunikationsprüfung teilnehmen. Diese kann als Einzel- oder Tandemprüfung stattfinden.
Mit einer Vielzahl an visuellen Impulsen bereitet *Challenge* auf diesen Prüfungsteil vor.

So gehen Sie vor

Lesen Sie zunächst die Aufgabe im Schulbuch und die entsprechenden **Skills files**.
Versuchen Sie dann, die Aufgabe im Schulbuch zu lösen.
Wie schätzen Sie sich dabei ein? In den Medien zum Schulbuch finden Sie in den Rubriken der jeweiligen Schulbuchkapitel Selbsteinschätzungstests und interaktive Übungen.

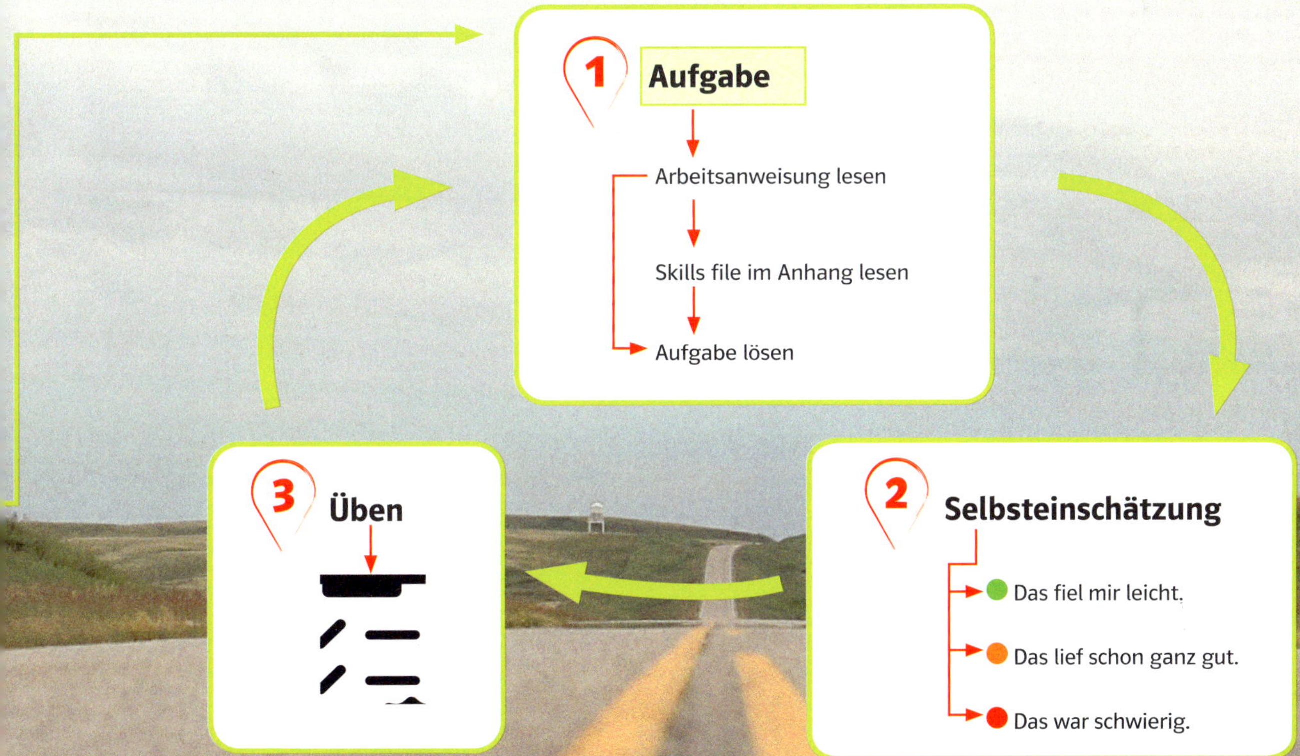

Ihren Wortschatz können Sie mit Hilfe des **Vocabulary** im Anhang des Schulbuchs erweitern.
Wenn Sie unsicher sind im Umgang mit der Grammatik, finden Sie passende Erklärfilme und Übungen in den Medien zum Schulbuch.

Ecological issues

A

B

C

D

1 Look at the pictures and collect ideas on how they might relate to the title of this topic.

2 Read the information below. Discuss with a partner which challenges the projected growth of the world population might bring. Share your ideas in class.

The **world population** keeps growing. In 2021 there were 7.9 billion people living on the earth. In 2050, there will be an estimated 9.74 billion.

GOOD TO KNOW

natural resources
= substances that occur naturally and are useful for humans (e.g. gold, coal, oil, arable land, forests, wildlife)

MK **3** Look at the infographic of Country Overshoot Days in 2021 on p. 13 and answer the following questions. You can go online.

1. Is there anything you find surprising? Why or why not?
2. Where is Germany in the infographic? How would you explain its position?
3. What might be possible reasons for the differences in the dates? → ○1
4. Why do you think Qatar would be the first country to reach Earth Overshoot Day?

Country Overshoot Days 2021

Earth Overshoot Day marks the date when natural resources used in a year exceed what the earth generates in that year. On which date would Earth Overshoot Day take place if the world's population lived like …

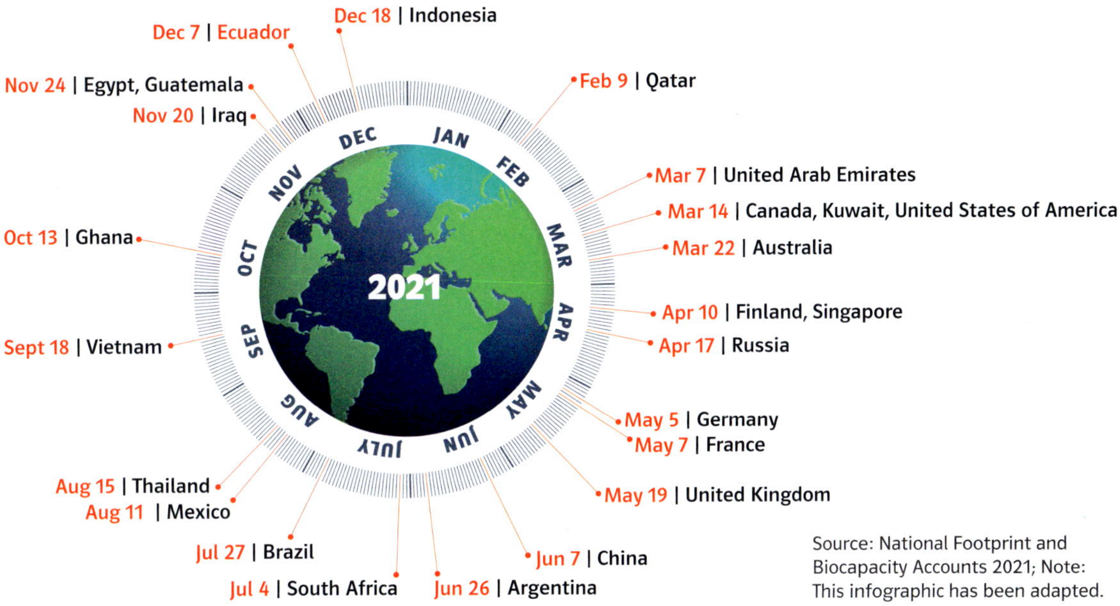

Source: National Footprint and Biocapacity Accounts 2021; Note: This infographic has been adapted.

A1 **4** Listen to the podcast "Forward Thinking: Eco-cities" and answer the following questions in keywords: → S 2, S 3 → WB, p. 5/2

1. Which overall goal does Jim Brandon pursue in his podcast?
2. What does Shalini Ghosh want to achieve by talking about eco-cities?
3. What efforts has San Francisco made to solve its waste problems? Name three.
4. Which measures are implemented in Singapore to make the city greener? Name two.
5. Which areas is Copenhagen working on to be more eco-friendly? Name three.

5 Discuss with a partner what makes up the ecologocial footprint of a person. → ◯ 2

6 Your school aims to improve its ecological footprint. Write an email to a group of students in England who are pursuing a similar goal in which you explain your ideas on how to reduce your ecological footprint and ask about their experiences. → S 6.4

USEFUL PHRASES

Saving resources in school

The cafeteria could serve organic / regionally produced food / …
Saving energy by turning off lights / electric appliances / heating / using renewable energy …
Encouraging students and teachers to use alternative / environmentally friendly forms of transport like …
Introducing a waste management by banning single-use plastic / recycling materials / using refillable bottles / …
Striving for a greener school by laying out a school garden / exploring vertical gardening / …

A How to feed the world

BEFORE YOU READ

1 Changing one's eating habits

a Read the text below and look at the picture. Explain in your own words what the planetary health diet is and what its goals are.

b Describe the diagram. Based on the information given, explain how following the planetary health diet might help to solve environmental problems.

c With a partner, collect ideas about changes which could be made in food production and sales to make it easier for consumers to stick to the planetary health diet.

The planetary health diet
An international study from 2018 found that if we change our eating habits, we can not only ensure that the world's growing population will have enough food and be healthier, but also prevent a destruction of the environment. The picture on the right shows what a person should eat in a day according to this flexitarian diet; including consuming less meat, dairy products, fat and sugar.

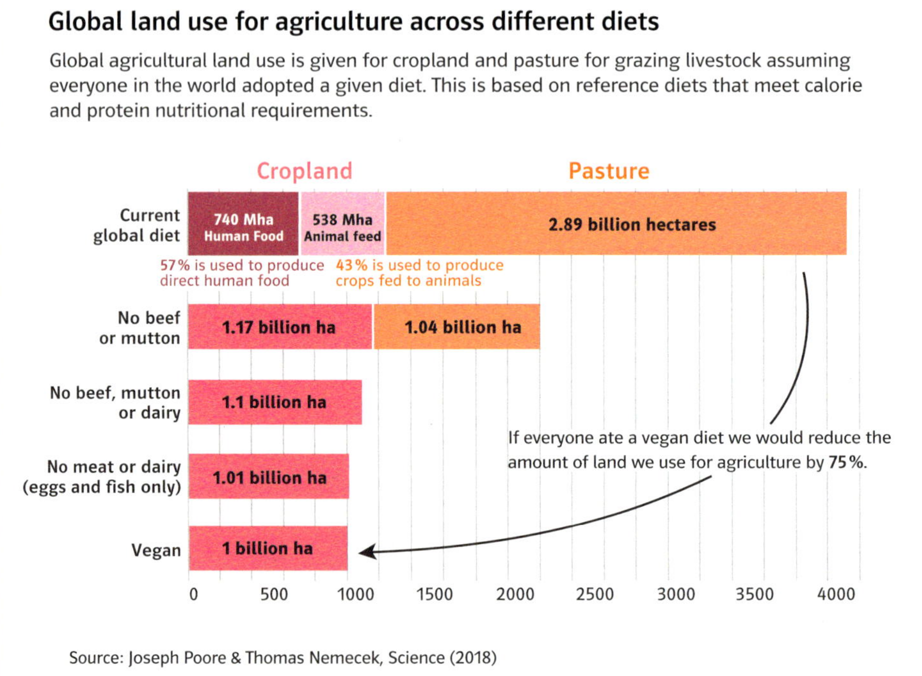

Going vegan: can switching to a plant-based diet really save the planet?

If politicians are serious about change, they need to incentivise it, say scientists and writers

The UK business secretary, Kwasi Kwarteng, is considering a "full vegan diet" to help tackle climate change, saying people will need to make lifestyle changes if the government is to meet its new emissions target of a 78 % reduction on 1990 levels by 2035. But how much difference would it make if everyone turned to a plant-based diet? Experts say changing the way we eat is necessary for the future of the planet but that government policy is needed alongside this. If politicians are serious about wanting dietary changes, they also need to incentivise it, scientists and writers add. The literature on the impact of reducing or cutting out meat from your diet varies. Some studies show that choosing vegetarian options would only reduce greenhouse gas emissions per person by 3 %. Others show a reduction in emissions per person of 20–30 % for halving meat consumption. [...]

The writer and environmental campaigner George Monbiot says the numbers on the impact of going vegan are different because of what scientists measure. "There are two completely different ways [to] look at the carbon impact of diet: one is carbon released by producing this or that food – that is 'carbon current account'. But another one is 'carbon capital account', which is the carbon opportunity cost of producing this food rather than another one," he said. "If you are producing meat, for example, what might land be used for if you took meat away? If you are growing forests there instead or peat bog there." Monbiot says what we eat is a "huge issue", alongside our transport habits. "Most of what you can do at an individual level is weak by comparison to what governments need to do ... but changing diet is not. That has a major impact," he said. "It is easier done if the government acts to change the food system but in the absence of that, we should still try and change our diets."

In 2018, scientists behind the most comprehensive analysis to date of the damage of farming to the planet found avoiding meat and dairy products was the single biggest way to reduce your environmental impact on the planet. The research showed that without meat and dairy consumption, global farmland use could be reduced by more than 75 % – an area equivalent to the US, China, European Union and Australia combined – and still feed the world. "There are lots of different sectors that have an impact on emissions and the food system is surely one of the most important ones as it is globally responsible for about a third of all greenhouse gas emissions," said Dr Marco Springmann, senior researcher on environmental sustainability and public health at the University of Oxford. He added that the overwhelming majority of emissions were due to foods such as beef and dairy, which "means that without changing emissions associated with those products it is hard to make progress". He said there were no good technical solutions for the fact that "cows emit methane emissions". "You can change feed composition but that does not change the animal and the need to feed the animal a lot of feed product," he said. He believes the government needs to offer price incentives for sustainable products, making beef and dairy more expensive.

Frank Mitloehner, professor and air quality extension specialist at the University of California [, Davis] said putting the onus on the individual was a distraction from policy changes that are needed. He said literature suggests "going vegan for two years has the same saving impact as one flight [from] Europe to the US would generate." [...] He believes the most important individual choice

3 **to incentivise** einen Anreiz schaffen
24 **greenhouse gas emissions** (*pl*) Treibhausgasausstoß
27 **to halve** halbieren
33 **carbon** Kohlenstoff; *hier:* Kohlenstoffdioxid
36 **current account** laufendes Konto; Leistungsbilanz
37 **capital account** Kapitalkonto; Vermögensbilanz
38 **opportunity cost** Ersatzkosten; Alternativkosten
43 **peat bog** Torfmoor
54 **to date** bislang; bis heute
90 **onus** Last; Pflicht

GOOD TO KNOW

A **sustainable system** can continue for a long time without interference. With regards to the earth and its natural resources, this means we cannot take more from it than it can supply without causing damage.

100 **silver bullet** Wunderwaffe
106 **anticipated** voraussichtlich; erwartet
108 **to occupy** einnehmen; füllen
108 **allowable** zulässig; erlaubt
114 **sufficient** genug; genügend; ausreichend
121 **directed** gezielt; gelenkt

someone can make is to "go and vote ... That is number one." Martin Heller, a research specialist at the University of Michigan, said: "There are no silver bullets for climate change. Nothing in isolation will be 'enough'". He added that studies showed that even with gracious assumptions in improvements in agricultural production, feeding an anticipated population at anticipated growing demand for animal-based foods by 2050 would occupy "all of the allowable emissions if we are to stay below a 2C temperature rise". "We have to change the way we eat," he said. "That certainly isn't saying that diet change – or even becoming vegan – will 'save the planet'. It's more of a necessary but not sufficient kind of thing." He added that "these diet shifts need to come with government, corporate and every other kind of action". "It's also probably naive to assume that people will just change these behaviours because it's good for the planet. It will require directed policy, changes in the restaurant and foodservice industries," he said. (808 words)

Sarah Marsh, *The Guardian* website, 2021

WORKING WITH THE TEXT

2 Reading for gist

a Scan the text and say what the following numbers refer to:

78 | 2035 | 3 | 20–30 | 75 | 2050 | 2

b Summarise the overall message of the text in one sentence.

3 Reading for detail

a Explain in your own words what the text says about ...

1. each individual's responsibility to help meet the emissions targets.
2. the concepts of 'carbon current account' and 'carbon capital account'.
3. the possible environmental impact of avoiding meat.
4. problems caused specifically by livestock.
5. the measures governments should take to reduce carbon emissions caused by food production.

b Point out the possible consequences of an increased demand for animal-based foods alongside continued population growth.

4 Words matter

Explain the meaning of the following expressions from the text. You may use a dictionary.

1. to incentivise sth (l.3)
2. sustainability (l.71)
3. to put the onus on the individual (l.90)
4. silver bullet (l.100)
5. allowable emissions (ll.108–109)
6. necessary but not sufficient (l.114)

A STEP FURTHER

5 Discussion

D12 Self-check 5.0

a Look at your ideas from exercise 1 c again and discuss how they relate to the arguments made in the text.

b Explain what you personally could do to fulfil the requirements of the planetary health diet. Discuss which other measures might help to solve environmental problems.

6 Listening → S 2, S 3

D11 I11 Self-check 4.0

A2 a Listen to the first part of the podcast "Forward Thinking: Veggie days" and answer the following questions in keywords:

1. What is Helen Cartwright's occupation?
2. What are Helen's arguments for a meat-free day per week? (two arguments)
3. In which two ways does deforestation and burning down rainforests have negative effects on the environment?
4. What can a weekly veggie day teach people?
5. What has Helen already done to reach her goal and what are the next steps?

A3 b Copy the table below. Then listen to the second part of the podcast and match the headings (A–E) to the speakers.

speaker	Margaret	John	Lilly	Zachariah	Helen
heading	...	...	...	...	...

A Impacts on the meat industry
B False expectations of the veggie day
C Transforming jobs in the meat industry
D Allowing people to choose their own diets
E Problems with using medicine in animal farming

7 Writing a personal letter → S 6.4

D10 I10 Self-check 3.3

a Your school and your partner school in England are planning to make changes to the food served in the cafeteria. Write a letter in which you outline the changes you are planning to make. Try to convince your partner school to follow the planetary health diet or to introduce a veggie day once a week.

b Exchange your letter with that of another student. Take on the role of the students from the partner school and write a letter in response.

Writing a speech

A speech is usually a formal talk that a speaker gives to an audience on a chosen topic. As part of your written exam, you might be asked to write the script for a speech. This means that you are expected to write a speech which could in theory be delivered in front of an audience. → S 6.6

GOOD TO KNOW

anaphora
= the repetition of one or more words at the beginning of two or more sentences

enumeration
= a list of several aspects

A Young people from Europe are taking part in a digital conference on how to make our lifestyles more sustainable. A discussion is planned and in order to prepare, the participants are asked to read the script of the main speech from the previous day of the event. Read the speech below and identify the following parts and elements of speeches:

1. introduction
2. main part
3. conclusion
4. personal motivation
5. direct address to the listeners (name five)
6. rhetorical devices (e.g. rhetorical questions, anaphoras, enumerations)

Hello everybody,
I'm very excited to be able to address you all today, across so many different countries, on an issue that is close to my heart. It has been my passion to fight for good food for many years now. And by good food I mean food that is good for us, and food that is good for our planet.
Climate change is real. You felt it in the past summers – the heat was terrible and there was either hardly any rain, or too much rain. And if you think summers are bad here in central Europe, take a look at the USA, Canada and Australia. Think of January 2020, when huge parts of forest were burning in New South Wales, and the summer of 2021, when in parts of the USA and Canada temperatures reached 50°C and above.
But there are also signs of hope. Millions of young people – people your age, and I'm sure, many of you are among them – march for climate justice, shout and demand political action to protect the climate, to protect our planet's future. And I want to encourage you to keep marching, keep shouting, keep demanding!
Yet, there is more that we can do. Things we can do in our everyday lives. Let's start by looking at what we literally do every day: What we eat. Since precisely because we do it every day – if we change it, there will be some real change!
We all know that animal-based food is bad for the planet. We know that in order to feed the livestock that is raised to feed us, rainforests are burned down. We know that this robs millions of species of their natural habitat. We know that we, humanity, are destroying the planet's green lung which we need to absorb the CO_2 that we are producing in abundance.
You may say, this is Brazil. There is nothing we can do about it. And I say, yes, it's Brazil. But no, it isn't true that there is nothing you can do. For one thing: Change the way you eat.

Does it help if you, and only you, do that? No, but if all young people today made a massive change, then yes, that would help a great deal. You make up a large part of today's consumers, and you're the mothers and fathers of tomorrow who can teach their children to eat in a way that is good for the planet.
So, should we all go completely vegan? Is that realistic?
I don't believe we need to. I believe that if we all drastically reduced the amount of meat and dairy we consume, we would come a long way.
Have you heard of the planetary health diet? Have you ever compared your eating habits with what it suggests? There you go.
How does it work? Basically – go plant-based, but still enjoy some of the cheese, eggs or even meat that you really like, every once in a while. One or two eggs a week, not two every day. A portion of meat every two weeks, not every day. A little milk, a tiny little bit of cheese. Enjoy those, and then learn to enjoy the great variety of plant-based foods that are out there. Meet up with your friends for a vegan cookout. Try something new every day. There is so much out there to enjoy that you may not even know about yet.
So, let us begin working for the climate on a daily basis, not just when we hit the streets with a banner in our hands. Let's start at our own kitchen table.
Let's take the first small steps to make a big impact. Let's not be the ones who are blaming others for failing us. Let's be the ones who did not fail ourselves, or any of the generations to come. (645 words)

B After the discussion, the participants are asked to form groups and to prepare a short speech in which they present their own ideas on what they can do to help protect the climate. Write the speech for one of the groups. → WB, p.7/1–3

1. Prepare your speech: Before you start, make sure you can answer the following questions:
   - What is the purpose of my speech?
   - What is the thematic focus of my speech?
   - Who is my audience? What do they already know about the topic?
   - How long should my speech be?
2. Create an outline and note down ideas for:
   - the introduction: Find a 'hook' to capture the audience's attention; introduce yourself; make clear what your speech is about
   - the main part: Present 3–4 main ideas; give details and use statistics, research findings, personal experience etc. to support your points; build up tension and present your arguments in a meaningful way; finish with the strongest argument
   - conclusion: Finish with a strong point or make an appeal, using well-chosen language
3. Write a first draft and add details to each part of your speech.
4. Revise your speech: Go through your draft to edit and improve it.
5. Write your speech: Think of how you can use language in a creative and interesting way to illustrate your points and involve your audience. Help your audience to follow you by using connectives. Engage your audience by using rhetorical devices (e.g. repetition, imagery) and addressing them directly when possible.

C Practise your speech and record yourself if possible. Make sure the length is appropriate and your arguments and thoughts are clear to follow.

D Present your speech to somebody you know. Use their feedback on the structure, arguments and language to further improve your speech.

B Facing climate change

BEFORE YOU READ

GOOD TO KNOW

Given that the terms 'global warming' and 'climate change' do not sufficiently express the severity of the situation, some people already promote the terms 'global heating', 'climate emergency' or 'climate catastrophe' instead.

1 Describing a picture

a Describe the picture and explain the message on the sign.

b Discuss with a partner what forms of change the sign may want to encourage.

c What do you know about global warming? Take notes and give at least three examples of the effects of global heating on the world and on your own lives.

2 Words matter

a Match the following words and phrases with the correct definitions. Use a dictionary if necessary.

1. to offset emissions
2. carbon capture and storage
3. 'net-zero' company
4. to violate sth
5. litigator
6. verdict
7. appeal (*law*)
8. to enforce sth

A to make sure sth is carried out
B capturing, transporting and keeping carbon dioxide underground
C sb who represents sb else in court
D a request to a court to change a decision
E to reduce, remove or avoid emissions
F to disregard/break sth
G an official decision made in court
H a business that drastically reduces emissions and implements methods of absorbing CO_2

b Find a suitable German translation for each of the words and phrases.

c Write a short text in which you use at least five of the words and phrases.

What a Dutch court ruling means for Shell and Big Oil

Climate lawyers are preparing to take on more fossil-fuel companies after a Dutch court ordered Royal Dutch Shell Plc to cut its emissions faster than planned, on the grounds that the oil giant is violating human rights by contributing to global warming. It was a turning point for climate court cases, which boomed after the Paris Agreement on global warming was reached in 2015. Initially, many cases challenged governments' plans, but litigators are increasingly targeting companies.

1 [...]

A Dutch court ruled on May 26 that Shell should slash its greenhouse gas emissions [by] 45 % by 2030 compared with 2019 levels, forcing the company to make some hard choices. The oil giant expects to appeal. [...]

1 **court ruling** Gerichtsentscheid; Rechtsprechung
13 **to target** zielen auf; anpeilen
17 **to slash** reduzieren; streichen
21 **to appeal** *hier:* Berufung einlegen

2 [...]

A big part of Shell's existing plans for cutting carbon rely, to some extent, on so-called nature-based solutions – planting trees, reforesting and restoring land to offset industrial emissions. Shell has a 2050 net-zero plan using natural offsets for about 120 million tons a year of carbon dioxide. Scientists and environmental groups are skeptical of such practices and argue companies should focus first on cutting emissions and offset only those that can't be eliminated. In Shell's case, opponents say it would have to plant an improbably large number of trees. The oil major's energy transition plans involve producing less oil, more gas and spending as much as $3 billion a year on renewables and business of exploration and production. It also plans to ramp up the emissions it puts in the ground using carbon capture and storage projects in North America and Europe.

3 [...]

If the ruling is upheld, the equivalent of 740 million tons a year of carbon dioxide, more than the emissions of Germany, will have to be removed from Shell's ledgers by the end of the decade. To hit the court-ordered emissions target, Shell would have to cut output of both oil and pipeline gas by 3% a year, keep liquefied natural gas production flat and cut oil product sales by 30% from 2020 levels, according to RBC Capital Markets analyst Biraj Borkhataria. Like many of its European peers, over the last year Shell has upped its targets to slash its carbon emissions and ultimately become a "net-zero" company by the middle of the century.

4 [...]

The ruling can be appealed, a process that could last many years. The decision was in line with the Paris Agreement to limit global warming. But it was countries, not companies, that signed up to that accord. Eric De Brabandere, a professor of international dispute settlement at the University of Leiden, said he understands the verdict as it currently stands, but would also see why another judge could reach another conclusion. While the Dutch government signed up to the Paris Agreement, Shell's existing targets don't violate Dutch law. [...]

5 [...]

Companies headquartered in the Netherlands could face similar cases, while those that have a subsidiary in the country can only be held responsible for their Dutch branches. Oil companies, or other big polluters, based in other countries may face similar cases; Milieudefensie is in touch with other nonprofit organizations and it expects the approach it took in this case will be replicated by others across Europe, its leader said. Jurisdictions differ, however, and the Dutch system provides more space for interpretation by the judge than most.

6 [...]

Two landmark cases have taken place in the Netherlands. In [another] case the Dutch government was told to step up its efforts to adhere to the Paris Agreement, while in the Shell case a similar verdict was applied to a corporation. Both cases were built on a 'duty of care' clause in the Dutch system which provided judges some liberty to interpret unwritten rules and consider links to human rights and the effect climate change has on the right to a healthy environment. A lawyer involved in both cases was Roger Cox, who wrote a book about judicial intervention and climate change, "Revolution Justified."

(668 words)

Diederik Baazil and Laura Millan Lombrana, *Bloomberg* website, 2021

26 **to offset** kompensieren; ausgleichen
35 **improbably** unwahrscheinlich
39 **exploration** Erforschung; Erkundung
40 **to ramp up** steigern; erhöhen
42 **carbon capture** Kohlenstoffabscheidung
48 **ledger** Konto; Bestand
57 **to up** erhöhen; hinaufschieben
68 **dispute settlement** Streitschlichtung; -beilegung
70 **verdict** Urteil
88 **jurisdiction** Rechtssystem; Rechtsprechung

GOOD TO KNOW

The Paris Agreement was signed by almost all countries of the world during the annual international climate conference (COP) held in Paris in 2015, pledging to work towards keeping the increase of global temperature levels to a maximum of 2°C – ideally below 1.5°C – compared to pre-industrial levels.

WORKING WITH THE TEXT

3 Reading for gist

Skim the text and match the following subheadings with paragraphs 1–6: → ◯ 3

A Why are Dutch courts leading on climate?
B What grounds for appeal does *Shell* have?
C What was the *Shell* verdict?
D How could *Shell* comply with the court?
E What about *Shell's* longer-term targets?
F What does it mean for other companies?

GOOD TO KNOW

to point out
= to give information about sth

4 Reading for detail

a Summarise what the *Shell* verdict is and the effects it may have on other companies.

b In your own words, say what *Shell's* original targets were and why they are problematic.

c Point out why *Shell's* appeal might be successful.

d Explain what is special about the verdict. What is it based upon?

5 Focus on analysis

a Answer the following questions for each argument given in the text:

1. What statement do the authors make?
2. How do they explain the statement?
3. What examples do they give to support their statement?
4. How do they introduce an opposing opinion? Give examples.

D2 12
Self-check 1.2

b Examine the authors' intentions by analysing how their arguments are structured in the text. Include examples and quotes. → S 10.3 → ◯ 4

D8 18
Self-check 3.1

6 Writing a speech → S 6.6

Using the information given in the text, write a speech on one of the following topics. Include quotations from the text in your speech. → ◯ 5

1. Shared responsibilities: Governments, companies and individuals

Or:

2. Avoiding or offsetting? – how best to reduce CO_2 emissions

A STEP FURTHER

D6 16
Self-check 1.6

7 Working with a diagram → S11.4

Look at the diagrams from the UK Energy Statistics. Describe and analyse the diagrams.

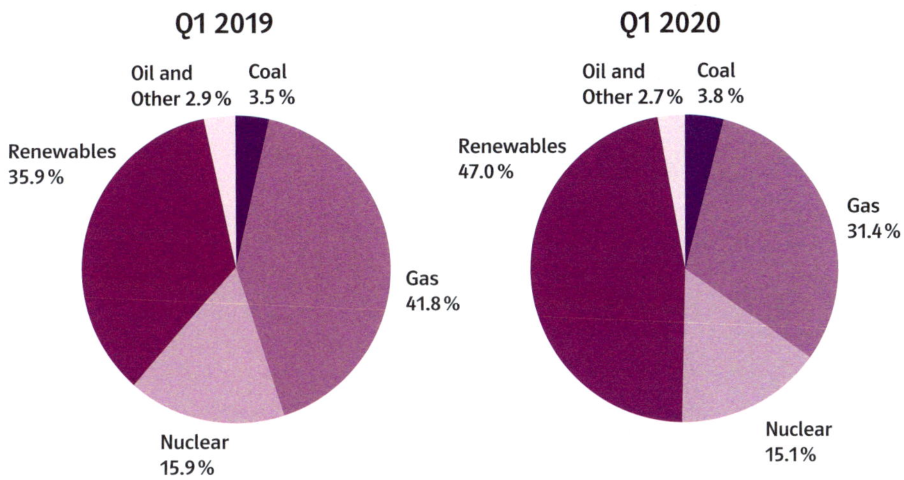

Source: Department for Business, Energy & Industrial Strategy, 2020. www.gov.uk

D12
Self-check 5.0

8 Giving a presentation

a Talk with a partner about when you use energy and take notes.

b The diagrams in exercise 7 give an overview of major sources of energy. Research renewable energies (e.g. solar energy) and make a list.

MK

c Form groups. Each group should be working on a different energy source. Go online to find information on one source of energy and take notes on:

- how it works
- its risks and benefits
- the costs
- its use in Germany and in the UK

d Prepare and give a 5-minute presentation, including a handout with the relevant information. → S14.1

9 Creating a flyer

a Work with a partner and collect ideas of how you as individuals can conserve energy.

b Compare your results with at least two other pairs and create a flyer to be distributed at your school with tips on saving energy.

Talking about ability, permission, necessity

A Identify the modal auxiliaries in the text below. Copy the table and sort the modal auxiliaries into one of the four groups of functions. Some modal auxiliaries can be used in more than one group. → G 8 → WB, p. 10/1–2

requests / orders / permission	ability	necessity	possibility
...	can (l. 1), ...	have to (l. 5), ...	...

Can we save biodiversity?

Looking at the world today, with the rise of extreme weather events, the loss of biodiversity and increasing water shortages, we have to ask ourselves: Are we still able to stop this? We cannot deny that the problems are getting more serious. While global warming is often discussed, we mustn't ignore the problem of biodiversity loss. We have to remember what different animals and plants do for us. Some insects might be irritating, but without bees we would not have honey and many birds would not be able to find enough food to live on. We ought to take a moment and imagine a world without birds. And then we should think of ways to protect them.

Some people think that we needn't worry because there are still so many insects and birds that we can see. But what we see may not reflect the truth. You might not know that every day around 150 animal species are dying out. So we must do something to stop this! And we shouldn't ignore the fact that our actions are causing this problem. We must act before it is too late!

B You are working on a brochure with tips on how to combat the loss of biodiversity. Work with a partner and put the following suggestions or demands into your personal order of importance. Use modal auxiliaries to express the urgency of each tip.

1. Buy organic food grown without using chemicals that endanger wildlife.
   Example: We need to buy organic food grown without using chemicals that endanger wildlife.
2. Buy fish from sustainable fisheries with the Marine Stewardship Council logo.
3. Reduce CO_2 emissions by using your bike or walking instead of taking the car.
4. Prevent habitat loss by eating less meat and other animal-based foods.
5. Put a bee hotel in your garden or on your balcony.
6. Do not grow any exotic plants in your garden.
7. Demand that politicians make legislations to protect natural habitats.

C Write a blog post in which you suggest measures that you as individuals can take to protect biodiversity. Use at least six different modal auxiliaries.

C The blue planet

1 Talking about using less plastic

a Read the following tips for reducing plastic waste in your everyday life. Talk with a partner about how practical these tips are. What else could you do? Come up with at least five more tips.

- Use loose-leaf tea with a tea strainer instead of teabags that are sealed with plastic.
- Make freshly squeezed juice instead of buying juice in plastic bottles.
- Give up chewing gum as most modern chewing gum is made of synthetic rubber.
- Avoid using disposable plastic pens and use fountain pens instead.
- Make your own cleaning agent with vinegar and water.

b Rank all of the tips from 'most helpful' to 'least helpful'.

c Note down your ideas on what firms and governments could do to reduce plastic waste.

d Exchange and compare your tips and ideas with the rest of the class.

USEFUL PHRASES

I think we should …
We need to …
We could all reduce …
In my opinion, we can do a lot …
We have to be more aware of …
I don't want to change my habits because …

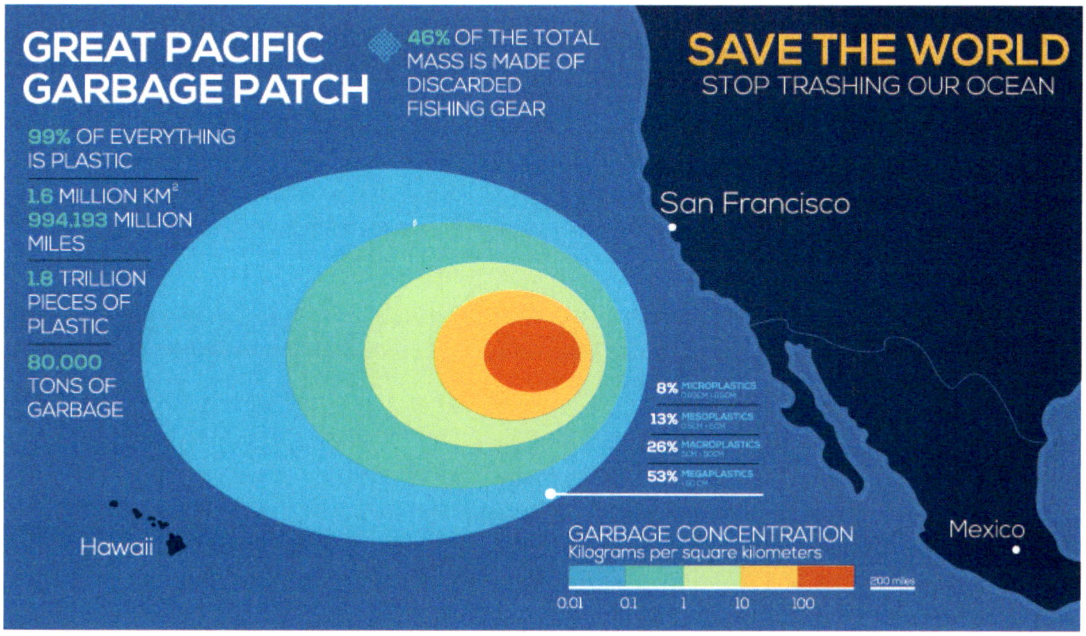

The Great Pacific Garbage Patch
Approximately 80 % of the debris in the Great Pacific Garbage Patch comes from land. The other 20 % of the debris comes from boats, oil rigs and cargo ships that either dump or lose debris in the water. Fishing nets make up the majority of this debris – about 79,000 tons of it. More unusual items, such as bath toys and computer monitors, come from lost shipping containers.

2 Working with an infographic

a Look at the infographic and read the text about the 'Great Pacific Garbage Patch' on p. 25. With a partner, discuss the different kinds of plastic in the infographic and give examples. Use a dictionary if necessary. → S11.4 → WB, p.11/1

b Discuss in groups whether the figures in the text and in the infographic surprised you.

10 **to call it quits** aufhören
11 **to plow one's way through sth** sich seinen Weg durch etw bahnen
12 **to swirl** wirbeln
12 **vortex** Strudel
12 **garbage** (*AE*) Müll; Abfall
26 **litter** Müll, Abfall
30 **current** Strömung
44 **to log** erfassen; aufzeichnen
67 **dinghy** kleines Boot; Beiboot
76 **to usher in** einleiten

A 52-year-old man is swimming through the Pacific Garbage Patch. He's caught disgusting trash, including a toothbrush and a toilet seat.

Somewhere in the Pacific Ocean, swimmer Ben Lecomte is kicking through trash. Lecomte swam across the Atlantic Ocean – from the US to France – in 1998, and he tried to become the first person to swim across the Pacific last year, traveling 1,753 miles before calling it quits.

This year, he decided to plow through a swirling vortex of garbage between Hawaii and California known as the Great Pacific Garbage Patch.

"I'm not trying to go for any record," Lecomte told *Business Insider* from the sailboat that's following him as he swims. "It's a unique opportunity to show exactly what is under the surface."

The human race dumps about 8 million pounds of plastic trash into the oceans every year. For context, the average 16.9-ounce bottle of water weighs less than 13 grams, so there are at least 35 water bottles in a pound of trash. But of course, bottles are not the only litter in the sea: there are abandoned fishing nets, laundry baskets, toilet seats, toothbrushes, and much more.

Currents sweep up a lot of this plastic and carry it to a handful of locations in the ocean. The Great Pacific Garbage Patch is the most well-known of these trash vortices – it's double the size of Texas and now holds 79,000 tons of trash.

That's what Lecomte is swimming through. He wants the effort to bring more awareness to the issue of plastic consumption and show people what the garbage patch really looks like.

"I want to share what it is through swimming and bring people with me," he said.

[...] Lecomte wanted to log at least 300 nautical miles in the garbage patch (roughly equivalent to 345 miles) because it's estimated that the world produces about 300 million tons of plastic every year. So he is swimming more than one mile for each million tons.

[...] In June, Lecomte set out from Hawaii in a 67-foot yacht, headed toward the patch. He's traveling with nine other crew members.

[...] According to his live tracker, Lecomte [...] has swum at least 323 nautical miles and spent 230 hours kicking through the waves.

"If I swim 400 or 500 or 200, it's just a number," Lecomte said. "What we are focusing on is particular areas – it's very important for us to get data – and also in those areas for me to swim, so we have a very unique perspective on what it is we find in the water."

When Lecomte starts swimming each day, a support dinghy follows him, making sure he doesn't get lost and feeding him soup and bread every two or three hours.

Lecomte said one of the greatest misconceptions about the Great Pacific Garbage Patch is that it's one big trash heap. "It's not a big floating island," he said.

Rather, it's an area of the ocean where the current conditions usher in trash.

"There is much more plastic debris floating here in the Great Pacific Garbage

Patch than anywhere that I ever swam," Lecomte said.

In addition to plastic bags and big pieces of trash, Lecomte also comes into contact with a lot of small particles in the water. [...]

On board the ship, scientists <u>periodically</u> drop a net in the water to capture and count microplastics in the patch. They leave the net in the waves for a half hour at a time, and Lecomte said the crew captures around 36 plastic pieces every minute.

"And that is just an average," he said. "Our biggest <u>tow</u> has been over 3,000 pieces in 30 minutes." (611 words)

Hilary Brueck, *Business Insider* website, 2019

85 **periodically** in regelmäßigen Abständen
93 **tow** *hier:* Fang

WORKING WITH THE TEXT

3 Scanning the text

a Scan the text and find out what the following numbers refer to in the text:

1998 | 79,000 | 300 | 300 million | 36

b Find other numbers in the text on pp. 26–27 which are important for the topic of waste in the ocean. Explain why.

4 Reading for detail → ○ 6

a Read the text and describe in your own words what the *Great Pacific Garbage Patch* is. Pay special attention to the quantity and the type of plastic garbage Ben Lecomte encountered on his swim.

b Explain why Ben Lecomte is swimming through the Great Pacific Garbage Patch.

c Outline how the swimmer is being supported during his attempt to swim through the vortex of garbage.

5 Words matter → ○ 7

Read the text again and identify words and expressions that belong to the word field "garbage". Make a word web.

garbage

to produce

6 Focus on grammar → G 8

a Complete the sentences with a suitable modal auxiliary.

1. We … reduce our use of plastic.
   Example: We must reduce our use of plastic.
2. You … continue to use so much plastic.
3. Plastic bottles … be replaced by reusable bottles.
4. All single-use plastic … be banned worldwide.
5. If we act now, we … still make a difference.
6. But we all … act together!

b Write six more tips for reducing plastic waste. Use a different modal auxiliary in each sentence.

D 8 18
Self-check 3.1

7 Writing a comment → S 6.1 → WB, p.11/2

Write a personal comment on Lecomte's initiative and whether you think this sort of venture is an effective way to raise awareness about the problem of plastic waste polluting our oceans. Include a reference to the picture and its message in your comment.

A STEP FURTHER

V1 ### 8 Working with a video → S 2

a Research where Henderson Island is. Write down five interesting facts about the island. Compare your facts with a partner's. Share your results with the class.

b Watch the video "Henderson Island". Give a brief summary.

c Watch the video again and answer the following questions:

1. In what sorts of wildlife has plastic waste been found?
2. What kind of plastic waste can be found on beaches?
3. How much rubbish did the clean-up team collect?
4. What was James Beard's lowest point during the clean-up?
5. Why couldn't the rubbish be removed from the island?

d In a group, discuss how you feel after watching the video. Do you feel motivated to use less plastic? Would you consider joining a clean-up expedition?

● ### 9 Creating an informative handout → S 6.7

MK **a** Research online how plastic production and waste are connected with rising sea levels.

b Create a fact sheet on the different ways in which plastic endangers the oceans and possible measures to preserve them. Include an infographic and/or statistics if possible.

D Water shortage

BEFORE YOU READ

1 Conducting a survey on water usage

a You are going to conduct a survey on water usage. Think of situations in which water is being used. What do you want to find out? Write down questions. In class, agree on six questions.

b Conduct the survey in class and document the results. Then discuss the results in class.

c Compare your water usage with the information in the box. Do you use more or less?

CULTURE BOX

Water usage worldwide
While the average German uses about 125 litres of water a day, US Americans use around 300 litres. In comparison, the average person in Nigeria uses 9 litres. It is estimated that 12–16 litres is the minimum a person should have per day. When taking a shower, we use 9–12 litres per minute. A standard toilet uses 6–9 litres to flush. The production of a cotton t-shirt uses about 2,500 litres of water and that of a smartphone about 12,000 litres.

The apocalyptic thriller *Dry* was written by American author Neal Shusterman and his son Jarrod. It is about water drying up in the US and the state of emergency that follows.

Dry

by Neal and Jarrod Shusterman

Day one

Saturday, June 4th

The kitchen faucet makes the most bizarre sounds. It coughs and wheezes like it's gone asthmatic. It gurgles like someone drowning. It spits once, and then goes silent. Our dog, Kingston, raises his ears, but still keeps his distance from the sink, unsure if it might unexpectedly come back to life, but no such luck. Mom just stands there holding Kingston's water bowl beneath the faucet, puzzling. Then she moves the handle to the off position, and says, "Alyssa, go get your father." [...]

"Dad," I shout out into the garage, "kitchen issues." My father's feet stick out from underneath his Camry like the Wicked Witch. Uncle Basil is hidden behind a storm cell of e-cig vapor. "Can't it wait?" my father says from beneath the car. But I'm already sensing that it can't. "I think it's major," I tell him. He slides out, and with a heavy sigh heads for the kitchen. Mom's not there anymore. Instead she's standing in the doorway between the kitchen and the living room. She's just standing there, the dog's empty water bowl still in her left hand. I get a chill, but I don't yet know why. "What's so important that you gotta drag me out of –" "Shush!" Mom says. She rarely shushes Dad. She'll shush me and Garrett all day, but my parents never shush each other. It's an unspoken rule. She's watching the TV, where a news anchor is blathering about the "flow crisis." That's what the media's been calling the drought, ever since people got tired of hearing the word "drought." Kind of like the way "global warming" became "climate change," and "war" became "conflict." But now they've got a new catchphrase. A new stage in our water woes. They're calling this the "Tap-Out."

5 **faucet** (*AE*) Wasserhahn
6 **to drown** ertrinken
9 **handle** Griff
13 **vapor** (*AE*) Dampf
17 **to get a chill** erschaudern
18 **to shush sb** (*ugs*) jdn zum Schweigen bringen
20 **news anchor** Nachrichtensprecher/-in
21 **drought** Dürre; Trockenheit
24 **woe** Kummer; Leid
24 **tap** Wasserhahn

27 **floodgate** Schleusentor
29 **spigot** Zapfhahn
33 **to broker** vermitteln
36 **precautionary** vorsorglich
37 **to reroute** umleiten
41 **to code** *(infml) hier:* stillstehen, zum Stillstand kommen
41 **resuscitation** Wiederbelebung
46 **gulp** Schluck
53 **premonition** Vorahnung
61 **reclusive** zurückgezogen lebend
65 **to piss off** (*vulg*) verärgern
67 **to hoard** (an)sammeln; horten
71 **produce** landwirtschaftliche Erzeugnisse

Uncle Basil emerges from his vapor cloud long enough to ask, "What's going on?" "Arizona and Nevada just backed out of the reservoir relief deal," Mom tells him. "They've shut the floodgates on all the dams, saying they need the water themselves." Which means that the Colorado River won't even reach California anymore. Uncle Basil tries to wrap his mind around it. "Turning off the entire river like it's a spigot! Can they do that?"
My father raises an eyebrow. "They just did."
Suddenly the image switches to a live press conference, where the governor addresses a gathering of antsy reporters. "This is unfortunate, but not entirely unexpected," the governor says. "We have people working around the clock attempting to broker a new deal with various agencies."
"What does that even mean?" Uncle Basil says. Both Mom and I shush him. "As a precautionary measure, all county and municipal water districts in Southern California are temporarily rerouting all resources to critical services. But I cannot stress enough the need to keep calm. I'd like to personally assure everyone that this is a temporary situation, and that there is nothing to be concerned about." [...]
I go to the kitchen to try the tap myself – as if I might have the magic touch. Nothing. Not even the slightest dribble. Our faucet has coded, and no amount of resuscitation will bring it back. I note the time, like they do in the emergency room: 1:32 p.m., June 4th. Everyone's going to remember where they were when the taps went dry, I think. Like when a president is assassinated.
In the kitchen behind me, Garrett opens the fridge and grabs a bottle of Glacier Freeze Gatorade. He begins to guzzle it, but I stop him on the third gulp. "Put it back," I tell him. "Save some for later." "But I'm thirsty now," he whines, protesting. He's ten – six years younger than me. Tenyear-olds have issues with delayed gratification. It's almost finished anyway, so I let him keep it. I take note of what's in the fridge. A couple of beers. Three more bottles of Gatorade, a gallon of milk that's down to the dregs, and leftovers. You know how sometimes you don't realize how thirsty you are until you take that first sip? Well, suddenly I get that feeling just by looking in the refrigerator. It's the closest thing I've ever had to a premonition.
I can hear neighbors out in the street now. We know our neighbors – run into them occasionally. The only time whole bunches of them come out into the street at the same time is July Fourth, or when there's an earthquake. My parents, Garrett, and I gravitate outside as well, all of us standing, strangely, looking to one another for some kind of guidance, or at least validation that this is actually happening. Jeannette and Stu Leeson from across the street, the Maleckis and their newborn, and Mr. Burnside, who's been eternally seventy years old for as long as I can remember.
And as expected, we don't see the reclusive family next door – the McCrackens – who have probably barricaded themselves inside their suburban fortress upon hearing the news. We all kind of stand there with our hands in our pockets, avoiding direct eye contact, like my classmates at the junior prom. "Okay," my dad finally says, "which one of you pissed off Arizona and Nevada?" Everyone chuckles. Not because it's particularly funny, but it eases some of the tension.
Mr. Burnside raises his eyebrows. "Hate to say I told ya so, but didn't I say they'd hoard what's left of the Colorado River? We let that river become our only lifeline. We should never have let ourselves become so vulnerable." Used to be no one much knew or cared where our water came from. It was just always there. But when the Central Valley started to dry up and the price of produce skyrocketed, people started to pay attention. [...] "Las Vegas still has water," someone points out. Our neighbor, Stu, shakes his head. "Yeah – but I just tried to book a hotel in Vegas. A million hotel rooms, and not a single one available." Mr. Burnside laughs ruefully, as if taking pleasure in Stu's misfortune. "One hundred twenty-four thousand hotel rooms, actually. Sounds like a whole lot of people had the same idea." [...] (1,030 words)

WORKING WITH THE TEXT

2 Reading for gist → WB, p. 12/1

Sum up the main events and what they mean for the people involved.

3 Reading for detail → WB, p. 12/2

a Illustrate the different emotions the family members go through in this extract. Quote from the text and give line numbers.

b Explain how the media and politicians talk about the water shortage in the text.

4 Focus on analysis → S 8.1

a Collect examples of the use of contrast and comparison in a table.

b Analyse the examples by considering the effect they have on the reader. Take the stylistic devices used into account.

5 Writing a diary entry → S 6.10

The next day Alyssa writes in her diary about the first 24 hours since the water stopped. She has found this cartoon and refers to it, describing it and discussing its meaning. Write her diary entry.

IN THE FUTURE, WARS WILL BE FOUGHT OVER WATER

A STEP FURTHER

6 Discussion

During an internship in a region that experiences frequent droughts, you are asked to suggest guidelines for your company on how to preserve water.

a Work in groups and make a list of measures.

b Present your ideas to the other groups and discuss which measures might be most effective and should therefore be included in the guidelines.

7 CULTURE Project: Worldwide water usage and preservation

a In class, decide which regions and countries with severe water shortages you want to choose (e.g. Ethiopia, Mexico, California). Form groups and assign a different country / region to each group.

MK b In your group, find your country / region on a map. Research online and answer the following questions:

1. How much water is used by the average household / person?
2. What production facilities are there that use large amounts of water?
3. What are the region's needs with respect to water supplies?
4. How could this region improve its water usage?

c Prepare and give a presentation on the facts and requirements as well as your ideas for improvement in this region.

d Consider how your own behaviour affects other regions and what you can do to counteract the worldwide water problem.

Sustainable Europe: A film project

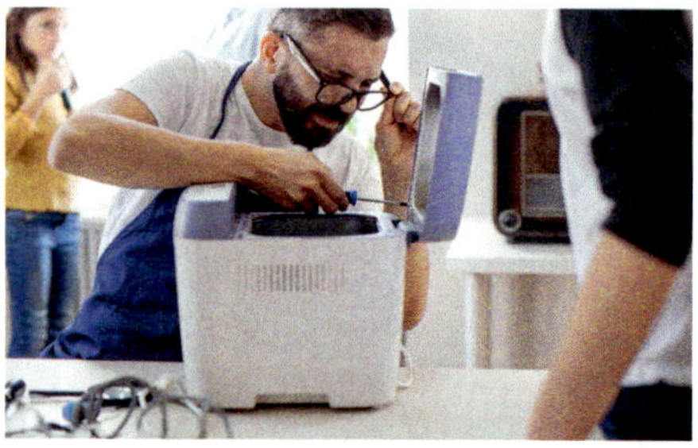

A European organisation has been formed to present European examples of sustainable development. The organisation is calling upon people from all over Europe to submit short film sequences that depict examples of initiatives for a sustainable development.

Step 1 Form groups and agree on a community where one of you lives. Find information on different initiatives (e.g. waste management, city planning and public transport) that have been made in that community to be more sustainable.

Step 2 Decide on one initiative that you would like to focus on. Take notes of aspects, places and institutions you would like to present in that context.

Step 3 Visit different places, institutions etc. Use your smartphones (or a video camera) to record film footage on your topic. → S 17
Consider these points:
- Try to cover as many different aspects as possible. The final film should be 3–4 minutes long.
- Make sure your footage is varied (close-ups, long shots, different forms of camera movement, include interviews where possible).
- Ask permission when you take film footage of institutions and people.

Step 4 Edit your film footage to make a coherent short film.
- Decide which shot is to be placed in which position in your film.
- Write a text to be recorded as a voice-over.
- Cut your film clips and put them together to make a film 3–4 minutes long.
- Combine soundtrack and film footage.

Step 5 In class, organise a film festival to watch your short films.
Give each other feedback on the content and the visuals.

Pressing ecological issues of today

"There is no reason to suppose that our stay here will be any more permanent than that of the dinosaur."
Sir David Attenborough, natural scientist and wildlife film-maker

Activism and hope in a time of crisis

The deforestation, plastic pollution, the over-exploitation of natural resources – it has become clear that the problems we are facing are manifold and severe. One of the greatest and most encompassing threats is that of steadily rising global temperatures. This alarming development has given rise to a massive, worldwide protest movement that started among, but is no longer limited to, young people. The movement demands that we concentrate on living more sustainably and reducing our ecological footprints in every area of our lives.

Why are global temperatures rising?

The cause of the rise of global temperatures is the 'greenhouse effect'. Certain gases in the earth's atmosphere trap the sun's heat, thus causing temperatures to rise. Human activity, especially since the onset of industrialisation, has caused the production of these gases to increase enormously. The main greenhouse gases are carbon dioxide (CO_2), methane, nitrous oxide and fluorinated gases. CO_2 levels are almost 50 % higher now than they were in pre-industrial times, and global temperatures have risen by 1.1 °C since then. CO_2 is emitted when fossil fuels such as oil, coal or gas are burned. Deforestation also causes a rise in CO_2 levels because with fewer trees to absorb CO_2, less of this gas can be taken from the atmosphere.

What are the effects of global warming?

- **Extreme weather events:** Rising global temperatures lead to an increase in extreme weather events, such as heavy rains and flooding on the one hand and extreme heat and drought on the other. The latter leads to increased forest fires, which in turn result in a rise in CO_2 levels. Due to both man-made and spontaneous fires, the Amazon rainforest has now been found to emit more CO_2 than it absorbs. Extreme heat can lead to uninhabitable temperatures which will displace billions of people in decades to come. Climate migration is already a problem and will increase in the near future.
- **Rising sea levels:** Rising temperatures lead to rising sea levels because glaciers and the polar ice caps are melting. This can result in coastal areas being flooded and millions of people losing their homes.
- **Loss in biodiversity:** Biodiversity is at serious risk because of global warming. Many species are endangered, not only from losing their habitat, but also as a result of forest fires and temperature changes that are hard for them to adapt to. When the climate of a region changes, invasive species from other regions can spread and displace indigenous species. For this reason, and due to increasing pollution, we are experiencing a loss in biodiversity which some people even refer to as a mass extinction.

6 **exploitation** Ausbeutung
15 **to trap** einfangen; einschließen
16 **onset** Beginn; Anfang
35 **glacier** Gletscher
43 **indigenous** einheimisch; heimisch
46 **extinction** (*no pl*) Aussterben

51 **summit** Gipfel
65 **crops** Nutzpflanzen
73 **charge** Gebühr

Steps towards a better future

Scientists point out that it is still possible to avert the worst effects of the climate crisis if emissions are drastically reduced and global temperatures are kept from rising more than 1.5°C above pre-industrial levels. In 2015, during the climate summit in Paris, the 'Paris Agreement' was signed by 196 countries all pledging to work towards reaching that goal. Net-zero carbon emissions need to be reached within a short period of time. For example by:

- **Sourcing of energy:** Renewable energy sources such as wind energy, solar energy or geothermal energy need to replace carbon-producing energy sources such as coal, gas and oil. The development of e-mobility has to go hand in hand with the development of renewable, emission-free sources of electricity. Emissions that cannot be avoided should be offset by investing in reforestation projects and other initiatives.
- **Changes in diet:** A major factor determining global warming is food production. A potential solution would be dietary changes favouring the planetary health diet thus reducing the amount of animal products we consume. Buying organically produced food and sticking to regional products are also be important measures.
- **Water conservation:** Rising temperatures as well as the scale of agricultural and private water usage are leading to water shortages. Growing water-intensive crops in naturally dry regions (e.g. almonds in California) uses excessive amounts of water. A route to more sustainable agricultural practices might include choosing crops that are suitable for the natural climate of a region. In addition, water can be conserved by acting responsibly when showering and washing dishes and by recycling waste water.
- **Waste: reduce, repair, reuse, recycle:** Waste – especially plastic waste – is a massive problem for the environment. One solution to this is avoiding using plastic whenever possible. Many governments have already banned certain plastic products or put charges on plastic bags. Alternatively, objects can be reused or sold second-hand. Another form of reusing objects is upcycling, i.e. altering an object to give it a new function. Things that cannot be reused at all should be recycled. Consumers can not only separate waste, but also look out for products made from recycled materials.
- **Eco-cities:** Many cities, such as Copenhagen, Singapore and San Francisco, are attempting to actively reduce their ecological footprints at various levels, e.g. by handling waste in a sustainable manner, developing sustainable transportation systems and supporting green roofs, vertical gardening and organic fashion.

MK **1** Research online to find out more about David Attenborough and his work. How does his statement on p.33 relate to the infographic on p.33? Share your findings in class.

2 Read through the texts on pp.33–34. Make a table in which you list the measures that can be taken by governments, companies and individual people against the climate crisis.

MK **3** Choose one measure to be taken by companies and governments e.g. in the USA and/or in Germany against global warming. Go online to find information on that measure. Present your findings in class.

Outlook: For further discussion, consider the following questions:
- What would it take on a local and global level to reverse global warming?
- What actions have politicians undertaken so far? What could be the next steps?
- What is the IPCC and what did they say in their latest report?
- What effects will changes in the gulf stream (AMOC) have on us and the world?

1 Lesen und Schreiben

Prince Charles's speech at the World Economic Forum 2020 in Davos, Switzerland

Ladies and gentlemen, [...]
We are in the midst of a crisis that is now, I hope, well understood. Global warming, climate change, and the devastating loss of biodiversity are the greatest threats humanity has ever faced – and one largely of our own creation. [...]
In order to secure our future and to prosper, we need to evolve our economic model. [...] I am delighted to be launching a Sustainable Markets Initiative [...]. For me, Sustainable Markets offer a new systems-level framework which ground markets in a higher purpose mission – in other words, putting people and planet at the heart of global value creation. Sustainable markets generate long-term value through the balance of natural, social, human and financial capital. [...]
The past decade has shown us just how quickly industry transformation can happen when you reimagine and re-engineer the business model – we need only look to mobile technology, electric vehicles, the space industry, e-commerce and online streaming for inspiration. [...]
I would like to outline 10 practical actions that will drive forward the sustainable markets approach.
First of all: shifting our default setting to "sustainable". [...] [P]ut simply, we need to put nature, and the protection of nature's capital – from which we draw an annual return – at the heart of how we operate. [...]
Second: [...] It is time for businesses, industries and countries alike to design and implement how they will decarbonise and transition to net zero. Moving together, with clear roadmaps, will create efficiencies and economies of scale that will allow us to leapfrog our collective progress and accelerate our transition. [...]
Third: [...] Using a sustainable markets framework, we have an incredible opportunity to create entirely new sustainable industries, products, services and supply chains, based on a circular bioeconomy, while in parallel helping to transition our existing systems. [...]
Fourth: [...] We need to identify, showcase and invest in the game-changing technologies and solutions that are emerging around the world. [...] Often, I have found, it is simply about bringing the right people together to help lift those roadblocks out of the way. [...]
Fifth: [...] To achieve scale within sustainable markets we must not be afraid to adapt our long-standing incentive structures if we are to reap the benefits afforded by a more sustainable world. [...]
Sixth: investing in STEM, innovation and R and D [research and development]. [...]
To move forward, we must acknowledge that sustainability and profitability are no longer mutually exclusive. Effective solutions must ensure that sustainable technologies and alternatives are competitively priced.
Seventh: investing in nature as the true engine of our economy. [...] Nature's contribution to the global economy is estimated to be worth more than $125 trillion annually – greater than the entire world's annual GDP, estimated at $85.91 trillion in 2018. [...] If, ladies and gentlemen, we valued our natural capital properly [...], our national and individual balance sheets might look very different indeed!
Eighth: adopting common metrics and standards. [...] People want to trust that the goods and services they buy are socially, environmentally and ethically produced. Through new technologies we have the ability to tag, track and trace supply chains in unprecedented ways – so it is time to make this level of supply chain transparency the norm.
Ninth: making the sustainable options the trusted and attainable options for

consumers. [...] [W]e cannot expect consumers to make sustainable choices if these choices are not clearly laid before them. [...] If all the true costs are taken into account, being socially and environmentally responsible should be the least expensive option because it leaves the smallest footprint behind. [...]

Tenth: connecting investments to investables using platforms that can rapidly scale solutions. On every pressing issue we face, there are solutions that are not just available, but increasingly cost effective. [...]

Now if we all accept that a profitable, yet sustainable, future is the desired end state – the questions we must ask are: How quickly can we get there and who are the leaders who will drive us forward?

[...] After all, ladies and gentlemen, do we want to go down in history as the people who did nothing to bring the world back from the brink in time to restore the balance when we could have done? I don't want to. [...]

When the right sustainable goods and services are developed, proved and affordable, the choice to adopt them will become obvious. Truly to seize these opportunities, we need to visualise the future and have the confidence to invest in it. [...]

And just think for a moment – what good is all the extra wealth in the world, gained from "business as usual", if you can do nothing with it except watch it burn in catastrophic conditions?

[...] We simply cannot waste any more time – the only limit is our willingness to act, and the time to act is now.

Thank you, ladies and gentlemen.

(826 words)

ASSIGNMENTS → WB, p. 13/1–2

1. Summarise Prince Charles's proposals for a more sustainable economy.
2. Analyse how Prince Charles uses stylistic devices to bring his message across.
3. Choose one of the following tasks:

   3.1 Comment on Prince Charles's ninth proposal (ll. 93–102).

   Or:

   3.2 Write a letter to Prince Charles in which you let him know what you think of his ideas. Give examples from your own experience and add further ideas.

2 Hörverstehen

ASSIGNMENTS → WB, p. 14/1–3

Listen to a radio report on green energy. You will hear each recording twice.

A4 1. Copy the table. Listen to part 1 and match the headings (A–E) with the speakers.

person	Martin Edwards	Juliet Davenport	Emma Pinchbeck	Baroness Brown
heading	...	...	...	...

A Reactions to the first wind farm in the UK
B Surprise about changing wind energy prices
C Change of laws for building wind farms necessary
D Massive increase in production of renewable energies
E Speedy development of technologies surrounding renewable energies

A5 2. Listen to part 2 and answer the following questions in keywords:

a) What are the two major problems with the net-zero target?
b) Why does shutting down steel plants not lower the UK's carbon footprint?
c) How does the universal price for carbon work?
d) What would happen if steel producers in the UK had to pay for the pollution they cause, and steel producers in China didn't?
e) How have carbon emissions developed since 1990?

3 Kommunikation → WB, p.15/1–4

Monologue

Your school is hosting a conference on the climate crisis. You are asked to give a 5-minute presentation based on the following graph, cartoon and quotation.

Graph

Describe and analyse the graph.

Final energy consumption by sector, EU, 2019

(% of total, based on tonnes of oil equivalent)

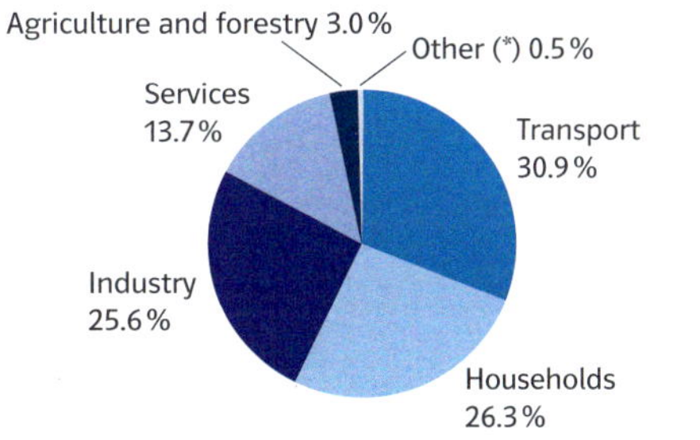

Source: Eurostat 2019;
*Data for 'international aviation' is included in this category.

Cartoon

Describe and analyse the cartoon and refer it to the graph.

If you cover your eyes, you can make it go away.

Quotation

Explain and comment on the quotation. Refer it to the visual materials.

"[R]eal success can only come if there is a change in our societies and in our economics and in our politics."

Sir David Attenborough, natural scientist and wildlife film-maker

Dialogue

In the conference other topics are brought up. Be prepared to discuss the pros and cons of recycling or the impact of food production on global warming.

D13 Progress report

Science and technology

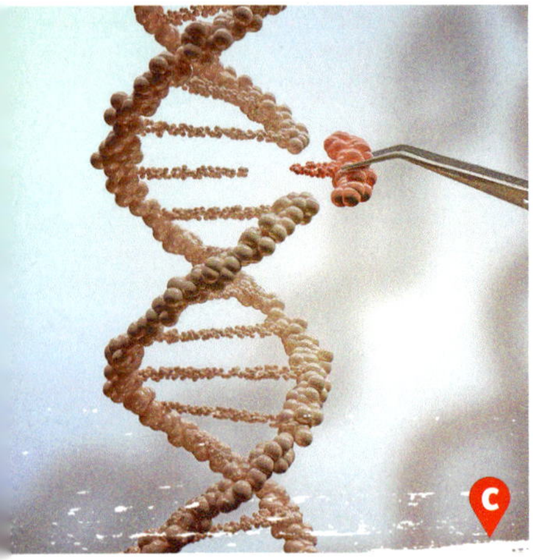

1 Look at the five pictures and describe each one. Say which topics related to science and technology are being shown and what effects they might have on society. Use the words below to help you. Compare your results with a partner's.

control panel | smart home | Internet of Things | 3D-printer | modern production methods | genetic engineering | DNA | creating more efficient organisms | ethical issues | genetically modified organisms | virtual reality | simulations | VR glasses

2 What are the most important technological inventions you can think of? Present your ideas to your partner and then in class. → WB, p.16

USEFUL PHRASES

On the one hand … On the other hand … | One of the advantages/disadvantages of … is … | In my opinion, … has more risks/benefits because … | In my mind, it is clear that … | Due to technological/scientific progress … | Another important aspect is (that) … | The main reason/result is that … | All in all, we can say (that) …

3 Discuss in groups which technological developments and inventions make your life easier. Make a list of at least five inventions you cannot imagine living without and give reasons for your choices. Share your ideas with the class.

4 You are going to listen to the podcast episode "Forward Thinking: Benefits and risks of technological developments". → S 2, S 3

D 11 I 11
Self-check 4.0

A6 **a** Listen to the first part and answer the following questions in keywords:

1. What is the title of Michael Southwater's book?
2. According to Carrie Fisher, what does technology offer us?
3. What does a smart factory use data for? Name two examples.
4. Which positive examples of facial recognition technology does Carrie mention? Name two.
5. What are the positives and negatives of drones mentioned? Name two each.

A7 **b** Listen to the second part of the podcast and choose the correct answer from the options given below (A, B or C). There is only one correct answer.

1. Carrie agrees that technology has always been used for …
   A making money.
   B doing unpleasant things and breaking the law.
   C communicating with people all over the world.
2. In Michael's opinion, …
   A driverless cars do not help the environment.
   B there will be no driverless cars on the road in ten years' time.
   C technology can help solve more important issues than driving cars.
3. The Internet of Things refers to …
   A a virtual marketplace where almost anything can be bought and sold.
   B a technology which can use virtual reality to enhance a real-world setting.
   C physical devices that are linked together and exchange information with one another.
4. According to Michael, augmented reality has been used positively for …
   A selling furniture and teaching.
   B improving the world as we know it.
   C exploring different historical periods.
5. When talking about genetic engineering, Carrie argues that …
   A the public should be informed about the potential health risks involved.
   B society should try to live in a more sustainable way before turning to science.
   C technology must be used immediately to modify crops and fight global hunger.

5 Look at the pictures on p. 38 again. Think of another image that in your view represents the modern world of science and technology and an increasingly interconnected society. Write a description of the picture and explain your choice.

A A smarter world

BEFORE YOU READ

1 Thinking about personal data

a Think about a typical day and brainstorm situations in which your personal data is recorded by someone else. Consider the kind of information you make available and what data you would consider private. Take notes and exchange your findings in class.

b Discuss why companies might be interested in accessing your data and for what purposes.

Andreas Weigend's work focuses on social mobile technology, big data and consumer behaviour. In the introduction to his book, he uses a first-person narrator, although it is a non-fictional text.

Data for the people: How to make our post-privacy economy work for you

by Andreas Weigend

7 **GPS receiver** GPS-Empfänger
9 **accelerometer** *(AE)* Beschleunigungsmesser
9 **barometer** Luftdruckmesser
13 **meter** (Verbrauchs-)Zähler
17 **cellular signal tower** Sendemast für das Mobilfunknetz
18 **carrier** *hier:* Mobilfunkanbieter
24 **land developer** Bauunternehmen; Bodenerschließer
29 **to log** erfassen; aufzeichnen
31 **on-board** fahrzeugeigen

How can we ensure that data are for the people?

At 6:45 a.m., the alarm on my mobile phone wakes me up. Eager to start the day, I carry my phone to the kitchen while I scan through my email and Facebook notifications. My phone's GPS receiver and wifi register the changes in location, logging my shift a few meters north and east. As I pour myself a cup of coffee and really start to get going, the phone's accelerometer tracks how quickly I walk and the barometer registers when I'm going up the stairs. Because I have Google apps installed on my phone, Google has a record of all these data.

After breakfast, I'm ready to make my way to Stanford University. The electricity company has put in a "smart" meter, which registers the decrease in electricity use as I turn off my lights and unplug my mobile devices. When I open the garage door, the meter detects the usage signature specific to it. Thus, as I pull my car out onto the street, my electricity provider has enough data to know I'm no longer at home. When my phone's signal gets picked up by different cellular signal towers, so does my mobile phone carrier.

On the road, a camera installed on a street corner takes a photo of my license plate in case I speed through a red light. Thankfully, I'm on my best behavior today so I won't be greeted with a ticket in the mail. But as I go on my way, my license plate is photographed again and again. Some of those cameras belong to the local government, while some belong to private companies that are analyzing the data to identify patterns of mobility – which they sell to police departments, land developers, and other interested parties.

When I get to Stanford, I use the EasyPark app on my phone to pay the parking fee. The money is automatically debited from my bank account, and the university parking team is notified that I'm paid up, so both the school and my bank can see that I'm on campus starting at 9:03 a.m. When my phone stops moving at a car's pace, Google infers this is where I have parked and logs the location, so that I can look it up in case I forget later. It's also time to check my Metromile insurance app, which has been recording data about my drive from the car's on-board diagnostic system. I can see in an instant that my fuel efficiency was lower today – nineteen miles per gallon – and that I spent $2.05 on gas for my commute.

After my day at Stanford, I'm planning to meet up with a new friend back in San Francisco. We "virtually" met each other when we both commented on a post by a mutual friend on Facebook, and liked each other's take on the topic. It turned out we had more than thirty Facebook friends in common, more than enough reason to meet up. Google Maps predicts that I'll get to my new friend's place at 7:12 p.m., and as usual the prediction is correct within a few minutes. As it happens, my friend lives above a store that sells tobacco products as well as various paraphernalia used for smoking marijuana. The GPS receiver on my smartphone doesn't differentiate between the apartment and the store, however. As far as my carrier and Google are concerned, I've ended my day with a visit to the head shop – a fact revealed to me by the ads Google shows when I check the weather forecast before going to bed.
Welcome to the social data revolution. (623 words)

36 **mutual** *hier:* gemeinsam
40 **paraphernalia** Zubehör
43 **head shop** Geschäft für Tabak, Cannabis etc.

WORKING WITH THE TEXT

2 Reading for gist → WB, p. 17

a In your own words, briefly describe the narrator's 'online day'.

b List the technical devices that send and receive the narrator's data.

3 Reading for detail → WB, p. 18

a Explain which conclusions can be drawn about the narrator by collecting and analysing his data.

b Compare the devices and apps the narrator uses for his own comfort and benefit with the devices that record his information for other purposes. → ○1

4 Focus on analysis → ○2 → S 8.2

a Decide if the text is written in a more informal or formal style. Give reasons.

b Find examples in the text that help to classify its style, tone and register. Keep in mind that texts can show characteristics of more than one category.

c Analyse the style, tone and register of the text. Explain its effect on the reader. Say why you think the author wrote his non-fictional text in the first-person perspective.

D1 I1
Self-check 1.1

5 Writing an email → S 6.4 → G 8

Write an email to the author in which you give him an answer to his initial question: "How can we ensure that data are for the people?" (l. 4)
Include the message of the cartoon in your text.

D10 I10
Self-check 3.3

"It's free, but they sell your information."

A STEP FURTHER

6 Working with a video → S 2

V2 a Watch the video "Big data: why should you care?" Explain the four aspects of big data.

V2 b Watch the video again and write down the different possibilities for the use of big data mentioned in the video. Exchange your findings with a partner's.

c With your partner, discuss the positive and negative aspects of the use of big data according to the video. Consider other opportunities big data might offer.

d Choose one of your ideas and research it in more detail. Prepare a 5-minute presentation in which you outline the basic concept, give examples and critically evaluate the use of big data in this area.

7 Project: Smart homes

a Work in groups of three or four students and choose one of the following areas of smart home technology, or one of your own choice, that you would like to focus on.

- home entertainment
- home security
- environmental controls like air conditioning, heating and lighting
- household appliances / Internet of Things
- home automation for elderly and people with disabilities
- baby, child and pet care

b Research your chosen area. Sum up the key information and collect images for a 3–5-minute presentation. Add further ideas to make homes 'smarter' using the figures on the right to help you.

c Give your presentations in class and discuss both the benefits and risks these technologies may have.

D 12
Self-check 5.0

Top factors leading to a positive attitude towards smart home devices, 2021

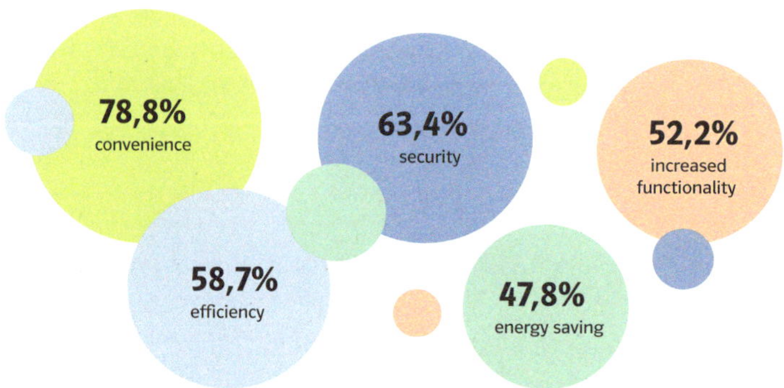

Quelle: Cinch Home Services, 2021

B Benefits of innovative technologies

BEFORE YOU READ

1 Thinking about revolutionary technology

a What does the term 'revolutionary technology' mean to you?

b List examples of what you consider revolutionary technologies in history.

c Look at the pictures and consider how revolutionary technologies might be used to increase prosperity in African countries.

GOOD TO KNOW

evolution
= a slow and gradual change

revolution
= a sudden, dramatic and complete change

Revolutionary technologies will drive African prosperity – this is why

Right now, we're at a tipping point in Africa's development. We're hurtling headlong into the Fourth Industrial Revolution (4IR), which has the potential to turbocharge the socio-economic development of the entire African continent. We've got the youngest continent in the world, with 60% of Africa's 1.25 billion people under the age of 25. If we make the right decisions in the next few years, we could pave a bold new path of African prosperity.

In Africa, 4IR's potential is limitless. Its technologies, like artificial intelligence (AI) and the internet of things (IoT), offer a new vision for economic growth, innovation, development and human well-being. It can solve a host of business and societal challenges, from providing better healthcare and basic services to creating more efficient governments, and helping businesses become intelligent enterprises that drive growth and prosperity.

Our governments and institutions have a massive opportunity to start using AI and digital platforms to do life-changing things: Like delivering safe drinking water to our people, improving the quality and reach of education, and even giving people the ability to identify themselves, to be able to access government grants, open bank accounts and vote in elections.

We know Africa suffers from a massive infrastructure deficit. But the beauty of 4IR's technologies is that you don't need big legacy systems and programmes in place to start rolling them out. We're already seeing numerous case studies and examples of how developing countries can move quickly to new digital approaches that can transform public service delivery in critical areas like farming, healthcare and education.

Take agriculture as an example. Today, small-scale agriculture accounts for about 80% of food production and nearly 70% of all jobs in Africa. Imagine what can be achieved if we use data to help small-scale farmers to improve their production: better use of land and water, less food being imported, improved food security –

3 **tipping point** Wendepunkt
4 **to hurtle** rasen; sich schnell bewegen
5 **headlong** kopfüber
40 **to roll sth out** etw starten; etw auf den Markt bringen

56 **revenue** Ertrag; Einnahmen
57 **surplus** überschüssig
58 **subsistence** Lebensunterhalt
81 **leakage** Leck; undichte Stelle
94 **to unlock** erschließen

and the ability for farmers to start generating revenues for themselves by selling surplus produce, and breaking free from subsistence.

We can use technologies like AI to improve access to healthcare across the continent for the most vulnerable and needy communities. It can even help make diagnoses in rural areas, where there are precious few doctors. And we're already seeing technology changing the face of education in countries like India, where they've launched a national teacher platform that builds capacity by allowing teachers to provide richer content, while giving administrators access to data about student study patterns. Digital platforms are not only transforming teaching, but changing the way we think about learning.

Another relatively quick win for Africa would be to roll out digital identification systems, as India has done with its Aadhaar system, which can play a major role in driving financial inclusion and reducing corruption through reduced fraud and leakages in social benefits payment systems. Once people have digital identities, they can do anything from getting a SIM card to arranging a bank account or pension.

If you empower people with their personal information and data, they can use this data to get better loans, get better skills and ultimately earn better salaries. On a continent like ours, developing a high-performing digital ecosystem will provide a unique chance to stimulate the economy and create jobs.

But the real promise of 4IR is to unlock a new future for Africa's estimated 700 million young people. We're going to have to move quickly, though. Today, fewer than 1 % of African children leave school with basic coding knowledge. We – big business, governments, NGOs and civil society – must do more to give our youthful workforce the skills they need to participate in the digital economy. This is vital if we are to avoid a situation where millions of people are unable to participate in our brave new technology-driven world. [...] (643 words)

Cathy Smith, *The World Economic Forum* website, 2019

WORKING WITH THE TEXT

2 Reading for gist

Summarise what the text says about the current social and political state of affairs in Africa.

3 Reading for detail → G 1.9–1.13, G 2 → WB, p. 19

a Identify the key statements made in the text on revolutionary technologies in Africa. Take notes and give line numbers.

b In your own words, illustrate the possibilities of 4IR and AI according to the text.

4 Words matter → G 5, G 6 → WB, p. 20/2

Copy the table and fill it with adjectives and adverbs used in the text. Note down whether these words have a positive or negative connotation and the contexts the words are used in.

adjective/adverb	connotation	context
revolutionary (l. 1)	positive	referring to the effect new technologies will have in Africa

5 Focus on analysis → S 8

D1 I1 Self-check 1.1

a Decide if the text is more informal or formal. Give reasons for your answer.

b Use the table in exercise 4 to examine the author's use of adjectives and adverbs in the text and the effects this has on the reader.

c Analyse how the language used in the text brings out the author's attitude to these technologies. Give quotes and examples.

6 Writing a comment → ◯ 3 → S 6.1

D8 I8 Self-check 3.1

Taking into consideration your background knowledge of big data and data analysis and using the information given in the text, comment on the view that these technologies "offer a new vision for economic growth, innovation, development and human well-being" (ll. 17–20).

A STEP FURTHER

7 Working with a diagram → S 11.4

D6 I6 Self-check 1.6

Work with a partner. Together compare the figures for Nigeria and South Sudan and interpret the results of your comparison.

Total population	Internet users	Active social media users	Mobile connections
Nigeria in 2021			
208.8 million	104.4 million	33.00 million	187.9 million
Urbanisation: 52.3 %	vs. population 50.0 %	vs. population 15.8 %	vs. population 90 %
South Sudan in 2021			
11.29 million	900.7 thousand	450.0 thousand	2.61 million
Urbanisation: 20.4 %	vs. population 8.0 %	vs. population 4.0 %	vs. population 23.1 %

Source: wearesocial, 2021

CULTURE BOX

Nigeria and South Sudan
Nigeria is located on the western coast of Africa. It is the most populous of all African countries. South Sudan is located in eastern Africa.

D 12 Self-check 5.0

8 Role play → S 1

Form groups and discuss the key statements made in the text (see exercise 3) in a role play. First brainstorm what each of the following protagonists might say about them. Then act out the role play.

- a representative of a company offering digital solutions for agriculture and farming
- a government representative planning to install a digital identification system
- a representative of a mobile phone / internet provider
- a healthcare official
- a representative of an organisation fighting for data protection issues

D 11 I 11 Self-check 4.0

A8 9 Listening → S 2, S 3

Copy the table. Listen to five people talking about the uses of drones in different fields. Match the headings (A–G) with the speakers (1–5). There is one more heading than you need.

speaker	1	2	3	4	5
heading	...	...	...	...	...

A Helping farmers
B Reaching people in need
C A danger to our private lives
D New developments, new risks
E Transporting important goods
F Helping to protect rare wildlife

D 6 I 6 Self-check 1.6

10 Working with a cartoon → S 11.3

Describe and analyse the cartoon.

My package arrived OK by drone, but I don't think we'll see the cat again.

11 Project: Applications of drone technology → S 6.7

MK

Work in small groups. Go online and find an example of how drone technology is being used in one of the following areas. Consider benefits and risks of the use of drones in this particular area. Prepare an informative handout that includes pictures and/or graphs as well as short informative texts. Present your handout to the class.

agriculture | conservation | disaster management | emergency services | entertainment | military and warfare | policing | sports | surveillance | transportation and logistics

Talking about processes → WB, p. 21

A Read the text and identify the passive verb forms. Write down line numbers. → G 3

Industry 4.0 is being discussed by scientists, politicians and industry experts. You cannot avoid it nowadays. But how has it developed and how has it influenced modern production?

The first industrial revolution came in the 18th century when steam and water were utilised to power machines. Throughout the 19th and 20th centuries, production methods were developed further. Many companies started to use electricity and mass production as early as the 1870s. This period became known as the second industrial revolution. Around 100 years later, fully automated assembly lines emerged as we entered the third revolution, where robotic systems were programmed to replace manual work. A lot of progress has been made since, as we find ourselves at the dawn of the fourth revolution: Industry 4.0.

The term Industry 4.0 refers to the integration of information and communication technology in industrial production. As a key element of Industry 4.0, companies are implementing artificial intelligence (AI) and the Internet of Things (IoT) to improve production processes and create intelligent systems. Industrial utilisation of IoT involves the use of sensors, software and electronics linked to industrial machines, allowing real-time data on performance to be collected and analysed. Many logistics companies have been using IoT to manage inventory. Similarly, 3D printing enables parts to be stored as design files in virtual inventories, so that they can be produced on-demand. Augmented reality (AR) is also influencing modern production. For example, a leading supplier of jet engines is currrently testing AR glasses to help their mechanics perform maintenance tasks.

These developments, along with others such as big data, cloud computing and advanced robotics, not only provide endless opportunities for modern production, they also put pressure on companies. If companies cannot move with the times, they will be left behind by those who can.

B Copy the table and note down examples of passive constructions in different tenses.

passive construction in the …	example
1. simple present	…
2. present progressive	is being discussed (l. 1), …
3. present perfect simple	…
4. simple past	…

C Choose four active sentences from the text and change them into the passive.

Example: You cannot avoid it nowadays. → It cannot be avoided nowadays.

● **D** Use the picture to write four passive sentences about Industry 4.0 using different tenses.

Example: Automation was introduced to make production more efficient.

Analysing the structure of a non-fictional text

Writers structure their texts deliberately to have a particular effect on the reader. In your exam, you might be asked to analyse the structure of a non-fictional text. To do this, you should use terminology that shows you understand how structural features influence what the reader takes from the text (see the table below). → S10.2

feature	intention	analysis
opening	to spark interest in the reader	How does the writer introduce ideas/ questions? e.g. *The writer begins with … In l.xx he/she introduces/asks … This highlights that …*
repetition or patterns	to emphasise or highlight an idea / a problem / a question	What do these repetitions / patterns stress? e.g. *In l. xx, repetitions/patterns of … are used. This stresses (lack of) development/ …*
direct speech and quotes	to show different points of view, to give the text more credibility or to add to the importance of issues raised	Are these elements used to give examples, to emphasise or to introduce points of view? e.g. *In l.xx., the author makes use of a strong direct quote by … This has the effect that …*
cause and effect	to describe the cause of an event and the consequences e.g. *is caused by …, for this reason, as a result, leads to …*	Does the writer use cause and effect-relationships to get his/her message across? e.g. *By using a cause and effect-relationship in l.xx, the author expresses her/his opinion …*
comparison and/or contrast	to show difference or similarity e.g. *Different from / to …, Same as …, Similar to …, As opposed to …, Instead of …, Compared with / to …, however, but, yet*	What effect does the use of comparisons and contrasts have on the text and the reader? e.g. *In l.xx, contrast is used to make the reader aware of … A comparison is presented in l.xx, where the author raises the issue of …*
problem and solution	to describe a problem and present possible solutions e.g. *The problem / question is …, A solution might be …, One answer is …*	Does the writer focus on problems, solutions or both? What effect does this have? e.g. *The author focuses on the problem of … in l.xx but also offers a solution straight away. This gives the reader the impression that …*
closing	to give the reader some food for thought, to make a final statement or to forge a bridge to the beginning	Is the reader provided with answers or left with open questions? How does the end relate to the beginning? e.g. *The text ends with …, leaving the reader … The end relates to the beginning in that …*

A Read the text on p. 49. Complete the following analysis of how the author tries to grab the reader's attention in the opening with the correct words.

describes | emphasises | feature | idea | implies | repetition

The author opens with the (1) that things which were unimaginable in the past are now reality. In ll. 8–10, she makes use of (2) by using the word 'smart' several times in one sentence. With this (3), she (4) the fact that because of AI, we nowadays have a very high technological standard. The opening (5) that this is a positive development, as she (6) in detail in ll. 5–7 what beneficial influence this 'smartness' has on our lives.

A different kind of intelligence
by Sara Khan

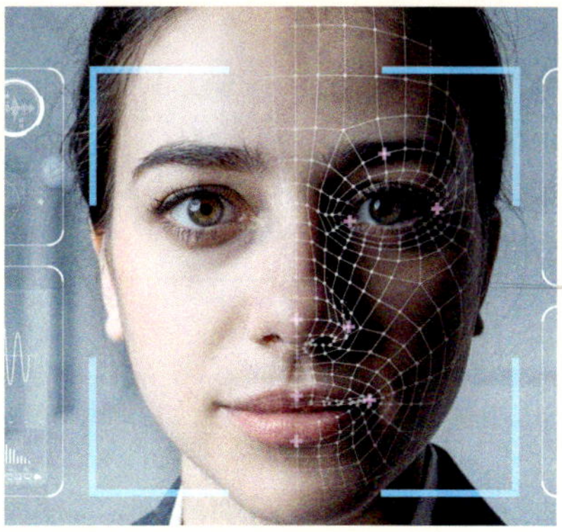

What used to be the subject of science fiction stories and comics is now a part of everyday life. Over time, artificial intelligence (AI) has been developed to make our lives easier, more convenient and more efficient. From the smartphones in our pockets, to the smart devices and smart cars in our smart homes, and the smart factories keeping our smart cities running, it seems that AI has all the answers.

But have things gone too far? What are the potential dangers of placing too much power and control in the hands of AI? As a society, it seems we are putting more faith and responsibility in machines and algorithms and are consequently giving up some control. Take facial recognition, for example. On the one hand, the police could use facial recognition to not only identify and catch criminals, but also find missing people or help tighten up security in airports and other public areas. However, others argue that such technology imposes on personal freedom. The problem is that some countries with questionable levels of state control, such as the UAE, North Korea and China, commonly use facial recognition technology to spy on their citizens, and such examples create mistrust. One solution is that the countries who intend to use this technology are completely transparent about their intentions. Trusting governments has been an issue since long before AI. This shows the complexity of the debate surrounding AI, and any technological advancement for that matter. Many people want the advantages it can bring but are worried about the potential threats to security, privacy or health. A leading British sociologist recently argued that "We are standing at the crossroads in terms of technological progress and ethics, and it's essential that we choose the right path. If we don't, there may be no way back."

The question is which path to choose. Can we find the correct balance of artificial and human intelligence? Can we make our lives easier without giving up too much control? Can we embrace technological progress and make the world a better place? The future is definitely bright, but we must be aware of what is lurking in the shadows. (366 words)

B Use the table on p. 48 to analyse the structure of the main part of the text (ll. 12–28). Find these structural features, listed in the order they appear. Give line numbers.

1. contrast
2. cause and effect
3. contrast
4. problem and solution
5. contrast
6. direct speech and quotes

C Explain briefly what effect the structural elements you identified in exercise B have on the reader. Use the table on p. 48 to help you.

D Analyse the closing of the text (ll. 29–32) and write a similar text as in exercise A. You can use the words below to help you.

contrast | figure of speech | question(s) | repetition | imagery | ambigous

E What do you think the overall purpose of the text is? Does the text want to describe, instruct, argue, persuade and/or inform? Discuss with a partner. Give reasons and examples from the text. → WB, p. 22/1–2

C Genetic engineering

BEFORE YOU READ

1 Know – Wonder – Learned

a Draw a table with three columns entitled "know", "wonder" and "learned". In the first column, note down in keywords what you already know about genetic engineering. In the second column, note down what you would like to find out about it.

b Exchange your prior knowledge as well as your questions in class.

c Leave the third column empty for the time being. After having worked through this text workshop, look at the second column again and see which of your questions were answered. Note down the answers to your questions in the third column.

2 Talking about genetic engineering

a Look at the pictures and describe them. Use a bilingual dictionary to help you. → ○ 4

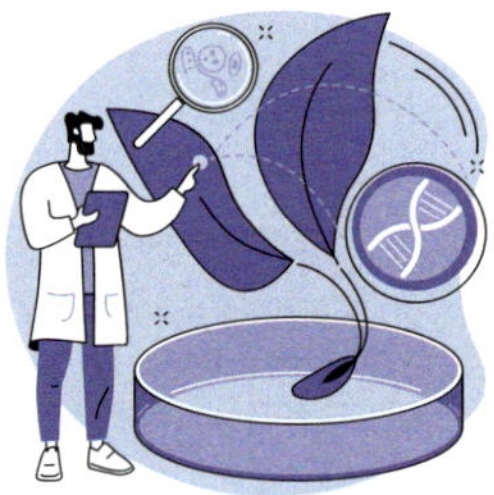

b Discuss with a partner how these pictures and the information in the box below relate to the topic of genetic engineering. Use the following keywords to help you. Report back to the class.

animal testing | cloning | curing diseases | decoding | designer babies | combating world hunger | experiments | genetic modification | genome | GM food | research and development | health and safety

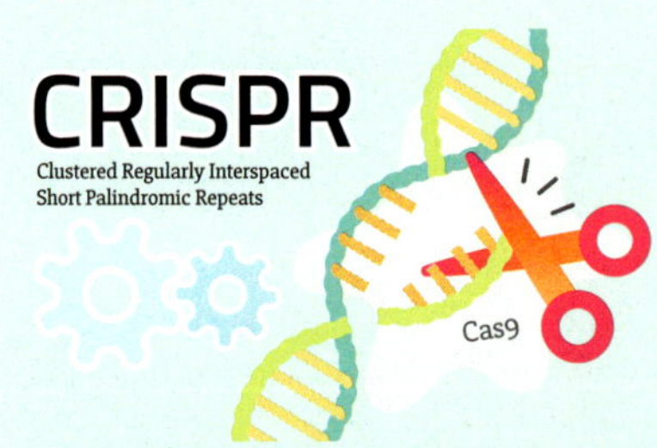

In 2012, the French microbiologist Emmanuelle Charpentier and the US-American biochemist Jennifer Doudna made a discovery that revolutionised the work in laboratories around the world. They described how a defence system that bacteria use against viruses can be utilised as a universal tool in genome editing. In 2020, Charpentier and Doudna were awarded the Nobel Prize in Chemistry for their discovery.
Crispr (Clustered Regularly Interspaced Short Palindromic Repeats), also called Crispr/Cas9, can modify the DNA of organisms more precisely than any technology before it. The tool consists of an enzyme called Cas9, which functions like a tiny pair of scissors that can cut DNA. Once the scissors have separated and removed a faulty gene segment, the cell's natural repair mechanisms patch the DNA back together. Gene sequences can be inserted or changed in the process.

Gene editing will let us control our very evolution. Will we use it wisely?

[...] We live in a time when science and technology are having an impact on our society in more and more ways. And the decisions that shape how these new fields of knowledge develop ultimately affect all of us.

When I studied biology in high school, I didn't learn about DNA for a very simple reason. The work of Francis Crick, James Watson, Rosalind Franklin and others who unlocked the structure of the basic code of life was still years away. The idea of engineering human beings? Well, that was firmly the stuff of science fiction, like Aldous Huxley's dystopian novel *Brave New World* (published a year after my birth). It seemed as likely as, say, going to the moon.

There are a few inferences you can make from this framing of my life. One is that I have been on the planet for a while. The other is the speed of change in what we know about what life is, and how we can control it, has accelerated at a rapid rate. Now we as a species are on the precipice of being able to manipulate the very building blocks of human evolution, not to mention wield unpredictable change on the greater world around us. Even as I commit that thought to paper, I pause in awe at its implications.

I have lived through eventful times and my job as a journalist has been to chronicle wars, presidents and sweeping social movements such as civil rights. I have seen a world in flux, but when I try to peer into the future I come to the conclusion that this story of humankind's ability to understand life on its most intimate level and be able to tinker with it for our benefit or detriment is likely to be the biggest one I will ever cover.

[...] This brings me to a term that has become a big part of my life over the last few years: Crispr. Perhaps you know of it. Perhaps you don't. When I first heard of it, I thought it might be a new brand of toaster. I now know it's an extremely powerful tool for editing genes in seemingly any organism on Earth, including humans. Scientists doing basic research have been uncovering the mechanisms of life for decades. They have been creating tools for modifying individual genes but Crispr is one of those revolutions where what researchers thought might be possible in the distant horizon is suddenly available now. It's cheap, it's relatively simple and it's remarkably precise.

I immediately knew that this was a story that needed telling. *Human Nature*, the resulting film – full disclosure, I am executive producer – came out of our conversations with scientists. They tend not to be the type of people who hype things but when they talk about Crispr you can feel the urgency in their voices. This is something you need to know about. All of you. If you are worried about your health or the health of your children. If you are concerned about how we might need to engineer our planet in the face of the climate crisis. If you are in finance, law or the world of tech. This will shape all of it.

And as we grapple with the unintended consequences of the internet and social media, as we try to make progress against a heating planet, I humbly submit that we as a species tend not to be good at thinking through where we are going until a crisis is already upon us. I fervently hope with Crispr that we can start the conversation sooner. That we can start it now. That's why we made the film.

To be clear, we are probably a long way from designing babies to be more intelligent or more musically inclined. Life is just too complex for that, at least right now. More immediately, there is so much about this technology that is very exciting. As someone who remembers a time when my classmates were struck down with childhood diseases for which we now have vaccines, I know science can have profound applications for human health. Crispr could cure genetic diseases such as sickle cell and Huntington's. It is being tested against cancers and HIV. It could also

27 **precipice** Abgrund
30 **to wield** *hier:* vornehmen
32 **awe** Ehrfurcht
38 **in flux** im Wandel
42 **to tinker with** herumbasteln
43 **detriment** Nachteil
64 **full disclosure** *hier:* ganz offen
77 **to grapple** ringen
80 **humbly** bescheiden; demütig
94 **struck down** niedergestreckt
96 **profound** umfassend
98 **sickle cell** Sichelzellkrankheit
100 **cancer** Krebs *(Krankheit)*

potentially be used to make crops more drought-resistant or food more nutritious. On the other hand, we are walking closer to a world Aldous Huxley foresaw. What does it mean to be human? Where should we draw the boundaries beyond which we dare not cross? The inspiring researchers we talked to for the film know that the ethical and moral questions this technology raises are not for them to decide. Science has given us the tools, but not the answers. This is up to us, all of us. We need to be informed. We need to be honest with what's real and what's not. And we need to add our voices to a global conversation. That's part of our responsibility as humans living on Earth today. (851 words)

Dan Rather, *The Guardian*, 2019

WORKING WITH THE TEXT

3 Reading for gist

Skim the text and find a suitable heading for each paragraph. → ○ 5

4 Reading for detail → WB, p. 23/1

a In your own words, outline why Crispr is "an extremely powerful tool" (ll. 50–51).

b Explain why Dan Rather felt compelled to make a film about Crispr.

c Illustrate why the author thinks that "there is so much about this technology that is very exciting" (ll. 91–92).

D2 12
Self-check 1.2

5 Focus on analysis → S 10.2 → WB, p. 23/2

a Describe how the author tries to grab the reader's attention in the opening (ll. 1–8).

b Identify the structural features the author uses in the main part of the text (ll. 9–86) and in the ending (ll. 87–117). Give line numbers. → ○ 6

c Analyse the structural features used and the effects they have on the reader.

D8 18
Self-check 3.1

6 Writing a blog post → S 6.2

Write a blog entry in which you comment on the article and give your opinion on Dan Rather's initial question as to whether humans will use gene editing wisely (l. 1–2).

7 Focus on grammar → G 3

Change these active sentences from the text into the passive.

1. There are a few inferences you can make from this framing of my life. (ll. 21–22)
2. This will shape all of it. (l. 76)
3. I fervently hope with Crispr that we can start the conversation sooner. (ll. 83–85)
4. Crispr could cure genetic diseases such as sickle cell and Huntington's. (ll. 97–99)
5. Science has given us the tools, but not the answers. (ll. 111–112)

A STEP FURTHER

8 Online research

MK

Do some research on Dan Rather and his documentary *Human Nature*. Prepare a fact sheet with the key information. Take different sources into account. Compare your fact sheet with another pair's.

9 Words matter

With a partner, use the following words related to the topic of food production and GMOs to create a word web. Add more topic-related words or phrases. → 7

benefits | concerns | crop yield | ethical issues | food security | GM crops | interbreeding | malnutrition | risks | sustainability

10 Working with a cartoon → S 11.3

D6 I6 Self-check 1.6

Describe and analyse the cartoon.

11 Listening → S 2, S 3 → WB, p. 24/3

D11 I11 Self-check 4.0

A9 Listen to a report about GMOs and answer the questions in keywords:

1. What exactly is a GMO?
2. What percentage of the world's population does not have enough to eat?
3. What are some benefits of GM crops? Name three.
4. Why was 'Golden rice' created?
5. How could GMOs endanger the ecosystem?
6. What is the difference between testing on animals and testing on humans?

12 Working with a diagram → S 11.4

D6 I6 Self-check 1.6

a Carry out a class survey on the question "Would you be prepared to exclusively consume GMOs for a month?" Note down the results.

b Describe and analyse the graph. Compare and discuss the results with those of your class survey.

Widespread skepticism about the safety of genetically modified foods

% who say genetically modified foods are generally ... to eat

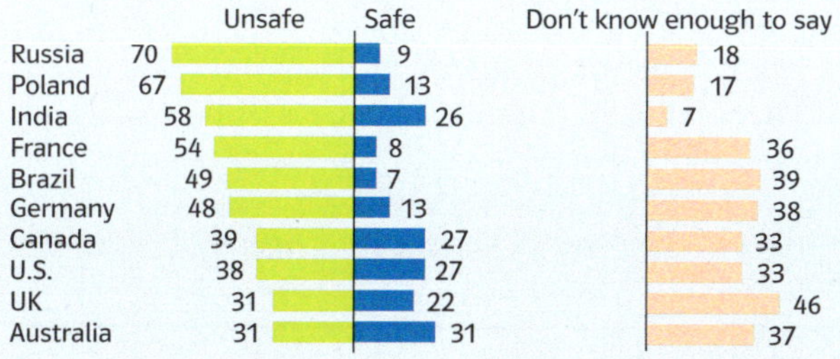

Source: International Science Survey 2019–2020. Q20. "Science and Scientists Held in High Esteem Across Global Publics"

D Surveillance and state control

BEFORE YOU READ

1 Talking about CCTV in schools

a Imagine your school is thinking about installing CCTV cameras with facial recognition technology in every area on school premises. Work with a partner and write down at least three pros and three cons.

b Exchange your ideas with another pair's and rank the three strongest pros and cons. Present your results in class.

GOOD TO KNOW

facial recognition technology = an AI-based technology which analyses a person's facial structure in order to detect their presence or identity

2 Discussion

Discuss in groups how it would affect your and your family's everyday life if the government decided to put CCTV cameras in private homes in order to monitor its citizens. Present and compare your ideas in class.

Inversion is a short story written by British author Colin Neville. It is set in a fictional society and deals with the issues of surveillance and state control.

Inversion

by Colin Neville

As George mounted the stairs the camera on each landing followed his progress, the soft clicking of its movement reminding him of its presence. [...] His wife, Helen, was there, preparing vegetables by the sink. She did not turn to greet him. Neither of them spoke. George poured some tea and sat down. Helen chopped at carrots, the sharp tapping on the wooden board the only sound in the room.

She stopped and turned to him. 'Well?'

'No chance.'

Helen returned to the chopping board; the tempo increased.

'What did you say to him?' She looked at his reflection in the window facing her.

He looked beyond her stiff back to her face in the glass. Anger stirred, rose and elbowed past his weariness. 'I told him. We need more money. Just a bit more to manage on, now Bobby's growing so fast.'

'A bit more!' She shook her head. 'What did he say?'

'He said that unless work picks up there's no chance of a wage increase at the moment, but to ask him again in three months. And I didn't push it. He could easily replace me.'

His wife clattered plates onto the table. One spun and slowly patted to a stop. He snatched the newspod and looked at the screen, but the words were a blur.

He had tried – he really had – to get a rise in wages. He hadn't had an increase in two years. But he was scared he would be replaced if he made a big deal out of it. There were four million unemployed now and his job was not skilled, and it was probably only his length of service at the factory that protected him these days.

3 **to mount the stairs** die Treppe hinaufgehen
3 **landing** Treppenabsatz
6 **to chop** hacken; klein schneiden
12 **anger** *(no pl)* Zorn; Wut
13 **weariness** Erschöpfung; Müdigkeit
19 **to snatch** schnappen; ergreifen

George looked at the tight face of his wife. He could not contain it. Fury spewed its prepared piece.

'Why don't you ever support me? Eh? You don't know what it's like for me. I know we need more money, but everyone is shitting themselves at the factory about losing their jobs if we don't get more orders. And I come home to this ... this ... this!'

He scraped the chair back and banged out of the kitchen. [...]

They had a visitor the following evening. It was a middle-aged woman in the green uniform of an Area Social Worker. She spoke in a neutral voice, her face expressionless in an attempt to appear objective. Complaints had been received about their frequent and loud quarrels in the presence of a child under five. The government, she said, had clearly established '... a link between children under five witnessing their parents' quarreling, and teenage crime.'

Helen shook her head. 'We quarrel because I'm stuck at home all day now because of this new law. We can't manage on George's money alone. We just about got by when I was working.'

The Social Worker had heard it before. 'Mothers looking after their young children full time are the best protection against juvenile crime.'

'But at what price? If mothers can't work now until their kids are school age, they're going to go crazy cooped up all the time with them. That's not going to do the children any good, seeing their mothers screwed up. And I don't believe this juvenile crime is the real reason', said Helen. 'It's about keeping the unemployment figures down, isn't it? Come on admit it, isn't that the real reason?'

'I'm not getting into a pointless discussion with you about this.'

George noted that her voice had changed; the objective tone dropped.

'Quarreling in front of your child is anti-social and selfish. You need to think about your son's long term welfare.'

A visual monitor would be installed in the flat. Their behaviour would be observed for a while at Area Office – discreetly – no one else would know. It was, she said, '... for the best. No one wants to see your child taken into care. But responsible parents think beyond their own needs and grievances.'

A Social Service Technician came and installed a monitor in every room. Each was contained within a small box with a cylindrical screen. A lens was visible inside. It followed their movements, clicking as it went, and seemed to cock its mechanical head to the side as they spoke. The monitors had a malevolent presence in the flat. [...]

After Bobby went to bed, Helen and George sat in silence. Helen spoke. 'Have you asked him again?'

'Wh ... what?'

'Have you asked him again? For a rise. It's been three months now.'

Her words, sharp as a siren, penetrated the fog in his head.

He looked with alarm at her. What was she doing raising this subject?

'No, no, the time's not right, still not right.' He struggled to keep his voice neutral.

'Yes, you're right, of course. O yes,' she continued pleasantly, 'always right.'

Her clown's smile leered. 'We haven't been close to each other much recently, have we? It's been a long time since we've really told each other our feelings, isn't it?'

George glanced at the monitor; it seemed to be eyeing them with even greater curiosity.

She went on. 'You've been a great strength and comfort to me you know, these last three months. My rock.'

He felt his anger coiling, but he pulled it back.

She persisted, 'I wish I had your strength. Yes.' She moved closer, put her arm around his neck. 'What a man to have. So strong.' He felt the taut hardness of her body against his.

24 **to spew** (aus)speien
29 **to scrape** schrammen
31 **expressionless** ausdruckslos
33 **quarrel** Streit; Auseinandersetzung
42 **cooped up** eingesperrt
56 **to cock** (den Kopf) schief legen
57 **malevolent** böse; übelwollend
66 **to leer** *hier:* heimtückisch blicken
68 **to glance at** einen Blick werfen; blicken
71 **to coil** *hier:* (sich) zusammenballen
73 **taut** angespannt

78 **knuckle** Knöchel
79 **to arc** *hier:* überbrücken

George looked at his wife: her lank and unkempt hair, her careless dress. He understood. He pulled his face into a rictus grin.

'Well, if I am strong, you're the reason for it. You're a woman to be proud of. I'm a lucky man.'

They grasped hands and squeezed until their knuckles whitened. They stared at each other, their smiles rigid. But their thoughts had arced the distance between them. He felt a familiar peak of tension that slowly ebbed away. He saw from her eyes that it was the same for her. She rested her head against his. He felt her body gradually relax into him. The room was quiet. The sounds of other tenants drifted up to them. Outside, a man tending the communal garden scraped mud from a spade. The monitor continued its stare. (1,059 words)

WORKING WITH THE TEXT → WB, p. 25/1

3 Reading for gist

Read the short story and sum up in a few sentences the situation the couple find themselves in.

4 Reading for detail → WB, p. 25/2

a Outline why George is worried that he will lose his job.

b Explain why monitors are installed after the social worker's visit.

c Describe the emotions Helen and George are going through in the last scene (ll. 58–84). Quote from the text to support your answer and give line numbers.

● 5 Words matter

Replace the underlined parts with words and phrases that express the same idea.

1. 'He said that unless work picks up there's no chance of a wage increase at the moment, ...' (l. 16)
2. But he was scared he would be replaced if he made a big deal out of it. (l. 21)
3. You don't know what it's like for me. (l. 26)
4. Complaints had been received about their frequent and loud quarrels in the presence of a child under five. (ll. 32–33)
5. But responsible parents think beyond their own needs and grievances. (ll. 52–53)

D5 I5
Self-check 1.5

6 Focus on analysis → S 8.1, S 9.4, S 9.6

a Characterise George and Helen as they are presented in this extract. Take the stylistic devices used by the author into account. → ○ 8

D3 I3
Self-check 1.3

b Examine the narrative perspective of the short story.

c Analyse the effect the narrative perspective has on the reader.

D10 I10
Self-check 3.3

7 Writing a letter → S 6.4

Write a letter to Helen in which you comment on her behaviour. Do you think she is responsible for the surveillance monitors? Is she right to complain about it? Will her play-acting be successful?

A STEP FURTHER

D6 16
Self-check 1.6

8 Working with a chart → S11.4

a Describe and analyse the chart.

b Work in groups and discuss your own opinions on the use of facial recognition technology in each situation mentioned in the survey. Report back to the class.

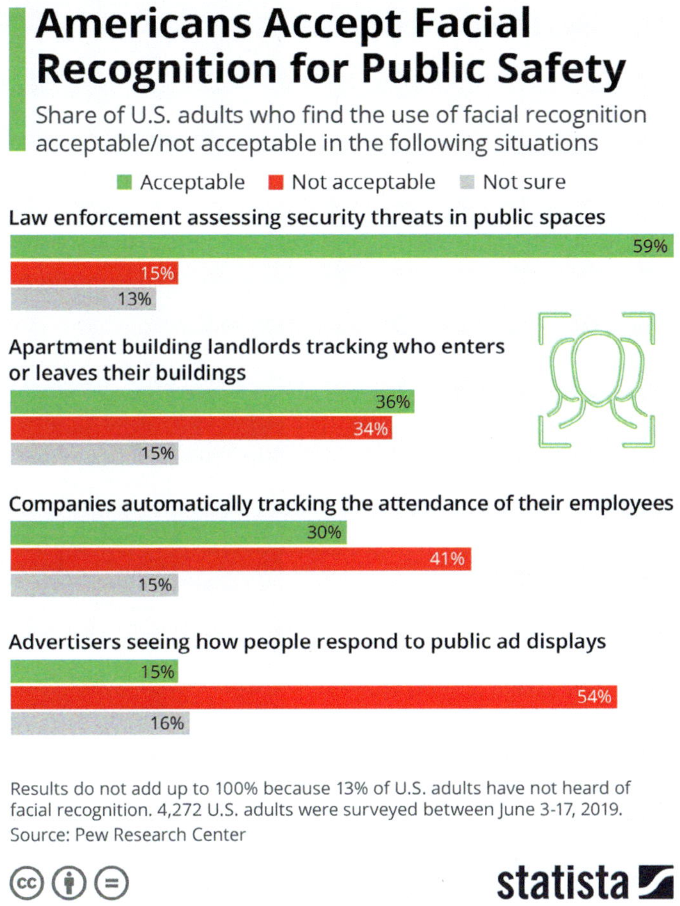

9 CULTURE Project: CCTV and facial recognition technology worldwide

a Work with a partner. Choose a country from the list below or make your own choice. Research the areas in which CCTV and facial recognition technology are used in your chosen country and to what extent.

Canada | China | Dubai | Germany | India | Japan | North Korea | Russia | Singapore | UK | USA

b Sum up the key information, including the positives and negatives and the effects on the local population, and prepare a 3–5-minute presentation.

c Give your presentations and say why you think your chosen country stands out in comparison to other countries. Discuss in class what forms of surveillance and supervision you have heard about would be acceptable or unacceptable for you as citizens of Germany. → S14.1

Analysing a film/series about the future

V3 **Step 1** Watch the video "How to recognize a dystopia" twice. Answer the questions in keywords.

1. What is the meaning of the word 'dystopia'?
2. What was one of the first dystopian novels ever written and who was the author?
3. Which technological developments and political movements between the late 18th and the mid-20th century inspired authors like H.G. Wells, Aldous Huxley, Jewgeni Samjatin, George Orwell and Sinclair Lewis? Name at least three.
4. What topics did dystopian literature and films focus on in the decades after WWII?
5. What does today's dystopian fiction focus on?

Step 2 Work in groups and choose a film/series that is set in the future. Prepare a presentation about the film/series and its depiction of life in the future, including the following parts:

1. A fact sheet with key information about the film/series
   - Title
   - Year of release
   - Director
   - Genre
   - Main actors
2. A summary of the plot
3. An explanation of which aspect of humanity or society the film/series focuses on
4. A characterisation of the protagonist(s)
5. An analysis of one or two scenes, including:
   - a short summary of the scene(s)
   - a characterisation of the characters in the scene(s)
   - an analysis of cinematic devices (e.g. camera shots, angles and movements)
   - an analysis of the atmosphere

Step 3 Take turns to present your films/series. Answer these questions in your presentation:
- What are the contrasts between the world portrayed and the situation today?
- To what extent have or may the predictions come true?
- How likely does the future scenario look based on the situation today?
- Is it an example of dystopian fiction as described in the video? Why or why not?

Step 4 As a class, decide on which film/series you would like to watch together.

Step 5 Once you have watched the film/series, write a review in which you:
- outline the plot
- explain the vision of the future portrayed
- say whether you liked the film/series or not

Opportunities and challenges of modern technologies and interconnected societies

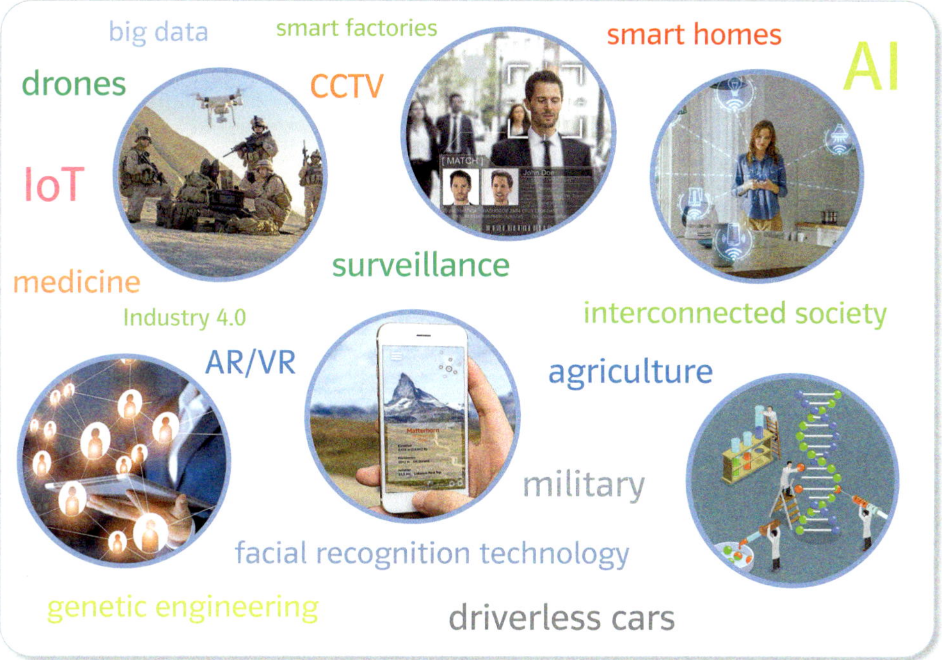

Most people associate **artificial intelligence (AI)** with human-like robots, but AI can also be found in many everyday life: for example, the personalisation of the news feed on your social networks, product recommendations on e-commerce platforms, spam filters in our email accounts as well as grammar and spellcheckers in word processing programmes. AI is also put to use in live mapping and navigation systems to analyse the traffic movement and consider real-time reports of construction or accidents in order to re-route or adjust arrival times accordingly.

What are characteristics of **big data**?

Volume: Big data sets typically include significant amounts of information, up to hundreds of terabytes, tens of petabytes or more.

Variety: This information comes from a wide range of sources in many formats.

Velocity: Big data arrives at speed, and for many applications it must be processed and analysed just as quickly – often in real-time.

The **Internet of Things (IoT)** not only connects devices via the internet, but it also helps create the **interconnected society** in which we live. Some of the main advantages of IoT are the access to real-time information, efficient communication and the chance to create smart cities where vast networks of devices can improve our living environment by sharing information and promoting energy-efficient and sustainable decisions. However, some argue there is a risk to data privacy when information is shared and transmitted through IoT devices. But perhaps the greatest risk is that we will get so used to the benefits and conveniences that IoT offers us, that we will become dependent on our increasingly smart devices, homes and cities – and what happens if the systems crash or are hacked?

9 **to adjust** anpassen
11 **volume** Menge
14 **velocity** Geschwindigkeit
22 **to transmit** übertragen

27 **selective breeding** gezielte Züchtung

Genetic engineering may be a relatively modern development, but people have been using selective breeding methods to modify living organisms for thousands of years, e.g. to create desired traits in crops, cattle and dogs. However, recent advances in biotechnology have meant that scientists can directly modify the DNA of organisms more precisely. While many of these organisms are used for scientific research in laboratories, others are produced for human consumption, such as a breed of salmon which has been modified to reach its full size in 18 months rather than 3 years.

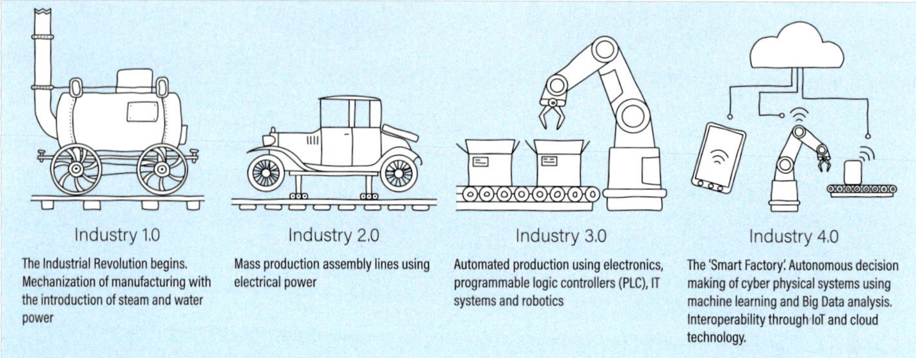

One thing is clear: The way we live, work, eat, communicate, entertain ourselves and move around has changed and will continue to develop. We have become an **interconnected society** and technological progress has the power to make us more efficient, but also more reliant on it. It can keep us safe, or under **surveillance**. It can feed the world, or put the control over nutrition in the hands of multinational companies. The future may not be entirely in our own hands, but it will play out before our eyes.

1 In pairs, choose one of the words from the word cloud on p. 59 and talk about it for 90 seconds. Your partner stops the time. Take turns and choose at least three words each.

2 Describe one of the pictures on p. 59 and analyse the extent to which it shows positive or negative aspects of technological progress.

3 Work with a partner and discuss the benefits and risks of the use of AI in everyday life and take notes. Present your findings in class.

4 Refer back to the word cloud on p. 59 and discuss in groups what you think are the most controversial areas of science and technology.

Outlook: For further discussion, consider the following questions:
- What changes should be made in education to give young people the best chance of success in the era of Industry 4.0?
- In your opinion, what are the most sensible ways to implement genetic engineering in the future?
- Try to imagine your life in 20 years' time. Describe a normal day in terms of how technology may influence your daily routine.

1 Lesen und Schreiben

Helsinki's huge VR gig hints at the potential of virtual tourism

[...] According to Finland's National Police Board, this year's Vappu Eve (the festive night before May Day, when the country traditionally enjoys public fun and frolics) was "exceptionally peaceful". Citizens largely respected calls to stay at home. And yet ... I found myself at a gig in Helsinki's Senate Square with almost 150,000 other people. I was dressed as a giant pineapple called Temperamenttinen Satuilija (Temperamental Fabulist!), and was tossing champagne at Finnish rap duo JVG as they performed live on a stage, in front of the city's neoclassical cathedral. Just another day in lockdown.

Though it happened in real time, the event was held in the virtual world. While Temperamenttinen – my avatar – was bopping in the Nordic twilight, I was at home, at my computer, cat on knee, finger on mouse, sending gestures and fizz-bottle emojis to the duo, who could see the feedback as they performed. I can't say it had the buzz of being at a "proper" concert. And JVG weren't my personal jam. But, technically, it was impressive. Without the requirement of a VR headset, I was watching humans, performing in real time, in front of an interactive audience, within a world of meticulously rendered make believe.

Virtual Helsinki – launched in late 2018 – is the physical capital's digital twin. It was built using 3D modelling from open data (supplied by the city), as well as drawings and images. It allows users to experience key landmarks as they choose, and it claims to be one of the world's most realistic VR experiences.

The platform is part of the city's bid to become the virtual capital of the world. "We are embedding digital innovation into all of the city's activities. Simply, digitalisation builds better cities – it means personalised services and more choice," says Laura Aalto, CEO of Helsinki Marketing. Helsinki is a good test-bed for VR: big enough to enable the development and trial of significant innovations, small enough for it to be feasible. The Covid-19 lockdown has spurred such a trial. [...]

The live show was watched on 460,000 computers. With a conservative estimate of 1.5 viewers per computer, that is almost 700,000 people – Finland's biggest online event. Of those, 149,403 attended by creating avatars, though the camera largely focused on the band and, with only 500 avatars visible at a time, you'd have been lucky to pick yourself out on screen – even dressed as a pineapple.

The gig was a success, but what does it – and virtual tourism more widely – mean for the future of travel? Helsinki is seeking to be a pioneer of sustainable tourism, and allowing people to visit without racking up carbon emissions certainly aids that.

"The travel industry needs to reinvent itself and I hope this encourages other destinations to experience with digital platforms," says Mikko Rusama, chief digital officer at City of Helsinki. "Some are suspicious and think no technology can replace a real visit – which in a way is true. But VR can bring about new experiences that are impossible in real cities."

Virtual Helsinki plans to develop its content – art exhibitions, shopping experiences, "re-lived" historical events – and to make it all multi-user. "Multiplayer functions enable visitors to become social in virtual cities," says Rusama. "That will have a big impact on people's interest to explore places virtually."

But, when we're permitted to move again, will the city have made actually visiting it feel unnecessary? "No, the idea is to offer visitors an alternative way of experiencing the city in addition to travelling here," says Aalto.

"Customer behaviour is likely to change radically post-corona[virus]. We won't stop travelling but the reasons will be different. We need a stronger "why"; visits will be more in line with what we stand for. The winners in the future tourism industry are those that can understand and meet the values of visitors."

[...] [D]estinations across the world are brainstorming ways to create virtual content to keep visitors interested [...]. There are 360-degree tours: we can scan the mountains of Switzerland, the skyscrapers of Dubai or the Great Barrier Reef; and 3D modelling allows us to take tours of Egypt's ancient wonders that offer such clarity we can see chisel marks on the walls. Also, festivals and events have moved online [...].

And we can expect more, believes Dr Timothy Jung, founder and director of the Creative AR & VR Hub at Manchester Metropolitan University. "The role of VR will increase," he says. "The tourism industry may need to consider hybrid experiences – a combination of real and virtual – in the future. And, after this forced isolation, people will be more open for virtual experience as an alternative way of socialising and enjoying life. It might be accepted as the new normal within tourism." (800 words)

Sarah Baxter, *The Guardian* website, 2020

ASSIGNMENTS → WB, pp. 26–27/1–4

1. Describe what Virtual Helsinki is and what it offers to its users.
2. Analyse the author's language, including the frequent use of quotes, and the effect it has on the reader.
3. Choose one of the following tasks:

   3.1 In the text, Dr. Timothy Jung says: "And, after this forced isolation, people will be more open for virtual experience as an alternative way of socialising and enjoying life." (ll. 120–123) Comment on how VR can have a positive effect on people's lives.

   Or:

   3.2 Write an email to the author in which you comment on the idea that virtual tourism has the potential to become a viable alternative to real-life tourism. Include opportunities and risks of virtual tourism.

2 Hörverstehen

ASSIGNMENTS → WB, p. 27/1

A10

1. Listen to a report about the testing of driverless cars. Answer the following questions in keywords:

   a) What service is Waymo testing?
   b) How do you contact the driverless car?
   c) How often does Shawn Metz use the service?
   d) What does he use the service for? Name three reasons.
   e) What do Shawn and his family hope to achieve by using this service?

A11 2. Listen to a discussion about the safety issues of self-driving vehicles. While listening, note down the correct answers (A, B or C). There is only one correct answer.

1. In March 2018, a woman was …
   A riding her bike.
   B locking up her bike.
   C walking with her bike.

2. The accident was caused by a self-driving …
   A test car.
   B car which was out of control.
   C vehicle which had technical faults.

3. Self-driving cars have …
   A special brakes.
   B a special sensor system.
   C a special ultrasound technology.

4. The accident happened because the …
   A warning system was damaged.
   B emergency braking system was turned off.
   C car did not detect the woman and the bicycle.

5. After the accident, the majority of people …
   A no longer had trust in this technology.
   B wanted to move away from the testing area.
   C were calling for a ban of all testing on public roads.

6. The self-driving vehicle operator Waymo has felt the public backlash because …
   A its self-driving vehicles were attacked.
   B the company's employees were verbally abused.
   C its services were temporarily suspended by the government.

7. Waymo is trying to …
   A move its testing area to a less populated location.
   B regain people's confidence through big marketing campaigns.
   C test as many different scenarios as possible to make their vehicles safer.

A12 3. Listen to a report about the future of self-driving cars. Take notes on the following points. You don't need to write full sentences.

1. Definition given of a fully driverless car	…
2. Difference between geofence driving and full driving automation	…
3. Estimated availability of driverless geofence driving	…
4. Estimated availability of full driving automation	…
5. Two potential problems with driverless cars in busy areas like Central London	• … • …
6. Two challenges that the developers of driverless cars have to meet	• … • …

Consumerism

Sammy_Spaniel · Follow

Sammy_Spaniel: Mum got me this new duck toy, so I don't have to chase after the real ones in the park anymore! It's so soft but still strong against my teeth. Get 10 % off with the code Sammy490@ Paws_for_Fun until Sunday!

Gianni_xo40: Cool, Sammy!
lola_dalyy: So cute. I just got one for my terrier Nino, too :)
dinowarrior: ♥♥

1 Describe each of the pictures.

2 With a partner, look at the pictures again and do the following tasks. Make notes.

a Which topics related to consumerism and advertising are shown?

b Do the pictures show a positive or negative aspect of consumption or advertising? Give reasons.

c Come up with a caption for each picture.

3 Which other positive and negative aspects of consumption can you think of? Choose one aspect and create a word web. Include your notes from exercise 2.

USEFUL PHRASES

advertisement (ad) | influencer | sales | shopping for fun / to pass the time | tiny house | shopaholic | owning too many things | fast fashion | online shopping | sustainable fashion | made from recycled materials | organic materials | greenwashing | promotion | minimalism

GOOD TO KNOW

Consumerism is the notion that increasing consumption of goods and services is a universal goal, and that happiness is directly linked to buying and owning things.

A13 **4** Listen to the first part of the podcast "Forward Thinking: Consumerism" and choose the correct answer.

1. Kasper Asgreen teaches and writes about consumerism and …
   A fitness.
   B money.
   C hygiene.
2. The most common online purchases in the UK are …
   A books.
   B fast food deliveries.
   C clothes, shoes and accessories.
3. According to Kasper, spending money has become a way of …
   A entertaining yourself.
   B gaining self-confidence.
   C getting a rush of adrenaline.
4. The average US household …
   A owns up to 3,000 pieces of clothing.
   B spends around $30,000 a year online.
   C has over a quarter of a million items in it.

A14 **5** Listen to the second part of the podcast and note down keywords to explain these terms. Then give a definition.

D 11 I 11
Self-check 4.0

1. linear economy
2. fast fashion
3. greenwashing
4. circular economy
5. vampire shopper
6. minimalism

6 Group discussion: How do you decide when to buy something and what you buy?
→ WB, p. 30/2

a Work in groups of two to three and discuss what inspires you to make a purchase – e. g. boredom, urgent necessity, appealing ad, spare money, current trend, peer pressure, etc.

b In the same group make a list of your favourite/least favourite brands. Discuss and write down what you think they stand for, what their image is, and what you like or dislike about them.

c Team up with another group to discuss your results before reporting back to the class.

USEFUL PHRASES

I often shop for things when I am …
I only buy something when …
I do/do not feel under pressure to follow trends.
I am often influenced by … when it comes to …
If I have money left over, I generally …
One brand I really like/dislike is …
In my opinion, this brand stands for sustainability/style/fitness/innovation/a healthy lifestyle/elegance/freedom.

A Shopping addiction

BEFORE YOU READ

GOOD TO KNOW

Compulsive is used to describe people or their behaviour when they cannot stop doing wrong, harmful, or just unnecessary habits.
A **disorder** is an illness of the mind or body.

1 Talking about compulsive shopping

a What do you think might be symptoms of compulsive shopping disorder (CSD)?

b What kind of person might be susceptible to developing this kind of addiction? Why?

Confessions of a 20-something man who found solace in online shopping (addiction) & overcame it

What is that one thing that gives you an unparalleled kick on a day-to-day basis? Most of you may be able to think of a number of quick responses to that, ranging anywhere from breaking a sweat in the gym at the crack of dawn, to downing a shot of espresso before you [kick-start] your day at work.

Now, while the reasons may vary for each of us, there can be no denying the fact that no matter the means, each of them serve the purpose of making us feel more prepared or equipped to take on the rest of the day, head on.

But this is where I must come forward and admit that I get my frequent doses of mental boost or "kick" out of another, a not-so-less ordinary form of activity – retail therapy, and more specifically online retail therapy. This is my story. My confession to being an online shopping addict [...]. For the longest time shopping as an indulgence has been attached to the notion that it's a woman's territory, that is to say, that "excessive" or "compulsive" shopping is more akin to a woman's behaviour, than it is to a man's. Yet, here I stand before you admitting to the possibility of #NotJustWomen and #YesMenToo.

A day in my life looks like any of yours on a given day - getting up, going for a run, quick shower and breakfast. Then I head to work, punch the keys on my keyboard for the next 8 hours, head out for a drink post work or have dinner at home. Browse through WWW/TV/Facebook. Call it a day. But then, so very often I experience these moments in a day, when all logic and reason evade me, and I feel there's no way to get past the intense need and craving, of picking items from the wishlist on an online shopping website/app and putting them into the cart. From then on, everything else kinda goes spiralling. One checkout leads to another, and I end up with multiple emails notifying me about all the goods that will soon be mine to claim.

For me, the rush, the thrill and the release comes with every buzz on my phone delivering a message of confirmation that I have bagged the items I had my eyes on, regardless of the need or use I'm expected to find in them. [...]

I let this exercise go on for as long as over two years, I started out as a 25-year-old, without ever stepping back to reconsider my shopping behaviour, until very recently, when I maxed out on all three of my credit cards within a fortnight. I had been rallying my frustration to a dear friend who finally put her foot down and pushed me to see things as they were. Apparently, I was addicted to online shopping, but I couldn't disagree with her more at the moment, I surely didn't think that was true. But isn't that just how all of us "think" when someone points out a shortcoming in us? But this was far more serious, she was calling me an addict and of course, I felt offended. But then she

1 **confession** Bekenntnis; Geständnis
1 **to find solace in** Trost in etw finden
4 **unparalleled** unüberbietbar
8 **at the crack of dawn** beim Morgengrauen; in aller Frühe
18 **dose** Dosis; Portion
20 **not-so-less ordinary** nicht so ungewöhnlich
28 **akin to** ähnlich; verwandt
39 **to call it a day** (*ugs*) Feierabend machen
47 **to go spiralling** *hier:* sich hochschrauben; ausufern
62 **to max out** das Limit erreichen
64 **to rally** *hier:* ausschütten
65 **to put one's foot down** ein Machtwort sprechen

pointed out the obvious "signs and symptoms" I had been apparently exhibiting [...]. A quick Google search and thirteen articles later, I found myself sitting across the table from my now therapist [...].

A survey conducted by Stanford University found that one in every 20 people suffer[s] from compulsive buying, and men featured in just as many numbers in the survey as did women. The only reason we don't hear about it as often is because men feel it isn't "manly" to seek help [...].

While every individual indulges in compulsive shopping for varying reason, a senior psychology lecturer at the University of Sussex, Dr. Hilga Dittmar stated that the 2 major factors are "materialist values and poor self-image", which is "taken care of" by buying things for self-improvement. For a layman, this may be translated to –

1. You enjoy shopping privately.
2. You appreciate the variety in styles and prices online shopping platforms have to offer.
3. You are big on instant gratification.

Because it makes you feel good about yourself, and life in general.

Just so you know, I ticked off each one of those points, and the following sessions with my therapist only helped me see things clearly. So here I am, still coping with the revelation, filing this confession post my diagnosis, and trying to survive each day without subconsciously reaching for my credit card every other moment. I wouldn't lie, the urge still persists, but I try to look past the pressing need to browse through every existing online shopping platform and checking out with all the good stuff, simply for the pleasure and satisfaction of it. It's true, my days seem incomplete, and most often I miss the feeling of accomplishment online shopping brought to my day, but you know what? At some point, I would have had to stop and I am glad it happened sooner than later, when it would have been too late. Thus, to simply reiterate, don't ignore your addiction and go about your day believing shopping addiction is a "woman's disease", 'cause it sure as hell isn't and you need to be aware of it.

(907 words)

Dev Sarkar, *MENSXP* website, 2018

84 **to feature** *hier:* Teil sein von
96 **layman** Laie
102 **gratification** Belohnung; Erfüllung
105 **to tick off** abhaken
109 **revelation** Enthüllung
125 **to reiterate** bekräftigen

WORKING WITH THE TEXT

2 Reading for gist → WB, p. 31/1

Briefly sum up Dev's problem and explain how it affected his life.

3 Reading for detail → WB, p. 31/2

a Explain why shopping addiction is seen as a female issue.

b According to the survey carried out by Stanford University, what percentage of people are shopping addicts and how many of them are male?

c Describe what happened when Dev started to look at things online.

d Outline how Dev came to realise that he had a problem and to what extent he is now 'cured'.

4 Replying to readers' reactions → ○1

Read the opinions on the article. Imagine you are Dev and want to reply to one of these statements. Choose one and write your reply based on the information from the text.

Matt_77 21:14
What's the issue? Just delete the shopping apps from your phone. Problem solved.

EddieM → Matt_77 21:29
If only it were that simple. I've struggled with this myself for many years and I know what Dev's going through. My problem is that I just can't ignore the sales.

Natalie → EddieM 22:01
Like Dev's story shows, we often need someone else to open our eyes. If you think you have a problem, pluck up the courage to talk to somebody you trust. It's the first step to changing your situation. Believe me, I speak from experience.

A STEP FURTHER

5 Project: Creating an informative handout → S 6.7

MK

a Work in groups of two to three. Go online to find advice on how to overcome a shopping addiction. Consider the following aspects:

recognising symptoms | self-help | therapy | changing patterns | finding support groups

b Collect all the relevant information and develop an informative handout for the person affected as well as for people wanting to support the affected person.

- Step 1: Start with general information about the addiction.
- Step 2: Focus on advice and suggestions for people affected.
- Step 3: Address people who want to support an addicted person.

c Present your informative handout in class. As a class, decide which handout you found most helpful. Give reasons.

6 Working with a cartoon → S11.3

D6 16
Self-check 1.6

Choose one of the following cartoons. Describe and analyse the cartoon. Explain how it is related to the text.

CartoonStock.com

USEFUL PHRASES

The cartoon consists of / is made up of …
There is a (short / an ironic) caption / speech bubble / thought bubble which says …
On the left-hand/right-hand side you can see …
In the foreground/background/middle/centre there is …
The cartoon criticizes/represents/is a caricature of …
This figure is a stereotype of … / is supposed to represent …
The cartoonist is making fun of …
The cartoon (only partly) achieves its aim of …
In my opinion, the cartoonist is (not) successful in presenting/criticising … because …
The cartoon appeals / does not appeal to me because …

B Sustainable consumption

BEFORE YOU READ

Aja Barber

1 Talking about shopping preferences

a Think about what's important to you when buying clothes. Put the following factors into your personal order of importance.

where it was made | quality | current trends | price | material used | how it was produced | brand

b Compare with a partner and report back to the class. Which factors were mostly at the top or bottom of your lists? Be prepared to explain your choices.

14 **ethical** ethisch; moralisch
15 **living wage** Lohn, der zum Leben ausreicht
24 **to biodegrade** (sich) biologisch abbauen
30 **garment** Kleidungsstück
36 **cruelty** Grausamkeit
36 **animal welfare** Tierwohl
40 **byproduct** Nebenprodukt
57 **hemp** Hanf
57 **silk** Seide
60 **irrigation** Bewässerung
62 **to wreak havoc on sth** sich verheerend auf etw auswirken

[...] A guide to the language of sustainable fashion

[...] Lately, shoppers have been faced with more decisions than ever when it comes to clothing and where to buy from, but one of the biggest dilemmas comes from confusion around the language of sustainability. [...] [T]he information on the label can sometimes be confusing and misleading [...]. So, here's a handy guide to help you figure out the difference between ethical and sustainable, and why you absolutely should ask for both from all your fashion purchases.

1 **Ethical** usually refers to the treatment of people. Are the workers paid a living wage? Are they given proper breaks? Is everyone of proper age? Does the company add positively to the communities in which it produces and help them to thrive? [...] Unfortunately, terms such as "ethical leather" and "faux fur" aren't always ethical for the humans that produce them and often these products do not biodegrade easily either. Can a product using PVC really be ethical if the workers who produce the PVC get sick? The best way to figure out how ethical a brand is to see how much information it puts out about the treatment of the workers who produce its garments. [...] If there is[, is] a brand you love and you're curious about worker treatment, I suggest you send a message or an email and ask what the lowest wage is in its manufacturing process.

2 **Cruelty-free** refers to animal welfare and whether any animals were hurt or harmed during the production of the garment. In fashion, it also means that the product contains no animal byproducts, but on beauty products it means the finished product wasn't tested on animals. If you want an item that is free of animal byproducts in regards to beauty, you need to look for a vegan product. [...] There are a number of cruelty-free leather options in development made from natural byproducts such as pineapple skin, but they aren't yet widely available.

3 **Organic** (in regards to materials) refers to natural fibres being grown and produced without the use of highly toxic materials such as chemical pesticides in the growing process. Cotton is probably the most common organic fibre you can buy, but it is also possible to find organic hemp, silk and jute [...]. Organic cotton has come under criticism, however, because it requires a lot more water and irrigation than conventional cotton. However, pesticides that go into conventional cotton wreak havoc on the environment, as well as the health of humans who drink from water supplies nearby. The solution isn't to discount organic cotton, it's for all of us to consume less cotton in general.

4 **Conscious fashion** is often used synonymously by the fashion industry with "ethical", "sustainable" or "eco" fashion. It's a bit of a catchall phrase that ends up being popular with brands that greenwash (see below). However, there are brands with the word "conscious" in their name [...] where the sustainability credentials do check out, so don't be deterred. A brand that has nothing to hide will have its sustainability record clearly displayed [...].

5 **Fair trade** is a partnership that refers to marginalised producers getting a fair wage for their product when it is sold in more affluent countries. [...] Fair trade has principles such as fair payment and ensuring good working conditions, which fair trade-certified clothing producers are encouraged to follow.

The problem with fair trade is that it's not a perfect solution for regulating the fashion industry. There are multiple fair-trade websites and getting a straight answer about fair-trade fashion often feels impossible. [... It] can often be better to research a company and learn how it operates, rather than rely on a certification. Even if a brand is awarded every certificate under the sun, it will still be a significant polluter if it is making 500 garments a minute.

6 **Sustainable** refers to the effect that production of a garment has on the world around us. How is it taken from the earth and how will it return to the earth? How much waste is involved in the manufacturing process? If it never biodegrades, it's not truly sustainable. In the words of Céline Semaan, founder of non-profit research team the Slow Factory, "everything you make returns to the earth as food or poison". Sustainable products should always return as food. Brands that make more sustainable products tend to use natural or recycled fibres in their creations. [...]

7 **Slow fashion** is the antithesis of fast fashion. It is high-quality garments that are designed with a long-term lifecycle in mind. In a perfect world, every item we bought would be slow fashion – but that would require us to no longer subscribe to a trend-driven market. Until the biggest fast-fashion producers in the world stop making so many garments so quickly (which, of course, means a smaller profit margin), they won't be slow or sustainable. Instead of buying into fast-fashion, research small labels and lend your support to those that are doing things the right way. [...]

8 **Greenwashing** is when a brand makes claims about something being ethical or sustainable that, upon further inspection, turn out to be false or exaggerated. An example of greenwashing is a brand claiming that a dress is eco-friendly because it's made of eco wool, when in fact it contains just 4% eco wool, along with other, less sustainable materials. Another example would be a brand loudly advertising a collection of 20 sustainable pieces while its inventory contains thousands of garments that aren't sustainable. Unfortunately, most big fast-fashion brands claiming sustainability credentials are guilty of greenwashing since they tend to produce too much product as a whole (some of which will remain unsold at the end of the season, when it becomes an additional environmental hazard). (963 words)

Aja Barber, *The Guardian*, 2019

76 **credential** Nachweis; Qualifikation
77 **to deter** abschrecken; abhalten
81 **to marginalise** *(BE)* an den Rand drängen
83 **affluent** wohlhabend
96 **to award sb sth** jmdm etw verleihen
117 **lifecycle** Nutzungszeit; Lebenszyklus (eines Produkts)
120 **to subscribe to** sich anschließen; folgen
141 **inventory** Warenbestand

WORKING WITH THE TEXT

2 Reading for gist

a Read the headings (A–H) and decide which paragraph (1–8) they fit with best.

A Back to the roots?
B Don't forget the people
C Don't believe the hype
D Better, but still not perfect
E A difficult partnership
F Don't be a slave to trends
G Being kinder to other creatures
H Watch out for greenwashing

b For each of the paragraphs 1–8, sum up in your own words which advice or tips the author gives to consumers who want to shop for clothes in a sustainable way.

3 Reading for detail → WB, p. 32/1

a Explain the difference between 'cruelty-free' and 'vegan' products in max. 100 words.

b Illustrate the link between 'conscious fashion' and 'greenwashing'. Include examples from the text. Give line numbers.

c Point out how clothing manufacturers could support 'slow fashion'.

4 Words matter → WB, p. 32/2

a Decide whether the words below are verbs, nouns, adjectives or adverbs. Then find corresponding words for the other categories. Use a dictionary if necessary.

1. sustainably
2. ethical
3. cruelty
4. organically
5. conscious
6. encourage
7. recycle

● b Use the words above to write five sentences about what is important for shopping sustainably.

A STEP FURTHER

D 11 I 11
Self-check 4.0

A15 ## 5 Listening

a You will hear five speakers giving their opinion on sustainable consumption. While listening, match the headings (A–F) with the speakers (1–5).

speaker	1	2	3	4	5
heading	…	…	…	…	…

A Power of ads
B Back to basics
C Easier said than done
D Keeping up
E No big deal
F We need transparency

b What is your opinion on sustainable consumption? Discuss with a partner.

GOOD TO KNOW

A **fact sheet** is a single-page document containing essential information about a product, person, service or other topic. Fact sheets are used to provide information in concise, simple language.

MK ## 6 Online research

Go online to find out more about Aja Barber, the author of the article. Prepare a fact sheet about her and her work.

7 Project: Sustainable clothes manufacturers

Get together in a group. Research a company producing sustainable clothes that fulfils some of the criteria mentioned in the article. Prepare a short presentation including as much of the following information as possible:

company name | location of company / production | company's mission | product range | production methods | level of transparency | availability of products

D 10 I 10
Self-check 3.3

8 Writing an email → S 6.4 → ◯ 2 → WB, p. 33/3

Write an email to Aja in which you explain to what extent her text and your research on the topic of sustainable fashion might affect how you shop for clothes in the future.

C Working in advertising

BEFORE YOU READ

1 Talking about jobs in advertising

Discuss the following questions with a partner. Take notes.

1. Which different jobs in the advertising industry can you think of?
2. What sort of skills do you imagine people working in an advertising agency might have?
3. Could you imagine working in advertising? Give reasons.
4. What do you think is the job of a copywriter?
   A to translate ads into different languages
   B to write original texts for ads or publicity material
   C to invent new ads by copying other comany's methods

Copygirl, by Anna Mitchael and Michelle Sassa, was published in 2015. It is the story of a young woman working at an advertising agency in New York. The novel is criticizing the advertising industry and an inspiring story about breaking through the glass ceiling.

Copygirl

by Anna Mitchael and Michelle Sassa

Cat lady

It's so hard to think when you have a gun pointed at your head. "First thing tomorrow, you'd better show me genius," Elliott had warned us earlier. Then he followed up with his very favorite threat: "Remember, I can fill your seats in five minutes." Come on, Kay, think. Think. THINK! I just need one good cat food slogan. It's not like I have to find the cure for cancer or invent some dome that will let us live on Mars. I type the first thing that comes to my head: Here, shitty kitty. And I am pretty darn sure that's not what Elliott has in mind. Here, shitty kitty is what Johnjoshjay say every morning when they see me coming down the hall of cubicles that comprise our ad agency's creative department. Here, shitty kitty. Here, shitty kitty. The boys' club loves to tease me, and this gem is their favorite catcall. (Pardon the pun. Occupational hazard.) It's because I'm the copywriter on Little Kitty, get it? Oh so clever. In retaliation, I refuse to call any of them by their individual name. At least, not in my own head. They deserve one generic identity since they all dress like identical little hipsters: sagging jeans, designer sneakers, ratty but overpriced T-shirts, hats on backward until they come in the door and then drop them next to their computers along with their matching leather satchels.
Those poser suck-ups think they're so great because they get to work on Superfine sneakers and Atlantis – the urban clothing line out of Brooklyn. And I'm stuck penning print ads for "pussy food". Another one of their wink-wink witticisms. But I'm not going to let any of that get me down. After all, Little Kitty is our biggest account. The proverbial cash cow. Our bread and butter. Its big budget keeps the agency lights on, so keeping the client happy keeps my bosses happy. And tonight I plan on coming up with mad genius ideas that wow the Little Kitty execs, so that Ben and I can finally get the recognition we deserve. Speaking of, where in Manhattan is my loyal work partner? I really thought he'd be back from the gym by now with the take-out dinner and brainstorming help he promised. My stomach swoons just thinking about my hunger ... and, okay, full disclosure ... thinking about him. As much as I want to nail this assignment, I secretly want to nail

8 **cancer** Krebs *(Krankheit)*
9 **to be pretty darn sure** (*ugs*) (sich) verdammt sicher sein
11 **cubicle** *an drei Seiten von halbhohen Wänden umgebene Arbeitsnische*
13 **gem** Edelstein
13 **pardon the pun** gestatten Sie dieses Wortspiel
14 **retaliation** Vergeltungsmaßnahme
17 **ratty** schäbig; verlottert
18 **satchel** Umhängetasche
20 **to pen sth** verfassen; schreiben
21 **witticism** geistreiche Bemerkung
25 **execs (= excecutives)** Direktoren/-innen; Geschäftsführer/-innen
28 **to swoon** flau werden; in Aufruhr geraten
29 **to nail sth/sb** etw schaffen; (*vulg*) jdn vögeln

35 **waking hours** Wachzustand
39 **edgy** *hier:* neu und cool
41 **to score this gig** (*ugs*) diesen Job landen

Ben even more. Cliché, I know. Girl copywriter falls for her hot art director partner. And it's quite possibly career suicide. But we've been a pair – in the work sense – since the second day of advertising school down in Atlanta, and now he's living with me, too. Granted, he sleeps on my couch, not in my bed like I wish. And, granted, the arrangement is temporary, just until he finds a place of his own. But whatever. The point is, he's totally grown on me, which is bound to happen when you spend almost all your waking hours breathing in someone's Axe body spray. Isn't there a name for that? The Axe Effect? You see, in addition to the cohabitation, Ben and I work side by side a lot. That's because we're the lucky new junior team in the creative department of Schmidt Travino Drew & Partners, one of the edgiest advertising agencies in the entire country. We must have beat out like a hundred other fresh-out-of-ad-school copywriters and art directors to score this gig. Just like creative teams at other agencies, we get paid to come up with ideas together, then Ben makes the pictures and I write the words. But unlike other agencies, ours was just named Advertising Age's Agency of the Year so we're "a big fucking deal". Tons of people would kill to steal our jobs, a fact that our creative director Elliott feels he must mention every time he briefs us on an assignment. Hence, the aforementioned gun pointing at my head. I know Ben likes me – why else would he have wanted us to take a job together after ad school? – but I'm hoping when he sees the brilliant headlines I come up with to save our asses, he gets so excited that he wants to kiss me full on the mouth. I just need to start writing. Now. [...] (728 words)

WORKING WITH THE TEXT → WB, p. 34

2 Reading for gist → ○ 3

a Skim the text and sum up the situation in two to three sentences.

b Briefly explain who the following people are and name their jobs and responsibilities. Write one to two sentences each about:

1. Kay 2. Elliot 3. Johnjoshjay 4. Ben

3 Reading for detail

Outline what Kay is thinking about while she is supposed to be inventing a slogan for cat food.

4 Words matter

Explain the following words and expressions in your own words. Use a dictionary if necessary.

1. occupational hazard (l. 13)
2. retaliation (l. 14)
3. generic identity (ll. 15–16)
4. witticism (l. 21)
5. cash cow (l. 23)
6. recognition (l. 25)
7. full disclosure (l. 28)
8. edgiest (l. 39)

D5 I5 Self-check 1.5

5 Focus on analysis → S 8, S 9.6

a Characterise Kay. Take the stylistic devices used into account. Give line numbers.

D1 I1 Self-check 1.1

b Analyse the author's use of slang words and colloquialisms and explain the effect this has on the reader. Use quotes from the text to support your answer.

A STEP FURTHER

6 Writing a diary entry → S 6.10

Write a diary entry in which Kay talks about her feelings about the working atmosphere as well as the behaviour of Elliot and "Johnjoshjay".

7 Working with a cartoon → S 11.3

Describe and analyse the cartoon and relate it to the text.

"Brilliant copy, it made me cry. It was more moving than Martin Luther King's speech. But Harris, there's one thing I keep asking myself – will it sell dog food?"

D6 I6 Self-check 1.6

8 Listening → WB, p. 35/2

A16 **a** Listen to the first part of the podcast "Forward Thinking: Marketing your business". Answer the questions in keywords. → S 2, S 3

1. What does Matilda lecture?
2. What is the idea behind her company *Fast Forward*?
3. How does she help entrepreneurs?
4. What is the most important part of running a company?
5. What does your advertising have to be like if you want to effectively reach the right audience?
6. How do companies promoting their products on social networks get users involved in their advertising campaigns?

A17 **b** Listen to the second part of the podcast and explain these marketing terms.

1. consumer benefit
2. USP
3. call to action
4. copy strategy
5. tonality
6. guerilla marketing

D11 I11 Self-check 4.0

GOOD TO KNOW

Marketing covers all the activities that help create interest in a business. It includes market research, pricing, product design and advertising.

Advertising is one element of the marketing process and includes the placement of ads in media like newspapers, magazines, direct mail, billboards, TV, radio and the internet.

9 Working with a video → S 2

MK

On the internet you can find many short video documentaries in which people working in advertising agencies talk about their jobs.

1. Work in groups of three to four. Go online and choose a video clip that you find interesting. The video should be no longer than seven minutes.
2. Write down what the people working in the advertising agencies say about their jobs, e.g. about their tasks, the pros and cons of having a creative job etc.
3. Prepare a short report about the content of the video clip and present it to the class.
4. In class, decide which clip(s) you would like to watch together.

Working with advertisements → WB, p.36

In the world of marketing and advertising, there are many different types of advertising strategies.

The **AIDA** strategy (print ads):
1. Attract immediate ATTENTION, e.g. with a surprising eye-catcher.
2. Arouse further INTEREST, e.g. with a new slogan or unusual layout.
3. Appeal to a special DESIRE or need, e.g. the need for health or comfort.
4. Finally, ask the target group to take a desired ACTION, e.g. to buy the product or to donate money.

The **KISS** strategy is good for all kinds of ads: KEEP IT SHORT AND SIMPLE.

The **PPPP** strategy says an ad should contain a PICTURE, a PROMISE, some PROOF and a PUSH to act.

The **USP** strategy concentrates on a UNIQUE SELLING PROPOSITION, i.e. a single message or piece of information about what makes the product special or desirable.

The **SUCCESS** principles are for radio/film ads:
Simplicity – find the core of your idea
Unexpectedness – grab attention by surprising
Concreteness – the idea is graspable, memorable
Credibility – make ideas believable and build trust
Emotion – make listeners respond emotionally
Stories – use true-to-life and realistic messages
Sound – build trust with a likeable voice

If you are asked to analyse a print advertisement (e.g. in your oral exam), you can use the following approach:

Introduction
Mention the following:
- advertiser
- target group
- what is being advertised (product, brand, company, person, organisation)
- main message

Main part
Explain the advertising strategy used (such as AIDA) and how the following elements contribute to the effect:
- layout (foreground/background, focus, text …)
- textual elements (heading, slogan, statement)
- relationship of language to visual content
- photographic elements
- visual element design (size/type, colours, logo)

Conclusion
Comment on the quality and effectiveness of the ad.

USEFUL PHRASES

Introduction:
The company advertising the product is called …
The ad is for a …
The ad is targeted at …
The main message of the ad is …

Main part:
In the foreground you can see …
The heading of the ad is …
The slogan suggests that …
The overall design of the ad can be described as …
The ad wants to convey the message that …
The ad uses … to get attention.
The … captures your interest.
Desire is created by …
The viewer is called to action by …

Conclusion:
In my opinion, the best/worst thing about the ad is …
This ad appeals to the intended target group because …
It is effective / not effective because …
What makes it interesting/boring/funny is …
I think it could be improved by …

A Look at the print ad below. Follow the guide on how to analyse it with the help of the AIDA strategy. Use the phrases on p. 76, add your own thoughts and write them down. Then present your analysis in class. → S 11.1

A18 **B** Listen to the radio ad and answer the following questions in keywords. → S 2

1. Who is the advertiser?
2. What product is being advertised?
3. Who do you think is the intended target group of this ad?

A18 **C** Listen again and analyse the radio ad with the help of the SUCCESS principles explained on p. 76. Answer the following questions. → S 2

1. Has this ad incorporated all the SUCCESS principles explained on p. 76 mentioned in the info box on the previous page? Give examples for each SUCCESS aspect.
2. How could this ad be improved? Give reasons.
3. Would you research or even buy the product after you have listened to the ad? Why (not)?

D Work in small groups and do the following tasks:

1. Choose a product (e.g. perfume, muesli bar) and design a magazine or newspaper ad with the help of the AIDA strategy. Make sure that your ad contains all four AIDA principles.
2. Swap your ad with that of another group. Analyse the other group's ad. Then give each other feedback (e.g. Is it effective?, What could be improved?).
3. Improve your ad in your group with the help of the feedback.
4. Present your ad in class. Decide which ad catches your attention most.

D Brands with purpose

BEFORE YOU READ

1 Think – pair – share → ○ 4

a Describe what the infographic illustrates.

b Compare your description with a partner's. Together, sum up in one sentence the message of the infographic.

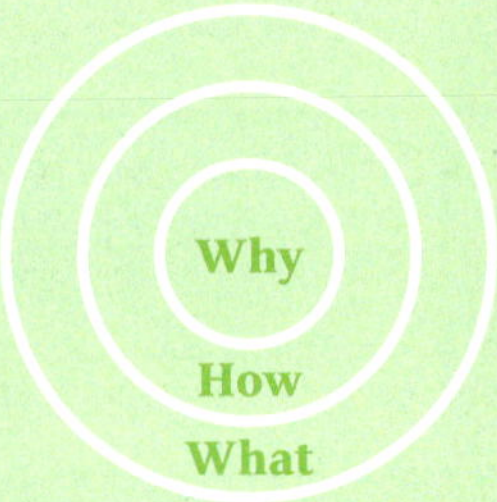

What	Every organisation on the planet knows WHAT they do. These are products they sell or the services they offer.
How	Some organisations know HOW they do it. These are the things that make them special or set them apart from their competition.
Why	Very few organisations know WHY they do what they do. WHY is not about making money. That's a result. WHY is about a purpose, cause or belief. It's the very reason your organisation exists.

16 **counter-intuitive** der Intuition widersprechend
30 **to stick with sth** bei etw bleiben
40 **stand** Haltung, Standpunkt
51 **incredibly** unglaublich

The power of purpose: How taking a stand helps brands to win customers' hearts (and business)

Black Friday is the busiest shopping day of the year in the U.S., with more than 116 million people hitting the shops in search of a great deal. But REI, an outdoor clothing and equipment brand, does Black Friday differently to other retailers. For the fourth year in a row, REI closed its doors on Black Friday [...], giving every one of its 12,000 employees the day off to enjoy the outdoors. "There are things more important than buying/selling tents – like going outside and actually using them," it explained on Twitter.

It might seem <u>counter-intuitive</u> to think that closing all your retail stores on the busiest shopping day of the year will be good for business. But that's exactly what REI has found. REI's CEO, Jerry Stritzke believes that the relationships between consumers and brands are changing – whilst you used to be able to win people over with deals, you now need "something more", he told *Business Insider.* [...]
"Since launching #OptOutside, we've watched more than 200 retailers go out of business," Stritzke told BestBlackFriday.com. "We've stayed healthy partly because we've <u>stuck with</u> our core values – like giving our employees time to do what they love with the people they love during the holidays. It's enabled us to add millions of new members and, most importantly, connect millions of people with the outdoors."
According to data from *Edelman*, sixty-four percent of consumers around the world will choose, switch, avoid or boycott a business based on its <u>stand</u> on societal and political issues. [...] "You have to be walking the walk before you talk the talk," Mike Dupree, Senior Manager for Media & Entertainment at Twitter, explained to me. Mike has been working with brands on their content and marketing efforts on Twitter for over six years [...].

Demonstration before communication
REI's *Opt Outside* campaign has been <u>incredibly</u> successful since it first launched in 2015 because it's not just a

marketing front – even REI's CEO takes Black Friday off to enjoy the outdoors. And Mike believes that this authenticity is key, not only to REI's success, but to any purpose-driven campaign: "Being authentic is always critical in marketing, but when it comes to brand purpose it becomes even more important."
"Any purpose-driven campaign shouldn't be viewed as a short-term thing," Mike explained. "The purpose has to be deep rooted in the company across all facets of the organisation – from marketing and customer service to communications and policy, and everywhere in between."
"In short, it's about demonstration before communication," Mike concluded.

This is exactly why *Opt Outside* has worked for REI. For years before it launched the campaign, and communicated its "Opt Outside" ethos, it had demonstrated it through its actions. Enjoying the outdoors is a part of REI's brand message, and over the years it has consistently supported nonprofit partners, and encouraged both employees and customers to make the most of the outdoors.

[...] To stand for something, and embrace a purpose, brands don't need to create campaigns that choose sides on political, or social topics. "We've seen numerous examples of brands taking a stand without taking sides," Mike told me. "The key is to find universal issues that strike a cultural chord with anybody – something that everybody can get behind." For example, [...] brands have consistently helped out with disaster relief efforts after hurricanes, superstorms, and earthquakes. [...]
Anheuser-Busch sent more than 300,000 cans of emergency canned drinking water to local communities in North Carolina, South Carolina, and Virginia as the states prepared for the expected impacts of Hurricane Florence.
This action wasn't a one-off, though. Water is incredibly important to Anheuser-Busch's brewing process, and it has been committed to conserving water for years as part of its Better World focus. Since 2010, it has partnered with the River Network to host a series of local river and watershed restoration and protection projects.

[...] The campaigns we've discussed [...] all have something in common: The purpose they support is fully aligned with their brand – and that's not an accident. [...] The best examples of purpose-driven marketing are when brands connect with issues and purposes that they have long supported or played a part in. Anheuser-Busch's water campaign worked for its brand because it has been supporting clean water-related causes since 2010 – it wasn't just jumping in during a moment of crisis to try and grab some attention. [...]

Take the REI "Opt Outside" campaign. [...] "REI is a retail brand that has a business interest in Black Friday. But it has more of an interest in embracing the outdoors lifestyle and culture than it does in one big shopping day each year," Mike explained. "It believes that this approach will keep customers coming back, and build loyalty that lasts years, and years." [...]

"It's never been harder for brands to stand out and make connections that are enduring if you can do that it'll help your business [in the long-term]," Mike concluded.
"We see that 75 percent of consumers expect brands to make a contribution to their well-being, and quality of life – if you aren't doing that you'll be left behind. [...]"

(872 words)

Ash Read, *Buffer Inc.*, 2019

61 **purpose-driven** zielgesteuert
64 **rooted** verankert, verwurzelt
64 **facet** Facette, Aspekt
80 **to embrace** etw annehmen
86 **to strike a chord** Anklang finden
93 **Anheuser-Busch** *a multinational drink and brewing company*
94 **can** Dose, Büchse
101 **brewing process** Brauprozess
106 **watershed** Wassereinzugsgebiet
110 **to align with sth** mit etw übereinstimmen
133 **enduring** bleibend, dauerhaft

WORKING WITH THE TEXT

2 Reading for gist → G 1.3, 1.4

In your own words, explain what the companies did to get the public's attention.

3 Reading for detail

REI's ad for Black Friday

a Find quotes in the text that reflect the following opinions. Give line numbers.

1. Why spend hours walking around shops when you can spend time outdoors?
2. We've stood by our fundamental beliefs, and that has kept us going.
3. You have to practise what you preach.
4. If you want a campaign with a purpose behind it to be a hit, it has to be long-term.
5. Find something everyone cares about, and you will succeed.
6. If you want to reach the majority of consumers, your brand has to enrich their life somehow, or else you will lose them.

b Sum up REI's and Anheuser-Busch's motivation behind their actions.

c Explain why their campaigns were so effective.

d Relate the message of the infographic on p. 78 to the two companies mentioned in the text. → ◯ 5

4 Words matter

Match the following words from the text with their definitions.

1.	counter-intuitive (l. 16)	A	to accept
2.	core values (l. 30)	B	contrary to what you would expect
3.	to boycott (l. 40)	C	long-lasting
4.	authenticity (l. 55)	D	fundamental beliefs
5.	to embrace (l. 80)	E	to actively avoid
6.	enduring (l. 133)	F	the quality of being genuine

5 Focus on analysis → S 8.2

a Note down the sentences in the text that contain numbers and figures.

b Analyse what effect the use of numbers and figures throughout the text has on the reader.

D1 I1
Self-check 1.1

A STEP FURTHER

D11 I11
Self-check 4.0

A19

6 Listening → S 2

Listen to the podcast "Forward Thinking: The ethics of advertising" and answer the following questions:

1. According to Prof Polly Bond, how has advertising changed recently?
2. What does Prof Polly Bond mean when she says that partnerships between companies and influencers are not always transparent?
3. What does ASA stand for?
4. What has ASA recently done and why?
5. Why do young people often become attached to the people they follow online?
6. How can advertisers and influencers ensure transparency?

Creating a marketing campaign

Step 1 Your head teacher receives an email from a high school in the USA and forwards it to all of the students. In groups, read the email, identify what needs to be done to apply and decide as a team how you want to proceed.

From: principal@statecollege.usa
To: rektorat@schule.net
Subject: US college looking for partnership in Germany

Dear friends in Germany,

We, State College in New York City, are looking to expand our international network. State College is one of the top 10 colleges in the USA and has a reputation worldwide for academic excellence. We already have over 50 partner schools and colleges around the world, and we are now looking to expand our network to Germany. We feel that we can learn a lot from each other and would like to establish a sustainable connection and give our and your students the opportunity to sample student life in another part of the world.

If you are interested, then show us why we should choose *you* to be our partner. We want to know about your school and your region. To help us decide, we have set up a committee of staff, students and parents to judge the entrants. Please send us the following:

1. A one-minute image film for our jury to watch
2. A social media campaign to catch the interest of our students
3. A flyer to show off your school to our students and their parents

The winning school will be invited to visit us here in NYC and your students will have the chance to take part in our exchange program.

We look forward to hearing from you.

Best wishes,
US State College team

Step 2 In your group, brainstorm ideas for your marketing campaign. Then allocate responsibilities to produce the following:
- an image film
- a social media campaign
- a flyer to advertise the school

Think about the tonality of your campaign, any USPs (*unique selling points*) of your school or the surrounding area and a slogan or something similar.

Step 3 Give a 5-minute presentation about your ideas to the class. The others: Note down questions. Then ask them after the presentation.

Step 4 Discuss in class which campaign is most likely to succeed. Give reasons.

The birth of modern consumerism

5 **necessity** Notwendigkeit
14 **assembly line** Fließband
17 **famine** Hungersnot
22 **commodity** Artikel; Ware
24 **prosperity** Wohlstand
29 **deprivation** Entbehrung
45 **purchasing power** Kaufkraft

During the 20th century, people were slowly transformed into consumers. But how did this happen? Of course, people have always 'consumed' things, such as food, clothing and shelter, and they have had to do some form of work to pay for these things. However, for a long time any **consumption** beyond the necessities to survive was unheard of for everyone but the very rich. For example, in Britain, a wider variety of foods became available in the late 19th century, but the majority of people still lived on bread and potatoes. Over time, though, more shops and even department stores began to appear throughout Europe, attracting more middle-class people. A variety of attractive products started to be displayed for people to see.

In the USA, things moved more quickly and by the 1890s, mail-order shopping became widespread and multi-storey department stores popped up all over the country. Small shopkeepers were quickly being replaced by large corporations as assembly line production was used to full effect. A shift had begun to take place from selling the goods people needed to chasing the goal of **profit**. Following the poverty and famine of WWI, production increased dramatically, which not only created more products, but also jobs for millions of people. However, **mass-production** can only be successful if the products are being sold. This led to an increase in advertising, so that the companies could create interest and demand for their commodities. Products such as radios, vacuum cleaners and refrigerators became symbols of wealth and prosperity in the 1920s and the number of car owners increased dramatically.

Consumerism took two big hits after this due to the Great Depression and then WWII. However, as the world emerged from war, people longed for a better standard of life after years of deprivation and rationing. While radio had been a valuable source of sending information and entertainment into homes, the new medium of television was arguably the most important factor in the explosion of **consumer culture** as it could use images and increase the impact of advertising.

Many of the products advertised were portrayed as commodities to improve your life one thing at a time and to offer everyday people the chance to own things previously only available to rich people. For example, by saving up to buy a new carpet, the consumer is encouraged to feel they are upgrading their life. Although people began buying more and more things, they were actually being sold status.

But for this to be successful, there has to be an appetite to consume. The consumers can never be satisfied or content, or else they will stop buying. That is why **advertising** soon became a billion-dollar industry. Corporations looked for creative ways to generate demand, as people were essentially persuaded to buy things they did not need, and often did not even know they wanted. And as families had more purchasing power into the 1950s and 60s, shops and homes soon filled with goods. Until the internet came into many homes, local shops, high-street chains and gigantic shopping malls around the world were available to cater for the needs created by ever more glossy and powerful advertisements.

Consumerism today

Fast forward to the 21st century and although the media available to advertisers have increased, the principle is still the same – create a need and desire for goods and services in order to make profit. The advent of smartphones and social media has made it almost impossible for people to ignore advertising, and at the same time **online shopping** platforms and apps have made it possible to buy things in seconds, wherever we are and whatever the time.

Social media has created multiple images of the perfect life, home, holiday and body for us all to aspire to, just like the first TV ads following WWII. **Influencer marketing** and the creation of things such as Black Friday and Cyber Monday have sent online sales through the roof as people spend more time on their devices.

However, as products are still produced in such high quantities, few things are designed to last and many products end up in landfills around the world, we can no longer ignore the **environmental impact** of how we consume. This has led to more support for **sustainability** in the way we produce, consume and dispose of commodities. Companies and customers are being forced to think differently, to produce and live with less, make more considered choices, and to attempt to put a stop to mindless consumerism. Hopefully it will not prove to be a case of too little, too late.

58 **to aspire to** anstreben
64 **to dispose of** beseitigen; loswerden

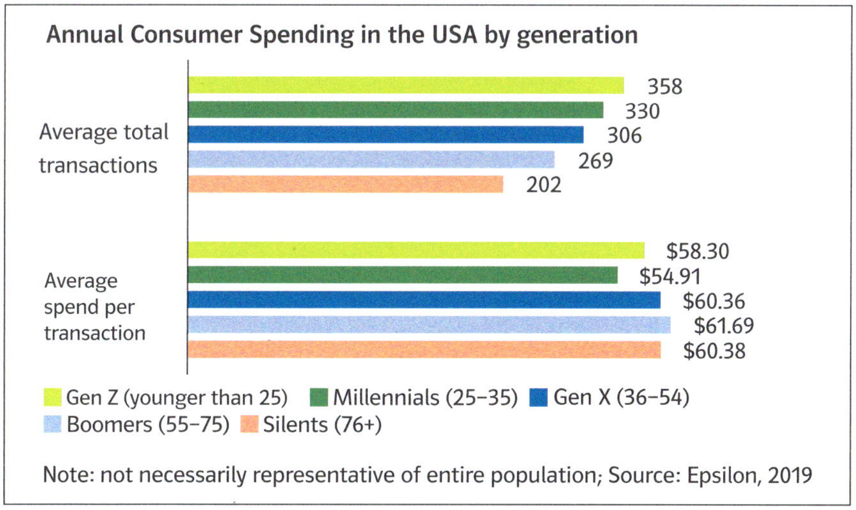

1 Read the text on pp. 82–83. Outline some of the driving factors of consumerism throughout history. Compare your findings with a partner.

2 Which different media have companies and shops used in order to advertise and sell products and services? Discuss with a partner.

3 Partner A: Describe and analyse the ad on p. 82 while partner B takes notes.
Partner B: Describe and analyse the graph on p. 83 while partner A takes notes.
Together, relate both visuals to consumerism in the past and today.

Outlook: For further discussion, consider the following questions:
- What are the pros and cons of increasing online shopping for consumers and enterprises?
- How might the advertising industry develop in the future?
- How can we become a 'greener' or more sustainable consumer society?

1 Lesen und Schreiben

When too much stuff gets in the way of all the good stuff

[...] When Hans and I relocated from Chicago to Ann Arbor, we wanted to live in a house with a big yard so we could plant flowers and get a dog. There were two backstories feeding these wants. I grew up on a farm and we always had a dog or two. And having lived in Chicago [...] for a decade, I was ready for some green grass. There were other things on our wish list, including enough space (to live in and for our stuff) and a garage (for the car and more stuff). [...] After looking at a dozen houses, we found our home. By today's standards, it was actually on the small side at 1,400 square feet (compared to the average size home of 2,500 square feet). There was a living room, family room, dining room, and kitchen. There were four bedrooms and two and a half baths. We don't have kids, so that's two bedrooms and a bathroom each – with half a bath left over! We earmarked a room for my home office, a workout room for the elliptical, a room at the far end of the house for Hans to loudly watch hockey ... It seemed there was a separate room designated for every possible activity. [...]

Filling the space

Conventional wisdom says when you have space, you fill it up. And we did. We brought furniture from Chicago and we bought furniture in Ann Arbor. We went to home stores and container stores and hardware stores. We acquired things to fill the space. Whether we needed all that stuff wasn't really discussed. We had the space and it needed to be filled (or so I thought back then). But a funny thing happened as we settled into our new home after years of apartment dwelling. We realized a couple things that would have been nice to have figured out beforehand. First, we hated yard work. Mowing the lawn felt like a huge waste of a weekend afternoon. My would-be green thumb forgot how much I dislike getting sweaty and dirty and toiling in the soil. And the dog? Yes, we really wanted a dog to love and pet and love some more. [...] But as we started to notice the disconnect between the dream of a big yard and the reality, we realized the doggie dream was much the same.

What freedom feels like

We started to embrace this about ourselves: The less commitment and obligation in our lives, the freer – and better – we feel. Initially, this was really uncomfortable for me to admit. I worried not wanting responsibility and obligations made me less of an adult. [...] I've realized being a mature adult is knowing who you are, what makes you comfortable in your own skin and at peace in your own mind – and then designing your life around what's true for you. In our more-is-better consumer culture, it's easy to buy into all the messages about what we're supposed to want and supposed to have. But what if you get those things and ... meh ... they just don't resonate. Then what?

Because that's what happened to Hans and me. Everything looked great from the outside, but just didn't feel quite right. It took us a while to figure out the disconnect between what we thought we wanted and what we really wanted. So, after the first year in our home, no flowers were planted. We paid someone to take care of the lawn. And I made sure to pet other people's dogs whenever I got the chance. But ... we couldn't unknow what we now knew: We're not house people. Or the landscaping-on-the-weekends type. And while we're totally dog people, we're dog lovers – not dog owners.

So now what?

Hans and I started to have the conversation:

- If we're not house people, who are we?
- If we're starting to have a different relationship to space and stuff, what does that mean?
- If we quiet the voices about how we're supposed to live and what we're supposed to want, what do we hear that's really true for us?

We began to realize we wanted less. Less space and less stuff. Less housework and less upkeep. Less overhead and less oversight. If you're on your own, making a life-altering change can be a solo decision. But when you're partnered up, it would be a tough compromise if one of you wants the McMansion and the other wants to go live in a Tiny House. Luckily, Hans and I were on the same page: We had a short list of new wants.

We wanted to downsize.

For us, this meant we wanted to significantly reduce our square footage. We made a conscious choice to define "enough" for ourselves. We rejected "more is better" as a default and really thought about how much space we need to be comfortable and how many rooms we want to clean.

All in all, we went from a house of 1,400 square feet to a hotel room of 300 (for six months while our apartment was under construction) to our current abode of 733 square feet. We have a kitchen, living room, bedroom, and bathroom.

And I can honestly say we've never been happier or felt closer. In fact, Hans and I joke that we could easily go lower, perhaps to 500 square feet. But, for now, our 733 square feet is home sweet home. [...]

(921 words)

Jennifer Bailey, *Tiny Buddha* website, 2017

ASSIGNMENTS

1. Explain why Jennifer and her partner Hans moved from a flat in Chicago to a 1400 square feet house, yet eventually ended up in a 733 square feet apartment.
2. Analyse the emotional journey Jennifer goes through. Quote from the text to support your answer. Give line numbers.
3. Choose one of the following tasks: → WB, p. 39

   3.1. Imagine you have won a competition to live in a tiny house with 18m² for one month. Write a blog post in which you report about your experiences after the month is over.

   Or:

   3.2. Discuss which 'home' would bring you more happiness and why: The mansion or the tiny house? Take the message of the cartoon into consideration when you write your argumentative essay.

"It's more than I can afford and less than I desire."

2 Hörverstehen

ASSIGNMENTS → WB, pp. 40–41/1–3

A20 1. In the podcast "Smart Consumer", the presenter is talking about the fashion industry with Helen Riley, Caroline Rush and Fee Gilfeather. While listening, choose the correct answers. There is only one correct answer. You will hear the podcast twice.

1. According to Helen, people are becoming more conscious of how their consumption …
   A impacts the environment.
   B influences climate change.
   C contributes to waste pollution.
2. Helen has noticed that there is an increase of vendors selling …
   A used clothes.
   B fair-trade clothes.
   C eco-friendly clothes.
3. According to Caroline, an event like "Fashion Week" has the potential to …
   A highlight the need to reduce textile rubbish in landfills.
   B persuade the consumer to buy more high-quality garments.
   C spread the message of environmentally conscious consumption.
4. Oxfam launched a campaign that encouraged people to …
   A stop buying clothes.
   B only buy pre-owned clothes.
   C donate their unwanted clothes.
5. According to Fee, Oxfam has always tried to …
   A generate more income from clothes.
   B convince consumers to boycott "fast fashion".
   C invest in sustainably managed high-street shops.
6. Fee thinks that social media has promoted …
   A the 'second-hand' hype.
   B the 'fast fashion' attitude.
   C the 'sustainable fashion' movement.

A21 **2** You will hear a teenager reporting about her money issues and an assessment of the problem. Take notes on the following points. You do not need to write complete sentences.

a) What are the reasons that have led to the teenager's financial problems (name three)?
b) What are the financial issues she is facing right now?
c) General reasons for young people's money problems (name three)
d) Indicators for a potential money problem (name two)
e) Examples of "good debt" (name two)

3 Kommunikation

Your boss asks you to work on an advertising campaign for a new fitness centre in town, which has a special focus on mindfulness.

Use the graph, quotation and cartoon to prepare a 5-minute presentation on possible marketing measures for the target group.

Monologue

Graph → WB, p. 41/1

Describe and analyse the graph.

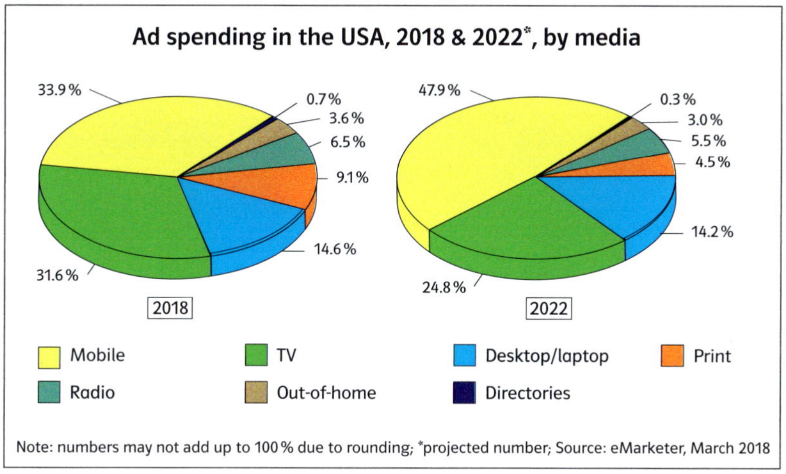

Quotation

Explain and comment on the quotation.

"You know when you look in the mirror and you think, 'Oh, I'm so fat, I'm so old, I'm so ugly.' Don't you know, that's not your authentic self? But that is billions upon billions of dollars of advertising, magazines, movies, billboards, all geared to make you feel awful about yourself so that you will take your hard-earned money and spend it at the mall [...]."

Margaret Cho, US-American comedian

Cartoon

Describe and analyse the cartoon and relate it to the quotation and the graph.

I'm so much more relaxed since I got this mindfulness app.

Dialogue

Be prepared to discuss further aspects with your boss such as consumer behaviour, sustainable brand images and marketing strategies.

Land of dreams?

1 Look at the pictures and match the following captions with the pictures. There are two more captions than you need.

1. Ground Zero
2. Westward expansion
3. Fighting for equality
4. Immigrants arriving in the USA
5. Native American life and culture
6. Economic success
7. Storm on the US Capitol Building

2 Get together in groups and do the following tasks.

a Take notes on what you know about the topics referred to in the pictures and in captions 1–7.

b Discuss how far the pictures and captions correlate with what you associate with the United States of America. Present your ideas in class.

A22 **3** Listen to the podcast "Forward Thinking: The USA – past and present". Answer the following questions in keywords. → S 2, S 3 → WB, p. 42

1. When did European immigration to North America start?
2. What reasons are given for people to immigrate to the USA? Name three.
3. When did the following events take place?
   - the protests after the murder of George Floyd
   - the arrival of the first enslaved people from Africa
   - the abolition of slavery
   - the Civil Rights Movement
4. What were the consequences of the terrorist attacks of September 11, 2001? Name three.
5. What event made a division in US society become apparent in January 2021?
6. What explanations does Sophia give for the large amount of things being invented in the USA? Name two.

GOOD TO KNOW

The September 11 attacks in 2001 were four terrorist attacks in the USA. Four airplanes were hijacked by Al-Qaeda and crashed into the World Trade Center in New York City and the Pentagon in Arlington. The fourth plane did not crash into its intended target. These attacks caused almost 3,000 victims.

V4 **4** You are going to watch the video of Amanda Gorman reciting her famous poem "The Hill We Climb". → S 2

a Watch the video and point out where and when Gorman recited her poem. Sum up the gist of her message. → ○1

b Watch the video again and answer the following questions.

1. What do you find out about Amanda Gorman as a person?
2. What does Amanda Gorman say about the past and the future of the USA?
3. What regions does Gorman name towards the end of the poem, and how does she characterise them?

5 Team up with a partner and choose an aspect connected with the USA (e.g. importance of sports; famous authors, musicians or artists; well-known musicals or movies; technological innovations). Prepare and give a 3-minute talk on the chosen aspect.

D 12 Self-check 5.0

USEFUL PHRASES

We would like to give you an overview of …
Our presentation is divided into … parts.
I'll start with … / First, I'll talk about …
Then we'll look at … / Next we'll explain …
We'd like to use this picture/diagram/newspaper headline to demonstrate …
If you have any questions, please feel free to ask.
I hope this enables you to understand the aspect/theme/situation.

A Shaping the USA

BEFORE YOU READ

1 Working with a picture

The picture shows a scene from a play that is set in the late 18th century. Describe the scene and the people in it (e.g. dress), and say what may be unusual about this.

2 Think – pair – share

a Research the following aspects and make notes:
- Alexander Hamilton
- The Founding Fathers: who they were and what they did
- The Federalist Papers

b Exchange your notes with a partner. Together, create a handout on the topics.

c Compare your handout with that of another pair and add more aspects to your handout.

3 **to take by storm** im Sturm erobern
4 **portrayal** Darstellung
9 **draw** Attraktivität
13 **polymath** Universalgelehrte/-r
14 **treatise** Abhandlung
14 **doctrine** Lehre
22 **maligned** verleumdet, schlecht gemacht
26 **ascent** Aufstieg
28 **to relate** erzählen, berichten
29 **orphan** Waise
30 **whore** *(vulg)* Hure, Nutte
39 **to boast** prahlen
39 **scrappy** kampflustig
54 **to woo sb** jdm den Hof machen

'Hamilton,' the musical now in Canada, tells the story of America's founding passions

[...] Four years after taking Broadway by storm, Lin-Manuel Miranda's portrayal of the life and times of Alexander Hamilton, one of the most colourful founding fathers, opens this month to sold out shows in Toronto.

Hamilton's main draws are its fabulous music and astonishing plot. Born a nobody on the British-ruled island of Nevis, Hamilton became a romantic polymath who fought wars and duels, wrote treatises and doctrines and helped turn 13 rebellious colonies into a rising empire. Inspired by Ron Chernow's 2004 biography, Miranda's masterpiece features a hip-hop soundtrack, a multiracial cast and powerful arguments, in theatrical form, for a more inclusive America.

More subtly, the play also explores ambition, a traditionally maligned passion in British North America that became a distinctive national ethic in the early United States.

Ascent from poverty

From the first scene to the last, *Hamilton* relates an incredible case of social mobility: "How does a bastard, orphan, son of a whore and a Scotsman ... grow up to be a hero and a scholar [and a] Founding Father?" The curtain parts as a teenaged Hamilton leaves his Caribbean birthplace and lands in New York City in 1772, determined to rise up in this "new land," where "you can be a new man." His destiny and that of the 13 colonies merge.

"Hey yo, I'm just like my country," he boasts, "I'm young, scrappy and hungry!" Both the man and the nation must throw off British rule to realise their mighty potential.

In the play – and in history – the young Hamilton's skills with the sword and pen catch the eye of George Washington, the statuesque leader of the Continental Army. As Washington's right-hand man, Hamilton helps keep the American Revolution alive after the British chase the outgunned rebels out of New York in late 1776.

Hamilton brilliantly captures the boundless energy of its main character. We watch Hamilton woo the daughter of a wealthy landlord, lobby the Continental Congress for more money, and outshine the other officers around Washington. "The Man is NON-STOP!"

With independence won, Washington entrusts his favourite officer with the new Treasury Department – and sides with Hamilton against Thomas Jefferson and most Americans, who don't understand that with the revolution over and done with, the new country must act a bit more like the self-interested, hyper-capitalist empire it just defeated. In the play's version of the chaotic 1790s, only Hamilton is smart enough to create a national bank and financial system while keeping the U.S. out of the French Revolution. [...]

[T]he play is accurate in its read of Hamilton's motivations. On stage as in real life, the man from Nevis doesn't seek money or office. He doesn't need creature comforts or cheap thrills. What he wants more than anything is for the world to know his name. He's defined and perhaps consumed by ambition, the desperate desire to be noticed by strangers and posterity.

Dangerous passion

The American patriots believed that republics required selfless and civic-minded citizens who were always on guard against those who lusted for power. The people had to "know ambition under every disguise it may assume," Jefferson warned in 1781. Otherwise, their republic would fall into corruption and tyranny.

In a society built on family labour, ambition often seemed useless as well as dangerous. Farm parents needed dutiful children, not ambitious dreamers.

Indeed, colonial Americans denounced ambition as a "fire" that threatened to destroy social ties and moral duties. They knew it as a radically selfish passion, a dark blend of pride, envy and rage.

By abolishing monarchy and aristocracy, however, revolutionary leaders also invited go-getters to reach for the sky. They celebrated their revolution as a grand theatre on which previously obscure people could do remarkable things.

In other words, they deliberately stoked ambition even as they worried about its destructive energies.

Ultimately, Americans like Hamilton solved this cultural riddle by turning ambition into a national virtue – something that was good and moral so long as it was in service to the United States, the only country (in theory) where merit found its reward. For young men, at least, the burning desire to rise up became not only a right but also a duty, something that would carry the nation as well as themselves to greatness.

American dreams

In this sense, *Hamilton* reflects the cultural moment in which the play is set. It is a celebration of a new and lasting marriage between individual and national ambition in American culture. It is a paean to patriotic ambition, set against the amoral careerism of the anti-hero, Aaron Burr, whom Hamilton ultimately confronts on the duelling ground.

And yet Miranda's play is also honest about ambition's costs. Hamilton's relentless pursuit of fame draws him away from his dutiful wife, Eliza, who can only wonder why she and the children aren't enough. His inability to respect other people's views – he assumes they can't keep up with him – alienates him from his peers. He's too busy to love anyone but himself, his country and their shared destiny.

In all these ways, *Hamilton* captures the national tendency to see history as a grand drama, in which the exceptionally driven and talented make things happen, for better and worse.

By its very nature, of course, this way of looking at ambition and history marginalizes the everyday concerns of most people, whose duties inevitably outweigh their dreams. That's yet another irony for a country that has long seen itself as the only real democracy.

(925 words)

J. M. Opal, *The Conversation*, 2020

56 **to outshine sb** jdn in den Schatten stellen
61 **Treasury Department** Finanzministerium
76 **creature comforts** leibliches Wohl, Annehmlichkeiten
82 **posterity** Nachwelt
85 **civic-minded** *hier:* politisch engagiert
87 **to lust for sth** gierig nach etw sein
94 **dutiful** pflichtbewusst
96 **to denounce sth** etw anprangern
103 **go-getter** tatkräftige Person
108 **to stoke** schüren
112 **riddle** Rätsel
117 **merit** Verdienst, Leistung
128 **paean** Loblied
139 **to alienate** entfremden
146 **driven** ehrgeizig
150 **to marginalize** *(AE)* an den Rand drängen

WORKING WITH THE TEXT

3 Reading for gist

a Briefly describe which time the musical is set in.

b Summarise what the musical is about in one sentence.

4 Words matter → S 16

Match the following words and phrases from the text with the correct definitions. There are two more definitions than you need.

1. polymath (l. 13)
2. to inspire (l. 16)
3. determined (l. 35)
4. to outshine sb (l. 56)
5. to entrust sb with sth (l. 60)
6. to be consumed by sth (l. 80)
7. go-getter (l. 103)
8. virtue (l. 113)
9. pursuit (l. 134)

A sb who is determined to succeed
B sb who knows a lot about many subjects
C good behaviour or attitudes based on strong moral values
D sb whose job it is to pick up things from one place and take them to another
E to give others the idea for sth, e.g. sth artistic
F to be more skilful and successful than sb else
G to have such strong feelings about sth that it affects everything you do
H intensely looking for sth or trying to get sth
I to make sure that sb has enough light directed at them on stage
J having made a decision to do sth and not letting anyone stop you
K to give sb a thing or duty for which they are responsible

5 Reading for detail → ◯ 2 → WB, p. 43

a In your own words, summarise what motivated Alexander Hamilton according to the text. → S 6.9

b Illustrate why colonial Americans thought that ambition was dangerous, and how it later became a national virtue.

D1 I1
Self-check 1.1

6 Focus on analysis → S 8.2

a Note down the parts of the text where the author quotes lines from the musical.

b Analyse the style and tone of the quotes and the effect they have on the audience.

D8 I8
Self-check 3.1

7 Writing a comment → S 6.1 → ◯ 3

"[…] *Hamilton* captures the national tendency to see history as a grand drama, in which the exceptionally driven and talented make things happen, for better and worse. By its very nature, of course, this way of looking at ambition and history marginalizes the everyday concerns of most people, whose duties inevitably outweigh their dreams." (ll. 143–152)
Comment on the author's statement on the role of ordinary people in shaping a country.

A STEP FURTHER

8 Listening → S 2, S 3

D 11 I 11
Self-check 4.0

A23 Listen to the podcast "Forward Thinking: The musical *Hamilton*" and choose the correct answer from the options given below. There is only one correct answer.

1. When talking about the musical *Hamilton*, Lin-Manuel Miranda said that it …
   A is more about the present than the past.
   B focusses more on the past than the present.
   C is a story about the past, told from the perspective of the USA today.
2. In what way are Alexander Hamilton's and Lin-Manuel Miranda's stories similar?
   A Both were born on a Caribbean island.
   B Both of them came to the USA to study.
   C They both impressed people with their ability to write well.
3. Miranda made a musical with rap music about Alexander Hamilton because …
   A Hamilton was a revolutionary and rap revolutionised American music.
   B Hamilton was musical and might have been a rapper if he had lived today.
   C Hamilton's early death in a duel reminded him of the rapper Tupac Shakur.
4. Miranda wrote the musical for people of colour because they …
   A made the musical more interesting.
   B are more comfortable with performing the rap songs.
   C often experience limitations in the roles they are cast for.
5. According to Terry Mulligan, many of the Founding Fathers …
   A opposed slavery.
   B were slaveholders.
   C married into slave-holding families.
6. What role does *Hamilton* play in the Black and Latino communities in the USA?
   A It is seen critically for not being realistic.
   B It raises hopes that people may continue to fight for racial equality.
   C It has been praised as an inspiration to write more musicals like this.

9 Creating a timeline of US history

Work in small groups and find information on one of the following topics. Considering the listed aspects, prepare and give a 5-minute presentation, including cards with keywords and images of decisive events. Put the cards on a timeline of US history. → ◯ 4

African Americans: the slave trade • the abolitionist movement • the Civil War • the Civil Rights Movement

Native Americans: Native American tribes • the Trail of Tears • Wounded Knee Massacre • reservations • situation today

Foundation of the USA: the arrival of European settlers in North America • the Boston Tea Party • the Revolutionary War • the Declaration of Independence

Westward expansion: the Oregon Trail • the frontier • the Louisiana Purchase • the California Gold Rush

The first Thanksgiving celebration, as depicted by European settlers.

B Dreaming the American Dream

BEFORE YOU READ

1 The US – a popular destination

In pairs, discuss why you think people choose to move to the USA today and what people might hope for when they migrate there. Agree on the five main aspects.

CULTURE BOX

The American Dream
The American Dream is a set of beliefs and ideals, based on the Declaration of Independence (1776), which promised that "all men are created equal" and have the right to "life, liberty and the pursuit of happiness". The term was coined in 1931 by James Truslow Adams and reflects the belief that God rewards hard work. For centuries people have been coming to the USA, attracted by the American Dream. For some this is the dream of economic success ("from rags to riches"), for some the hope for equality, democracy and justice, for some the dream of self-realisation and freedom.

GOOD TO KNOW

The **Diversity Visa Program** offers 55,000 permanent immigrant visa, also called 'Green Cards', based on a lottery system. The aim is to diversify the immigrant population and to encourage immigration from countries from which relatively few people have immigrated to the USA in previous years.

Abdi Nor Iftin was born in Somalia. After he fled to Kenya because of a civil war in his home country, he gained entrance to the US through the annual visa lottery. In his biographical book *Call me American*, he tells his story.

Call me American

by Abdi Nor Iftin

Every day we batted different houses and buildings in different towns. Ten miles, twenty miles, and sometimes as far as eighty miles. We had to finish batting a whole house within the same day, so we moved fast. Lunch break was only thirty minutes. Milton and Sean ate doughnuts, sometimes burgers they brought with them. I always sought a clean place and prayed. They both would come look at me bowing my head and reciting the Koran.

"What are you doing?" Milton asked me. During the prayer I am not supposed to speak, so I was quiet and answered when I finished. "I was praying." Milton picked up his phone and called everyone else who worked at the company and even his old lady.

He made fun of the whole thing. "This dude bows and says he's praying," he said with a laugh.

I had to tell them that I am Muslim, I have to pray five times a day. "They got Muslims in Africa?" Sean asked. Of course they thought all Muslims look like Osama bin Laden.

After work, Milton and Sean would stop at a convenience store to buy beer and cigarettes. Often they would ask to borrow money from me until the next payday. I always gave them a few dollars when they asked, but they never paid me back. I wasn't sure if it would be polite to remind them on payday.

One day on the job my hard hat disappeared. Another day my staple gun, then my winter coat. When I asked what could have happened, Milton laughed and said, "That's what happens when you're new here." The boss said he couldn't do anything. I had to buy a new hard hat and a new staple gun from the shop. I had no idea who was stealing my stuff until one day I found my hard hat in the back of Milton's pickup truck. The same

3 **to batt a house** ein Gebäude mit Glaswolle isolieren
7 **to bow** neigen
7 **to recite** auswendig aufsagen
12 **dude** *(ugs)* Kerl, Typ
16 **convenience store** Gemischtwarenladen
20 **hard hat** Helm
20 **staple gun** Tacker

guys I'd been working with for months, and when I asked, they said nothing! It was humiliating, and it felt as if my American dream was shrinking.
I asked Joey to put me on a different batting squad, and I was told to work with a guy named Tom. He was respectful to me, rolling down his window when smoking weed. He had been to prison several times, due to drugs, and he said he wanted to stop. But he explained that he needed the weed to do his job. [...]
Tom and I got along well. I felt it was safe to leave my things in his truck. He wanted to see the world outside the United States; he wanted to explore. He told me he liked watching National Geographic TV shows. He watched shows about the Maasai Mara and Serengeti national parks in Kenya and Tanzania. We talked about lions, hyenas, and wildebeests. I told him stories about my mom and dad facing lions in real life. I liked Tom, but I noticed the drugs he took to cope with work also seemed to cause his troubles. [...]
Many of the guys on the batting squad had lost their licenses from drunk driving, so they all gave each other rides home. Milton gave Sean a ride, and Tom picked up two other people. I asked if someone could give me a ride home, and Milton said I would have to pay him gas money. None of the other guys gave him gas money, but he wanted twenty dollars a week from me. I told him I was happy to walk home, even though I was so tired and dirty after work.
I don't know if the guys on the batting squad were racist; I hadn't been in America long enough to know about that. But it did feel like something I understood very well: the tribalism of Somalia. I have heard Americans complain that Africans bring on their own problems with their tribal feuds, and there is some truth to that. But these Maine guys had a tribe too. Maybe they didn't call themselves Darod or Hawiye, but it was a tribe, and I definitely was not a member. So I had to walk home, up Main Street, looking like some homeless guy in my filthy work clothes and covered in pink fiberglass threads. Fortunately, the people of Yarmouth got to know me and realized I was just a hard-working guy. When I got home, I took off my rough clothes, took a warm shower, dressed up nice, and walked back toward Main Street to relax at the Dunkin' Donuts. People waved and smiled. I started to feel like part of the community and not just an outsider like I felt at work. (789 words)

26 **humiliating** erniedrigend
27 **batting squad** Bauarbeitertruppe
28 **to smoke weed** kiffen
39 **to give sb a ride** jdn mitnehmen
46 **tribalism** Stammeswesen
47 **feud** Konflikt, Fehde
50 **filthy** schmutzig, dreckig
50 **thread** Faden

WORKING WITH THE TEXT

2 Reading for gist → S 6.9

Summarise the main ideas of the text in two sentences.

3 Reading for detail

a Point out the reactions of Abdi's co-workers to his religious practices.

b Describe situations in which Abdi feels he does not know American culture.

c Illustrate how Abdi compares the way he is treated with what he knows from Somalia.

d Explain in which way Abdi is treated differently in his neighbourhood and at work.

4 Focus on analysis → S 8, S 9.4

a List phrases that express Abdi's feelings and explain why he feels this way.

b Identify the narrative perspective and how feelings are expressed directly or indirectly.

c Analyse how the way Abdi talks about others adds to his description of his feelings.

D1 I1
Self-check 1.1

D3 I3
Self-check 1.3

D6 16
Self-check 1.6

A STEP FURTHER

5 Working with a graphic novel → S 9.1

a Look at the extract from a graphic novel and sum up what it is about.

b Compare the situation of the people in the graphic novel with that of Abdi in the text.

c Point out what role the American Dream plays in the lives of Abdi, Aarna and Kabir.

The graphic novel *Aarna's story* tells the story of Aarna and her husband Kabir, who are undocumented immigrant workers in the USA. Both Aarna and Kabir came from India and now find themselves working for much less than the minimum wage.

GOOD TO KNOW

graphic novel
= a book that tells a complete story by combining pictures and words

GOOD TO KNOW

It is estimated that about 3 % of the US population consists of **unauthorised immigrants** – that's around 10.3 million people

6 Writing a dialogue → WB, p. 47/2

Write a dialogue between Aarna and Abdi in which they talk about their hopes when deciding to immigrate to the USA and about what has or has not come true.

7 Listening → S 2, S 3 → WB, p. 47/3

A24 Copy the table. Listen to the podcast "Forward Thinking: DREAMers" and match the headings (A–F) with the speakers. There is one more heading than you need.

D 11 I 11 Self-check 4.0

speaker	Aiza	Juanita	Carlos	Luis	Isabella
heading	...	...	...	...	...

A Hope for DACA?
B Successful DREAMers
C Unauthorised or undocumented?
D Family separation
E A brief explanation
F The American Dream

Analysing style, tone and register

GOOD TO KNOW

style
= the use of language to express an identity and to give the text a specific quality

tone
= the emotional quality of the text

register
= the way language is adapted to a specific social situation

One task in your final exam is an analysis task. You are expected to examine how language is used in a non-fictional text to make a specific impression on the reader and to bring across the message of the text effectively. → S 8.2 → WB, p. 48

A Look at the definitions on the left. Which of the following words describe style, tone or register? Copy the table and sort the words into the correct column.

academic | alienating | elaborate | engaging | enthusiastic | formal | hopeful | humorous | informal | negative | neutral | personal | positive | sentimental | serious | witty

style	tone	register
simple, …	optimistic, …	colloquial, …

B Analyse style, tone and register of the speech below and the effect this has on the reader.

1. Read the speech and select passages that you find particularly moving or impressive.
2. Analyse the style, tone and register of these passages. Consider the stylistic features, emotions, attitude and formality expressed in the speech. → S 8.2
3. Describe the effects these passages have on you. Support your findings with quotes.
4. Present and compare your texts in class.

Reverend Jesse Louis Jackson, Civil Rights activist, politician and Baptist minister

Address by The Reverend Jesse Louis Jackson

[…] Common ground. America is not a blanket woven from one thread, one color, one cloth. When I was a child growing up in Greenville, South Carolina my grandmama could not afford a blanket, she didn't complain and we did not freeze. Instead she took pieces of old cloth – patches, wool, silk, gabardine, crockersack – only patches, barely good enough to wipe off your shoes with. But they didn't stay that way very long. With sturdy hands and a strong cord, she sewed them together into a quilt, a thing of beauty and power and culture. Now, Democrats, we must build such a quilt.

Farmers, you seek fair prices and you are right – but you cannot stand alone. Your patch is not big enough. Workers, you fight for fair wages, you are right – but your patch of labor is not big enough. Women, you seek comparable worth and pay equity, you are right – but your patch is not big enough. […]

Women, mothers, who seek Head Start, and day care and prenatal care on the front side of life, relevant jail care and welfare on the back side of life – you are right – but your patch is not big enough. Students, you seek scholarships, you are right – but your patch is not big enough. Blacks and Hispanics, when we fight for civil rights, we are right – but our patch is not big enough.

Gays and lesbians, when you fight against discrimination and a cure for AIDS, you are right – but your patch is not big enough. Conservatives and progressives, when you fight for what you believe, right wing, left wing, hawk, dove, you are right from your point of view, but your point of view is not enough.

But don't despair. Be as wise as my grandmama. Pull the patches and the pieces together, bound by a common thread. When we form a great quilt of unity and common ground, we'll have the power to bring about health care and housing and jobs and education and hope to our Nation. […]

We, the people, can win! […] (353 words)

The Reverend Jesse Louis Jackson, 1988

C Space and innovation

BEFORE YOU READ

1 Talking about inventions

a Find out who came up with the invention shown in the photo, and where and when it was invented.

b Do some research on what the following Americans invented.

Mary Anderson | Henry Ford | Bill Gates | Stephanie Kwolek | Elon Musk

First microwave presented to the public

c Find five more inventions that Americans came up with and take notes.

d Present your findings in class and rank all of the inventions in order of importance.

The space race is back on – but who will win?

[...]

Liu Boming took in the dizzy view. Around him lay the inky vastness of space. Below was the Earth. "Wow," he said, laughing. "It's too beautiful out here." Over the next seven hours Liu and his colleague Tang Hongbo carried out China's second spacewalk, helped along by a giant robotic arm. [...]

Meanwhile, on Mars, a Chinese rover was exploring. Video shows the vehicle trundling over a rocky surface. [...] China is only the second country to land and operate a rover on the red planet, after the US. The frantic tempo of the China National Space Administration's (CNSA) recent programme is reminiscent of the cold war, when Moscow and Washington were superpower rivals scrambling to put the first man in space and land on the moon.

Half a century on, space has opened up. It is less ideological and a lot more crowded. About 72 countries have space programmes, including India, Brazil, Japan, Canada, South Korea and the UAE. The European Space Agency is active too, while the UK boasts the most private space startups after the US.

Space today is also highly commercial. On Sunday Richard Branson flew to the edge of space and back again in his Virgin Galactic passenger rocket. On Tuesday, Branson's fellow billionaire Jeff Bezos is due to travel in his own reusable craft, New Shepard, built by the Amazon founder's company Blue Origin and launched from west Texas.

Non-state actors play an increasingly important role in space exploration. Elon Musk's SpaceX vehicles have made numerous flights to the International Space Station (ISS), and since last year they have transported people as well as cargo. Later this year Musk is due to send his own all-civilian crew into orbit – though he isn't going himself.

Even so, space still reflects tensions on Earth. "Astropolitics follows terrapolitics," says Mark Hilborne, a lecturer in defence studies at King's College London. Up there anything goes, he adds. "Space governance is a bit fuzzy. Laws are few and very old. They are not written for asteroid mining or for a time when companies dominate."

The biggest challenge to US space supremacy comes not from Russia – heir to the Soviet Union's pioneering space programme, which launched the Sputnik satellite and got the first human into space in the form of Yuri Gagarin – but from China. [...]

4 **inky** tiefschwarz
4 **vastness** (unermessliche) Weite
13 **to trundle** rollen
16 **frantic** rasant; wild
20 **to scramble** drängeln; nachjagen
32 **edge** Rand, Kante
41 **space exploration** Weltraumforschung
46 **cargo** Fracht, Ladung
55 **mining** Bergbau
58 **supremacy** Vorherrschaft; Überlegenheit

72 **to accrue** ansammeln
76 **bifurcation** Zweiteilung
81 **aligned** verbunden
89 **intermittently** zeitweilig; unregelmäßig
96 **staging post** Zwischenstation
101 **accusation** Anschuldigung
111 **surgeon** Chirurg/-in
120 **to transcend** übertreffen; übersteigen
128 **pre-eminent** herausragend
131 **nimble** wendig, flink
138 **boldly** mutig, kühn

In its annual threat assessment this April, the office of the US Director of National Intelligence (DNI) described China as a "near-peer competitor" pushing for global power. It warns: "Beijing is working to match or exceed US capabilities in space to gain the military, economic, and prestige benefits that Washington has accrued from space leadership." […]

According to Alanna Krolikowski, an assistant professor at the Missouri University of Science and Technology, a "bifurcation" of space exploration is under way. In one emerging camp are states led by China and Russia, many of them authoritarian; in the other are democracies and "like-minded" countries aligned with the US. […]

These rival geopolitical factions are fighting over a familiar mountainous surface: the moon. In 2019 a Chinese rover landed on its far side – a first. China is now planning a mission to the moon's south pole, to establish a robotic research station and an eventual lunar base, which would be intermittently crewed.

Nasa, meanwhile, has said it intends to put a woman and a person of colour on the moon by 2024. SpaceX has been hired to develop a lander. The return to the moon – after the last astronaut, commander Eugene Cernan, said goodbye in December 1972 – would be a staging post for the ultimate "giant leap", Nasa says: sending astronauts to Mars. […]

Moscow's state corporation for space activities, Roscosmos, has faced accusations of being more interested in politics than space research. Last month the newspaper *Novaya Gazeta* reported that Roscosmos's executive director of manned space programmes, former cosmonaut Sergei Krikalev, had been fired. His apparent crime: questioning an official decision to shoot a film on the Russian section of the ISS.

The film, *Challenge*, is about a female surgeon operating on a cosmonaut in space, and has been backed and financed by Roscosmos. It stars Yulia Peresild, who is due to head to space in October with director Klim Shipenko. The launch seems timed to beat Tom Cruise, who is due to shoot his own movie on board the ISS with director Doug Liman. […]

"Space is one of the areas that has traditionally transcended politics. The Mir space station worked at a time of east-west tensions. There was symbolic cooperation. Whether this will continue in the future is really up for debate," Hilborne says. "The US is very sensitive about what happens in space."

Most observers think the US will remain the world's pre-eminent space power, thanks to its innovative and flourishing private sector. China's Soviet-style state programme appears less nimble. Despite ambitious timetables, and billions spent by Beijing, it is unclear when – or even if – an astronaut will return to the moon. The 2030s, perhaps? Will they be American or Chinese? Or from a third country?

It may well be that the first person to boldly go again doesn't merely represent a nation or carry a flag. More likely, they will emerge from a lunar lander wearing a spacesuit with a SpaceX logo on the back – a giant leap not only for mankind, but for galactic marketing. (905 words)

Luke Harding, *The Guardian*, 2021

WORKING WITH THE TEXT

2 Reading for gist

Scan the text and say what the following numbers refer to.

72 | 2019 | 2024 | 1972 | 2030s

3 Reading for detail

a Summarise what is said about the space race during the Cold War.

b Outline what steps in space exploration have been taken by different countries in recent years, and what future plans and prospects are mentioned in the text.

c Describe the role of the private sector in space exploration according to the text.

d Explain the extent to which the USA has an advantage over China when it comes to space exploration.

4 Focus on analysis → S 8.1, S. 8.2 → WB, p. 49/2

a Identify the different registers used by the author. Give examples from the text.

b In the text the term "giant leap" is quoted twice (l. 97, l. 142) which refers to the famous quotation by Neil Armstrong, the first human to set foot on the moon: "That's one small step for man – one giant leap for mankind." Another famous quotation is "to boldly go …," (ll. 137–138) which alludes to the intro to *Star Trek*: "to boldly go where no man has gone before …". Explain the context in which these quotations occur and the effect they have on the reader.

c Analyse the stylistic devices used by the author to bring across his message.

D 1 I 1
Self-check 3.3

A STEP FURTHER

5 Writing a letter → S 13.1 → ○ 5

Imagine, the billionaires Elon Musk, Jeff Bezos and Richard Branson had created a programme to send particularly motivated young people into space. In order to participate, you have to write a motivational letter in which you give reasons why you consider space travel important for the world, and where you see its innovative potential. You decide to apply for the programme. Write a motivational letter in which you also consider political, economic and scientific aspects of space travel. Write at least 200 words.

D 10 I 10
Self-check 3.3

6 Working with diagrams → S 11.4

a Get together with a partner and choose one of the diagrams each. Describe and analyse the diagrams to each other.

b Together, compare the messages of the diagrams to what the text says about the role of the USA and China in the global economy.

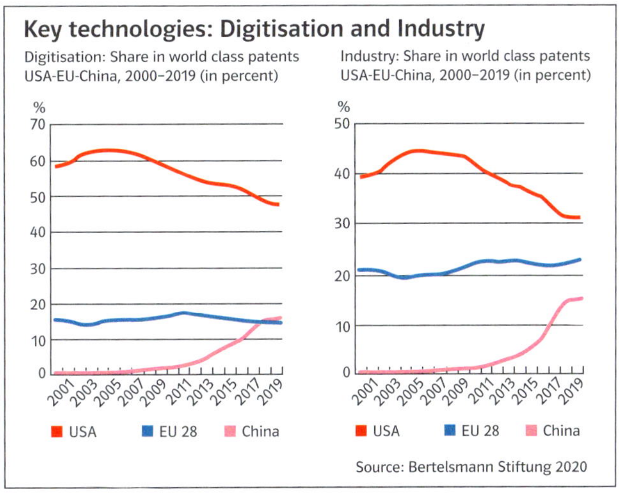

D 6 I 6
Self-check 1.6

GOOD TO KNOW

patent
= an official document stating that its owner has the exclusive right to produce and market a particular invention

D The USA and the world

BEFORE YOU READ

1 Talking about the United States

a In groups, discuss the role of the USA in the world. What changes have occurred in recent years in the US economy, the relations to other countries etc.? Take notes. → ○ 6

b Exchange your ideas with the rest of the class.

USEFUL PHRASES

Expressing an opinion	Agreeing	Disagreeing
I (really) think …	I (completely) agree.	I'm not sure I agree with you on …
I (strongly) believe …	You're (absolutely) right.	I'm sorry but I don't agree.
It seems to me that …	I can go along with that.	I see what you're saying but …
I would say …	You're right to a point.	You have a point there but …

2 Words matter

Match these words with their definitions. There is one more definition than you need.

1. alliance
2. authoritarianism
3. ally
4. adversary
5. credibility
6. bipartisan

A an opponent
B trustworthiness
C when two opposing parties agree on sth
D a group or country that helps another one in a conflict
E an agreement between countries or groups to work together
F a system forcing people to follow its rules without dissent
G a country run by an absolute ruler, e.g. a monarch or dictator

Remarks by President Biden on America's Place in the World

[...] [T]he message I want the world to hear today: America is back. America is back. Diplomacy is back at the center of our foreign policy.

As I said in my inaugural address, we will repair our alliances and engage with the world once again, not to meet yesterday's challenges, but today's and tomorrow's. American leadership must meet this new moment of advancing authoritarianism, including the growing ambitions of China to rival the United States and the determination of Russia to damage and disrupt our democracy.

We must meet the new moment [...] – accelerating global challenges – from the pandemic to the climate crisis to nuclear proliferation – challenging the will only to be solved by nations working together and in common. We can't do it alone.

That must be this – we must start with diplomacy rooted in America's most cherished democratic values: defending freedom, championing opportunity, upholding universal rights, respecting the rule of law, and treating every person with dignity. That's the grounding wire of our global policy – our global power. That's our inexhaustible source of strength. That's America's abiding advantage.

Though many of these values have come under intense pressure in recent years, even pushed to the brink in the last few weeks, the American people are going to emerge from this moment stronger, more determined, and better equipped to unite

6 **inaugural address** Ansprache zur Amtseinführung
15 **to disrupt** (stark) durcheinanderbringen; stören
19 **proliferation** Verbreitung; Weitergabe
24 **to cherish** (wert)schätzen
28 **dignity** *(no pl)* Würde
28 **grounding wire** *(fig)* Schutzleitung, Erdung
31 **abiding** dauerhaft

the world in fighting to defend democracy, because we have fought for it ourselves. [...]

Over the past two weeks, I've spoken with the leaders of many of our closest friends – Canada, Mexico, the UK, Germany, France, NATO, Japan, South Korea, Australia – to [begin] reforming the habits of cooperation and rebuilding the muscle of democratic alliances that have atrophied over the past few years of neglect and, I would argue, abuse.

America's alliances are our greatest asset, and leading with diplomacy means standing shoulder-to-shoulder with our allies and key partners once again. By leading with diplomacy, we must also mean engaging our adversaries and our competitors diplomatically, where it's in our interest, and advance the security of the American people. That's why, yesterday, the United States and Russia agreed to extend the New START Treaty for five years to preserve the only remaining treaty between our countries safeguarding nuclear stability. [...]

And we'll also take on directly the challenges posed by our prosperity, security, and democratic values by our most serious competitor, China. [...] We will compete from a position of strength by building back better at home, working with our allies and partners, renewing our role in international institutions, and reclaiming our credibility and moral authority, much of which has been lost.

That's why we've moved quickly to begin restoring American engagement internationally and earn back our leadership position, to catalyze global action on shared challenges.

On day one, I signed the paperwork to rejoin the Paris Climate Agreement. We're taking steps led by the example of integrating climate objectives across all of our diplomacy and raise the ambition of our climate targets. That way, we can challenge other nations, other major emitters, [...] to up the ante on their own commitments. I'll be hosting climate leaders – a climate leaders' summit to address the climate crisis on Earth Day of this year. America must lead in the face of this existential threat. And just as with the pandemic, it requires global cooperation.

We've also reengaged with the World Health Organization. [...] We've elevated the status of cyber issues within our government, including appointing the first national – Deputy National Security Advisor for Cyber and Emerging Technology. We're launching an urgent initiative to improve our capability, readiness, and resilience in cyberspace. [...]

We also face a crisis of more than 80 million displaced people suffering all around the world. The United States' moral leadership on refugee issues was a point of bipartisan consensus for so many decades when I first got here. We shined the light [...] of liberty on oppressed people. We offered safe havens for those fleeing violence or persecution. And our example pushed other nations to open wide their doors as well. So today, I'm approving an executive order to begin the hard work of restoring our refugee admissions program to help meet the unprecedented global need. [...]

There's no longer a bright line between foreign and domestic policy. Every action we take in our conduct abroad, we must take with American working families in mind. [...] When we invest in economic development of countries, we create new markets for our products and reduce the likelihood of instability, violence, and mass migrations.

When we strengthen health systems in far regions of the world, we reduce the risk of future pandemics that can threaten our people and our economy.

When we defend equal rights of people the world over – of women and girls, LGBTQ individuals, indigenous communities, and people with disabilities, the people of every ethnic background and religion – we also ensure that those rights are protected for our own children here in America. [...] (837 words)

Joe Biden, The White House, website, 2021

48 **to atrophy** verkümmern
77 **to catalyze** *(AE)* beschleunigen
82 **objective** Ziel
86 **to up the ante** noch einmal nachlegen; erhöhen
95 **to elevate** anheben; erhöhen
102 **resilience** Belastbarkeit, Stabilität
110 **haven** Zufluchtsort
111 **persecution** Verfolgung
119 **conduct** *(fml)* Auftreten

CULTURE BOX

Isolationism and interventionism
Since the beginning, the foreign policy of the USA has shifted between isolationism and interventionism – either the effort to abstain from any involvement in other countries and their conflicts or the effort to form alliances and even take on a policing role in other countries' conflicts. In his speech on the USA joining World War I, President Woodrow Wilson spoke the famous words: "The world must be made safe for democracy," which represent American interventionism. On the other hand, the slogan "America first", taken up by former President Donald Trump, is an extreme expression of American isolationism.

WORKING WITH THE TEXT

3 Reading for gist

Choose the statement that best sums up President Biden's speech.
Give reasons for your decision and the relevant line number(s).

A The US should be predominantly looking after its own interests.
B The US is intending to put foreign involvement ahead of its own interests.
C The US seeks to combine taking global responsibility and pursuing its own interests.

4 Reading for detail → ○7

a Explain how Joe Biden intends to restore a positive image of the USA in the world.

b Outline three pressing issues that the USA is planning to confront.

c Describe how Joe Biden sees the mutual influence of US foreign and domestic affairs on each other.

5 Focus on analysis → S10.3 → WB, p. 50

a Explain in your own words what the following quote by Thomas Jefferson from his first inaugural address in 1801 means: "Peace, commerce, and honest friendship with all nations, entangling alliances with none." Use a dictionary, if necessary.

b Collect instances from Biden's speech that either match or contradict Jefferson's message.

c Compare the message of Biden's speech with the quote by Jefferson.

GOOD TO KNOW

Thomas Jefferson was one of the Founding Fathers of the USA and the country's third president (1801–1809). He was also the main author of the Declaration of Independence.

A STEP FURTHER

D 11 I 11
Self-check 4.0

6 Listening → S 2, S 3

A25 **a** Listen to the first part of the podcast "Forward Thinking: US military activities since World War II". While listening, note down the correct answers (A, B or C). There is only one correct answer.

1. The invasion of Normandy by the allied forces resulted in the …
   A liberation of Paris.
   B immediate end of World War II.
   C withdrawal of the US army from the war effort.

2. Compared to the time directly after World War II, the number of US soldiers posted in Germany now is …
   A much lower.
   B much higher.
   C roughly the same.

3. Tensions in the Middle East …
   A only began in the 1990s.
   B were strongest in the 1990s.
   C started long before the 1990s.

4. During the Cold War, the Soviet Union and the USA …
   A fought each other directly.
   B avoided fighting each other directly.
   C engaged in a war using nuclear weapons.

5. After World War II, different parts of Korea were under the influence of …
   A Vietnam and the USA.
   B the Soviet Union and China.
   C the USA and the Soviet Union.

6. In 1965, …
   A the Vietnam War started.
   B the USA began fighting openly in Vietnam.
   C Vietnam was divided into North and South Vietnam.

A26 **b** Copy the table. Listen to the second part of the podcast and take notes on the following points.

	duration	reason	result
Gulf War			
Iraq War			
War in Afghanistan			

The USA seen from abroad – Creating a podcast

An American youth organisation is conducting a project on "The USA seen from abroad". The goal is to find out how young people from other countries worldwide view the USA. They are asking for contributions in the form of a 5-minute-long podcast on one of the following topics:

- The American Dream
- America and the world
- America now and then

Step 1 Form small groups and choose one of the topics above. Note that all three topics should be addressed by at least one group.

Step 2 Plan your podcast.

- Decide on the function of your podcast (e.g. to inform, to entertain, to convince).
- Plan the content of your podcast. Collect what you already know about your topic and also find further information. Add ideas on how this topic relates to your home country and in what way this influences how you see the USA.
- Note down the questions you want to ask in your interviews.

Step 3 Carry out a survey.

- Find out what people around you think about your topic by conducting interviews with at least three other students.
- Summarise the results of your survey for your podcast.

Step 4 Structure your podcast.

- Agree on a title for your podcast and its general message.
- Select aspects from the information you have collected that are helpful in bringing across your message.
- Decide how many speakers should be involved. Either speak as yourselves or create characters and give them a backstory.

Step 5 Write a script.

- Take notes on the main ideas and arguments you want to convey in your podcast.
- Structure the ideas and arguments.
- Write notes on what you want to speak about and copy passages from the interviews that you want to quote. Make sure your podcast fulfils its function (see step 2).
- Plan for a length of 5 minutes.

Step 6 Perform and record your podcast. Speak without using your notes and only read off the quotes.

Step 7 Present a few podcasts in class and upload the rest to a platform. Each student gives feedback on three podcasts, commenting on their content, structure, language and style.

The promised land?

From its beginnings, the United States of America has attracted people who had dreams – dreams of economic success and prosperity, the chance to make a living, freedom from political or religious persecution, a life in peace, or the promise to start a new life, reaching their full potential – in short: the American Dream.

The first European settlers

A little more than a century after the Americas were 'discovered' by European explorers, British settlers began to form settlements in North America. The first settlement, Jamestown in Virginia, was started in 1607 by people growing tobacco. In 1620, a ship of Puritans landed further north in what is now Massachusetts, bringing Puritans who were fleeing religious persecution in Europe, and who formed colonies strictly ruled by religious regulations.

Independence

Until the late 18th century, the settlements on the east coast in North America were largely under British rule. Governors who ruled the colonies were sent from England, and taxes had to be paid to the English Crown. From the late 17th century onwards, dissatisfaction with being ruled by a government thousands of miles away, without having any say, grew steadily. In 1773, this dissatisfaction erupted in the Boston Tea Party, when colonists protested taxation by throwing tea from a ship into Boston Harbor. This resulted in growing tensions between the British and the colonists, culminating in the Revolutionary War (1775–1783) and the Declaration of Independence in 1776.

Waves of immigration

Following the establishment of the first settlements, people started immigrating to the USA in growing numbers. Difficult circumstances such as war, famine, poverty and persecution in the countries of origin caused waves of immigration. Throughout the 19th and into the 20th century, people from very diverse backgrounds came to the USA, whose society is often described as a 'melting pot', where many different cultures merge to form something new. Others prefer the term 'salad bowl', where each element retains its specific qualities. Most immigrants were driven by the hope for a better life and the dream of unlimited opportunities.

US immigration flows by country

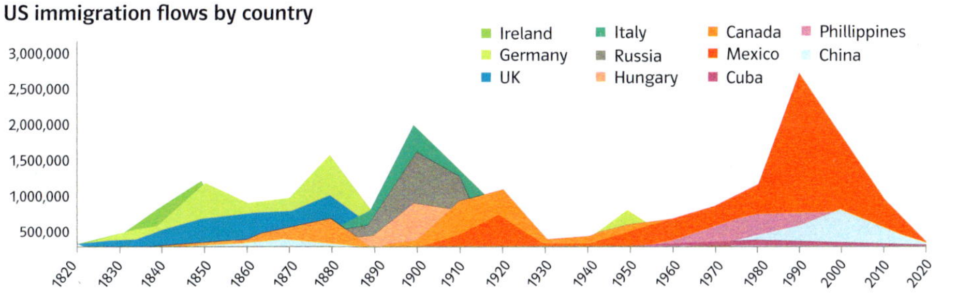

Max Galka, *Metrocosm* website, 2021

The displacement of Native Americans

During the 19th century, immigrants increasingly moved westwards and occupied the land, until setttlements reached the west coast. During this process, millions of Native Americans were displaced when their land was taken by mostly European settlers. Fierce battles between the two groups ensued, but the Native Americans eventually lost most of the land they used to live on.

16 **tax** Steuer
17 **dissatisfaction** Unzufriedenheit
23 **establishment** Gründung
24 **famine** Hungersnot
29 **to retain** behalten
35 **to ensue** (nach)folgen

56 **rift** Spaltung; Zerwürfnis
70 **fur** Fell; Pelz
71 **staple crop** *hier:* wichtigste Anbaupflanze
76 **conveyor belt** Fließband
85 **realm** Bereich

Slavery and racism

From 1619 on, African people were enslaved and brought first to the colonies, and later to the USA to work on the tobacco and cotton fields in the southern colonies and later states. The institution of slavery continued to exist until it was abolished in 1865 as a result of the Civil War which was fought between the Southern states, who relied on slavery for their economic success, and the more industrialised North, where a majority of people opposed slavery.

However, even after slavery was abolished, inequality and injustice continued for Black Americans. During the first half of the 20th century, the system of segregation kept white and black Americans separated in the public sphere. Only in the 1960s, as a result of the Civil Rights Movement, was inequality on any grounds declared illegal with the Equal Rights Act (1964). The situation of black Americans has improved slightly since then, and some have made it into high positions – most notably Barack Obama, who became president of the USA in 2009. Yet, continuing police brutality and other forms of discrimination show that the struggle for equality has not come to an end yet. There is a growing understanding that slavery was a significant historical development for the USA, and the contributions to society of Black Americans are receiving increasing attention.

The USA – a unified nation?

Although the USA carries the word 'united' in its name, there have always been rifts between various groups. The Civil War is a particularly striking illustration of such a rift in the history of the USA. However, even today the idea of the USA as a torn nation is often discussed. There is a clear rift along political lines, supported by the two-party system, with Republicans, who tend to oppose a strong government on the one hand, and Democrats, who tend to support government regulations on the other hand. The controversy over whether gun ownership should underlie state control is an example of this division. There is also what is called the urban-rural divide. In rural areas people adhere more to traditional values, while in urban areas they tend to be more open to innovative ideas. Differences in education and related job opportunities are also linked to the racial and the urban-rural divide. Finally, religion is a dividing factor, especially with fundamentalist Christians questioning liberal policies.

Economic success and innovative spirit

The USA developed gradually from a farming community to a highly industrialised economy. The colonists started an economy based on fishing, trading in furs and growing tobacco. Gradually, cotton became a staple crop in the southern states, while in the northern states, industrialisation led to a boom in manufacturing.

The later 19th century saw numerous technological inventions and innovative developments in industry and communication, such as the telegraph, the refrigerated

rail transport, the typewriter and many more. In the early 20th century, the conveyor belt was introduced by Henry Ford. This made mass production of goods possible and led to further economic growth. The saying "from rags to riches" captures success stories like Henry Ford's where a person could come from humble origins and make it to great wealth.

Over the years the US economy has shifted towards a service economy, with only some manufacturing. Agriculture plays a minor part in the US economy today. In the realm of innovation, however, the USA continues to be a leading force in the world, most notably in digital technology and space exploration.

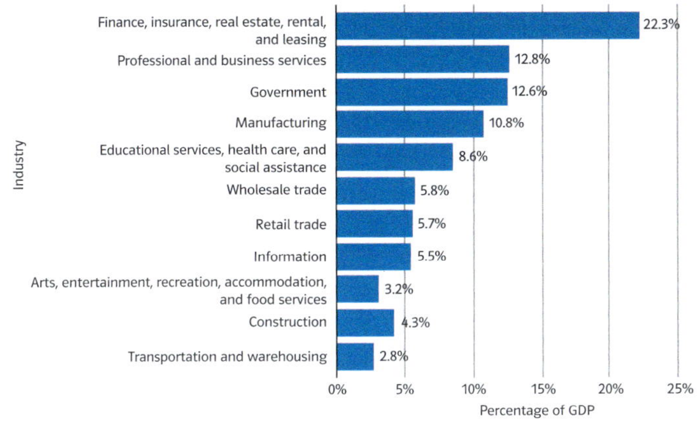

Percentage added to the Gross Domestic Product (GDP) of the United States of America in 2020, by industry (as a percentage of GDP)

Source: BEA; US Department of Commerce @Statista 2021

Foreign policy and military involvement

From its beginning, the USA has shifted back and forth between isolationism and interventionism. Isolationism, which was the dominant mode during much of the 19th century, means staying away from military interference in other countries. Interventionism means that the USA understands itself in a controlling position as a 'global police', intervening in other countries' conflicts. US involvement in World War I and II are examples of interventionism, as are the conflicts during the Cold War (e.g. the Korean and Vietnam Wars from the 1950s to the 1970s). In the early 21st century, military involvement in the Middle East (e.g. the wars in Iraq and Afghanistan) are further examples.

1 Read the text and study the statistics. Use the information to create a mini-quiz. Ask a partner your questions and answer theirs in turn.

2 Work with a partner and describe the statistics on p.107. Choose three immigration peaks and research the reasons for the rise in immigration at those particular points in time.

MK **3** Look at the statistics above which provide figures for the year 2020. Go online and research more recent figures and describe the continuities and changes since 2020.

4 Discuss what influence the USA has on your own lives and what cultural, economic and political role the USA play in the world. Do you see its influence more positively or more negatively? Use information from the text and give reasons for your evaluation.

Outlook: For further discussion, consider the following questions:
- What role does the USA play in international organisations (e.g. UN, NATO, WHO)?
- What position do you think the USA will/should take in the world in terms of economic, political, military and ecological issues?
- Is the American Dream still alive or is it just an illusion?
- How does the role of the USA compare with that of China? What are possible predictions for the future?

1 Lesen und Schreiben

Americans reflect on a divided nation: "This doesn't feel like America"

Time doesn't move any differently at Independence Hall, the birthplace of America. It's the building where both the Declaration of Independence and the U.S. Constitution were signed in colonial Philadelphia. If you travel there, you can learn something about America today.

"America is in turmoil right now," Billy White told "CBS This Morning" co-host Tony Dokoupil. Most people who journeyed to Independence Hall from all across the country had similar viewpoints. "This doesn't feel like America. The America I was raised to love and believe in," Victoria Johnson said. President-elect Joe Biden will face a daunting task after Wednesday's inauguration – reuniting Americans after a bitter election. "I'm not exactly sure that we're in the place that the Founding Fathers would have wanted us to be in," Laura Wilson said.

A CBS News poll found that 54% of Americans today say the biggest threat to our way of life isn't economic collapse, natural disasters or foreign invasions – but our own fellow Americans. "It should be America under one nation under God, indivisible. But I don't see it that way in my eyes right now," White said. The national mood, not to mention the 220-year-old American tradition of peaceful transfers of power, took a blow in January after rioters overran the U.S. Capitol in Washington, D.C. But Jessica Roney, professor of early American history at Temple University in Philadelphia, says America has had some turbulent times before.

"We've never been a unified country. We've always had these huge fractures. If anything, what we have now is a recognition of them. And in some ways, that's hard and painful and scary. And in some ways, it's the only way forward," she said. Roney agreed that divisiveness is American history, not the exception to American history. With that in mind, she said the goal of the Constitution was to somehow prevent the country from collapsing. "They thought it would decay inevitably?" Dokoupil asked.

"This is a world that believes in corruption. Like, right now, we think about our conspiracy theories as a 21st-century thing. It's not. The 18th century was all about conspiracy theories," Roney said. "It was all about this idea of tyranny and the usurpation of liberty ... and the same kind of heated rhetoric that we're used to today, there's a lot of that in the 1780s and '90s where people are really concerned about the imminent demise of the Republic right now, tomorrow, if the other guy is elected." CBS News asked people to put today's America in context with America's past and people responded with answers some might have feared.

"Is there any moment from American history that comes to mind as a point of comparison with today?" Dokoupil asked. "Maybe the American revolution? ... Or the Civil War. There's a fracture that I don't think ... we've seen in over a century," Wilson replied. Another person agreed and said it feels like America is back in a Civil War.

"I guess the Civil War when it was, like, the North versus the South. That's what it feels like again. It's just, it's not a matter of locations fighting each other. It's people fighting against people over a president," Nia King said. But Roney says there's actually a lesser-known moment in American history that may give us hope: "What I'm proud of in American history, what's a moment that I look to, I always said, 'The election of 1800.' I think it's just a phenomenal moment."

That election, which marked the exit of John Adams and the entrance of Thomas Jefferson, was the first peaceful transfer of power between opposing sides in American history. In his inaugural address, Jefferson made a now-famous appeal for unity among the parties of the time uttering the lines "We are all republicans, we are all federalists." As President-elect Joe Biden prepares to hit a very similar note in his inaugural address, not every American is ready to believe him. "How is he unifying America when he was supporting everyone who started the riots back over the summer? I don't see that as unifying at all," Johnson said. Others are hopeful about what Mr. Biden's election will mean for the state of the country but they have their doubts. "Are you hopeful that he will be president for all Americans, not just the people who voted for him?" Dokoupil asked.

"I hope so. I hope so," White said. When Dokoupil followed up and asked if White believed it was likely or if he expected it would happen, he replied back no. But in front of Independence Hall stood Susan Sandler. She was optimistic in part because of the decisions made long ago inside the building.

"I personally was not a Trump supporter, I supported the right of other people to believe in him and to give him a chance. I personally don't like how that worked out. So what did we do? We voted. That's what we do in the United States, right?" Sandler said. "And then we respect that vote. And then we move forward. And if we don't like it, we vote again. That's what we do in the United States. So there we are. Back to our basics." (877 words)

CBS News, website, 2021

ASSIGNMENTS → WB, pp. 51–52

1. Summarise the examples of division in the history of the USA mentioned in the text.
2. Analyse the style, tone and register of the article and say how language is used to engage the reader.
3. Choose one of the following tasks:

   3.1. Comment on the following quote from the text: "A CBS News poll found that 54% of Americans today say the biggest threat to our way of life isn't economic collapse, natural disasters or foreign invasions – but our own fellow Americans." (ll. 24–28)

   Or:

   3.2 Write a blog post in which you discuss the divisions within the USA.

2 Hörverstehen

ASSIGNMENTS → WB, p. 53

A27 Listen to a radio report on the question whether the USA has a civil religion. Copy the table and match the headings with the speakers.

speaker	Tom	Lynn	Shadi	Myles	Nicole	Katie	Philip
heading	…	…	…	…	…	…	…

A A settler state
B Teaching children
C American ideals for all
D The 'American' religion
E The Charters of Freedom
F An ever changing tradition
G Exploitation of Christian teachings

D16 Progress report

The UK and its people

1 Look at the pictures and do the following tasks.

a Work with a partner. Describe what you see in the pictures and consider which aspects of UK society are shown in each.

b With regard to what you came up with in exercise 1a, do you think the pictures are an accurate representation of the UK? Are there any other important aspects of British culture you can think of?

MK **2** Go online and try to find answers to the following questions.

a Choose one of the pictures and research background information about it. Use the following points to structure your research:
- are there any big events related to the picture throughout the year?
- is the content shown popular all across the UK or only in certain parts?
- how does the picture relate to your perception of someone British?

b In class, discuss possible pictures about Germany. Would the pictures be similar to the ones for the UK?

D 11 I 11
Self-check 4.0

A28 **3** You are going to listen to four speakers talking about the United Kingdom.
→ S 2 → WB, p. 56/1

a Listen to the recording once and note down keywords for each speaker's opinion.

b Copy the table below. Listen to the recording again and match each speaker with the correct heading. There is one more heading than you need.

person	Sura	John	Dave	Lottie
heading	…	…	…	…

A Drifting apart
B Family rivalry
C A common culture
D Politically disunited
E Tolerance and acceptance

4 Look at the cartoon. → S 11.3

a Describe the cartoon.

b With a partner, analyse it and discuss what the cartoon suggests about the relationship between the UK and the EU.

GOOD TO KNOW

The United Kingdom joined the European Economic Community (which later became the European Union) on 1 January 1973. In the 2016 EU referendum, 51.9 % of the people in the UK who voted chose to leave the EU. The UK left the EU on 31 January 2020, beginning an 11-month transition period, during which the UK and EU negotiated their future relationship. The withdrawal agreement became fully operational on 1 January 2021.

5 In class, discuss how united (or unified) you think Germany is. Consider the following aspects: → ○1

history | standard of living | politics | dialects | prejudice

USEFUL PHRASES

Germany seems united by … but it seems apart when it comes to …
The integration of East and West has been …
Many things have changed for the better / the worse / have not changed …
Dialects vary / are similar / sound different in / are perceived as …
While the North of Germany is …, the South tends to be …

A English and its regional varieties

BEFORE YOU READ

1 Talking about dialects

a Which dialect is spoken in your area? Do you speak this dialect? Give reasons. Exchange your ideas with a partner.

b What do you know about regional dialects in the UK? Do you know any example words?

GOOD TO KNOW

accent
= a way of pronouncing the words of a language that shows which country, area or social class a person comes from

dialect
= the form of a language that is spoken in one area with grammar, words and pronunciation that may be different from other forms of the same language

If you can't embrace regional dialect, you can kiss my chuddies

The Oxford English Dictionary's inclusion of regional terms shows off what the UK has in common – linguistic ingenuity

In a rare piece of happy news to distract us momentarily from all the chaos, those lovely linguists at the Oxford English Dictionary have announced an abundance of new words all taken from regional dialects.

The new entries include the Indian-English phrase "kiss my chuddies"; the delicious word "jibbons", which is what spring onions are called in Wales; and the Scottish words "sitooterie", which is (obviously) a place to sit out, and "bidie-in" ("a person who lives with his or her partner in a non-marital relationship"), which surely should have been in the dictionary ages ago, since the author Val McDermid, a fine connoisseur of the English language, uses it in her Twitter bio.

That the wise custodians of the English language are actively embracing regional variation is pleasing for many reasons. A recent report revealed "accent softening" lessons are becoming big business in the UK, especially since the Brexit referendum. Regional accents really are "a bar to social mobility", according to experts at the University of Manchester, who have found: "We can still sound regional in the workplace, but not too regional." But I'm with the linguists: now, if ever, we should come together with our fellow Brits, celebrate our diversity and make an extra effort to understand each other. Even people who say "scone" instead of "scone". Perhaps that would have avoided the sort of consternation that was caused recently when certain London-based commentators realised that Jess Phillips MP wasn't necessarily dragged up in a barn just because she speaks with a West Midlands accent. So, people in Birmingham can have office jobs, too? Well – as they say in Yorkshire – I'll go to t'foot of our stairs.

In middle-class offices around London last month, all eyes were on the New York Times's dialect quiz with which an American newspaper delighted British and Irish readers by reminding us that we'll always have our cute accents, no matter what else might be jiggered. After reading it, half the country vowed to use the magnificent word "nithered" (cold) more often; scousers wondered why nobody else has a special word for "scally"; northerners tried to figure out what's special about the word "put" that makes southerners pronounce it properly (despite saying "but", "cut", nut", etc, all wrong); and nobody managed to resolve whether the evening meal is called dinner or tea. (Tea. It's tea.) We can learn a lot about people from the things they say and how they say them. Only Scotland, for example, would have so many unique

1 **you can kiss my chuddies** (*ugs*) du kannst mich mal
3 **ingenuity** Einfallsreichtum; Genialität
17 **non-marital** nicht ehelich
22 **bio (= biography)** Biografie
29 **bar** Hemmnis; Hindernis
35 **fellow Brits** britische Mitbürger
40 **consternation** Fassungslosigkeit; Verwirrung
43 **to drag up** (*ugs*) (ein Kind) lieblos aufziehen
44 **barn** Scheune
56 **to vow** geloben

ways of describing folk with "an exaggerated sense of [their] own importance". (The OED mentions "bigsie", and "fantoosh", meaning showy or flashy.) It feels reassuring to learn that, linguistically at least, Britain is embracing difference and change. Periodically, lovers of variation in the English language fret that regional idiosyncrasies are being ironed out by some sort of ugly, modern, homogenous tone.

In the 1990s, linguists talked about "upspeak", or "high rising terminals", which made young people talk with an upward inflection at the end of sentences as though they were constantly asking questions. One theory was that they'd got it from watching *Neighbours*, and that it was all the fault of new towns where nobody had any proper English roots. Some observers thought that upspeak sounded ridiculous and infantile, until Tony Blair and George Osborne came along with their fake glottal stops, and then young people asking questions suddenly didn't seem so silly anymore.

My own voice comes from Yorkshire, where children getting in the way of adults were told, "Eee, tha's like 'oss muck – allus in t'road"; the Wirral, which scousers think is dead posh; Plymouth, whose locals are called janners; and Derby, where I learned to appreciate a flat pint of Bass in a jug, please, duck. I'm a linguistic shapeshifter, a fan of a neat phrase and an in-joke, and a proud citizen of all over t'shop.

The OED promises to continue its search for regional terms, showcasing all the diverse glory of British English, as well as reminding us of everything we have in common – our wit, our ingenuity, our endless enthusiasm for a bum metaphor. I for one am all in favour of upspeak, variety, linguistic inventiveness and chuddies. And maybe, if the expert team at the OED keeps investigating, one day they might even figure out what Jacob Rees-Mogg is on about. (756 words)

Katy Guest, *The Guardian* website, 2019

74 **reassuring** beruhigend
77 **to fret** sich sorgen
78 **idiosyncracy** Eigenart; Besonderheit
82 **terminal** *hier:* Endung; End-
84 **upward** aufwärts; steigend
84 **inflection** Tonfall
91 **ridiculous** lächerlich
93 **glottal stop** Knacklaut (ein stimmloser, glottal gebildeter Verschlusslaut)

GOOD TO KNOW

Tony Blair was prime minister of the UK from 1997 to 2007 and leader of the Labour Party from 1994 to 2007. Jacob Rees-Mogg was Leader of the House of Commons from 2019 to 2022. He is a controversial figure, often mocked for his old-fashioned, upper-class mannerisms.

WORKING WITH THE TEXT → WB, p. 57

2 Reading for gist

Skim the text to find out what these dialect words and expressions mean and where they can be heard:

bidie-in | bigsie | janners | jibbons | nithered | sitooterie

3 Words matter → S 16.3

a Look up the following words in a dictionary and write a definition for them. If the dictionary lists information about the (in)formality or origin of the word, note it down.

1. custodian (l. 23)
2. jiggered (l. 55)
3. scouser (l. 58)
4. scally (l. 59)
5. to fret (l. 77)
6. upspeak (l. 82)

4 Reading for detail → WB, p. 58/2

a In your own words, explain why the author is pleased that the *Oxford English Dictionary* is including words from regional dialects.

b Illustrate what the author means by "linguistic ingenuity" (l. 3).

c Summarise what the author says about her "own voice" (l. 96) (speech).

D1 I1
Self-check 1.1

5 Focus on analysis → S 8 → G 5, G 6 → ◯ 2 → WB, p. 58/3

a Examine the author's use of adjectives and adverbs in the text. Are there more words with a positive or negative connotation?

b Analyse how the language used in the text brings out the author's attitude to regional varieties of English. Include quotes from the text and give line numbers.

D10 I10
Self-check 3.3

6 Writing a letter to the editor → S 6.5

Write a letter to the editor in which you comment on the following statement from the text: "Regional accents really are 'a bar to social mobility', according to experts at the University of Manchester, who have found: 'We can still sound regional in the workplace, but not too regional.'" (ll. 29–33)

A STEP FURTHER

D6 I6
Self-check 1.6

7 Working with a graph → S 11.4

A29 **a** You are going to listen to two people talking about pronunciation. Listen to the recording twice. Take notes and then answer the following questions in keywords:

1. How do the speakers pronounce 'scone'?
2. Why do the speakers pronounce 'scone' differently?
3. What is a sociolect?
4. Why is there prejudice towards working-class accents?
5. What is 'The Great Scone Map'?

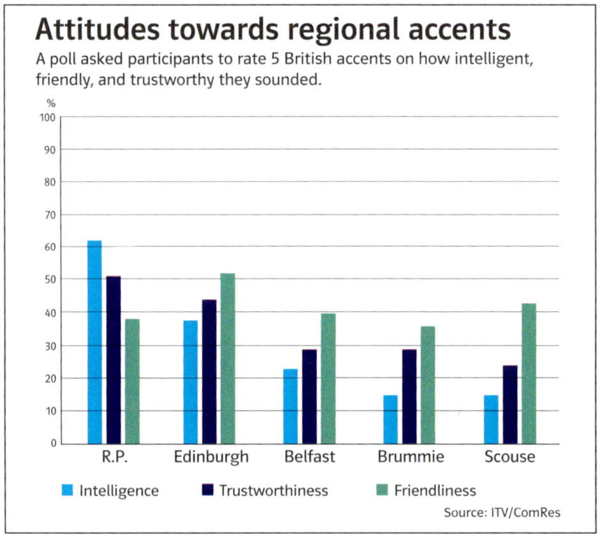

b With a partner, describe and analyse the information presented in the graph. Relate it to the text on pp. 114–115.

D12
Self-check 5.0

8 Having a discussion

Get together in a small group. Discuss attitudes to regional dialects in Germany.

a Identify and talk about the different German dialects and what they sound like.

b Discuss if German institutions should reinforce the use of dialects or if High German should be the only way to communicate.

GOOD TO KNOW

Brummie
= from or connected to Birmingham in England

Scouse
= from or connected to Liverpool in North West England

RP
= the abbreviation for "received pronunciation", which is an accent of British English, associated with education, broadcasting and the South of England

B National identity

BEFORE YOU READ

1 Talking about a baking competition

MK **a** Look at the list of baked items below. Can you guess which are sweet and which are savoury? Go online to find out if you guessed correctly. Share your findings with the class.

Bakewell tarts | Battenberg cake | Chelsea buns | Eccles cakes | millionaire's shortbread | parkin | sausage rolls | Victoria sponge | Yorkshire pudding

b Would you enter a baking/cooking competition on TV? Give reasons. What kind of person do you think might enter such a competition? Discuss your thoughts with a partner.

'The Great British Bake Off' Can Win Any Culture War

It is a place where heritage and culture stand proud, enriched but not diluted by the traditions of immigrants. Some of its denizens roam the world, exploring foreign cultures; others stick close to home; neither invites scorn. An island of confident identity in a fractured and contentious world, it celebrates cosmopolitan curiosity and deep-rooted traditions, local custom and diverse origins. It is a big tent – quite literally. I refer, of course, to "The Great British Bake Off" or, as it is known on American shores, "The Great British Baking Show."

A baking competition held in a giant white tent decked out with Union Jack bunting and a dozen kitchens' worth of equipment, the program is an institution in the U.K. It has been credited with sparking a boom in home baking and raising standards in the shops. The 10th season aired this fall and, available on Netflix, the show has attracted passionate U.S. fans as well. Earlier this month, Florida-based TV critic Andy Dehnart, who covers non-scripted programming on his site Reality Blurred, named it "the reality TV show of the decade".

Set in the countryside, with establishing shots of sheep grazing, songbirds chirping and bees buzzing among the wildflowers, the program could be peddling nostalgia for village life in England's green and pleasant land. The jokes are silly puns and double entendres, gentle and exceedingly British.

Commentators on both sides of the Atlantic emphasize its good nature as a respite from political conflict. A British critic calls it "a weekly therapy session. It is a last remnant of sanity in an increasingly crazy country; an oasis of niceness in a desert of vileness."

The welcoming atmosphere is "so different from the picture Brexit painted, that the British want their nation back and that they want us out," Chetna Makan, a 2014 contestant who moved to the U.K. from Mumbai, told the New York Times.

With its polyglot mix of regional accents, class backgrounds and national origins, the show is not nostalgic. But it is still "The Great British Bake Off," unabashedly so. And therein lies its cultural genius. In the famous tent, we see a culture changing without losing coherence or rejecting the past. You can keep your nation, the show suggests, while adding new elements. The constant reinforcement of Britishness, from Union Jack cakes and Gran's old recipes to Dr. Who references and Liverpool pride, is as essential to the

3 **diluted** verwässert
5 **denizen** *hier:* Gast; Teilnehmer/-in
7 **scorn** Spott; Verachtung
10 **deep-rooted** fest verwurzelt
17 **decked out** herausgeputzt
17 **bunting** Fahnentuch; Wimpel
20 **to credit** zuschreiben; zugutehalten
22 **to air** ausstrahlen
26 **non-scripted** nicht im Drehbuch geschrieben
33 **to peddle sth** etw verbreiten
35 **pun** Wortspiel
36 **double entendre** Doppeldeutigkeit
40 **respite** Ruhepause
44 **vileness** Niederträchtigkeit
54 **unabashedly** ungeniert; unerschrocken

64 **caster sugar** extra feiner Zucker
72 **presumption** *hier:* Anmaßung
80 **to shoot (a film)** (einen Film) drehen
82 **cake platter** Kuchenplatte
92 **venture** Projekt; Unternehmen
106 **treat** Leckerei
118 **ingredient** Zutat
120 **ginger** Ingwer
125 **self-effacing** zurückhaltend; bescheiden
134 **to mend** flicken; reparieren
139 **dietary custom** Essgewohnheit
142 **to meld** kombinieren

program as cardamom and caster sugar. GBBO, as fans refer to it, rejects the choice between openness and national identity.

Unlike most U.S. cooking competitions, with their professional chefs and substantial winner-take-all cash prizes, the show is in the great tradition of British amateurism, minus the aristocratic presumptions. Contestants bake because they love it, and, although everyone wants to win, they play fair and help each other out. Bakers include retirees and full-time parents (male as well as female), and a wide range of professions, from builder to geography teacher, garden designer to veterinary surgeon, with the occasional student juggling exams. (The show shoots mostly on weekends.) The winner gets a glass cake platter and, along with the other finalists, a bouquet of flowers. That's it.

Of course, success brings another valuable currency: public renown. Many finalists go on to at least semi-professional status, writing cookbooks and columns and appearing on TV. But career advancement seems a rare motivation, and coming in second doesn't make you a loser. Treating baking as a common venture where good ideas can come from anyone or anywhere, the show welcomes global citizens and the flavors they introduce. At the same time, it celebrates distinctively British baking and honors British history. The show's inclusive spirit embraces local traditions and the people who made them. It's as patriotic as it is cosmopolitan.

Maybe it takes an American (or an Indian immigrant) to recognize that Victoria sponge, Chelsea buns, sausage rolls, Battenberg cake, millionaire's shortbread and parkin (which I had to Google) are culturally specific treats. Traditional British baking, it turns out, can be pretty yummy – or scrummy, as former judge Mary Berry would say. "Before the bake-off, it was nearly impossible to find classic British sweets like Victoria sponge sandwiches, Eccles cakes and Bakewell tarts unless you or your granny made them at home," writes New York Times food columnist Melissa Clark. The show has introduced a new generation to old-fashioned baking. It also reminds viewers of how once-exotic ingredients became as British as Yorkshire pudding. When charged with making a ginger cake, Rahul Mandal, the eventual winner in 2018, explained that his mother back in India was surprised at the assignment. "In India we normally use ginger for savory things," said the self-effacing research engineer. "The first time I had ginger cake," he recalled, "was during a Bonfire Night celebration."

For non-Brits, he's referring to the Nov. 5 festivities marking the failure of the 1605 Gunpowder Plot to blow up parliament and kill the king. Ginger may not be British, but ginger cake certainly is.

A cooking contest alone can't mend a society's divisions, of course. But the success of this one suggests they may not be as deep as they seem. Food is, after all, one of the most powerful tribal markers, with dietary customs and taboos separating us from them. A hit show dedicated to the idea that specifically British baking can meld old and new, regional and national, local and foreign, without losing its distinctive identity is a powerful indicator of cultural health. [...]

(924 words)

Virginia Postrel, *Bloomberg* website, 2019

WORKING WITH THE TEXT

2 Scanning the text

Scan the text and note down clues that reveal the author's cultural background.

3 Reading for detail → WB, p. 59/2

a Explain the concept behind *The Great British Bake Off*.

b Write down three examples from the text that illustrate how Britishness is reinforced in the show.

c Summarise the ways in which the show has achieved its "inclusive spirit" (l. 98).

4 Words matter

In your own words, explain the following expressions from the text.
Use a dictionary if necessary.

1. diverse origins (ll. 11–12)
2. national identity (l. 66)
3. public renown (l. 86)
4. career advancement (l. 89)
5. tribal marker (l. 138)
6. cultural health (l. 145)

A STEP FURTHER

5 Working with videos

MK a Go online to find out more about *The Great British Bake Off*. Find answers to the following questions. Take notes.

1. On which channel/platform can you watch the show in the UK?
2. How many seasons have there been to date?
3. Who are the judges?
4. Who are the presenters and what is their role?
5. Are there any well-known former contestants? Who are they and what do they do now?

MK b Work in small groups. Go online and look for short *Great British Bake Off* clips. Each member in your group should watch a different clip. Take notes on the clip's content as you watch.

c Watch your clip again. Take notes on the type of humour used in the clips. Pay attention to the use of humour as described in the text: "The jokes are silly puns and double entendres, gentle and exceedingly British." (ll. 35–37). → ○ 3

d Take it in turns to share your findings in the group. Then discuss which clip represents 'British humour' best.

CULTURE BOX

In *The Great Celebrity Bake Off*, celebrity contestants take part in special versions of the popular British baking competition to raise money for charity. The charities are *Sport Relief*, *Comic Relief* and *Stand up to Cancer*. Each season of *Celebrity Bake Off* focuses on one charity. Celebrities have included actors James McAvoy and Daisy Ridley, Youtuber KSI and athlete Dame Kelly Holmes.

D8 18
Self-check 3.1

6 Writing a blog post → ○4 → WB, p. 60

13 **to encompass** umschließen
15 **MBE** (Member (of the Order) of the British Empire)
16 **to come full circle** zum Ausgangspunkt zurückkehren
25 **to entertain** *hier:* beantworten
36 **hotpot** Eintopf
40 **to rip apart** verreißen
44 **to own sth** *(infml) hier:* sich etw zu eigen machen
54 **to be up for scrutiny** auf dem Prüfstand stehen

Nadiya Hussain: 'I want to blend in. But the truth is, I'm never going to blend in'

Nadiya Hussain has never published a baking book. She has never fronted her own baking show before either, having had her life changed by appearing on the big one, the one which put her under the national spotlight as she transformed from a shy, uncertain home cook into a Great British Bake Off winner, the best-loved winner in the history of the series. Now, after five years of fame, her career, which has encompassed books, documentaries, cooking shows, a memoir, an MBE, and much, much more, has come full circle, and she is ready to focus on baking again. [...]

"What I've learned in the past five years is that the change I want to see, I have to see in myself first. I am a brown Muslim woman, working in a very male-dominated, Caucasian industry. And if you'd asked me five years ago, what does it feel like to be a Muslim, I wouldn't have entertained it. I would have said, look, can we just talk about the cooking and the baking? [...] Having worked in it for five years, there's no space [in the industry] for someone like me. I've learned that if I don't create that space, who will? Someone has to do it." [...]

"I also understand the responsibility of needing to talk about these things. It comes with great responsibility, but it's also quite exhausting, at the same time, because I can't do a Lancashire hotpot without somebody saying, why do you get to do a Lancashire hotpot? Why do you get to make a Cornish pasty? [...] I get bits of my books ripped apart because, am I English enough to be writing these things? It upsets me because there are cooks out there who... Jamie can do Italian. He's allowed to own that as something he loves to do and something that is his, but I can't do a Cornish pasty. That's what's wrong with this industry and that's what's wrong with this society and that's what's wrong with the world. Because I'm a daughter of an immigrant, because I am bilingual, because I'm a Muslim, because I'm a brown woman, because I don't fit into that industry or fit into these worlds, I'm constantly up for scrutiny. I'm constantly up for questioning. I'm kind of fed up of it." She smiles, her big, famous, winning, national treasure smile. "But I also really enjoy saying, does it look like I care?"

(425 words)

Rebecca Nicholson, *The Guardian* website, 2020

a Read the text and complete the following tasks:

1. Briefly state who Nadiya Hussain is and what she does.
2. Note down the words Nadiya uses to describe herself.
3. Summarise the reasons why Nadiya says she is "never going to blend in" (ll. 1–2).

b Write a blog post in which you compare the impression you get from the text on pp. 117–118 about how immigrants are accepted in the UK with Nadiya Hussain's experience.

Nadiya Hussain

Working with maps → WB, p. 61

In your exam you might be given a map to describe or you may need to include a map in your analysis.

A30 **A** You are going to listen to a report which briefly explains the history of the British Empire. Copy the table and complete it with the key events from each century. You will listen to the recording twice.

17th century	18th century	19th century	20th century
…	…	…	…

B Look at the map and read the description. Write down words and phrases that you would find useful when you have to describe a map. Add more words and phrases.

Countries colonised by the British
Areas controlled by other European colonial powers
Independent countries
Current international borders

The map shows the continent of Africa. The colour blocks represent the countries which were colonised by the British or other colonial powers. The grey lines show the borders of each country today. According to the legend, the countries that are green in colour were colonised by the British, while the orange areas represent countries that were "controlled by other European colonial powers", such as France, Germany, Portugal, Spain and Italy.
Great Britain ruled Egypt, Sudan, South Sudan, Uganda, Kenya, Tanzania, Nyasaland, Northern Rhodesia, Southern Rhodesia, Botswana, Swaziland, Lesotho, South Africa, Ghana, Gambia, Sierra Leone and Nigeria. The names of the countries as they are known today are in brackets below the colonial names. The British colonies stretched from Egypt in the north to South Africa at the southern tip of the continent. Two countries on the map are grey in colour, which means that they were independent; Liberia in the west and Ethiopia in the east. The map does not include a reference of time when the African countries were British colonies.

C You are going to listen to a short report which explains the origins of the Commonwealth.

A31 **a** Listen to the report and take notes on which events took place in the following years:

1926 | 1947 | 1948 | 1949

A31 **b** Listen again and answer the following questions in keywords:

1. How many countries are there in the Commonwealth?
2. Why is Ireland not a member of the Commonwealth?
3. What are the requirements for joining the Commonwealth?
4. Which Commonwealth members are not former British colonies?

D Describe and analyse the map below, including the information from the recording.

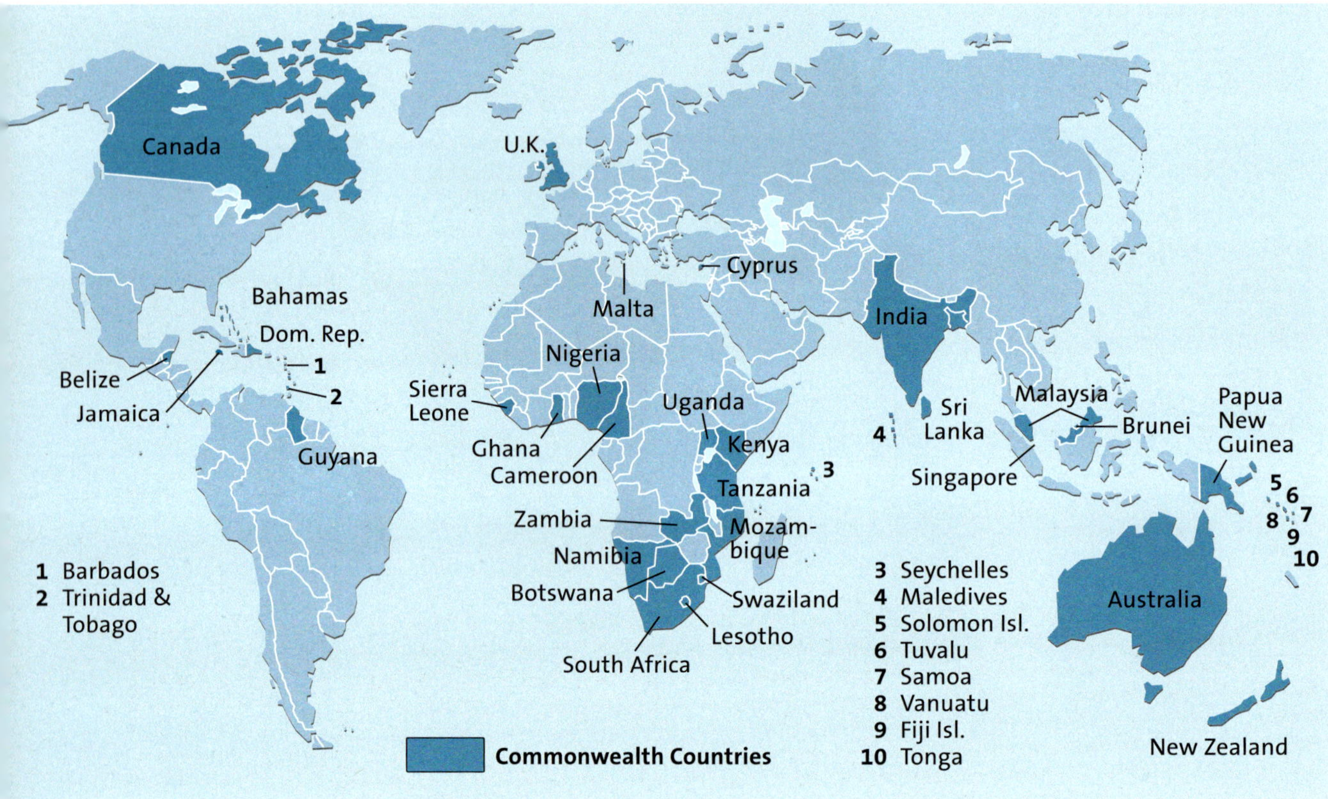

CULTURE BOX

The Republic of Ireland Act 1948 came into force on 18 April 1949 and thus Ireland was no longer ruled by British monarchy but lead by an Irish president. At the time, a declaration of a republic terminated Commonwealth membership. Ireland did not reapply when the rules were altered. Hence, it does not take part in the Commonwealth nowadays.

C History from another perspective

BEFORE YOU READ

1 Talking about slavery

a What is slavery? Who was involved and in which way? In your opinion: Is it still important to talk about slavery today? Talk to a partner. Then discuss the questions in class.

b Write down a definition for each of the following terms:

1. abolition
2. absentee owner
3. Middle Passage
4. plantation
5. slave trade
6. underground railroad

Compare them in class.

Blonde Roots (2009) is a satirical novel by the British author Bernardine Evaristo. In the novel, Evaristo reverses the historical roles during the transatlantic slave trade. "Whyte Europanes" are enslaved by "blak Aphrikans". They are either brought to plantations or serve rich ‚blak' families. The narrator is Doris, who, as a 10-year-old child, was stolen from England. She now tries to escape from Chief Kaga Konata Katamba I, after two decades of slavery.

GOOD TO KNOW

'White' and 'Black' are purely socio-cultural labels given to people. They do not represent actual skin colours and are only used as a justification of power.

Blonde roots

by Bernardine Evaristo

Chief Kaga Konata Katamba I [...] made his fortune in the import-export game, the notorious transatlantic slave run, before settling down to life in polite society as an absentee sugar baron, part-time husband, free-lance father, retired decent human being and, it goes without saying, sacked soul.

My boss is also a full-time anti-abolitionist, publishing his pro-slavery rants in his mouthpiece The Flame – a pamphlet distributed far and wide – as a freebie.

In spite of myself, I'd just begun to flick through the latest godawful issue, feeling my stomach constrict and my throat tighten, when a hand shoved a folded note through the open office window and vanished before I could see who it was attached to. I opened the note, read the magic words and felt my head suddenly drowning. Waves crashed and thundered inside my skull. I let out the most almighty, silent howl. Then I passed out.

How long for, I've no idea, maybe a few minutes, but when I came to I was slumped in my seat, my head dropped forwards, the note still in my hand. I read it again through a film of water. It was real and it was true – I was being given the chance to escape. Oh Lord. After so many years on the waiting list the thing I most desired was in the palm of my hand. Yet it was all too quick. I sat there frozen. A thousand what ifs ran through my mind. In returning my life to its rightful owner – me – I would also be putting my life at stake. If I wasn't careful or lucky I'd end up at the local whipping post or chopping block.

Then my survival instincts kicked in. My head cleared. I was back again. I ripped the note to shreds. I stood up and looked at the wooden mask of Bwana's face on the wall. And I gave it the right, royal one finger salute.

6 **to be a sacked soul** (*ugs*) *hier:* seine Seele verkauft haben
7 **rant** Schimpftirade
8 **mouthpiece** Sprachrohr
8 **as a freebie** kostenlos
12 **to drown** ertrinken; überschwemmen
13 **skull** Schädel
13 **howl** Geschrei
14 **slumped** zusammengesackt
20 **to whip** schlagen; peitschen
23 **right royal** *hier:* ordentlich

25 **derailment** Entgleisung
38 **flaming** *hier:* verflixt
44 **to get it in the neck** einen auf den Deckel bekommen
46 **vivid** lebendig; lebhaft
47 **flint** Feuerstein
49 **tartan** Schottenkaro (bestimmtes Muster eines Clans); karierter Schottenstoff
50 **knickers** (*ugs*) Schlüpfer

The note told me that the Underground Railroad was operating again after service had been suspended owing to derailment. It was often the case when energy couldn't be filched from the city's power station or the train broke down due to the overload of escaping slaves wanting to cadge a safe ride out of the city, to begin the long journey back to the Motherland. I hoped I could trust the message because the Resistance was often infiltrated by sleepers who eventually went operational to betray whole rebel cells. Deep down I knew that the slave traders were never going to give up their cash cow. It was, after all, one of the most lucrative international businesses ever, involving the large-scale transport of whytes, shipped in our millions from the continent of Europa to the West Japanese Islands, so called because when the 'great' explorer and adventurer, Chinua Chikwuemeka, was trying to find a new route to Asia, he mistook those islands for the legendary isles of Japan, and the name stuck.

So here I am in the United Kingdom of Great Ambossa (UK or GA for short), which is part of the continent of Aphrika. The mainland lies just over the Ambossan Channel. It's also known as the Sunny Continent, of course, on account of it being so flaming hot here. Great Ambossa is actually a very small island with a growing population to feed and so it stretches its greedy little fingers all over the globe, stealing countries and stealing people. Me included. I'm one of the Stolen Ones. That's why I'm here. [...]

Slavery had taught me that promises never came with a money-back guarantee and if you complained to customer services they'd report you to management and then you'd really get it in the neck. But I am a firm believer in hope. I am still alive, after all. [...] For the first time since I had been taken away, I could seriously consider that I might be returning home. Was it possible? I still had such vivid memories of my parents, my three sisters, our little flint cottage on the estate. [...]

The Ambossans called us tribes but we were many nations, each with our own language and funny old customs, like the Border Landers, whose men wore tartan skirts with no knickers underneath.

But oh, how I longed for those cloudy grey skies.

How I longed for the incessant drizzle and harsh wind slapping my ears. [...]

How I longed for England.

How I longed for home.

(751 words)

GOOD TO KNOW

The fictional character Chinua Chikwuemeka, mentioned in the excerpt, is based on the Italian explorer, Christopher Columbus, who reached the Americas in 1492. He thought he had actually landed in the "Indies" (Southeast Asia). After his voyage, Europeans began using the term "West Indies" to distinguish the region from the original "Indies". This explains also, why native Americans were called 'Indians'. However, this term is inaccurate.

CULTURE BOX

Transatlantic slave trade
Between 1532 and 1832, at least 12 million African people were captured and taken to the Americas, most of them by British slave traders. For the latter, it was a three-legged journey also called the triangular trade.
British enslavers sailed from Great Britain to West Africa. There, British goods such as linen, alcohol and guns were exchanged for captives. The second leg of the journey was transporting the captives across the Atlantic, and selling them at auctions to plantation owners in the Americas and West Indies. The third leg was the journey back to Britain to sell the cargo of rum, sugar, and other goods cultivated by slaves in the Americas and West Indies.

WORKING WITH THE TEXT

2 Scanning the text

a Scan the text and complete the names of the imaginary places that come up in the text.

1. W... J... I...
2. G... A...
3. A...
4. A... C...

b State where the narrator is originally from and where she is trying to escape from. Give line numbers.

3 Reading for detail → WB, p. 62/1

a Summarise the narrator's reaction to the note she received.

b Point out how the narrator plans to escape back to her motherland.

c Illustrate the narrator's feelings about her imminent escape.

4 Words matter → ○ 5

Find the words or phrases in the text that match the following definitions. Give line numbers.

1. a person who is not at a place where he or she was expected to be
2. a person who is against the abolition of slavery
3. to risk losing one's life
4. in this case: a block of wood on which a person's head was cut off as a punishment
5. a word used in parts of East Africa to address a man who has authority over you
6. to steal something, especially something small or not very valuable
7. the part of a business that always makes a profit and that provides money for the rest of the business

5 Focus on analysis → WB, p. 62/2

a Note down words and expressions from the text which describe Chief Kaga Konata Katamba I.

D1 I1 Self-check 1.1

● **b** Analyse the language the author uses to describe the narrator's boss. Assess the effect this has on the reader.

c Discuss in class possible reasons why Evaristo decided to reverse the historical roles. What is the effect of this reversal?

D4 I4 Self-check 1.4

A STEP FURTHER

6 Working with a map

a Look at the map. What is it about? Describe it and relate it to the excerpt. Share your findings in class.

MK b Speculate about the reasons why those places on the map have more tributes than other places in the UK. Go online to find out if you were correct.

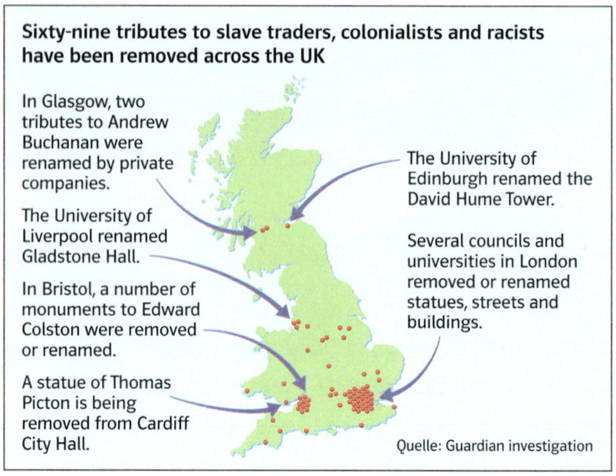

7 Having a discussion

CULTURE BOX

Modern implications of the slave trade
Edward Colston (1636–1721) was a 17th-century slave trader who was responsible for the enslavement of 84,000 Africans. He earned large sums of money through slave trade. In Bristol there are many schools, streets and buildings named after him and a statue of him was erected in 1895. During a Black Lives Matter protest in June 2020, protestors tore his statue down, sparking a debate about what should happen to the damaged monument.

a Prepare a discussion about the way in which historical figures who were slave owners/traders should be remembered in the UK. Think about the following questions and take notes. You can research online.

1. Should statues of slave traders such as Edward Colston and Cecil Rhodes be removed from public spaces?
2. Should street names bearing names of slave traders be changed?
3. Are there other ways to inform people about the history of the slave trade without erasing or revising history?

b Discuss the topic in small groups. Then share your results in class.

c Do you know of any similar tributes in Germany? What do you think about them?

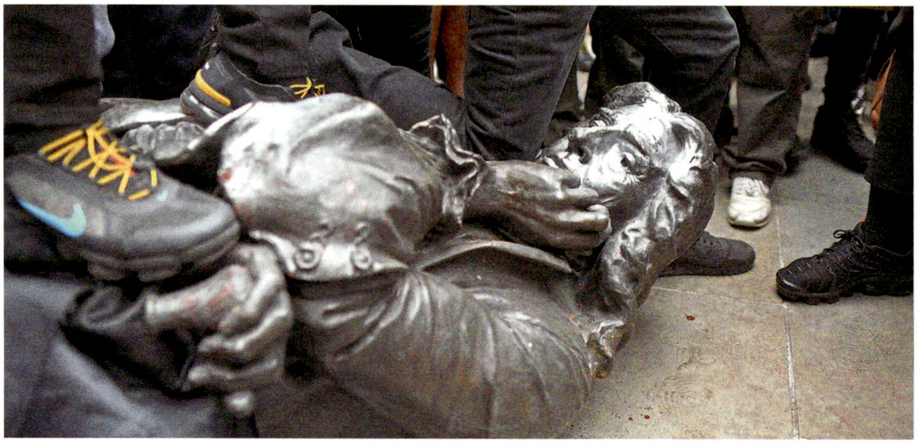

D Food poverty in the UK

BEFORE YOU READ

1 Talking about food poverty

MK **a** What do you know about food poverty? Go online and answer the following questions. Share your findings in class.

1. What is food poverty?
2. What is the cause of food poverty?
3. How many people suffer from food poverty in the UK?

b Speculate why football player Marcus Rashford wrote a letter to UK Members of Parliament about child food poverty. Exchange your ideas with a partner.

'Protect the vulnerable': Marcus Rashford's emotional letter to MPs

I encourage you to hear the children's pleas and find your humanity. Please reconsider your decision to cancel the food voucher scheme over the summer holidays

To all MPs in parliament,

On a week that would have opened Euro 2020, I wanted to reflect back to 27 May 2016, when I stood in the middle of the Stadium of Light in Sunderland having just broken the record for the youngest player to score in his first senior international match. I watched the crowds waving their flags and fist-pumping the Three Lions on their shirts and I was overwhelmed with pride not only for myself but for all of those who had helped me reach this moment and achieve my dream of playing for the England national team.

Understand: without the kindness and generosity of the community I had around me, there wouldn't be the Marcus Rashford you see today: a 22-year-old black man lucky enough to make a career playing a game I love.

My story to get here is all-too-familiar for families in England: my mum worked full-time, earning minimum wage to make sure we always had a good evening meal on the table. But it was not enough. The system was not built for families like mine to succeed, regardless of how hard my mum worked.

As a family, we relied on breakfast clubs, free school meals, and the kind actions of neighbours and coaches. Food banks and soup kitchens were not alien to us; I recall very clearly our visits to Northern Moor to collect our Christmas dinners every year. It's only now that I really understand the enormous sacrifice my mum made in sending me away to live in digs aged 11, a decision no mother would ever make lightly. [...]

As many of you know, as lockdown hit and schools were temporarily closed, I partnered with food distribution charity FareShare to help cover some of the free school meal deficit. Whilst the campaign is currently distributing three million meals a week to those most vulnerable across the UK, I recognise it's just not enough.

This is not about politics; this is about humanity. Looking at ourselves in the mirror and feeling like we did everything we could to protect those who can't, for whatever reason or circumstance, protect

5 **food voucher scheme** Programm zur Verteilung von Lebensmittelgutscheinen
30 **minimum wage** Mindestlohn
38 **coach** Trainer/-in
38 **food bank** Lebensmittelausgabe; 'Tafel'
44 **to live in digs** zur Untermiete wohnen, oft mit Vollverpflegung

61 **affiliation** Zugehörigkeit
72 **to evaporate** *hier:* sich auflösen; verdampfen; verdunsten
77 **nutritional needs** Nahrungsbedarf; Nährstoffbedarf
80 **hardship** Entbehrung; Not
107 **to be on a knife's edge** Spitz auf Knopf stehen (*Redensart*)
109 **driver** *hier:* Auslöser; Verursacher
119 **rest assured** seien Sie versichert (*fml*)
133 **furlough scheme** Kurzarbeit; Zwangsurlaub

themselves. Political affiliations aside, can we not all agree that no child should be going to bed hungry?

Food poverty in England is a pandemic that could span generations if we don't course correct now. Whilst 1.3 million children in England are registered for free school meals, one quarter of these children have not been given any support since the school closures were ordered. We rely on parents, many of whom have seen their jobs evaporate due to Covid-19, to play substitute teacher during lockdown, hoping that their children are going to be focused enough to learn, with only a small percentage of their nutritional needs met during this period.

This is a system failure and without education we're encouraging this cycle of hardship to continue. To put this pandemic into perspective, from 2018-2019, nine out of 30 children in any given classroom were living in poverty in the UK. This figure is expected to rise by an additional one million by 2022. In England today, 45% of children in black and minority ethnic groups are now in poverty. This is England in 2020...

I am asking you to listen to their parents' stories as I have received thousands of insights from people struggling. I have listened when fathers have told me they are struggling with depression, unable to sleep, worried sick about how they are going to support their families having lost their jobs unexpectedly, headteachers who are personally covering the cost of food packages for their vulnerable families after the school debit card has been maxed out; mothers who can't cover the cost of increased electricity and food bills during the lockdown, and parents who are sacrificing their own meals for their children. In 2020, it shouldn't be a case of one or the other. [...]

During this pandemic, people are existing on a knife's edge: one missed bill is having a spiral effect, the anxiety and stress of knowing that poverty is the main driver of children ending up in care, a system that is designed to fail low-income families. Do you know how much courage it takes for a grown man to say, "I can't cope" or "I can't support my family"? Men, women, caregivers, are calling out for our help and we aren't listening.

I also received a tweet from an MP who told me: "This is why there is a benefit system." Rest assured, I am fully aware of the Universal Credit scheme and I am fully aware that the majority of families applying are experiencing five-week delays. Universal Credit is simply not a short-term solution. I also know from talking to people that there is a two-child-per-family limit, meaning someone like my mum would only have been able to cover the cost of two of her five children. In April 2020, 2.1 million people claimed unemployment-related benefits. This is an increase of 850,000 just since March 2020. As we approach the end of the furlough scheme and a period of mass unemployment, the problem of child poverty is only going to get worse.

Parents like mine would rely on kids' clubs over the summer break, providing a safe space and at least one meal, whilst they work. Today, parents do not have this as an option. If faced with unemployment, parents like mine would have been down at the job centre first thing Monday morning to find any work that enables them to support their families. Today, there are no jobs.

[...] The government has taken a "whatever it takes" approach to the economy – I'm asking you today to extend that same thinking to protecting all vulnerable children across England. I encourage you to hear their pleas and find your humanity. Please reconsider your decision to cancel the food voucher scheme over the summer holiday period and guarantee the extension. [...]

Yours sincerely,
Marcus Rashford

(1,034 words)

Marcus Rashford, *The Guardian* website, 2020

CULTURE BOX

The Universal Credit scheme is a financial aid for low-income households which is paid monthly. The scheme was introduced to replace six other benefits and merges them into one payment. Universal Credit is claimed by more than 6 million households across the UK (2022).

WORKING WITH THE TEXT → WB, p. 63/1

2 Reading for gist → WB, p. 63/2

a Explain in one sentence why Marcus Rashford is writing to MPs. Were you correct in exercise 1b?

b Based on the text, briefly describe who Marcus Rashford is.

3 Reading for detail

a Point out how the Covid-19 pandemic has affected the lives of many families.

● b Summarise the "system failure" (l. 78) Rashford describes in his letter. Give line numbers.

4 Words matter

Copy the table and complete it with words and phrases from the text that are related to these aspects. Give line numbers.

work and employment	food	poverty
…	…	…

5 Focus on analysis → WB, p. 64/3

a Make a list of all the stylistic devices (rhetorical question, repetition, etc.) used, that are typical for a persuasive text. Give line numbers. → S 8.1

D1 I1
Self-check 1.1

b Analyse the style of the letter and examine the effect it has on the reader. → S 8.2

A STEP FURTHER

6 Writing an informative handout → S 6.7

MK a Go online to find out more about Marcus Rashford. Collect information on the following aspects:

1. his background and education
2. his football career
3. his activism and achievements

D9 I9
Self-check 3.2

b Create a timeline of key events in Rashford's life.

c Write an informative handout about his life history and defining characteristics.

7 Working with a video → S 2

a Before you watch the video, "How to Break into the Elite", read and comment on the following quote from the clip:

"75 % of the top judges are private-school-educated, about 50 % of the cabinet are private school educated. 7 % of the nation's kids go to [a] private school."

V5 **b** Watch the video. Then give a short summary of the conversation the presenter Amol Rajan has with his former boss and mentor Matthew Wright.

c Watch the video again and answer the following questions:

1. Why does Amol say he was incredibly lucky?
2. Why did Matthew give Amol a job?
3. What does Matthew mean when he says that he "punctured a glass ceiling"?
4. Why does Matthew consider class to be the last barrier to break into the elite?
5. What does Amol suggest people from working class backgrounds need in order to break into the elite?

d Discuss with a partner: Based on what you heard in the video, how far do you think people are judged on their skills, achievements or qualifications in the UK? What about Germany?

D6 16
Self-check 1.6

8 Working with a cartoon → S 11.3

Describe and analyse the cartoon and relate its message to the video about the class system in the UK.

"It's not my fault. Bad grades wouldn't matter if I had been born rich."

Staging a talk show

Groups of students in your class are going to prepare and stage a talk show with well-known British figures to discuss the following question: How much does your family background influence how well you can expect to do in life?

Emma Watson

Sadiq Khan

Jamie Oliver

Mhairi Black

MK

Step 1 Look at the pictures of these well-known Brits. With a partner, go online and research each person's family background and education. Share your findings with the class.

Step 2 Look at the words in the list below and discuss the following question in small groups: How do you think these things affect people's lives?

academic ability | access to resources | discrimination | education | employment | ethnic background | health | housing | income | life span | motivation | privilege | social class | wealth

Step 3 In your group, prepare to stage your talk show about how much your family background influences how well you can expect to do in life.

a Choose a host to present and moderate the talk show. It is the host's job to make sure each participant can put their views forward.

b Decide which of you will take on the roles of the four famous people A–D.

c Take notes about what your person's standpoint would be and prepare your arguments.

Step 4 Now stage the talk show in front of the class. The rest of the class represents the audience. They can ask questions or make comments. The audience takes notes (e.g. on the use of body language) to give feedback after the discussion.

Step 5 Assess the talk show. Include the following aspects:
1. Participants: Report how you felt. What was difficult, surprising, challenging, …?
2. Audience: Give feedback to the participants concerning content and performance. What was good? What could be improved?
3. Reflect on the impact the talk show had on you and your perspective on (in-)equality in British society.

A brief history of the British Empire

1600
British East India Company is established.

1607
The first permanent British settlement is installed in the Americas at Jamestown, Virginia.

1620s
The first British colonies in the Caribbean are founded.

1661
The first permanent British settlement on the African continent is made at James Island. It becomes a key post in the trans-atlantic slave trade.

1655
The British invade Jamaica, previously a colony of Spain.

1664
The English take over the Dutch colony of New Netherland, including New Amsterdam, which they rename New York.

1666
The first colonies are established on The Bahamas.

1670
Jamaica officially becomes a British colony.

1757
British colonial administrator Robert Clive overthrows the ruler of Bengal in the Battle of Plassey.

1775–1783
The American War of Independence takes place. Britain recognises the United States as an independent nation.

1787
First shipment of transported prisoners from the UK to Australia.

1807
Shipment of slaves in British ships or to British colonies is prohibited.

1833
Slavery is abolished throughout the British Empire.

1840
New Zealand officially becomes British.

1857–1859
Indian Mutiny – the first, but unsuccessful rebellion by Indians against the British rulers.

1867
Canada is given 'dominion' (self-governing) status.

1876
Queen Victoria takes the title 'Empress of India'.

1881–1919
The 'Scramble for Africa' – Britain and other European colonial powers acquire colonies stretching from Cairo to Cape Town.

1901 and 1907
Australia and New Zealand are given 'dominion' status.

1920
Mahatma Gandhi becomes a leading member of the Indian National Congress. He eventually leads India to independence.

1926
British Commonwealth of Nations is created through the 1926 Balfour Declaration.

1947
Indian Independence Act is proclaimed.

1948
The Republic of Ireland Act is signed, ending British monarchy.

1960s–1970s
Most of Britain's African and Caribbean colonies achieve independence.

1997
Hong Kong, a former British colony, is handed back to China.

The influence of the past on today's Britain

The British honours system is a system in which people are given special titles by the government or the monarch as a reward for achievements in public life and/or committing themselves to serving and helping Britain. In 2004, a House of Commons Select Committee recommended changing the names of the titles so that the 'E' in OBE (Officer of the Order of the British Empire) and MBE (Member of the Order of the British Empire) stood for 'Excellence' rather than 'Empire'. However, Tony Blair, the prime minister at the time, ignored its findings.

In 2019, George the Poet, the spoken word artist and award-winning podcast creator, said he was unable to accept an MBE because of the "pure evil" of the British Empire and the "colonial trauma inflicted on the children of Africa". George delivered the message in the last episode of his BBC Sounds series *Have You Heard George's Podcast?*, in which he discusses the legacy of colonialism. George the Poet, whose real name is George Mpanga, was born in London and is of Ugandan heritage. He said that while "the gesture is deeply appreciated, the wording is not".

2 **honours** Ehren-; Ehrung
3 **reward** Belohnung
11 **to inflict sth** etw zufügen
29 **to impede** behindern

In January 2021, English market research company Ipsos MORI conducted a survey in which it asked British adults what they thought about the impact of the UK's decision to leave the European Union. The results of the survey show diverse opinions on the outcomes of the Brexit referendum in 2016 across different aspects of day-to-day life, practices and cooperations.
According to news reports, the main impact of the withdrawal agreement can be felt in the economy due to increased customs controls for imported and exported goods, laws regulating trade agreements and conditions for private or business travel within the EU. Reduced international participation in scientific and educational projects, for example, can also be observed. Supplies and logistics between the UK and mainland Europe have also at least partially been impeded.
Perhaps as a result of these combined factors, social change may also be felt in the attitudes and relationships between the British people and their European neighbours. On the other hand, some Britons report positive feelings towards the increased autonomy in decision-making on British laws and regulations – for example regarding the COVID-19 pandemic. Others say that their daily lives are unaffected by the change. In terms of social change, supplying food to the UK has become more difficult due to a shortage of staff who can transport goods from the mainland to the UK.

1 Read the timeline and the text. Use the information to create a mini quiz.

2 Ask a partner your questions and answer his or hers in turn.

3 Note down three aspects you found interesting or surprising about this topic. Get together with a partner and exchange your views.

Outlook: For further discussion, consider the following questions:
- How are British attitudes towards the Empire changing in today's Britain?
- In how far does the UK value its multiculturalism (e.g. in daily life)?
- How important is social class in Britain today?

1 Lesen und Schreiben

Ethnic diversity makes Britain's culture great. It would be a disaster if we lost it

Figures show nearly 40% of our top cultural figures come from migrant or minority ethnic backgrounds – but barriers still exist

A couple of weeks ago, a young black man from south London stood up in front of tens of thousands of people and delivered one of the most celebrated performances in the history of Glastonbury. A few days later, an England cricket squad – almost half of whom were born abroad or are from an ethnic minority background – made it into the semi-finals of the World Cup. Meanwhile over at Tate Modern, a British artist of Nigerian origin is displaying an artwork made up of thousands of books imprinted with the names of migrants who have made significant contributions to British culture.

Today, some of our most brilliant prospects in art and culture are from minority ethnic or migrant backgrounds. We present a gloriously multicultural face to the world. And that is important not just for the story we tell to others, but for the stories we tell ourselves. Think of the cultural power of the first Asian families on EastEnders, the breakthrough of Soul II Soul in the 1980s, or the nation-defining literary output of Zadie Smith.

The British actor Riz Ahmed refers to this as "stretching the flag, so it's big enough to embrace all of us". He is talking about how art can remould how we see ourselves and the country that we live in. The Pakistani-British heritage of his youth is just as much a part of our modern national story as the playing fields of Eton, remote Shetland communities or the multi-ethnic melting pots of Leicester, Birmingham and London. But it is only through the representation of that experience in our national culture that those truths are cemented across the whole country.

We should be confident and proud about this story – yet it is too rarely told.

Now a report from Global Future does exactly that, demonstrating not only the increasing diversity of our cultural industries, but how popular that diversity is. According to the report, nearly 40% of our leading cultural figures are from migrant or minority ethnic backgrounds. In other words, diversity is making an outsized contribution to British culture. And the size of the contribution is going up all the time: five years ago, it was less than a third.

Global Future's survey of 2,000 UK adults suggests nearly seven in 10 of us agree that diversity has improved our culture, against 15% who disagree. Food, music and sport are the cultural industries where people believe diversity has had the greatest impact. This is music to my ears, of course. Britain is my home. I was born here, I have lived my whole life here, and I have pursued my life's passion here. As a dancer, Britain has been my stage. It is our culture that makes me most proud to be British. That same culture has been a welcoming home for my own work: where a British dancer of Bangladeshi origin can pursue a career blending the Indian kathak style with contemporary forms.

This openness to diversity is visible in many arenas: just look at the Notting Hill carnival every year. Or take the Turner prize, where the artists shortlisted in the last two years have been of German, Fijian, Israeli, Zanzibari, Palestinian, Jamaican and Bengali heritage.

Diversity is what makes Britain's culture great. But recently it has felt as though we have lost sight of this self-evident truth. Brexit, polarisation and the poisonous debate about immigration threaten to turn our diversity into division. That would be a historic disaster for the country.

And yet when it comes to our culture, we are not really divided at all. We are united in our admiration for the acting of Idris Elba, the athleticism of Jessica Ennis-Hill and the artistry of Anish Kapoor and many more. It is essential that we remind ourselves of that fact, at a time when our politics seems geared towards making us forget it.

We can – and should – always do more. There are still serious barriers to entry for people of a minority ethnic background into our major cultural industries. In some cases, exclusivity in the arts is increasing rather than decreasing. Our culture should be ours collectively, not reserved for a few – and we have to work tirelessly to make sure that is the case.

But let's never lose sight of what makes Britain so special. Our differences fuel our creativity. And our exposure to all the cultures of the world does nothing but improve our own. (778 words)

Akram Khan, *The Guardian* website, 2020

ASSIGNMENTS → WB, pp. 65–66

1. Summarise the findings of the Global Future survey.
2. Examine how the author persuades the reader that ethnic diversity makes Britain's culture great. Include examples from the text.
3. Choose one of the following tasks:

3.1. Discuss the following question: "Can Britain be seen as a successfully diverse society?"

Or:

3.2. Write a letter to the editor in which you comment on the author's statement that "diversity is making an outsized contribution to British culture".

2 Hörverstehen

ASSIGNMENTS → WB, pp. 66–67

Listen to an interview with Afua Hirsch. You will listen to the recording twice.

A32 1. Listen to the first part of the interview. Take notes on the following points. You do not need to write full sentences.

1. Two ways the empire is talked about	• …
2. Aspects of partition	• …
3. Other empires which failed	• …
4. Positive effects of the British Empire for the British	• …
5. Two wishes for the future	• …

A33 2. Listen to the second part of the interview. Answer the following questions:

1. What did Afua Hirsch learn about in her history lessons at school?
2. What was the argument Afua Hirsch made in her column for *The Guardian*?
3. What does Afua Hirsch aim to achieve by writing columns and articles?
4. Who is Winsome Pinnock?

D17 Progress report

6 GETTING STARTED

Diverse identities

GOOD TO KNOW

identity
= who you consider yourself (character and personality of an individual) to be

diverse
= including many different people with different identities

1 Look at the pictures. Which picture makes the biggest impression on you? Describe it to a partner and say why you have chosen this picture.

2 Team up with another pair and exchange your findings.

3 Look at the pictures again in your group. Which issues do these pictures represent? Relate them to the heading of this topic.

4 Together with your group, find another picture that shows another aspect of diverse identities. Present it to the class, explaining which aspects of social relationships and/or identities are displayed. → S 11.1

A34 **5** Listen to the podcast "Forward Thinking: Diversity in society". While listening, take notes on the following aspects: → WB, p. 69/2

1. the history of multiculturalism in the US
2. the status quo in the US
3. Virginia's hope for the future
4. the plus sign in 2SLGBTQ+
5. HIV and AIDS
6. the Pride Parade

A34 6 Listen to the podcast again. Are these statements true or false? Correct the wrong ones.

D11 I11
Self-check 4.0

1. Virginia descends from Irish immigrants.
2. Initially, immigrants in the US stayed within their ethnic groups.
3. Some states still ban interracial marriage today.
4. Approximately 80 % of hate crimes are based on race and religion.
5. The *Davie Street Cooperative* deals with gender issues.
6. The letter "G" in the abbreviation 2SLGBTQ+ stands for gender.
7. Homophobia means prejudices against people's sexual orientation.
8. The *Davie Street Cooperative* painted rainbow-striped crosswalks.

GOOD TO KNOW

HIV is spread primarily by unprotected sex, but also e.g. by contaminated blood transfusions or from mother to child during pregnancy. AIDS is the final stage of HIV. While numbers of HIV-affected people are higher in the LGBTQ+ community, it is important to know that everyone (regardless of their sexual orientation) can get HIV.
Race, as a concept is based mainly on physical attributes or traits (e.g. skin colour). It is frequently used in open dialogue (e.g. articles, books, etc.) in the English-speaking world. The word in itself does not carry unpleasant connotations. However, the term can be seen as a social construct (a classification invented by humans) which can be used to justify movements like White supremacy.
Ethnicity is a label used to refer to a group with shared cultural background, e.g. due to a common language, religion, etc. Many people feel it is important to consider how their ethnicity has shaped their life, since it can help them to learn more about themselves or about others.

7 Get together in groups of three to four. Select a question below and note down possible answers to the question. Discuss your answers in class.

1. Why do you think immigrants in the US initially lived in ethnic neighbourhoods?
2. Do you think the plus symbol at the end of the gender abbreviations is a good idea? Why (not)?
3. Do you think enough is being done to integrate people with disabilities into our society? Why (not)?

USEFUL PHRASES

to offer a sense of security
to make someone feel at home
to share common goals
to celebrate differences
to become aware of inequality
to appreciate diversity
to identify as/with
to live with a disability
to debunk prejudices

I think it includes/excludes …
It's (im-)possible to embrace …
By throwing light on …, we can see that …
Being different can …
Identification in society can be linked to …
Actions speak louder than words.
Knowledge is power.
Debunking prejudices is nearly impossible / is possible.

A Challenging identities

BEFORE YOU READ

1 Talking about identity

a Add more terms to this word web for 'identity'.

IDENTITY – family, traditions, gender

GOOD TO KNOW

'Black' and 'White' are purely sociocultural labels given to people. They do not represent actual skin colours and are only used as a justification of power.

b Take notes on the kinds of possibilities there are for changing your identity if you are dissatisfied with it. Consider elements such as a change of appearance, career, mindset etc. Discuss your notes with a partner.

The novel *The Vanishing Half* was written by Brit Bennett in 2020. It is set between the 1940s and the 1990s and covers three generations of a 'Black' family. The main storyline centres on Desiree and Stella Vignes, who are identical twins. They were born and raised in Mallard, Louisiana, a fictional town proud of its light-skinned 'Blacks'. In this excerpt, Stella is considering passing over into the 'White' world and ends up working for a marketing agency with a 'White' boss, who later becomes her husband.

11 **redheaded** rothaarig
18 **to line up** (sich) aufstellen
20 **boldness** Dreistigkeit; Mut
22 **to wink** zwinkern

The Vanishing Half
by Brit Bennett

A week after Stella disappeared into the city, Willie Lee [...] had something to tell Adele – something he should've told her weeks before Founder's Day. One afternoon he'd driven Stella into Opelousas. [...] He had to make deliveries and figured, hell, she might want to get out of town for a bit. He'd given her a nickel to buy a Coke, and when he'd finished unloading, he found her standing beside his truck, breathless and flushed. She'd gone inside some shop called Darlene's Charms, where the shopgirl mistook her for white. "Isn't it funny?" she'd said. "White folks, so easy to fool! Just like everyone says." "It ain't no game," he told her. "Passin' over. It's dangerous." "But white folks can't tell," she said. "Look at you – you just as redheaded as Father Cavanaugh. Why does he get to be white and you don't?" "Because he is white," he said. "And I don't wanna be." "Well, neither do I," she'd said. "I just wanted to look at that shop. You won't tell my mama, will you?" [...]

She'd been caught before. Only once, the second time she'd ever pretended to be white. During her last summer in Mallard [...] she'd gone to the South Louisiana Museum of Art on an ordinary Saturday morning, not Negro Day, and walked right up to the main entrance, not the side door where Negroes lined up in the alley. Nobody stopped her, and again, she'd felt stupid for not trying this sooner. There was nothing to being white except boldness. You could convince anyone you belonged somewhere if you acted like you did. In the museum, she'd glided slowly through the rooms [...] when she noticed a Negro security guard in the corner of the room staring. Then he'd winked, and, horrified, she rushed past him, head down, barely breathing until she stepped back into the bright morning. [...] Of course passing wasn't that easy. Of course that colored guard recognized her. We always know our own, her mother said. [...]

GOOD TO KNOW

Until the civil rights movement, 'Negro' was often used to refer to Afro-American people, but people like Malcolm X objected to the word because it is associated with slavery, segregation and discrimination.

In New Orleans, Stella split in two [...] after she got fired from Dixie Laundry. She'd been daydreaming during her shift, thinking, again, about the morning she'd visited the museum as a white girl. [...] She'd never felt so free. [...] Then, the Sunday before rent was due, she spotted a job listing in the paper. Maison Blanche was looking for young ladies [...] to fill an opening in the marketing department [...]. She'd always gotten good marks for her typing, but a department store would never hire a colored girl to do more than put away shoes or spray perfume at thc counters. Still, Desiree told her she had to apply. [...] She almost said no. Told Desiree, forget it. So what if she could type? Why subject herself to the humiliation of some prim white secretary telling her that colored girls need not apply? Still, she woke up the next morning, put on her nice dress, and rode the streetcar to Canal Street. [...]

The elevator carried her to the sixth floor, where she stepped into a waiting room filled with white girls. She halted in the doorway, wondering if she should just turn back. But the blonde secretary waved her over. "I need your typing sample, dear," she said. Stella could have left. Instead, she carefully filled out the application and typed up the sample paragraph. Her hands trembled as she pressed the keys. She was terrified of being discovered, but almost more afraid that she wouldn't be. And then what? If she was hired, she would have to be white every day, and if she couldn't sit in this waiting room without her hands shaking, how could she ever manage that? When the secretary announced that the position was filled, she felt relieved. [...] She quickly gathered her coat and her pocketbook, heading toward the elevator when the secretary asked if Miss Vignes could start tomorrow. [...]

At work, Stella became Miss Vignes or, as Desiree called her, White Stella. [...] Soon she no longer felt nervous as the elevator glided skyward and she stepped into the office. You belong here, Blake had told her. Soon she thought of him as Blake, not Mr. Sanders, and she began to notice how he lingered at her desk now when he said good morning, how he invited her to lunch more often, how he began walking her to the streetcar after work. [...] When she was with Blake, no one bothered her. The leering white men who'd tried to flirt with her at her stop now fell suddenly silent; the colored men sitting in the back didn't even look in her direction. [...] If Blake knew who she truly was, he would send her out of the office before she could even pack her things. But what had changed about her? Nothing, really. She hadn't adopted a disguise or even a new name. She'd walked in a colored girl and left a white one. She had become white only because everyone thought she was. [...] Sometimes she wondered if Miss Vignes was a separate person altogether. [...] Maybe Miss Vignes was already a part of her, as if she had been split in half. She could become whichever woman she decided, whichever side of her face she tilted to the light. [...]

"Jesus," Desiree said. "I still can't believe you did it, Stella." "It isn't so hard. You could've done it." "You didn't want me to. You left me." [...] "It wasn't that," Stella said. "I met someone." "You did this all for a man?" "Not for him," she said. "I just liked who I was with him." "White." "No," Stella said. "Free." Desiree laughed. "Same thing, baby." (960 words)

28 **to be due** fällig sein
29 **job listing** Stellenanzeige
30 **opening** *hier:* freie Stelle
33 **to subject oneself to sth** sich etw unterwerfen
34 **humiliation** Demütigung; Erniedrigung
45 **relieved** erleichtert
46 **to head** gehen; zusteuern auf
57 **disguise** Verkleidung

WORKING WITH THE TEXT

2 Reading for gist → WB, p.70/1

a Write a short summary about Stella's journey. Write about 150 words. → ○1

b List the main events that had led to Stella "passing over" and write a definition of the term.

3 Reading for detail → WB, p. 70/2

a Note down words from the text which describe Stella's thoughts and feelings.

b Illustrate how Stella's lifestyle choices impacted her sense of identity.

c Explain Stella's worries about "passing over".

4 Words matter

Read the definitions and find the corresponding words in the text.
Give line numbers.

1. red in the face
2. to trick someone into believing something that isn't true
3. too neat, formal and proper in talk and behaviour
4. to shake in response to a powerful emotion, particularly fear
5. to stay longer because you don't want to leave
6. looking at someone in a sexually interested way

D1 I1
Self-check 1.1

5 Focus on analysis → WB, p. 71/3

a Consider the idea that Stella faces an "inner" and "outer" conflict. How would you describe each one?

b Collect quotes which express the inner and outer conflict Stella faces throughout her journey. Give line numbers.

Example: "She'd never felt so free." (l. 28); "She was terrified of being discovered …" (ll. 41–42)

c Examine the quotes from exercise b and how language is used here to convey Stella's inner and outer conflicts.

GOOD TO KNOW

inner conflict
= a character's internal struggle, possibly involving emotional problems
outer conflict
= a conflict between a character and external forces (e.g. a group)

CULTURE BOX

The concept of 'White privilege'
The term 'White privilege' defines advantages 'White' people have due to their skin colour. Peggy McIntosh published a paper in 1988 in which she listed 46 examples of 'White privilege', including being accepted by neighbours when moving to a new neighbourhood or finding oneself represented in the media and textbooks. After the killing of George Floyd in May 2020, the topic of 'White privilege' has come back to the attention of people worldwide.

D8 I8
Self-check 3.1

6 Writing a comment → ◯ 2

Choose one of Stella's statements from the novel. Discuss her attitude and give your opinion.

1. "Because she knew that, if it came down to her word versus Loretta's [a 'Black' woman], she would always be believed. And knowing this, she felt, for the first time, truly white."

Or:

2. "Why wouldn't you be white if you could be? Remaining what you were or becoming something new, it was all a choice, any way you looked at it. She had just made the rational decision."

A STEP FURTHER

D 12 Self-check 5.0

7 Having a discussion

a With a partner, note down several aspects that shape a person's identity.

Example: past experiences, ethnic background

b Get together with another pair and exchange your notes. Discuss the differences and similarities in your notes about aspects that shape a person's identity.

c In class, disuss the following: Which role does a person's background play in determining their place in society?

USEFUL PHRASES

to consider yourself to be	It doesn't depend on …	Upbringing is important.
to show one's colour	inclusion	Education is key.
to view sb as	From my point of view …	Taking into account that …

8 Working with a video → WB, p.71/4

a Match these words and phrases with their definitions.

1. to be raised
2. fair complected
3. in the service
4. to wait something out
5. elementary school
6. junior high (school)
7. to tan

A to be patient until something ends
B to have light skin
C to be brought up
D school for students aged 11–14
E to get browner skin from the sun
F in one of the armed forces (army, navy…)
G school for students aged 5–11

V6 b Watch the video "You don't have to look black to be black". While you watch, take notes on the following aspects:

1. Why does Bert call herself 'Black'?
2. How does Bert explain how their community came to be?
3. Summarise the main conflict between Bert and her daughter Jessica.
4. Describe Bert's facial expressions while Jessica is talking.
5. Do you think Jessica is betraying her family? Support your answer.

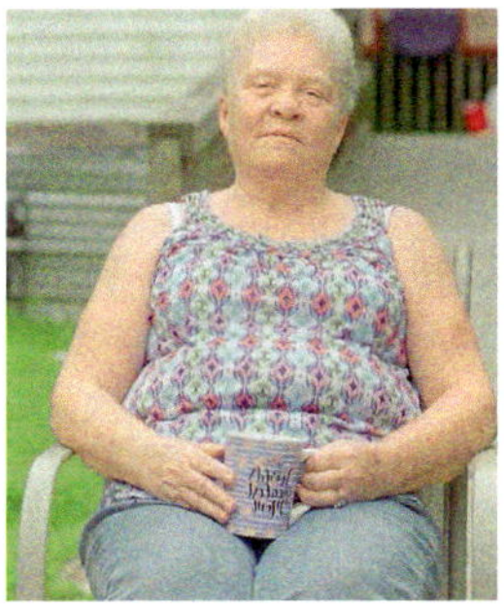

c Watch the video a second time. Double-check your answers and correct them if necessary.

d Compare the video to the novel excerpt on pp. 138–139.

1. What are the differences between the fictional town of Mallard, Louisiana and the real East Jackson, Ohio?
2. Contrast Bert's and Stella's attitudes regarding their skin color.

B Diversity in gender

BEFORE YOU READ

1 Talking about gender stereotypes

a Which gender stereotypes do you know? Make a list and compare your findings with a partner.

b What do you think: Is this division into 'male' and 'female' behaviour and attitude based on reality? Give reasons.

Changing more than pronouns: a non-binary teen fights education laws

Santi Ceballos worked to change Arizona's curriculum laws that focused sex education on heterosexuality and left them out

1 **non-binary** nicht-binär *(Geschlecht, das weder weiblich noch ganz männlich ist)*
11 **to be gender nonconforming** nicht gender-konform sein
19 **hormone blocker** Hormonblocker
22 **condominium** Eigentumswohnung
34 **pre-service teacher** Lehrer/-in in Ausbildung
48 **to enrol** einschreiben; anmelden
50 **gender spectrum** Bandbreite der Geschlechter
53 **to assign** zuweisen; zuordnen
58 **immediate** direkt; unmittelbar; spontan

Sometimes, other kids call Santi "it". "It's sort of like treating me as a different species," said Santi Ceballos, who goes by they/them pronouns, looking straight into the camera for a video [...] last year. The video was made in an effort to educate others about what it means to be gender nonconforming. "There's not only two genders!" Santi continues. "Just let us be who we want to beeee ..."

Santi Ceballos, right with mother Carol Brochin and brother Joaquin Ceballos.

Today, at 13, they have let their wavy, golden-brown hair grow past their shoulders, with thick bangs over eyelashes long enough to graze oversized aviator glasses. Hormone blockers have staved off puberty, leaving Santi's face round and their skin clear and hairless. Outside of their small condominium in central Tucson, near the University of Arizona campus, Santi wears the classic teenager outfit: an oversized windbreaker and black skinny jeans with ripped knees.

Santi has had a long and sometimes painful journey, says their mother, Carol Brochin, an education professor. She teaches future public school teachers, and has seen what she calls a real lack of empathy and understanding of the issues facing non-binary and transgender kids. "I tell my pre-service teachers, 'You have to be prepared. The kids are going to transition,'" Brochin says.

Although there's no official data for Arizona, Brochin estimates there are about 140 families in the Tucson area with kids who identify as non-binary or trans. In 2017, a study by the Williams Institute at the UCLA School of Law estimated that 0.7% of kids in the US between ages 13 and 17 – about 150,000 teens – identify as transgender.

When Brochin realized her own kid was struggling with identity, she looked for support. In 2017, she enrolled Santi in a popular program outside of Tucson for kids who identify all over the gender spectrum called *Camp Born This Way,* [...] funded by the *Southern Arizona Aids Foundation.* As campers were assigned name badges with preferred pronouns at orientation, Santi asked for a name badge with he/him. They had never met a non-binary person until that day at camp, and the impact was almost immediate. The next day, Santi asked to switch their pronouns to they/them.

"That's when I came out, kind of," they said, smiling shyly. Brochin says it's not uncommon for kids to transition at *Camp Born This Way*. (She's now a member of the camp's steering committee.) "People often talk about it as, like, you come down the mountain and there's lots of tears and then you have to re-enter society," she says.

Re-entry was not easy for Santi. They came home feeling empowered – and, at the same time, more vulnerable than ever. A few weeks later, Santi transferred from a traditional public school with uniforms and kids who teased them for playing with the girls but using the boy's bathroom, to a charter school with a gender neutral restroom and overall more progressive views, such as a focus on social justice and environmental sustainability.

Joaquin, their brother who is 20 months older, changed schools, too. He didn't like the "busy work" at his old school. But he also wanted to protect Santi. "Because of this," he says, gesturing up and down dramatically at his sibling sitting next to him. Everyone at the table laughs, including Santi.

Seventh grade was going so much better than sixth, for both kids. But then it came time for sex education. The boys and girls were separated. Santi was told to pick, which was very upsetting to them, and the curriculum included nothing beyond heterosexual basics, thanks to a 1991 Arizona law called *No Promo Homo*. Arizona was one of seven states in the US with such laws.

Santi's backslide after that was evident. "It caused a lot of dysmorphia and suicidal ideation," Brochin recalls. She got Santi counseling and they got better, she says. But she wanted to make a change. So did Santi. In March, a group called *Equality Arizona*, backed by the *National Center for Lesbian Rights and Lambda Legal*, filed a lawsuit against the state, claiming that by focusing sex education only on heterosexuality, Arizona was violating the Equal Protection Clause of the 14th amendment of the US constitution. The plaintiff, along with the *National Center for Lesbian Rights and Lambda Legal*, was Santi.

Within days, the state legislature had voted to repeal the law. Governor Doug Ducey immediately signed the repeal – and *No Promo Homo* was gone. [...]

(771 words)

Amy Silverman, *The Guardian* website, 2019

65 **steering committee** Führungskomitee; Leitungsgruppe
71 **to feel empowered** sich bestärkt fühlen
77 **charter school** *(AE)* *in den USA: Schule, die mit öffentlichen Mitteln finanziert wird, aber nicht den Schulbehörden untersteht*
99 **backslide** Rückfall
100 **dysmorphia** Dysmorphophobie *(psychische Störung, bei der Betroffene sich hässlich fühlen)*
100 **suicidal ideation** Selbstmordgedanken
106 **to file a lawsuit** eine Klage einreichen
110 **amendment** (Verfassungs-) Zusatz
111 **plaintiff** Kläger/-in
114 **state legislature** gesetzgebende Versammlung auf Bundesstaatsebene

WORKING WITH THE TEXT

2 Reading for gist

a Briefly describe who Santi Ceballos is.

b Say which other people are mentioned and how they are connected to Santi.

3 Reading for detail → WB, p. 72/1

a Explain why Santi and Joaquin changed school.

b Point out the differences between the "old" and the "new" school the two attended.

c Name the reasons why Santi took the state to court.

4 Words matter

Collect quotes by the author that show understanding and sympathy for Santi and the difficulties they had to face. Give line numbers.

5 Focus on analysis → S 8 → G 10 → WB, p. 72/2

a Note down who is speaking in the text through direct or indirect quotes.

b Examine the language the author uses to describe Santi and what they went through.

c Analyse the style and tone of the text. Assess the effect this has on the reader.

D 10 I 10
Self-check 3.3

6 Writing a personal letter → S 6.4

Write a letter to a friend in which you comment on how the family reacted on Santi being non-binary.

A STEP FURTHER

V7 **7 Working with a video** → S 2

a Watch the video "Horizon, Being Transgender" and give a short summary of the main character Charlotte's story.

b While watching for a second time answer the following questions:

1. Why is social transition "the hardest part" for Charlotte?
2. How does Charlotte explain the term "transgender woman"?

c Charlotte says she was "concerned going out in a masculine environment". Describe the reaction of Charlotte's colleagues and how they behave in the short conversation in the video. Are you surprised by their behaviour? Why (not)?

8 Online research and discussion → S 1, 14.1

The fact that there are not only two genders (male and female) is widely accepted in many societies. New laws have been established to avoid discrimination of non-binary people and we are encouraged to change our use of language (for example by using "they" instead of "he" or "she").

GRAPHIC DESIGNER

We accept applications from all backgrounds.

MK a Research online to find information to answer the following questions:
- Which legal regulations do already exist in the UK?
- What kind of obstacles can you think of concerning communication in the world of work?
- What do non-binary persons wish or demand to make their situation more equal?

D 12
Self-check 5.0

b In small groups discuss the topic of acceptance non-binary people in society. Prepare a short presentation. Consider the following aspects:
- difficulties in private as well as in working life
- opportunities for a more open society without discrimination
- areas where changes are necessary to achieve equal conditions for everyone

Talking about conditions

A Copy the table. Read the text and find examples of the tenses used in the three different types of if-clauses. Write them in the table. → G 1–3 → WB, p. 74

type	example	tenses used	use
1	if you are given the gift of a diverse background, you should be proud of it (ll. 11–12)	…	…
2	…	…	…
3	…	…	…

Growing up, I tried everything I could to fit in with the other kids at school. Each day I thought to myself some variation of, "if mum had packed me English food like sandwiches, I'd finally feel normal". If my mum or dad spoke to me in Hindi in public, I would respond in English. I avoided wearing a traditional Indian dress to my prom like my mum had always wanted; I felt that if I showed any hint of my background, I could become an outcast. That was my teenage philosophy. If I erased it, it couldn't come back to hurt me.
What I didn't know back then was that you can't erase who you are. In fact, if you are given the gift of a diverse background, you should be proud of it. Ironically, if I had taken the time to think properly, I might have realised that curry is as English as fish and chips, or that a sari is a beautiful reminder of my family's culture. If I had thought about my future career or adult life, I would have used every opportunity to practice speaking Hindi with my parents, so that I could mention it in my CV.

B Decide which type of if-clause you would use when you …

1. think something is highly likely to happen.
2. think something is possible but unlikely to happen.
3. talk about something that happened in the past and is impossible.

C Form sentences and questions using the words in brackets and the correct tense. Pay attention to which conditional type you have to use.

1. What (you / do) if you win the lottery tomorrow?
2. We (be) travelling to South Africa, if it wasn't so far away.
3. If they hadn't come to the party, (you / call) them?
4. She would visit all of India if she (have) enough time and money.
5. If you went to Madrid, (you / visit) the multicultural districts?

D Write a blog post about diversity in your neighbourhood. What has changed in the past years? Which initiatives to enhance diversity would you like to support? Use if-clauses to highlight the changes which have taken place and the wishes for the future. → S 6.2

Example: If the mayor welcomes many refugees, my city will be …

C Two worlds?

BEFORE YOU READ

1 Talking about family conflicts

a Make a list of the top five priorities in your life right now.

b What topics do you and your parents disagree about? Make a list.

c Are there things in these two lists that conflict with each other?

The film *The Big Sick* (2017) is based on a true story about the relationship between Kumail and Emily. Kumail was born in Pakistan but moved to the United States when he was 18. He wants to be a stand-up comedian. He and Emily meet in Chicago. In this excerpt from the film script, Kumail speaks with his brother about his new girlfriend, Emily discovers a selection of potential brides and both Emily's mother Beth and Kumail's parents discuss the ins and outs of marriage.

2 **tiffin** *Behälter für vorab gekochtes und geliefertes Essen in Indien und Pakistan*
2 **ramekin** *kleines Schälchen zum Servieren von Saucen etc.*
9 **to not give a shit about sth/sb** *(vulg)* sich einen Dreck um etw/jdn scheren
15 **hit and run** Unfallflucht
16 **to forge** fälschen
19 **to mow a few lawns** *(ugs)* sexuelle Erfahrungen machen

1 INT. BATTING CAGE SNACK SHACK

LATER Kumail and Naveed eat from tiffins & ramekins. They fork-fight over their meal. [...]

KUMAIL These cookies are really good.

NAVEED They're biscuits! Listen to yourself. You hardly sound Pakistani. "Cookies"? [...] You're such a burger.

KUMAIL I'm not a burger.

NAVEED Yes, you are. You're a big fat burger.

KUMAIL I'm not a burger and biscuit is actually a British term.

NAVEED Well thank you for that information that no one gives a shit about and you should listen to mom and grow a beard.

KUMAIL It gets really itchy, I've tried. It's all patchy. [...] You know, I have to tell you something, Bhai.

NAVEED Here we go. Yeah?

KUMAIL I've been dating this girl. [...] She's white.

NAVEED I thought you were going to say you were involved in a hit and run or you got caught forging some checks. But a WHITE GIRL? Such a [cliché].

A white family stares in their direction.

KUMAIL It's okay! We hate terrorists!

NAVEED Listen. I understand. You're in America. You wanna mow a few lawns and see what it's like. But eventually you have to marry a Pakistani girl. Like I hung out with other girls. But then I married Fatima. We hardly spoke two words to each other the first few months! But now, Kumi, she's like my best friend. You have to break up with her immediately.

KUMAIL If I find someone who's as good for me as Fatima is for you, Mom would understand, right? I mean, she wouldn't love me less?

NAVEED She would definitely love you less. Slowly, you'd sort of -- what's the word when guys stop returning girls' calls?

KUMAIL Ghosting?

NAVEED Yes. *(dead serious)* You have to end it now or Mom will fucking ghost you. [...]

2 *Emily opens the cigar box and sees the headshots of the women. She flips through them. [...] Kumail enters.*

KUMAIL *(sees her with the box)* I was going to tell you about that.

EMILY Are you like judging Pakistan's Next Top Model or something? Seriously, who are these women?

KUMAIL You know how we have arranged marriage in my culture? These are those women.

EMILY These are women in Pakistan who want to marry you?

KUMAIL They're not in Pakistan.

EMILY You've met these women?

KUMAIL Just with my parents. We haven't like –

EMILY You're not serious about this, are you?

KUMAIL It's my mom's thing, I just go along with it.

EMILY So what does your mom think about you and me, then? [...] She doesn't know about me, does she?

KUMAIL No.

Emily storms out of the bedroom. [...]

3 KUMAIL How did you and Terry meet?

BETH I was going to East Carolina University [...]. We met at this coffee shop, I was waiting on him. I liked his hair. He was a teacher already. Thick New York accent like nobody I'd ever met. Totally wrong for me. So naturally we fell in love. My family could not stand him. We're all military people, army pilots. All my brothers played football. Terry couldn't even change a tire. My father got so mad he broke every dinner plate we had. [...] And Terry just stuck around. Eventually they just all got over it.

KUMAIL They just got over it. How?

BETH Lots of fucked up dinners. How'd your parents meet, Kumail?

KUMAIL So we have arranged marriage as you know. A big group got together to see a movie, but really it was just a set up so my mom and dad could meet.

BETH What movie did they see?

KUMAIL I have no idea. I never asked. [...]

4 SHARMEEN [...] We have sacrificed everything for you.

KUMAIL I know, okay?

SHARMEEN We have left our family. We have left our home. [...] I have not seen my mother for fifteen years. [...]

KUMAIL I know that. I really appreciate everything you did for me, but can we talk about this another time?

SHARMEEN Kumi, if you don't want to be a lawyer, fine. If you want to do the [stand-up] comedy and embarrass us as a family, fine. There is only one thing that we have ever asked from you: [...] that you marry a Pakistani girl. That is it, one thing!

KUMAIL Can I ask you something that has never made sense to me? Why did you bring me here if you wanted me to not have an American life? We come here but we pretend like we're still back there? That's so stupid! [...] You don't care what I think. You just want

30 **headshot** Portrait(foto)
42 **to go along with** etw mitmachen
51 **can't stand sb/sth** jdn/etw nicht ausstehen können
52 **tire** *(AE)* Reifen
53 **to stick around** *(ugs)* dableiben
53 **to get over sth** über etw hinwegkommen
55 **fucked up** *(vulg)* beschissen

79 **selfish** selbstsüchtig; egoistisch

me to follow the rules. But the rules don't make sense to me. [...] And I can't marry someone you find for me.

SHARMEEN And why not?

KUMAIL Because I'm in love with someone. I am. Her name is Emily and she's gonna be a therapist. And right now she's very sick but I couldn't tell you that. [...] I really appreciate everything you've done for me. [...] I just need to figure it out on my own.

SHARMEEN You're not my son. [...]

AZMAT Kumi, you're being selfish. You're not thinking about us. [...] In fact you're not even thinking about that girl that you are in love with. You think American Dream is just about doing whatever you want and not thinking about other people? You're wrong! [...]

(899 words)

WORKING WITH THE TEXT

2 Reading for gist → WB, p.75/1

a Sum up each of the four scenes.

b Briefly describe the characters from the excerpts above.

GOOD TO KNOW

Romantic comedy
= (film) genre that presents love in an amusing way. It often presents its characters through clichés and stereotypes.

3 Reading for detail → WB, p.76/2

a Find elements that make this film a romantic comedy. Take notes.

b Explain what Emily's and Kumail's opinion on arranged marriage is. Support the explanations with quotes from the text. Give line numbers.

CULTURE BOX

Around the world today, about 55 % of marriages are arranged marriages. In India, an astounding 90 % of marriages are arranged. Even Indians living in the US are most likely to marry another expat Indian – 86 %. Parents and family play a large role in arranged marriages. Criteria like family reputation, financial situation, career, appearance, values, religion, and health are taken into consideration. Just like there are online dating services and apps, there are also such services for arranged marriages. Parents can register on behalf of their son or daughter for the help of a digital matchmaker.

4 Focus on grammar → G 2

Choose the correct verb form in brackets.

1. If I (were / am) you, I (would / will) tell him straight away.
2. If you (will take / take) part in tomorrow's challenge, you (will get / get) a ticket to the winners' ceremony afterwards.
3. If I (knew / had known), I (would never have done / will never do) it.

D1 I1
Self-check 1.1

5 Focus on analysis → WB, p.76/3

a Analyse Kumail's sentence "We hate terrorists!" (l.19) in the first scene. Consider the historical and cultural significance and if it is appropriate to use humour in this context. → ○ 3

b Explain the irony in Beth and Terry's relationship.

6 Writing a comment → S 6.1

D8 18 Self-check 3.1

Comment on the question Kumail asks his parents in the last scene: "Why did you bring me here if you wanted me to not have an American life?" (ll. 69–70)

A STEP FURTHER

7 Working with pictures

a Think about different ways a neighbourhood can look like and how the people there can live together. Describe these pictures, say what society constellation they represent and to what extent they describe integration.

A

B

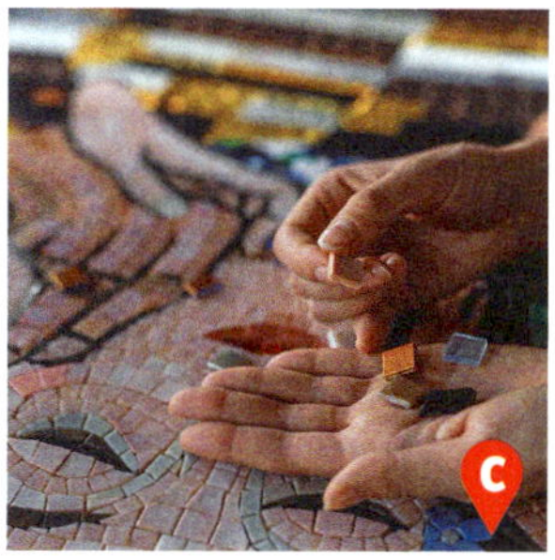
C

USEFUL PHRASES

salad bowl | melting pot | mosaic | to become assimilated into a society | to integrate | to blend in | to adapt | to isolate oneself | forced assimilation | to respect differences | to show tolerance | to uphold traditions | to maintain individuality | to coexist | to cooperate

b Choose a picture from exercise a for each of the following statements. Explain why you think they fit.

1. Interracial marriage became legal in the US in 1967.
2. 67.7 % of Chicagoans identify as non-'White' ('Black', Hispanic, Asian and other).
3. In the NBA 74 % are 'Black' players, playing together with 'Whites', Latinos and Asians.

8 Project: Multicultural neighbourhoods

a Get together in a group of three students and choose one of Chicago's multicultural neighbourhoods (e.g. Chinatown, Little Italy, Pilsen). Research answers to the following questions:

1. Who lives there? How long have they lived there?
2. Where can you see/experience the culture?
3. Has the neighbourhood changed in recent years?

b Give a short presentation about this neighbourhood. → S 14.1

D Invisible identity?

BEFORE YOU READ

1 Talking about mental health

a Give a definition of the term 'mental health'.

b Exchange your ideas with a partner. Discuss the following questions:

1. How can mental health affect your physical health?
2. Which issues can bad mental health cause/provoke in your daily life?
3. Which illnesses have you heard of that are associated with mental health?

c Read this definition of 'stigma':
"a cluster of negative attitudes and beliefs that motivate the general public to fear, avoid, and discriminate against people with mental illnesses"
What could some of the negative attitudes and beliefs be?

GOOD TO KNOW

Depression is a serious medical condition in which a person feels sad, unimportant and hopeless. It can make it hard to function at school, at work, in a family or other relationships. Basic tasks like getting up in the morning or riding a bus can become major challenges. Depression has been more openly discussed since cases have risen significantly.

My employer made me feel my depression was invalid

People won't always know if you're struggling. Sometimes it feels like being silent is the only viable option. After all, why would you want to burden someone else with your problems?

1 When I was at sixth form college, I found it hard to balance college assignments with my part-time work. Evening and weekend shifts were taking up a lot of free time. I was burning myself out. The anxiety around achieving the right grades for uni was making me stressed. My workplace was not supportive when it came to my mental health challenges. Feeling depressed wasn't a choice. It was a natural reaction to my personal circumstances.

My GP recommended activities to help me feel better. Some of these involved going outside. Work penalised this by issuing written and verbal warnings. The reason being that I wasn't housebound during my sick leave. The worst moment was when I tried to confide in my line manager that I was experiencing severe depression.

My sick note had "stress" as the reason because that is what I asked my GP to write. I asked them to write this because I found it embarrassing to be honest about the true nature of my illness. My line manager scoffed when they saw "stress" on my sick note. How could someone of my age feel stressed?

When I said it was depression, they started laughing at me. This made me feel like a joke. My depression felt invalid.

I ended up dropping out of college during the second year. At this moment in time, it wasn't right for me.

4 **viable** brauchbar; möglich
7 **sixth form college** *College in GB, das Schüler/-innen auf den britischen A- oder AS-Level-Abschluss vorbereitet*
19 **GP (general practicioner)** Hausarzt/-ärztin; Allgemeinarzt/-ärztin
33 **to scoff** sich verächtlich äußern; spotten

2 It wasn't until a few years after when I moved on from my part-time job and started an apprenticeship in the public sector. This was a different experience. I found it easier discussing my personal circumstances with my new line manager. My circumstances included ongoing domestic abuse and long-term consequences from historic abuse. This was affecting my performance at work, and even my ability to arrive [on time]. I ended up sharing a lot with my line manager over the course of my apprenticeship.

They never laughed at my circumstances, nor any of my speculative diagnoses. My depression was not invalidated.

I learned something valuable from these two very different experiences. Both involved me opening up about my struggle with mental illness. Both involved line managers, who provided contrasting reactions. What I learned was that the reaction you receive says more about that person than it does [about] you.

3 In 2017, I attended a mental health hospital as a voluntary inpatient. I am not afraid of telling you that the reason for my admission was acute psychosis. My anxiety was getting out of control and I was experiencing delusions. I believed that I was not safe outside. I believed that everyone was watching me. This time, I was honest from the beginning about why I needed time off work.

My line manager was understanding. They had the emotional intelligence not to penalise me for a lapse in my mental well-being. I was in hospital for over one month before being discharged back to my GP. I met with my line manager outside of work for lunch. We talked about the best way to help me return to work and college without burning myself out.

We agreed on a phased return to work plan. I received flexible time off to attend mental health-related appointments. I could not have asked for a more understanding and empathetic line manager during this time.

The same can be said of my college tutors. They were aware of the recent events, and had regular check-ins with me. I didn't always feel like I deserved their time and attention. I even said this to them at times. They always assured me that their job is to help me achieve the best of my ability. I am grateful for the time and efforts from my line manager and college tutors. It is thanks to them that I not only completed my apprenticeship, but also developed the skills to progress to a new position. I'm still in the public sector so that pension pot is still growing ;)

4 You can't assume everyone will react the way you want when you open up about your mental health challenges. But you won't get any reaction unless you speak up.

Hold on. What if I'm on the receiving end? What's the correct thing to say? What kind of reaction is right?

It might be easier to first tell you what kind of reaction I believe is wrong. It's one that dismisses what you've been told as nonsense or something silly. For example, I recently revealed some details about my anxiety to a work colleague. I told them that I am always on edge. No matter where I go, I can't seem to relax.

They told me to "just chill out".

This was a bad response and demonstrates weak emotional intelligence. In this scenario, it would have been acceptable, and intelligent, to ask questions like:

"Has there ever been a time when you didn't feel like this?"

"How do you manage those feelings?"

Or, and this one works in many situations,

"Is there anything I can do to help you?"

A simple offer of help can go a long way. It could even prevent someone from taking their own life. It's why I'm still here.

(905 words)

Jamil, *Time to change*, 2021

49 **domestic abuse** häusliche Gewalt
68 **voluntary** freiwillig
72 **delusion** Wahnvorstellung
79 **to penalise** bestrafen
81 **to discharge** entlassen
116 **to dismiss sth** etw abtun; etw zurückweisen
120 **to be on edge** nervös sein; auf der Kippe stehen

WORKING WITH THE TEXT

2 Reading for gist

a Skim the text and decide where these headings fit best. There are two more headings than you need.

A Here's where to get help
B Understanding is key for change
C Avoiding mental health hospital
D Reactions are important
E My problems aren't taken seriously
F Being honest with oneself

b Summarise the difference between the two line managers' reactions to Jamil's health problems.

c Briefly describe the Jamil's relationship to his second line manager.

3 Reading for detail

a Note down key words that describe the author's time during sixth form college.

b Outline how the author recommends reacting to someone with a mental health problem.

● **c** Which factors contributed to the author's success in his apprenticeship?

d What lesson(s) does the author want his readers to learn?

4 Words matter

a Match the words to form collocations that are used in the text.

1. viable
2. sick
3. true
4. phased
5. to be
6. emotional

A return
B on edge
C intelligence
D option
E nature
F leave

b The text contains many words with a negative connotation e.g. "struggle" (l. 61). Create a table with these words on one side. Then find positive words for the other side.

D2 I2
Self-check 1.2

5 Focus on analysis → S 8.2, 10.2 → WB, p. 77/1

a What do you think the intention of the text was: to inform, describe, instruct, argue or persuade? Analyse the text accordingly and give examples from the text that support the intention. → ○ 4

D1 I1
Self-check 1.1

b The author uses a problem-solution-structure. Explain how this structure is used in the text and the effects it has on the reader.

c The text is written in a very personal style. Examine the language the author uses in order to appeal to the reader's feelings. Give line numbers.

D10 I10
Self-check 3.3

6 Writing a letter → S 6.4

Write a letter to the author and comment on his journey. Think of questions you might want to ask the author or any personal experiences you have had with perceptions/stigma about mental health issues. Write at least 150 words.

A STEP FURTHER

7 Project: Having a discussion → WB, p.77/2

a Read this quote from an article on mental health and do the tasks 1.–3.

> "To reduce mental health stigma, action must be taken at all levels of society. [...] Everyone can change the way they refer to those with mental health conditions by avoiding labels. Instead of saying, "she's anorexic", for example, say "she has anorexia." Individuals can learn how to offer reassurance and acceptance. [...] Therefore, this means we need to express concern and let go of preconceptions."
>
> *Newport Academy* website, 2021

1. Explain the alternative label shown in the quote.
2. Make a list of other labels and possible alternatives, like in the quote.
3. Look back at the text and find examples of offering reassurance and acceptance.

b Form a group. Choose one group of participants in society from the options below. Brainstorm about and research their connection to mental health issues. Consider their potential influence on reducing mental health stigmas, helping those with mental health challenges, but also their limits. Take notes.

media | political leaders | researchers | mental health organisations | employers

c Have a discussion. One pair represents the chosen group and argues in its interest. The other pair argues on behalf of mental health patients. Discuss this statement: "Mental health patients are solely responsible for their well-being." → S 14

D 12
Self-check 5.0

USEFUL PHRASES

to say you're against something: We completely disagree with … / The facts show that … / Recent studies show the opposite.
to say you're for something: We strongly support … / Research supports our idea that … / We are in favour of … / We stand for …
to review: We've clearly shown that … / Our arguments plainly illustrate … / The other team has failed to … / We have offered strong arguments for/against …

8 Working with a cartoon

a Describe and analyse the cartoon. → S 11.3

b Relate the cartoon to what you have learned about mental health and stigma.

He seems to be depressed. Let's label him and see if several years of unemployment, hopelessness and poor relationships helps his condition.

D 6 16
Self-check 1.6

Talking about stereotypes

We are all influenced by stereotypes. For example, when you ask people around the world about Germany, they usually have stereotypical pictures in their head. Do you own a pair of lederhosen or a cuckoo clock? Have you been saving up money for your retirement since you were a child?

Step 1 In a small group, decide which of the pictures representing Germany reflect common stereotypes. What other stereotypes do you know of?

Step 2 Which countries do you associate with these stereotypical souvenirs? Give reasons.

Step 3 Now that you have looked at several stereotypical representations of nations, write a definition for the term "stereotype".

- In which contexts are stereotypes often used?
- Why do they exist?
- To what extent do they help in intercultural interaction?
- To what extent do they hinder us?
- Which stereotypes apart from cultural ones do you know of?

USEFUL PHRASES

cliché | negative attitude | discrimination | to label a group | to judge someone by | to cause misunderstandings | pigeon-hole thinking | to have something in common | to simplify life | to predict someone's behaviour | stigma | prejudice | to feel treated (un-)fairly/outcasted/misunderstood | open-/narrow-minded

Step 4 Compare your definitions in a group. Discuss how you could overcome stereotypes. How can you best find out about people/places? Which things accurately represent people/places?

Step 5 Create a poster about stereotypes. Find pictures that represent different aspects and give examples. Present the posters in class in form of a gallery walk. Decide on a poster which you would like to show in school. Give reasons.

All men are created equal?

This famous phrase is part of the U.S. Declaration of Independence. It was written by Thomas Jefferson in 1776. The whole sentence is: "We hold these truths to be self-evident, that all men are created equal, that they are endowed by their Creator with certain unalienable Rights, that among these are Life, Liberty and the pursuit of Happiness". Since then, more progress has been made.

Several milestones on the path to equality

1807 Slave trade is prohibited in British Empire

1863 Emancipation Proclamation states: "all persons held as slaves within any State [...] shall be [...] forever free"

1920 19th Amendment (U.S. Constitution): "The right to vote shall not be denied or abridged on account of sex"

1928 Women in England, Wales and Scotland are given the right to vote on the same terms as men

1947 Jackie Robinson becomes the first 'Black' player in a Major League Baseball team

1954 U.S. Supreme Court ruled unanimously (9–0) that racial segregation in public schools is unconstitutional

1960 First Paralympics in Rome with 400 athletes in wheelchairs

1964 U.S. Civil Rights Act: aimed at ending discrimination based on race, colour, religion, origin or gender

1979 In 1979, California becomes first state to allow gay couples to adopt a child

1980 Vigdís Finnbogadóttir (Iceland) is elected the first female president of a country

1990 Americans with Disabilities Act: Discrimination against people with any disabilities is unlawful, including mental disabilities (e.g. depression)

1994 Apartheid (racial separation) is officially ended in South Africa

2000 Homosexual citizens are allowed to serve in Her Majesty's Armed Forces (Great Britain)

2001 Marriage equality is granted to same-sex couples in the Netherlands

2007 Pratibha Patil becomes the first female head of state in India, a patriarchal country

2008 The first 'Black' U.S. president – Barack Obama – is elected

2018 Plus-size model Tess Holliday is featured on the cover of *Cosmopolitan*

2019 Transgender model, Valentina Sampaio, is booked for *Victoria's Secret* fashion show

2020 New Zealand introduces a highly diverse cabinet including an inidigenous female foreign minister

February 2018
Kareem Abeed: Syrian producer nominated for Oscar but denied entry into US

June 2018
Women in Saudi Arabia no longer banned from driving

October 2020
Victim of homophobic attack thought he would die

Diversity in society

17 **to accompany** begleiten
23 **to withdraw** (sich) zurückziehen

"Privilege isn't the presence of perks and benefits. It's the absence of obstacles and barriers. That's a lot harder to notice. If you have a hard time recognising your privileges, focus on what you don't have to go through. Let that fuel your empathy and action."
Marie Beecham

People from different backgrounds – like a particular social class or with a certain type of education – and with a large variety of identities such as transgender or 'Black' can determine how diverse a society is. Another form of identification in society can be via physical or mental disabilities, for instance living with a depression. In recent years, migration has gained more and more influence on how a society is shaped. Cultural diversity can have both positive and negative effects on society.
The language barrier can lead to social segregation simply because groups or individuals can't communicate. Luckily, language barriers are temporary in most cases since immigrants eventually learn the language of their host country. The physical segregation, however, may persist despite the newly acquired language skills. Immigrants may continue to live in segregated neighbourhoods.
Diversity and the accompanying cultural differences can also be the cause of social tension. This is sometimes due to religious and secular values colliding with each other, which, in turn, can cause resentment. However, opening up about one's cultural or other identity can encourage intercultural communication and raise awarenesss about different forms of privileges. Sometimes, people from a minority group may have fewer or worse employment opportunities because they have not had equal educational opportunities. Feeling disadvantaged can cause a minority group to withdraw from the integration process. On the positive side, it might be an advantage for certain jobs if you speak niche languages and understand how deals are made in a certain culture.

1 Choose three of the issues addressed in the timeline and find out when similar changes happened in Germany. Where does Germany stand on these issues today?

2 Read the headlines. With a partner, discuss what image they paint of diversity and tolerance.

3 Read the comment on diversity in society. In a small group, think of examples from your surroundings where diversity has a positive impact or is perceived negatively.

Outlook: For further discussion, consider the following:
- Which benefits do you think you have in your life? Why do you have them?
- When is your identity dertermined by factors such as rules, political decisions or labels that other people assign to you?
- What kind of action can you take to support and encourage diversity in your class/ neighbourhood?
- What limits do you see in expressing your identity? How tolerant are you towards other social identities?

1 Lesen und Schreiben

Shared skin colour doesn't equal connection

WHETHER THE CARIBBEAN, LATIN AMERICA, OR AFRICA, traveling to a predominately black location can be difficult as a black traveler. The cultural and historical diversity within the African diaspora has created uniquely connected yet disconnected cultures, traditions, and identities. As a black traveler in countries with an African presence, your skin [colour], race, identity, and racial authenticity are constantly being shaped, challenged, and broadened.

I have always been black. Blackness has been ingrained in me since I was a youngster in Chicago, and it is very much so a part of my identity. However, my blackness was constantly challenged this past semester when I had the opportunity to study abroad and live with host families in a variety of communities in South Africa. As a black woman in Cape Town, South Africa, given their racial theories and categories, my race, ethnicity, and heritage were confronted on a daily basis.

Black Americans are a diverse community that have a variety of skin tones and hair textures, but because of this diversity we can occupy a complex position in South Africa. My identity oscillated between black and coloured, a racial group in South Africa that denotes black, European, and Asian ancestry. Many times, it was through my voice rather than my appearance that people realized I wasn't from there. Unlike members of my cohort, I had a privilege of ambiguity, where onlookers questioned my identity.

Until I opened my mouth and South Africans realized I was American, the ways in which I was perceived and classified solely based on phenotypical characteristics impacted the ways in which people responded to me and uniquely shaped my overall experience. I recall a particular day when my friend CJ (who happens to be white) and I got on a taxi in Langa, a black township right outside of Cape Town. The driver turned around and began to speak Xhosa to me. Even after I told him I only spoke English, he continued to speak in Xhosa. After a minute of talking in Xhosa and me responding in only English, he finally spoke to me in English and told me I should accept my blackness and not conform. Clearly, he did not hear my American accent, but he consistently wanted to push his conceived identity on me despite my own as a black American.

When I lived in Langa, my host-family accepted me as a black person in their community. When I arrived, I wore my hair in either a big afro or braided. My Langa mother's friend even told me "I could be a part of the family." They knew I was an American, but I was able to physically blend with them and the people in the neighborhood.

Interestingly enough, when I moved to the Cape Malay "coloured" community I was again accepted, but now as a part of the coloured community. In Bo Kaap, a Cape Malay coloured neighborhood, I was blatantly told (mind you, by someone who was darker then me) that I should stop saying I was black, and in South Africa I was coloured. To them, they believed saying I was black was denigrating — one of the worst insults. Their perceptions were obviously influenced by the history of the place, but it was also reflective of the different perspectives of blackness around the world. I was able to oscillate at any point from being black to being coloured to being who knows what else. These experiences highlighted the fact that there is no clear boundary or definition of who is considered black or coloured.

While this is my experience, all of the black American experiences cannot be summarized within a tightly constructed paragraph. The ways in which blackness is understood abroad is unique. Yet, each person's experience is informed by a multitude of factors. The complexity and plurality of the black American experience abroad provides a narrative of the complex intertwining of race, class, and nationality. There have been countless accounts of black Americans returning to the "motherland" and not being accepted as they thought they would be. It's a mind-f*ck to say the least when you visit nations of the African Diaspora and people look exactly like you, but there is little if any acknowledgement of similar roots and culture.

Saidiya Hartman says it best as she recounts her sojourn to Ghana, "Old and new worlds stamped my face, a blend of peoples and nations and masters and slaves long forgotten...[but] A black face didn't make me kin." A golden thread connects people of the African diaspora – we have flourished independently and our cultures have been nurtured by the various influences, environment, and desires of that distinct diasporic group. The complex interplay of skin [colour], nationality, and class all emerge through the black American's experience in countries with a black presence. It is up to you as a global trekker to open your critical lens and be aware of the possible impacts your skin [colour] and nationality has on your experience.

To the black traveler: Don't expect to be welcomed with open arms, and understand blackness is not necessarily transferable. (857 words)

Tayler B Ulmer, *Matador network* website, 2014

ASSIGNMENTS → WB, p.78

1. Outline which different attitudes towards her appearance the author experienced in South Africa and from whom.
2. Analyse the means the author uses to bring across her experiences as a Black traveller.
3. Choose one of the following tasks:

   3.1. "No matter how you look, where you are from or how you were raised, it is possible to find something in common with any other human."
   Assess this statement and discuss whether you agree or disagree with it.

   Or:

   3.2. Write a blog post about a recent travel experience and comment on how travel does or does not determine your identity.

2 Hörverstehen

ASSIGNMENTS → WB, p.79

You will hear a report from Dina Nayeri, who was born in Iran, talk about what it was like living and growing up in England and the United States. You will hear each recording twice. After each listening, you will have time to complete your answers.

A35 1. Listen to the first part of the narrative. Answer the following questions in keywords.

a) When did Dina first leave Iran to live abroad?
b) How did her family expect her to react after the accident with her little finger?
c) Why does she think children in London started being mean to her?
d) What were the reasons that Dina and her family left Iran in 1988?
e) How does she describe her time as a refugee in Dubai and Rome?
f) Why does Dina think the school children in Oklahoma made Chinese jokes about her?
g) How did she deal with the teasing and jokes?

A36 2. Listen to the second half of the narrative. Choose the correct answer (A. B or C). There is only one correct answer.

1. Dina first encountered a negative side to gratefulness …
   A when she was being bullied in London.
   B in a conversation with her American teacher.
   C when she heard it mentioned at her grandmother's church.

2. Generally, Dina feared that if she didn't show her gratefulness …
   A her teachers would dislike her.
   B she would be left out by the other children.
   C she would lose freedom from religious control.

3. Dina's mother was not accepted by her new coworkers and bosses because …
   A she used to be a doctor.
   B she had too little experience.
   C the language barrier made them feel she was inferior.

4. Over time, Dina's family were accepted once …
   A they converted to Christianity.
   B they gave up their past identity.
   C they introduced the others to their culture.

5. When speaking with Dina's family, most people were interested in …
   A their escape story.
   B their life and family back in Iran.
   C when they were returning to Iran.

7 GETTING STARTED

Issues of globalisation

1 Copy the table and note down how globalisation affects these aspects of our lives. Work with a partner.

culture	politics	economy	technology	trade
international sport events	…	…	…	…

2 Relate the aspects of globalisation you collected to the pictures. Compare your ideas with a partner. → WB, p. 82

USEFUL PHRASES

The effects of globalisation can be observed …
The movement of goods / people / ideas is rapid / free-flowing / increasing.
Different places / products in the world are becoming more similar / less unique / more integrated / more connected / less independent / more competitive.

A37 **3** Listen to the podcast "Forward Thinking: Globalisation".

a Copy the table. Listen to the first part of the podcast and take notes on the positive and negative aspects of globalisation mentioned by Kathleen Whitehead.

Positive effects of globalisation	Negative effects of globalisation
...	...

A38 **b** Now listen to the second part of the podcast. Add further aspects to your table.

A37 A38 **c** Listen again to both parts of the podcast and answer the following questions in keywords.

1. Why do many global players have a bad image?
2. What has the UN achieved so far?
3. Which arguments are given by those who deny a collective spirit of globalisation?
4. How could globalisation become fair according to Kathleen Whitehead?

4 Read the quotes below. Choose two of the quotes and explain them.

"Globalization is a fact, because of technology, because of an integrated global supply chain, because of changes in transportation. And we're not going to be able to build a wall around that." *Barack Obama, former US president*

"Globalization is a fact of life. But I believe we have underestimated its fragility." *Kofi Annan, former Secretary General of the United Nations*

"Globalization has changed us into a company that searches the world, not just to sell or to source, but to find intellectual capital – the world's best talents and greatest ideas." *Jack Welch, American business executive*

"It is time to draw the economy anew, embedding it within society and within nature, and powered by the sun." *Kate Raworth, British economist*

5 Choose one of the quotes you explained in exercise 4 and do the following tasks:

a Which issues of globalisation are highlighted by your chosen quotes? Take notes.

b Think of a real-life example (e.g. lack of medicinal equipment in some countries) that demonstrates the main point of your chosen quotes and discuss it with a partner.

c Find a picture or a statistic that illustrates each of the different ideas mentioned in the quotes about globalisation. Present your picture or statistic in class and explain why you chose it.

A Global work

BEFORE YOU READ

1 Ideas about the text → G 5

Look at the quote from the text you are going to read:
"Whenever a seat became free he willed someone else to take it, the illogical hope growing inside his chest that by staying very still and quiet he could preserve himself, would not have to pass through any of the three frosted-glass doors." (ll. 33–36)
Speculate on what the text might be about.

Hari Kunzru is a British journalist and novelist. In *Transmission*, he tells the story of Arjun Mehta, a Delhi computer geek who wants to live the Amercian Dream and has to learn that he knows little about the world around him.

Transmission
by Hari Kunzru

For a moment Arjun Mehta, consumed by hesitation, was the only stationary figure in the crowd. He was visible from a distance, a skinny flagpole of a boy, hunching himself up to lose a few conspicuous inches before making his entrance. The face fluttering on top wore an expression of mild confusion, partly obscured by metal-framed glasses whose lenses were blurred with fingerprints. Attempting to assert its authority over his top lip was a downy moustache. As he fiddled with his collar, it twitched nervously, a small mammal startled in a clearing. Finally, feeling himself as small as he would ever get, he clutched his folder of diplomas to his chest, stated his business to the chowkidar, and was waved up the steps into the air-conditioned cool of the office lobby. Marble under his feet. [...]
He frowned at the man, who stared unapologetically back as he continued his progress across the lobby. At the desk the receptionist directed him to a bank of elevators. Stepping out at the eighth floor, he walked up and down a corridor searching, with rising panic, for Office Suite E. Just as he was beginning to think he had been given an incorrect address, he came to a door with a handwritten sign taped over the nameplate: INTERVIEWS HERE. He knocked, received no reply, knocked again, then shuffled about for a while wondering what to do. The shuffling did not seem to help, so he kneeled down and polished his smudged shoes with his handkerchief.

'Excuse me please?' He looked up at a prim young woman in a peach-coloured salwar-kameez.
'Yes?'
'Would you mind moving out of the way?'
'Sorry.' She brushed past him and unceremoniously pulled the door open to reveal a waiting room filled with nervous young people, sitting on orange plastic chairs with the peculiar self-isolating stiffness interview candidates share with criminal defendants and people in STD-clinic reception areas. The woman swept in and announced herself to a clerk, who checked her name on a list and assigned her a number. Consumed by his own inadequacy, Arjun followed. [...]

There were three interview rooms in simultaneous operation; and, as people were called in and others arrived, the scene around Arjun changed like a time-lapse photograph of

4 **skinny flagpole** *hier:* Bohnenstange
4 **to hunch up** (sich) kauern
8 **downy moustache** flaumiger Schnauzbart; Milchbart
8 **to twitch** zucken
10 **chowkidar** (*Hindi:* watchman) Wache
13 **unapologetically** *hier:* unbeeindruckt
20 **smudged** beschmutzt
21 **prim** förmlich; korrekt
22 **salwar-kameez** *(Hindi) ein längeres Hemd, das locker über einer Hose getragen wird*
27 **stiffness** Steifheit
28 **STD (Sexually Transmitted Disease)** sexuell übertragbare Krankheit
32 **time-lapse photograph** Zeitrafferaufnahme

some uncertain natural process, neither generation nor decay. Whenever a seat became free he willed someone else to take it, the illogical hope growing inside his chest that by staying very still and quiet he could preserve himself, would not have to pass through any of the three frosted-glass doors. 'Mehta A. K.?' He stared hard out of the window. 'Mehta A. K.?' It was no use. The woman with the list was speaking to him. Weakly he put up his hand and allowed her to show him into an office, where she indicated a seat in front of a pine-veneer desk. On the far side, legs ostentatiously crossed, lounged a man who appeared to be less a human being than a communications medium, a channel for the transmission of consumer lifestyle messages. [...] Arjun tugged at his collar. 'Sunny Srinivasan,' said the channel, leaning over the desk and shaking hands. 'So how are you today?' Sunny Srinivasan's features were regular and well defined. He had the polite yet aggressive air of a man who enjoys competitive racket sports. [...]

As Arjun considered skincare, Sunny flicked through his certificates, holding one or two up to the light. 'So,' he concluded, 'it all looks *most* excellent. What I need to know from you now is how much you're bullshitting.'

'Bull –? What do you mean?'

'Well, Arjun K. Mehta, educated to B.Sc. standard at North Okhla Institute of Technology, on paper your qualifications look good. Not great, but good. The question is, are they real?'

'Entirely. One hundred per cent.'

'Glad to hear it. Half the losers out there in the waiting room bought their diplomas in the bazaar. Another quarter have completed some two-bit nightschool computer course and faked it up to look like a college education. But you, Arjun, you're telling me you're the real deal. Right?'

'Absolutely Real deal. Thumbs up. As I said on my application, I can provide references. I am skilled in all major areas – networking, database –'

'Let me stop you there.' Sunny held up his smooth, lipid-nourished hands. 'You don't need to wow me with all that. I'll tell you a secret, Arjun: I don't know the difference between SQL and HTML. And I don't care. To me it's all letters. What I care about is butts, good properly qualified desi butts sitting on good American office chairs, earning good consultancy dollars for Databodies and for me. Understand?'

'Absolutely,' murmured Arjun. Sunny Srinivasan was appearing more impressive by the minute.

Sunny leaned back in his chair and clasped his hands behind his head. 'So what I'm going to do is this,' he announced, as if the thought were the product of long rumination. 'I'm going to take your application, get you checked out by my people, and, if you're telling the truth, I'm going to send you to America and start making you rich.'

Arjun could not believe it. 'Just like that?'

'Just like that, Arjun. When you're a Databodies IT consultant, things happen. Your life starts moving forward. You start to become who you always dreamed of becoming. That's our mission, Arjun. To help people become their dreams. That's what we stand for.'

'And you can guarantee me a job in America?'

'Boy, good programmers like you are gold dust over there. Everyone knows American college students are only interested in cannabis and skateboarding, right? You leave it with me. If you're telling the truth, you're going to be raking in the dollars just as soon as we can get you on a flight.' Arjun could barely contain his gratitude. He reached across the desk and clasped Srinivasan's hand. 'Thank you, sir! Thank you! Have a nice day!'

'No, thank you, Arjun. Good to have you aboard.' (1,000 words)

36 **frosted-glass** Milchglas-
39 **pine-veneer** Kieferfurnier
39 **to lounge** liegen; sich fläzen
45 **to flick through** durchblättern
47 **to bullshit** *(ugs)* Blödsinn erzählen
62 **desi butts** *(ugs)* indische Hintern
67 **rumination** Grübelei
76 **gold dust** *(fig)* Goldstaub
78 **to be raking in the dollars** die Dollars scheffeln

WORKING WITH THE TEXT

2 Reading for gist

a Sum up the situation Arjun finds himself in.

b Briefly describe the encounter between Arjun and Sunny Srinivasan.

3 Reading for detail → WB, p. 83/1

a Explain Sunny Srinivasan's business model.

b Illustrate what Arjun's immediate future will look like according to Sunny Srinivasan.

D5 I5 Self-check 1.5

4 Focus on analysis → S 9.6 → G 4, G 5 → WB, p. 83/2

a Find the passages in the text relevant for characterising Arjun. For each passage, find one adjective that best summarises it. Give line numbers.

b Characterise Arjun as he appears in the extract on pp. 162–163.

c Describe the relationship and interaction between Arjun and Sunny. → ○1

D10 I10 Self-check 3.3

5 Writing a personal email → S 6.4

"That's our mission, Arjun. To help people become their dreams." (l. 73)
Write a personal email to Arjun in which you comment on Sunny's behaviour and warn him about the promise he makes.

A STEP FURTHER

D11 I11 Self-check 4.0

A39 6 Listening → S 2 → WB, p. 84/3

Listen to the podcast "Forward Thinking: Outsourcing" and answer the following questions in keywords.

1. What does outsourcing mean to a business or an organisation?
2. Why did outsourcing become so important?
3. In which ways do developing countries benefit from outsourcing?
4. What are the downsides of outsourcing for developing countries?

D12 Self-check 5.0

7 Giving a presentation → S 14.1

Research countries and cities that are particularly important for or rely heavily on global outsourcing (e.g. Vietnam, China, Ethiopia). Choose one location and prepare a presentation in which you:
… provide basic facts about the country/city.
… list the business services the country/city offers.
… say what makes it attractive in terms of outsourcing.
… explain what outsourcing means for the local economy.

D8 I8 Self-check 3.1

8 Writing an argumentative essay → S 6.3 → ○2

Discuss the following question:
Is outsourcing a win-win situation for all countries, companies and organisations involved? Think about global players, countries with a lot of natural resources etc.

Writing a blog post

In your exam you may be required to write a blog post about a specific topic. A blog post is usually an informal piece of writing. Like in any written piece, it is important to grab your audience's attention from the very beginning.

A Copy the table. Then read Allison's blog post and note down examples for each of the categories from the text. Give line numbers.

Exclamation	Rhetorical question	Exaggeration	Connectives	Adjectives	Adverbs
Wow! (l. 3)	...	...	...	...	...

GOOD TO KNOW

exclamation = word or phrase to express a strong emotion
rhetorical question = question where no answer is expected
exaggeration = making sth bigger/better/worse than it actually is/was

My adventures as an office intern

Sunday, 3rd July 20...

Wow! My new adventure is about to begin. Tomorrow I start my three-month internship at one of the biggest consulting companies in the world. I've been eagerly awaiting this day for over a year. I'm so incredibly excited! I think I'm going to get to know some amazing people who will teach me about the world of business.

It's hard to completely prepare for something like this, but I've tried to do my homework. Even though I've carefully read through the company's website several times, I'm feeling a little overwhelmed by all the information. A multinational company that operates in at least 17 different countries can offer a multitude of services to its customers. And here I am – just one little, lonely intern in a huge organisation. Will I make any mistakes? Who will I eat lunch with? Are my clothes okay? Will people understand my English or will they just ignore me if they don't understand what I'm saying?? Help me!

So yes, in case you couldn't already tell: I'm nervously waiting for today to end and tomorrow to start. I just hope that in the office tomorrow they won't see my shaking hands, hear my heart pounding loudly or feel my wavering confidence. The helpful advice from my careers counsellor will come in handy – speak clearly, look people in the eye and listen carefully. And perhaps most importantly: Ask questions if you don't understand tasks, processes or how the coffee machine works – anything really. I might feel embarrassed ... Well, nothing shows interest and willingness to learn like asking questions.

sigh I think it's time to turn off my brain and get some sleep before my big day. Are you ready? All together now – take a deep breath, exhale, relax and goodnight!

(304 words)

B What kind of person do you think Allison is? Write down several characteristics about her that are evident in the blog post. Give line numbers. → WB, p. 85/1

C Get together with a partner and discuss the following questions:

1. What structure can you see in Allison's blog post (e.g. headline, paragraphs)?
2. What are the functions of the different structural elements? Give reasons.
3. Who is Allison's target audience? Explain.
4. What attracts your attention the most in Allison's blog post?
5. Is there anything you miss in the blog? Give reasons.

D Get together with another pair and imagine Allison's first day as an intern. Look at the pictures and write down things that may have happened to Allison on her first day. Add your own ideas.

E Imagine you are Allison and you want to tell the readers about your first day as an intern. Write the next post on Allison's blog. You can use the pictures as inspiration or your own ideas. Write at least 200 words. → S 6.2 → WB, pp. 85–86

USEFUL PHRASES

(I'm) back again after my first day … / Welcome back to my blog about …
My first day was great/brilliant/awful/boring …
Can you imagine what happened to me today?
My colleagues welcomed me / ignored me / went to lunch with me …
I spilled my coffee/tea/drink …
The tasks I was given sound interesting/boring/challenging …

B Working across cultures

BEFORE YOU READ

1 Talking about collaborations

MK **a** Find out the meanings of the words "cooperation" and "collaboration" online or with the help of a monolingual dictionary. Explain the difference in your own words.

b Discuss possible benefits and challenges of collaborations across different countries. Think about the organisation of work, communication and cultural differences. Take notes and exchange your ideas in class.

2 Thinking about cultures

Which other cultures do you know about? Which ideas come to mind when you think about them? Then consider which factors or events could make you change the way you think about them. Exchange your ideas with a partner.

Working Across Countries and Cultures: Collaboration Tips and Tricks […]

More and more companies are becoming remote and international.

I currently work with a team of designers, located in California, Poland and Ukraine. There are many benefits that come from having designers in […] different places. For example, my designer teammates in Poland are able to perform usability research on people from Europe more readily than the designers in California can. […] Working across these different countries provides us all with a more open perspective.

Benefits are often accompanied by obstacles and collaborating across the globe may pose some challenges. Drawing from my personal experience, I've got some advice on how to mitigate these hurdles:

#1 – Dealing with different time zones

This is one of the most common and difficult challenges when working across different countries. […] This heavily impacts the flow of how you work together with your team as it affects meetings, response times, and communication efficiency. […] Depending on your time difference, you may wake up to full inboxes or go to sleep with your email blowing up. This can cause stress as you have to deal with many questions at one time. Organize your inbox to bundle or tag related emails. This way you can bucket different topics you are a part of and focus on one at a time. […] Take into account the time difference and note that this equates to delayed response time. The time difference between our two teams is 8 hours, so we have at least that amount of time before we receive any response from our Polish teammates. In the case that you are unable to plan ahead, prioritize things so team members understand what they should be focusing on first. […]

#2 – Figuring out meeting logistics

Organizing meetings across different time zones can be a hassle. The time difference could be so large that few hours work equally for everyone. Compromises will need to be made. […] Be flexible: figure out what works best for the team. […] Find meeting times that are acceptable for all sides and be sensitive to working hours.

4 **currently** derzeit; zurzeit; momentan
9 **usability research** Nutzbarkeitsstudie
16 **obstacle** Hürde; Hindernis
25 **to impact** sich auswirken auf
33 **to bundle** bündeln; zusammenfassen
54 **sensitive** verständnisvoll; sensibel

56 **alternating** wechselnd
60 **disruption** Unterbrechung; Störung
77 **to be bound to be** zwangsläufig entstehen
96 **rationale** Gründe; Grundgedanke
101 **to enunciate** sich artikulieren
105 **to discern** wahrnehmen; erkennen
107 **inherently** grundsätzlich; von Natur aus

If you aren't able to locate times that work for everyone, consider alternating times each week. Check your tech. [...] Make sure you have a stable connection as technical problems are a common source of disruption for virtual meetings and can take up a lot of precious time.

#3 – Communicate communicate communicate

Communication is the one thing that can make or break your team. Without clear communication, productivity dissolves. This can be tough in any workplace and is especially tough for teams working across countries. [...] You may have to spend extra time clarifying your thoughts and asking questions. If you're not sure about something, just ask. I would rather ask too many questions than work on something I'm unsure about. This also helps develop patience, which is always helpful.

#4 – Understanding cultural differences

There's bound to be differences when working with people all around the world. [...] Being sensitive to cultural differences will go a long way in establishing good relationships with your coworkers. [...] Our company participated in a workshop on cultural differences between the US and Poland. This helped employees on both sides better understand our differences and set realistic expectations. [...] While there may be some general cultural characteristics to keep in mind, keep an open mind when someone acts in a way that is different from what you would expect. For example, our Polish counterparts are more open and straightforward, while we are more "polite" and like to make small talk. Talk through your differences so you can hear the explanations and rationale behind why someone acts the way they do. Remember that English (or whichever language you speak) may not be someone's first language. [...] Accents vary and I have found that enunciating more clearly helps with better understanding all around. The more you get used to listening to a particular accent, the better you will be at discerning what is being said.

#5 – Getting to know each other

This is inherently more difficult when you have only met virtually. There can be a barrier in the beginning especially if some teammates aren't as open or social as others. [...] Turn on your webcam during meetings, so you can see facial expressions and body language along with hearing voices. This helps everyone develop a better understanding of what someone is saying because nonverbal communication provides supporting information. [...] Despite having some challenges to overcome, it is a beneficial learning experience to work with [...] teams that span two or more countries. Working across countries expands your skill set and helps you develop an understanding you might not otherwise have the chance to. [...] (793 words)

Angela Ng, *User Interviews* website, 2019

WORKING WITH THE TEXT

3 Reading for gist → WB, p. 87/1

Decide where these subtitles fit in the text. Give line numbers.

1. Be culturally aware.
2. Set your calendar up to show all the necessary time zones.
3. Plan ahead.
4. Final thoughts
5. When in doubt, over-communicate.
6. Don't typecast or stereotype your teammates.
7. Space out the times you allot for email correspondence.

4 Words matter

Paraphrase these phrases from the text using context clues.

1. to mitigate hurdles (ll. 19–20)
2. to bucket different topics (ll. 34–35)
3. to be a hassle (l. 48)

5 Reading for detail

a Illustrate the author's motivation for writing this blog post.

b What are the authors top five tips for good cross-cultural colloboration?

6 Focus on analysis → WB, p. 87/2

a Analyse what could go wrong in a cross-cultural collaboration if you do not follow the advice from the blog post. Include examples from the text and give line numbers.

b Read the scenario described below. Speculate what went wrong and explain how an "open perspective" from the article could have saved the situation. → ○ 3

A high-level executive from Spain is invited to fly to California to negotiate a business deal with a large corporation. The executive arrives at the airport at 7:00 pm to find only a company car and a driver waiting for him. He is immediately driven to his hotel. There is a bottle of Californian wine waiting for him in his room and a friendly welcome note but no food. He doesn't see any of his US counterparts until the next morning after breakfast when he is driven to the company where the negotiations are to take place. His hosts notice that he is irritated but don't comment. They attribute it to jet lag.

7 Writing a blog post

D6 16
Self-check 1.6

Write a blog post about working across cultures. Include information from the text and the message of the cartoon below. → S 6.2, S 11.3

The American intern who served his boss coffee for the afternoon tea break

A STEP FURTHER

8 CULTURE Working with pictures

a Gestures, facial expressions and body language can mean different things in different cultures. Decribe what the gestures below mean in your culture. Find out what they mean in other cultures.

MK **b** Go online and research one of the aspects below. Then share your results in class.

greetings around the world | table manners | business clothes

9 CULTURE Project: Cultural differences in schools around the world

a Get together in small groups. Each group chooses one of these regions:

North America | South America | Europe | Northern Africa | Southern Africa | Middle East | Asia | Australia

b Narrow down your region by choosing a country, state or city. Collect facts and pictures about the place. Make sure you cover each of the following aspects:

- **location of schools:** What kinds of buildings or structures are used? Where are they located? How do the students and teachers get there?
- **school materials:** What do the students and teachers use in the classroom?
- **clothing:** Is there a school dress code?
- **level of education:** How much schooling is available in the country? How many students reach which level?
- **value of education:** How is education viewed in society? Who is able/allowed to get an education?
- **cost of education:** Who pays for education? Who can afford it?

c Create a poster summarising the information you collected. Present the posters in class.

C Global trade

BEFORE YOU READ

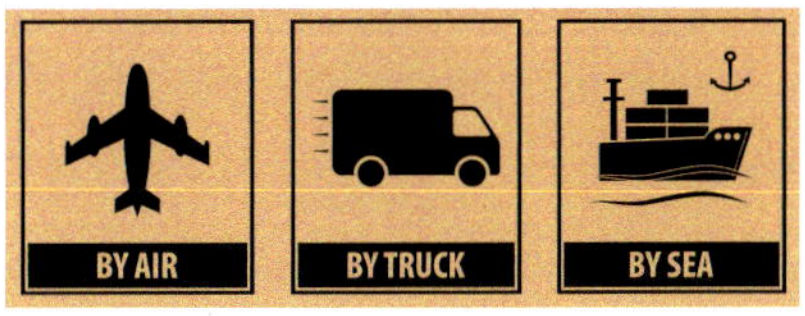

1 Talking about packaging

a Make a list of different kinds of transport goods, small and big, that you know and the advantages and disadvantages of each one.

b Think about the role that packaging can play in globalisation. Discuss the following questions in class:

1. How does packaging influence global markets?
2. What needs to be taken into account in terms of packaging and global cooperation?
3. How do companies interact in terms of packaging?

Today's global economy runs on standardized shipping containers, as the Ever Given fiasco illustrates

A Perhaps you're snacking on a banana, sipping some coffee or sitting in front of your computer and taking a break from work to read this article. Most likely, those goods – as well as your smartphone, refrigerator and virtually every other object in your home – were once loaded onto a large container in another country and traveled thousands of miles via ships crossing the ocean before ultimately arriving at your doorstep.

Today, an estimated 90% of the world's goods are transported by sea, with 60% of that – including virtually all your imported fruits, gadgets and appliances – packed in large steel containers. The rest is mainly commodities like oil or grains that are poured directly into the hull. [...]

In short, without the standardized container – like the thousands that helped to keep the Ever Given stuck in the mud along the Suez Canal, snarling traffic for almost a week – the global supply chain that society depends upon would not exist. About 30% of global container shipping volumes transit through the Suez Canal. [...]

B Since the dawn of commerce, people have been using boxes, sacks, barrels and containers of varying sizes to transport goods over long distances. Phoenicians in 1600 B.C. Egypt ferried wood, fabrics and glass to Arabia in sacks via camel-driven caravans. And hundreds of years later, the Greeks used ancient storage containers known as amphorae to transport wine, olive oil and grain on triremes that plied the Mediterranean and neighboring seas to other ports in the region.

Even as trade grew more advanced, the process of loading and unloading as goods were transferred from one method of transportation to another remained very labor-intensive, time-consuming and costly, in part because containers came in all shapes and sizes. Containers from a ship being transferred onto a smaller rail car, for example, often had to be opened up and repacked into a boxcar. [...]

C [...] [I]t was not until the 1950s that American entrepreneur Malcolm McLean realized that by standardizing the size of the containers being used in global trade, loading and unloading of ships and trains could be at least partially mechanized, thereby making the transfer from one mode of transportation to another seamless.

This way products could remain in their containers from the point of manufacture to delivery, resulting in reduced costs in terms of labor and potential damage. In

4 **to sip** schluckweise trinken; schlürfen
18 **steel** Stahl
24 **to snarl** *hier:* durcheinanderbringen
30 **dawn** *(fig) hier:* Morgengrauen; Beginn
34 **to ferry** befördern
39 **trireme** Triere; Schiff mit drei Ruderreihen
39 **to ply** regelmäßig fahren
51 **boxcar** Güterwagen
59 **mode** Art und Weise
60 **seamless** nahtlos

78 **to soar** sprunghaft steigen; in die Höhe schnellen
85 **surge** plötzlicher Anstieg
89 **to haul** transportieren
97 **predicament** missliche Lage; Klemme
102 **logjam** Stillstand
104 **fierce** *hier:* rau; heftig
105 **bank** Ufer
117 **vessel** Schiff

1956, McLean created the standard cargo container, which we basically still use today. [...]

This dramatically reduced the cost of loading and unloading a ship. In 1956, hand-loading a ship cost $5.86 per ton; the standardized container cut that cost to just 16 cents a ton. [...] One of the key advantages is that whatever size a ship uses, they all, like lego blocks, fit neatly together with virtually no empty spaces. This innovation made the modern globalized world possible. The quantity of goods carried by containers soared from 102 million metric tons in 1980 to about 1.83 billion metric tons as of 2017. Most of the containerized traffic flows across the Pacific Ocean or between Europe and Asia – usually through the Suez Canal.

D The standardization of container sizes has also led to a surge in ship size. [...] In fact, the average size of a container ship has doubled in the past 20 years alone. The largest ships sailing today are capable of hauling 24,000 containers [...]. Put another way, a ship named the Globe with a capacity of 19,100 20-foot containers could haul 156 million pairs of shoes, 300 million tablet computers or 900 million cans of baked beans – in case you're feeling hungry. [...]

E But the growing size of ships has a cost, as the Ever Given's predicament showed.

Maritime shipping has grown increasingly important to global supply chains and trade, yet it was rather invisible until the recent logjam and blockage of the Suez Canal. As the Ever Given was traversing the narrow 120-mile canal, fierce wind gusts blew it to the bank, and its 200,000 tons of weight got it stuck in the muck.

About 12 % of the world's global shipping traffic passes through this canal. The blockage had, at one point, at least 369 ships stuck waiting to pass through the canal from either side, costing an estimated $9.6 billion a day. That translates to $400 million an hour, or $6.7 million a minute.

Ship-building companies continue to work on building ever-larger container vessels, and there's little evidence this trend will stop anytime soon. Some forecast that ships capable of carrying loads 50 % larger than the Ever Given's will be plying the open seas by 2030.

In other words, the standardized shipping container remains more popular – and in demand – than ever. (795 words)

Anna Nagurney, *The Conversation* website, 2021

WORKING WITH THE TEXT

2 Reading for gist → WB, p. 88/1

a Match these headings to the correct paragraphs (A–E) in the article.

1. Trade before the container
2. A trade revolution
3. Cost of success
4. Take a look around you
5. Ships get huge

b Think of an alternative title for the article. Discuss your title suggestions with a partner.

c Briefly describe the effects the standard cargo container has had on world trade.

3 Reading for detail

a Answer the following questions:

1. What does the article say about efficiency in relation to the movement of goods?
2. Why has the ship size increased so dramatically?
3. What does "just-in-time" have to do with the logjam in the Suez Canal?

b Using the information in the article, create a timeline for the development of the international movement of goods. → ○ 4

GOOD TO KNOW

In the manufacturing sector, **"just-in-time"** is used to describe a system where parts or goods arrive at the factory just as they are needed and not before. The products are also manufactured as they are ordered and not in advance. These two steps reduce storage costs, for example.

4 Words matter

a The text includes many different verbs to express the movement of goods, e.g. to travel or to transfer. Find at least eight more verbs in the text related to this word field. Give line numbers.

b Find synonyms for these words and phrases in the article. Give line numbers.

1. a sudden or unexpected disaster
2. small electronic device
3. beginning of day
4. in many varieties
5. without interruption
6. a sudden strong increase
7. a situation that is hard to get out of

5 Focus on analysis → WB, p. 89/3

D1 I1
Self-check 1.1

a Note down the figures used in the article. Give line numbers. Then analyse what effect the use of numbers and figures throughout the text has on the reader.

b Examine whether the author is more critical or in favour of globalisation. Include examples from the text to support your opinion.

● **c** Find examples in the text where the author praises the standardised shipping container. Then examine whether this praise is justified or not. Say whether the author has convinced you as a reader.

A STEP FURTHER

6 Working with a video

Economists and politicians frequently debate the advantanges and disadvantages of free trade and protectionism in a globalised world. You are going to watch a video which explores how political and economic ideas affect the average citizen.

a Before you watch the video, match the following words with their definitions:

1. free trade
2. protectionism
3. tariff
4. import
5. export
6. trade agreement

A bringing in goods from another country
B charge for services or goods entering a country
C international buying and selling of goods withouth limits or restrictions
D arrangement between countries to improve buying and selling conditions
E the principle of protecting the economy of one's country (e.g. by taxing foreign goods)
F taking goods to a different country

V8 b Watch the video "Impact of tariffs on small US business" and answer the following questions. Take notes.

1. What is Kevin Rapp's business?
2. Why did the USA put tariffs on European wine?
3. What could be possible solutions for Kevin Rapp's business strategy?
4. Why do the tariffs affect businesses in the USA more than in European countries?
5. To what extent do the tariffs affect consumers?

c Get together in a small group and discuss how national and international decisions on tariffs or trade agreements can affect people in different parts of the world.

7 Role play

Get together with a partner and put yourselves in the position of a business owner who is affected by tariffs. One of you is affected by the tariffs and the other gives advice on how to proceed. Act out the role play. The phrases below can help you.

USEFUL PHRASES

I don't know how to keep my business afloat …
Do you have any advice on how to keep my customers / proceed?
Maybe you could import from / export to other countries …
I would suggest waiting for updates from world leaders / branching out / asking for professional help …

D Global economy?

BEFORE YOU READ

1 Talking about a diagram → WB, p. 90/1

Describe the diagram and explain in simple terms in 1–2 sentences which economic goal it aims to illustrate.

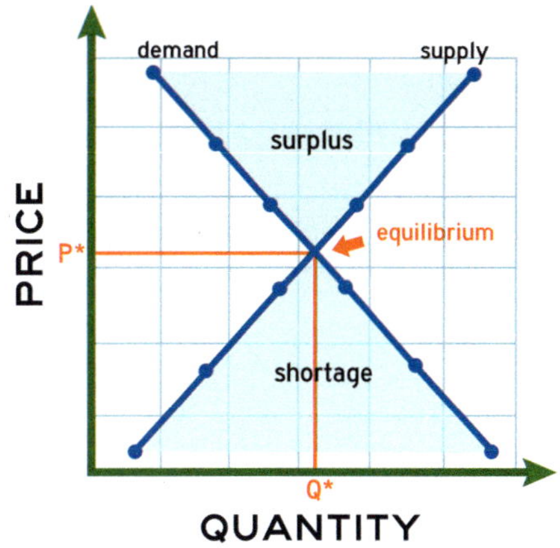

2 Working with a dictionary

Work in small groups and choose three of the economic terms below. Find out what the terms mean and write definitions in your own words.

capital goods | consumer price index | gross domestic product | inflation | liquidity | recession | trade deficit | unemployment rate

"Doughnut Economic" model arrives in California

If a doughnut isn't the first thing that pops into your head when you think about saving the planet and fixing the economy, I wouldn't blame you. But, as it turns out, a doughnut might be just what we need right now.

As the world continues to crumble around us, communities and cities have been turning to an economic model known as "Doughnut Economics." The "doughnut" is an idea that was first presented by renegade economist Kate Raworth in her bestselling 2017 book, "Doughnut Economics: Seven Ways to Think Like a 21st-Century Economist." The idea is based on an image that contains two rings. The inner ring represents our social foundation and the outer ring represents our ecological ceiling. The goal of the "doughnut" model is to get humanity into the doughy center — the space where we are meeting our economic needs while remaining within planetary boundaries. The most prominent image that is associated with economics is probably the supply and demand curve. And while useful in certain contexts, Raworth wants to replace this image with that of a doughnut. Her vision is one which rejects our current attachment to endless economic growth while making sure that humanity is thriving.

"What is the goal of the economy?" Raworth says. "The old diagram that told us that the goal of the economy was that of GDP growth, which is just an ever rising line going up and up – this deeply rooted notion that forward and up is good. But we know that GDP growth and growth itself is not bringing all the wellbeing that we want in the world. The process we have now is leading to extraordinary environmental degradation and extraordinary inequalities as well."

By creating policies and frameworks which reject blind, endless growth – policies that lie within the doughnut's sweet spot, Raworth believes that we can structure our societies in a way that provides communities with the economic securities they need while maintaining a habitable planet.

"The doughnut is trying to represent a vision of the world in which we can meet the needs of all within the means of our planet," Raworth says. "That is the vision of human wellbeing that it's depicting. So that every person has the resources and abilities to meet their needs and their rights to food, water, health, education,

5 **to blame** vorwerfen; übel nehmen
8 **to crumble** zerfallen; zerbröckeln
23 **to meet the needs** den Bedarf decken
37 **GDP (gross domestic product)** BIP (Bruttoinlandsprodukt)
38 **deeply rooted** tief verwurzelt
39 **notion** Idee; Vorstellung
46 **framework** Rahmenbedingungen
53 **habitable** bewohnbar

69 **public policy** öffentliche Ordnung
108 **folks** (*infml*) Leute
114 **to amass** ansammeln; zusammenbringen
122 **to take the lead** die Führung übernehmen
127 **holistic** ganzheitlich

housing, community, connection, energy, and political voice."

And Raworth is not alone in her vision. Many communities and even entire cities have begun exploring the "doughnut" model as a goal for community and environmental wellbeing as well as for public policy. And although the goal is a global doughnut, all of them will not look the same.

The model is flexible and can be applied in a grassroots way by a diversity of communities, cities, states, and even countries. After realizing how much interest there was in the doughnut model, Raworth and co-founder Carlota Sanz launched the Doughnut Economics Action Lab, or DEAL to create a global network of communities that want to embrace doughnut economics.

Most recently, residents of the state of California have been gathering in Zoom meetings in an attempt to bring the "doughnut" model to their state. "I read Doughnut Economics when it came out and honestly it was the first glimmer of hope," Jared Ruiz Bybee told Shareable. "It brought together lots of different threads that I knew were important individually but didn't have a mental map for them being together. So when Kate Raworth and the DEAL team launched the DEAL platform and were making some of these tools and concepts available to people I was really hopeful that I could participate in something happening in California and later around the world." Bybee has been spearheading the efforts to bring the "doughnut" to his state.

"We are trying to stay really broad and open about what it might mean to apply Doughnut Economics in the state of California," Bybee told Shareable. "Whether that's at a very grassroots level or whether a statewide policy level. I'm most interested in statewide politics and policy, but other folks from the group are interested in much more grassroots type efforts. And we're hopeful to create a big enough tent that there's a space for each of those and everyone in between."

After setting up a Slack channel and amassing around 100 people, the group created different working groups that focus on the different dimensions of bringing the doughnut model to California, including the ecological dimension, the social dimension, and the business dimension.

"I'm hopeful that, like with a lot of things, California can take the lead," Bybee told Shareable. "That we can show other states and other places what is possible if there was political will to think about economics and to think about our economy in more holistic ways." (804 words)

Robert Raymond, *Shareable* website, 2021

WORKING WITH THE TEXT

3 Reading for gist → WB, p. 90/2

a Briefly describe the doughnut model and its goal in your own words.

b Summarise which steps the state of California has taken so far. → S 6.9

4 Reading for detail → WB, p. 91/3

a Find passages in the text that express the following ideas. Give line numbers.

1. Bigger, faster, stronger is not always beneficial to everyone.
2. The model shows how to satisfy peoples' basic needs without overtaxing the earth.
3. Doughnut economics is adaptable to different kinds and sizes of organisations.
4. Our plan is to broaden the appeal and make it open to people on all levels.
5. Being willing to take a more all-inclusive look at economics is a first step in setting a good example.

● **b** Look at the diagram below and the words between the social foundation and the ecological ceiling. Attempt to rank these needs. Would you add needs to or subtract needs from the "doughy center"? → S 11.4

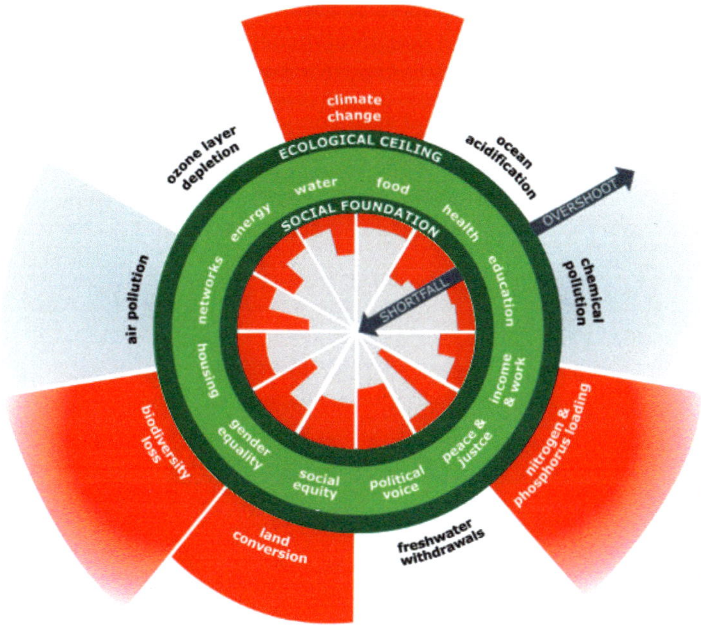

Source Raworth, K. (2017), Doughnut Economics: Seven Ways To Think Like a 21st Century economist London: Penguin Random House.

5 Words matter

a Find these metaphors and concepts used in the article and explain their meanings. Discuss with a partner what helped you understand them: The context or the visuals that come to mind?

1. renegade   2. doughy   3. grassroots   4. to spearhead   5. tent

b Look at these other economic metaphors and discuss their meanings.

1. economy on steroids
2. financial weapons of mass destruction
3. the financial crisis was an economic tsunami

● **c** Use a dictionary and note down the definitions for the following verbs which all have their own intention:

1. to argue   2. to describe   3. to inform   4. to instruct   5. to persuade

6 Focus on analysis → WB, p. 91/4

D1 I1 Self-check 1.1

a Look at the text and find a paragraph that matches each of the verbs and their intentions in exercise 5 c. Compare your results with a partner. Discuss the cases where you disagree.

b Collect words and phrases from the text that represent each of the intentions. → ○ 5

c Examine whether the author has argued for or against the doughnut model. Include examples from the text that highlight his intentions. Give line numbers.

A STEP FURTHER

7 Giving a recommendation

Dairy milk or soy milk? This decision seems to be about food, not global impact. However, if you look more closely at the doughnut model, you can see that other areas like health, water and energy can be affected by this decision.

a Look at the information collected here and at the doughnut model again. Based on this information, what would you recommend to your partner?

Soy milk:
- good source of protein, calcium, and iron
- has fewer calories than cow milk
- all nine essential amino acids
- no problem if you're lactose intolerant
- can reduce blood pressure and cholesterol levels
- US and Brazil biggest suppliers
- "beany" taste
- some people are allergic
- carbon footprint high if grown on land converted from forest

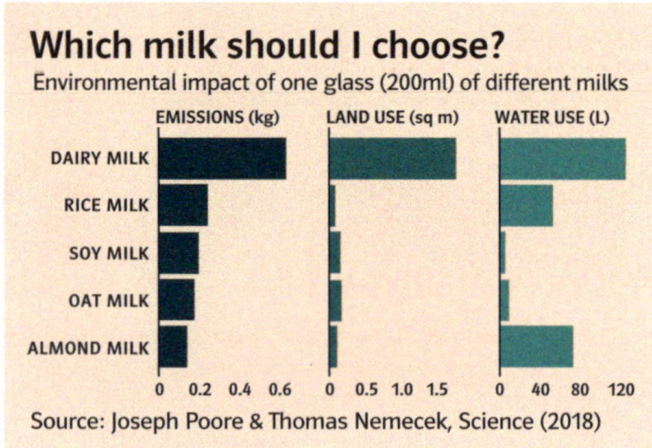

Dairy milk:
- high in calcium, vitamin B12 improves memory power
- good source of protein
- strengthens immune system
- all the amino acids and nutrients make it a complete meal
- nitrous oxide – a by-product of cow manure – depletes the ozone layer
- may reduce blood pressure and risk of heart disease

b Choose another everyday aspect and research the pros, cons and alternatives. Examine where this aspect and the alternative fit into the doughnut model.

c Write a short recommendation based on your research. The phrases below can help you.

USEFUL PHRASES

Based on the doughnut economic model …
This aspect fits well into the social foundation as described …
In addition, the amount of emissions …
The amount of land and water required leads to …
One possible alternative is …
Take into account the transport from …
The main argument for me is that …
I believe I can compensate for …
Nevertheless, my recommendation is …

A survey on English as a company language

You are working at the German branch of an internationally operating American company. The company's management is considering introducing English as the company's language. It wants to find out if this will be accepted by the employees and how far the introduction of English should go (e.g. Should English be the general language of communication or should it be the rule only in certain situations?).

As a member of the works council you have been asked to develop a questionnaire for a survey among the staff in the German branch. Since the staff consists of people from many different countries, the questionnaire should be in English. Also, an English questionnaire will make it easier for you to write up the results of the survey for the company's management.

Step 1 Work in groups.

a Define the goals of your survey.

b Think about the aspects you want to cover in your survey (e.g. benefits and drawbacks of the transition; possible exceptions and limitations to the transition; how prepared employees feel; what employees might need to manage the transition). Take notes.

c Look at the different types of questions below and consider the influences they have on the possible answers. Think about how free or limited the participants are in the answers they can give.

1. closed-ended questions in which one option needs to be ticked (e.g. yes-/no-questions)
2. multiple-choice questions in which one or more options of a list of choices may be selected
3. rating questions in which the participant is asked to rate an opinion or experience (e.g. on a scale from 1 to 5)
4. open-ended questions in which the participant has an opportunity to formulate their opinion or concerns freely

d Use your ideas so far and design a questionnaire with eight questions.

e Present your questionnaires in class and choose the eight best questions.

Step 2 Work in groups.

a Imagine you are an employee of the company and fill in the questionnaire.

b Collect and analyse the surveys. List facts and figures that speak for and against introducing English as the company language.

c Discuss the arguments mentioned. Agree on a recommendation for the management.

Step 3 Write an email to the company's management in which you outline the key arguments for and against introducing English as the company language and include the recommendation you have agreed on in your group.

Different faces of globalisation

"We are aware that globalization doesn't mean global friendship but global competition and, therefore, conflict. That doesn't mean we will all destroy each other, but it is no happy global village, either."

René Girard, French literary scholar and anthropologist

7 **silk** Seide
16 **to assemble** zusammenbauen; montieren
41 **interconnectedness** Vernetzung

A statue of camels caravan in Uzbekistan. A reminder of the Silk Road which went through the country.

Global trade

Historically speaking, one of the first global trade routes were the so called "Silk routes" between the Chinese and Roman empires. Goods traded from West to East included wool and gold. The Romans favoured receiving products like silk, paper and spices from the Eastern world. In 2013, the Chinese president Xi Jinping announced plans for the so called "One Belt, One Road" initiative, which is often referred to as the new **Silk Road**. Although it would open up major routes from Asia to Europe and Africa and within these continents, the project is seen critically due to the **global power** it attributes to China. Nowadays, we associate global trade with finished products. However, it is easy to forget that our mobile phones or cars or kitchen appliances were made from parts that are traded across the globe and finally assembled and shipped to where we live. Thus, it is hard to say where a finished product really comes from. The **World Trade Organisation** was established in 1995 to manage trade agreements between nations and ensures that all phases of global trade run as smoothly as possible.

Global players

Global players are companies that impact and/or influence business worldwide. An example are companies such as *Tesla* and *Space X*. The CEO of these companies, Elon Musk, pushes **global innovations** such as hybrid cars. He is well known for his business attitude globally and visits production sites, for example in Germany. Another global player could be a football club such as Real Madrid, which attracts both football players and sponsors from all over the world.

International communication

Originally, English was commonly known as THE global language due to the far reach of the former British Empire and the United States of America, the global superpower. However, Mandarin (Chinese) and Spanish are more widely spoken than English, which is particularly significant in terms of emerging trade in/with China and Latin American countries.

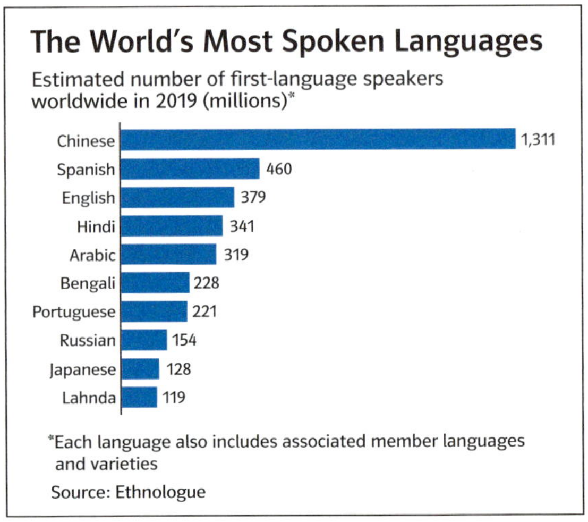

International collaboration

Digitalisation and the interconnectedness of the world via travel opportunities have enhanced global collaboration. With the help of online communication tools, people from different areas can cooperate easily and enrich projects with technological, scientific, and cultural **expertise**. This is important when it comes to international research collaboration. Scientists from the USA and Germany for instance, are able to work together on new medication or an expedition in the Arctic – like MOSAiC – can combine the knowledge of people from over 20 different countries.

Culture

From the 1940s into the 2000s, cultural globalisation was dominated by the English language and US culture. While this may encourage integration among different societies, it also has negative effects. It can lead to countries and cultures losing their uniqueness, forgetting their identity, and even giving up their own language. In the 16th century there were 14,500 spoken languages worldwide. Today, less than half of them are left. That is why it is refreshing to observe the **global success** of pop groups performing in Korean. One band was even named Entertainer of the Year by *Time Magazine* in 2020 and has been called a "global music sensation". **Cross-cultural bonds** and exchanges are important to enrich our lives in this shrinking world, but preserving cultures is equally important.

68 **to shrink** schrumpfen

All these different aspects impact our daily lives, but our daily lives and decisions can also have global impacts. Production models like "just-in-time" may impact how quickly our consumer products are manufactured and where, or the simple act of working with colleagues in Bangkok while taking different time zones and communication methods into account can determine when and how we work. Global **consumption** has highlighted two major impacts of globalisation: Trade wars including **tariffs** and increased pollution of the environment. Tariffs affect countries, companies and, in the end, individual consumers, reflected in higher prices. Consumers' constant demands for goods and a throwaway culture have increased the effects of climate change – not just where we live, but worldwide.

1 Copy the table. Get together with a partner and come up with at least three examples for the categories.

global trade	global players	international communication	international collaboration	culture
global brands produce in different countries	...	...	...	...

2 Get together in small groups and choose one company that you consider to be a global player. Research your company and find out what the company has done to be considered a global player. Have its globalisation activities been perceived positively or negatively? Give reasons.

3 Think about your daily life and make a list of things that you think are linked to globalisation. Take notes, give reasons and share them in class.

Outlook: For further discussion, consider the following questions:
- What impact will increased digitalisation have on global trade?
- Are we heading towards a global culture rather than one unique to each country?
- What opportunities and challenges do you see regarding language in a global business world?

1 Lesen und Schreiben

Experienced planner with talent for improvisation

As logistics coordinator of the largest Arctic expedition ever, Verena Mohaupt ensured smooth and safe operations on board the “Polarstern”. She enjoyed seeing how her concepts worked out in practice – even though the Corona pandemic threw many plans out of kilter.

“I don’t really like superlatives,” says Verena Mohaupt. And yet big projects seem to attract her. Already at the age of 31, the physicist took charge of the joint polar research base of the Alfred Wegener Institute (AWI) and the [French Polar Institute Paul-Émile Victor] in Ny-Ålesund on Spitsbergen, one of the northernmost settlements in the world. And then MOSAiC: a research vessel, hundreds of researchers, collecting data for a whole year and getting closer than ever to the North Pole in the middle of the Arctic winter. Verena Mohaupt coordinated the logistics for the entire undertaking. For this, the trade magazine Nature named her one of the ten people who had a decisive impact on science in 2020. “Of course, the task initially instilled respect in me,” says the 37-year-old. 70 tons of equipment from over twenty countries had to arrive on time in Tromsø, Norway, and be stowed on the ship. […]

In addition to coordinating the expedition procedures, Mohaupt was responsible for the safety of the participants together with her colleague Bjela König. […] To prepare themselves and the scientists for the Arctic conditions during the expedition and to test their equipment, König and Mohaupt organized safety training courses in Tromsø, Norway, and on Spitsbergen. For example, participants practiced pulling themselves or others out of the icy water back onto the ice after an accident. Many of the scientists also learned how to look out for polar bears in the permanent darkness of the polar night […] in order to support the safety team in the polar bear watch. […]

“It was great to see how what we had designed at the desk worked in training,” Mohaupt says. She likes the mix of planning and the research work in the field. “Being in the field is incredibly fun for me,” she says. “Still, there are boring moments there, too.” […]

The physicist spent almost nine months on board the “Polarstern”. In order to survive even strenuous facets of the expedition in the confines of the ship, the cold of the Arctic and months of darkness of the polar night well, the AWI researcher took two things with her: Knitting and pomegranates. “Knitting allowed me to switch off from the rigidly structured routines of the work days, when we were almost never alone,” she says. Taking something with you to enjoy all to yourself is something she recommends to anyone going on an expedition. […] And the pomegranates? “They kept in the fridge for months, and then every now and then I celebrated having fresh fruit.”

[…] She coordinated an information tour of the German Greenpeace ship on the topic of Arctic protection before taking over the management of the research station on Spitsbergen. “My experience naturally helped me to keep track of things and plan ahead when coordinating MOSAiC,” says the scientist. […]

The key to successfully running a business in these dimensions is “as much preparation and planning as possible,” she says. That allows participants to react flexibly in critical situations, she adds. “And, of course, a good dash of spontaneity.” She proved that herself time and again. For example, when she realized on the trip to the Arctic that she couldn’t use the carriers for the power grid as planned. “We then improvised and [sawed …] what we had to size and tied it together so that it fit again,” Mohaupt recounts. […]

In the spring of 2020, the Corona pandemic shook up the entire Arctic expedition schedule. "There you have a plan B, C, D and X," Mohaupt says. "And then a virus like this comes along and just thwarts all the plans." At times, the continuation of the venture was at stake. Many researchers' round-trip routes were cut off and visas expired, while operations were delayed. "There were uncertainties and question marks everywhere," Mohaupt recalls. When colleagues dropped out, she unceremoniously returned to the "Polarstern" from her shore leave two months earlier than planned. "Just ten days before I had to go into quarantine, I decided: okay, I'm already going," she says with a laugh.

[...] Readjusting after months in the ice and at sea isn't easy for her. [...] She has swapped her polar bear guard post for her desk at the Alfred Wegener Institute; instead of sitting among stacks of boxes, she sits in front of potted flowers and white bookshelves. "I allowed myself a longer vacation without a rigid daily structure and like to take my time in the morning," she says. She is currently coordinating the work of the research station on Spitsbergen. "But I'm also excited to see what new adventure is in store for me." (825 words)

Ulrike Schneeweiß, *Hemholtz Association* website, 2021

ASSIGNMENTS → WB, p.92

1. Illustrate Verena Mohaupt's journey from getting the job to work on the MOSAiC expedition to her return.
2. Examine the style, tone and register of the text and the effect these elements have on the reader.
3. Choose one of the following tasks:

   3.1 Discuss the pros and cons of a global expedition such as MOSAiC in terms of experience, travel and cultural misunderstandings based on the examples given in the text.

   Or:

   3.2 You are asked to make a pledge for/against climate change research in front of the local council. Write a speech highlighting the challenges portrayed in the cartoon below.

Ironically, it wasn't just the sceptics or the anti-climate movement that obstructed climate change research ...

2 Hörverstehen

ASSIGNMENTS → WB, p. 93/1–2

You are going to listen to an interview with a French scientist, Zoe Koenig. She is an oceanographer who was part of the MOSAiC expedition and led Team Ocean. She also previously participated in an Arctic expedition called N-Ice 2015. You will hear each recording twice. After each listening, you will have time to complete your answers.

A40 1. Listen to the first track and choose the correct answer.

1. Which small "tricks" did Zoe use on the expedition?
   A She did not pack too many clothes.
   B She brought several changes of clothes.
   C She did not plan everything before the trip.

2. Which ship brought Zoe's team to Polarstern?
   A Kapitan 93
   B Fram Strait
   C Tryoshnikov

3. In which way were people transferred from one ship to the other?
   A They had to walk across a gangway.
   B They were transferred with a mummy chair.
   C They went on another small boat to get from one ship to the other.

4. What goods where exchanged?
   A Fuel and food.
   B Eggs, fuel and cakes.
   C Fuel, cheese and clothes.

A41 2. Listen to the second part of the interview and answer these questions in keywords.

1. What was the team on leg 5 responsible for?
2. What impressed Zoe about the MOSAiC expedition?
3. What was challenging to pack before returning home and why was it difficult? Name two reasons.
4. Which things did Team Ocean not pack?
5. How much cargo did Zoe carry throughout the packing?

3 Kommunikation

Monologue → WB, p.93/1

You are participating in a panel discussion about outsourcing in the context of globalisation. Give a 5-minute presentation on outsourcing based on the following cartoon and quotation.

Cartoon

Describe and analyse the cartoon.

Quotation

Explain and comment on the quotation. Refer it to the cartoon.

"If globalization is to succeed, it must succeed for poor and rich alike. [...] It must provide social justice and equity no less than economic prosperity and enhanced communication."

Kofi Annan, Secretary-General of the United Nations from 1997–2006

Dialogue

In the panel discussion other topics are brought up. Be prepared to talk about global trade, cross-cultural collaborations and the effects globalisation has on your daily life.

8 GETTING STARTED

The world of work

1 Look at the four pictures and do the following tasks.

a Describe each picture. Say which topic(s) related to the world of work is/are being shown.

b Explain whether each picture shows a positive or negative aspect of the world of work.

c Write down a caption for each picture and exchange them with a partner. Do the captions differ? Why? Discuss.

2 Go online to find another picture that you think represents the modern world of work. Share your picture with another pair and explain your reasons. Report back to the class.

GOOD TO KNOW

A **trade union** is an organisation formed by workers in order to represent their rights and interests.

USEFUL PHRASES

The picture represents … / The topic shown in this picture could be … / In my opinion, it shows a positive/negative aspect because …
video conference | automation | technological advances | loss of manual jobs | standing up for workers' rights | gender pay gap | inequality | career barriers | trade union

D 11 I 11
Self-check 4.0

A42 **3** Listen to the first part of the podcast "Forward Thinking: The world of work" and answer the questions below. → S 2, S 3

1. What was the name of the online lecture Melanie Bishop recently gave?
2. How many participants and countries were involved in Melanie's lecture?
3. What is the gender pay gap?
4. What is the surprising fact about Germany?
5. What are some reasons for the gender pay gap?
6. Which statistic does Melanie give to show the gap between the rich and the poor in the UK?
7. What does BAME stand for?

A43 **4** Listen to the second part of the podcast and decide whether the following statements are true or false. Correct the false statements. → S 2

1. The rise of automation will start to cause major unemployment in around 20 years.
2. Melanie argues that new technologies could have a positive effect on employment.
3. The human cloud refers to networks of people who work on different projects rather than for one company.
4. Many graduates are highly motivated by financial gains when choosing a company to work for.
5. Trade unions have lost their influence in the modern working world.
6. Melanie believes that more online communication means employees need to gain new skills.

5 Look at the chart and do the following tasks.

MK **a** Look at the skills mentioned and check if you understand what they mean. Go online if necessary.

b Explain the difference between soft skills and hard skills.

c With a partner, choose three of the skills you think will be important for your future and explain why.

d Share your results with the class and talk about which skills were mentioned the most.

e Come up with two to three other skills or personal traits that you think are important in the world of work today. Share your ideas with the class.

The Skills Companies Need Most

Top 5 Soft Skills

1 Creativity
2 Persuasion
3 Collaboration
4 Adaptability
5 Emotional intelligence

Top 5 Hard Skills

1 Blockchain
2 Cloud computing
3 Analytical reasoning
4 Artificial intelligence
5 UX design

Source: LinkedinLearning, 2020

A Why do we work?

BEFORE YOU READ

1 Talking about work motivation

When a survey asked the question "What is your motivation to work?", the most popular answers were the following:

A Lifestyle reasons
B Following a passion
C I do not want to rely on others now or in the future
D Ensuring financial security for my family

a Rank the answers from "reason most mentioned" (1) to "reason least mentioned" (4) and compare your ranking with a partner's. Does this ranking reflect your own attitude? Discuss.

b What other reasons would be on *your* list?

D 20 Survey

c Compare your results with those in the original survey in D20.

The following text is taken from the preface to the book *How much is enough? Money and the Good Life* by the economist Robert Skidelsky and his son Edward Skidelsky, who is a lecturer for philosophy.

How much is enough?

by Robert Skidelsky & Edward Skidelsky

How much is enough? A reply to our critics

Why do we work? Work, the standard view goes, is the cost of getting things we want. As people get richer – able to afford more of the things they want – they will work less. This in a nutshell was the theme of Keynes's essay 'Economic Possibilities for our Grandchildren', published in 1930. Keynes thought that about a hundred years hence – i.e. not far off from now – developed countries would be about four times richer on average than they were in 1930, and that therefore their inhabitants, on average, would work only a quarter as long, say fifteen hours a week rather than fifty or sixty. The demand for leisure would increase proportionately with income. In fact, though Keynes was not wrong in his forecast of economic growth, hours of work have fallen much less than he thought they would. We now work about forty hours a week and have been stuck there since the 1980s. To be sure, people have more leisure, but not nearly as much as he thought they would want.

So our book is really an enquiry into why Keynes got it wrong. He thought people would work only enough to enable them to live 'wisely, agreeably, and well' – to enjoy what we call 'the good life'. They seem to work much more than this. What did he miss? [...]

In the book we highlight two interlocking reasons for the continued dominance of the work ethic: one psychological, the other institutional.

The psychological explanation appeals to the perennial facts of human nature, particularly to the relative character of human wants. It is not just that we want more but that we want *more than others*, who at the same time want more than us; this fuels an endless race. [...] Human wants are insatiable because they are relative. And the more goods we want, the more we have to work to earn the money to acquire them.

6 **in a nutshell** in aller Kürze
7 **a hundred years hence** *hier:* hundert Jahre später
11 **proportionately with sth** proportional zu etw; etw entsprechend
19 **interlocking** ineinandergreifend
19 **dominance** Dominanz
20 **work ethic** Arbeitsmoral
21 **perennial** immerwährend
24 **insatiable** unersättlich

Economic insatiability is as old as money itself, but it has been greatly exacerbated by the institutions of capitalism. [...] Capitalism promises us the moon – provided we work hard! It brings an increasing range of goods and services under the sway of money exchange, thus inflaming the love of money itself. [...]

The thesis of our book is that the pursuit of money as an end in itself is bad not just because it is detrimental to happiness or the environment (though it may be to both these things) but because it is absurd. It rests on a misunderstanding of the nature and function of money. Money is essentially a means to the good; to treat its accumulation as an ultimate goal is to fall victim to delusion.

So what can we do to free ourselves from this delusion? The problem has two aspects, one intellectual, the other political.

The intellectual problem is to try to recover an idea of what money is for, because it is only in relation to such an idea that it makes sense to talk about 'having enough'. What money is for is, we argue, 'the good life', which can be broken down into the seven basic goods of health, security, respect, personality, harmony with nature, friendship and leisure. To possess a sufficient quantity of these seven basic goods is to live well; to lack a sufficient quantity of one or more of them is to be deprived. If this account holds up, then the question 'how much is enough?' has a non-vacuous answer: it is 'enough for the good life.' Of course, precise figures are going to vary widely according to age, circumstance and temperament. The needs of a twenty-year-old student are not those of a forty-year-old householder. But at least we have something more than the shifting fortunes of 'the Jones's' to guide us.

The political problem is to organize our collective existence so as to make it easier for people actually to live the good life. The state has a positive role to play here; it should not pretend to be 'neutral' between rival conceptions of the good. In the last part of our book, we outline a number of policies for bringing this about, including working hour regulation, work-sharing, stricter controls on advertising, an unconditional basic income and – drawing on the work of the economist Robert Frank – a progressive consumption tax. An unconditional basic – or 'citizens'' income – equivalent to the 'unearned' income enjoyed in the past by small minorities only – is probably the most important of these, as opening up individual choice between work and leisure. [...]

(770 words)

26 **exacerbated** verschärft; verschlimmert
28 **to bring sth under the sway of sth** etw unter die Herrschaft von etw bringen
29 **to inflame sth** etw entfachen
30 **as an end in itself** als Selbstzweck
34 **to fall victim to delusion** einer Täuschung zum Opfer fallen
43 **non-vacuous** *hier:* eindeutig
47 **the Jones's** *from the expression "keeping up with the Jones's"* = Nachbarn, mit deren Besitz man stets den eigenen vergleicht und mit denen man mithalten möchte
48 **collective existence** gemeinschaftliches Dasein
53 **progressive consumption tax** progressive Verbrauchssteuer

WORKING WITH THE TEXT

2 Reading for gist

Read the text and explain in short what the authors are trying to achieve in their book.

3 Reading for detail

Answer the following questions on the text. Use your own words as far as possible.

1. What predictions did Keynes make in 1930 regarding future income and working hours in developed countries?
2. What is "economic insatiability" (l. 26)?
3. Why do the authors think that "the pursuit of money as an end in itself is bad" (l. 30)?
4. According to the authors, what do we need to "live well" (l. 41)?
5. Why can't the authors state a precise figure regarding the question "how much is enough?" (l. 43)?
6. What can the state do to help people "live the good life" (l. 49)?

4 Words matter → S 16.1

Below is a list of words from the text. Find relevant verbs, nouns or adjectives which can express either the same or opposite idea as specified next to the word. Use a dictionary if necessary.

1. perennial (*opposite adjective*) (l. 21)
2. insatiable (*opposite, noun*) (l. 24)
3. to acquire sth (*same noun*) (l. 25)
4. accumulation (*same verb, adjective*) (l. 33)
5. sufficient (*opposite, noun, verb*) (l. 41)
6. deprived (*opposite, noun, verb*) (l. 42)

D 2 I 2 Self-check 1.2

5 Focus on analysis → S 10.2

a Collect passages from the text in which the authors mention their book.

b Explain the function of these passages in the text.

c Analyse the structure of the text and explain how the structure supports the authors to get their message across.

D 10 I 10 Self-check 3.3

6 Writing an email → ○1

In the authors' blog, they ask for readers' opinions on the question "How important is a work-life balance to you?" Write them an email answering the question. Give reasons for your answer.

You can start your email like this:

Dear Robert and Edward,
In your blog you asked about the importance of a work-life balance, and this made me think. In my opinion, …

A STEP FURTHER

D 11 I 11 Self-check 4.0

A44 ## 7 Listening → S 2, S 3 → WB, p. 96

Copy the table. You will hear six speakers with different views on working from home. While listening, match the headings A to H with the speakers 1 to 6. There are two headings you do not need.

speaker	1	2	3	4	5	6
heading	…	…	…	…	…	…

A A lack of connection
B Perfect for night owls
C More home than office
D Benefits on many levels
E Not without its problems
F Suits me down to the ground
G Difficult to make an impression
H More of a challenge for women

B The future of money

BEFORE YOU READ

1 Talking about financial security → ◯ 2

What would you do if you received a fixed amount of money per month for life? How would that affect your career and lifestyle choices? Discuss your thoughts with a partner and present them in class.

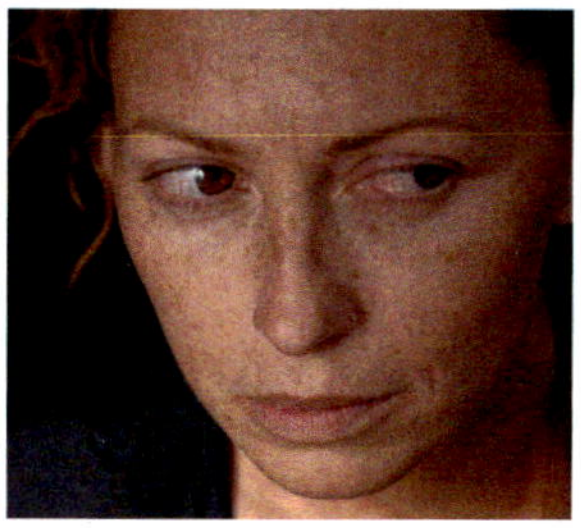

Rosalyn Kelly is a British writer of novels and short stories.

One wage

by Rosalyn Kelly

There it was, in her hand. Ready to be spent. Ready to do what it was meant to do, be what it was meant to be. But she couldn't do it. She couldn't fight this urge any longer and she stuffed it back in her pocket and left the shop. She was going to save it. Hoard it. Gather it until she had piles hidden in her flat. Illegal, of course, and shameful. But Roo had made up her mind, this money, her money, was not being spent today.
She walked home. Through the happy streets of London, everyone smiling at her. She smiled back, the money weighing heavily in her jeans. She'd already spent most of her wage that month, as required by Fair State, and this was a tiny amount, an eighth of the total. Hardly significant.
Deep down, she knew the state would find out. Every working person in England was paid the same monthly wage, no matter the job, as all were equal, whether cleaning the streets or engineering the latest robot. And they were each given access to free services including healthcare, education, childcare, cultural activities and gyms. Every able person was expected to work. Those who couldn't, through disability or illness, were still paid their salary. But those who wouldn't, through laziness, were sent for reconditioning and, if that failed, were eliminated. Fair State knew who was working and who was not, who was on parental leave, who was starting work at eighteen or taking a one year sabbatical from work to study, who was retiring at sixty-five. They were all paid the same wage until they died, in cash every month, the corrupt banks long ago demolished.
The state analysts would crunch the data and know that someone, somewhere, hadn't spent their full salary that month. The paid-out figure differing from the total spent in shops and on services, as all sales were reported meticulously back to the state. But they couldn't know it was her. Out of fifty-five million people in England, they couldn't know.
She let herself into her flat, unlocked of course, the one universal wage eradicating crime as everyone had the money to buy exactly what they wanted, whenever they wanted it. [...] Every person had a standardised home, a single, like Roo, had a one bedroom flat. A couple or family had corresponding bedrooms to their numbers. Green space was a five minute walk from every home. There were no empty buildings or second homes, or palaces with two people living in them. A fair distribution of wealth and life to all. People were happy, Roo was happy. At least, she thought she was. But, sitting on her luxurious sofa, with all the latest technology and trinkets glimmering around her, she pulled out the unspent coins. [...]

4 **urge** Drang
5 **to hoard** (an)sammeln; horten
6 **to gather** sammeln; zusammentragen
11 **hardly** kaum
17 **reconditioning** *hier:* Umerziehung
22 **to crunch (the) data** Daten verarbeiten
24 **meticulously** akribisch
26 **to eradicate** auslöschen
33 **trinket** Zeug; Kinkerlitzchen

35 **barely** kaum
42 **sprightly** beweglich; lebhaft
45 **to wince** zucken; zusammenzucken
50 **to be worked to the bone** hart arbeiten; schuften
57 **takeover** (Macht-)Übernahme
61 **to seize** beschlagnahmen
63 **to inherit sth** etw erben
66 **to drag** ziehen; zerren
67 **to flaunt sth** *hier:* etw offen missachten
74 **tatty** zerschlissen

[S]he'd need to replace the sofa soon, although it was barely used. To ensure people kept spending their wages, the law stated that one year old items were dropped off at one of the many R&R (Restore & Regenerate) centres to be broken down, recycled and used again to create new products with zero waste [...].

A knock at the door and then the voice of her elderly neighbour, Janice. "Are you home, Roo?"

"Yes, come in!" Roo jumped up and arrived at her lounge door just as Janice did; she was surprisingly sprightly for eighty-one.

"I'm sorry, dear, I've caught you in the middle of dinner."

[...] Janice chuckled and then lowered herself onto Roo's sofa, right on top of the hoard. Roo winced, praying Janice wouldn't feel it through the cushion. For the first time, she wanted her neighbour out of the flat.

"I won't stay long. Just wanted to say a quick hello. Please, continue." Janice waited for Roo to sit and take a mouthful of food. "Had a good weekend?"

Roo nodded, chewing, and Janice continued. "In my day, the weekend was only two days, not three. Can you imagine! We were worked to the bone, and for what? Terrible wages and a fear of growing old in poverty. But this new government is the best, truly. Don't you think? You're too young to remember how it was. A shocking wealth divide, no time for family or leisure just work, work, work."

This was Janice's favourite topic, about how awful the time before the revolution was, twenty-three years earlier. Before the One Wage party took control of Government and introduced the Fair State. Roo had been two. Her mother was part of the revolution and died during the Takeover of Westminster. Roo's father, Dinesh, was a staunch resister of the One Wage ideology (her parents had divorced when she was six months old, due to their conflicting opinions). Dinesh was "filthy rich", according to her official heritage report, and didn't want to share his wealth. [...] Like many others, Dinesh was eliminated, his wealth seized and distributed amongst every person in England. Roo barely remembered him, she'd been six when he died and she'd moved to the children's care home. A flash passed behind her eyes – perhaps I have inherited my father's love of money?

"You know, dear, I saw another inspection yesterday, when I was visiting my daughter. A Money Addict dragged from his house, screaming how the money wasn't his, and taken away to be reconditioned. I just can't understand why anyone would flaunt the rules! They are in place to keep the fabulous system running smoothly, to give us all the same shelter, food, jobs, quality of life. Why would anyone want to hoard money? It's evil."

Roo choked on a noodle and dropped her fork with a clatter. "Take a sip of water, dear. That's it." Janice shuffled on the cushion and frowned. "I think it's time you got a new sofa ..."

Roo's eyes widened. "Yes, it's coming up to one year. It's terribly uncomfortable and tatty now isn't it. Here, let me help you up."

"No, no, I can make it." Janice heaved herself up. "I should be getting on." [...]

(1,009 words)

WORKING WITH THE TEXT

2 Reading for gist

a Describe where the scene takes place and who the characters are.

b Sum up what happens in the extract.

3 Reading for detail → S 4 → WB, p. 97

a Find sentences that outline Roo's behaviour and emotions in the extract.

b Describe the relationship between the state and its citizens as portrayed in the text.

c Explain how money is distributed in the system described in the text and what happens to people who keep money.

d State why Janice prefers things today to how things were before the revolution.

4 Words matter

a Read the definitions and search for the corresponding words in the text. Give the line numbers.

1. a strong desire or impulse
2. to accumulate and hide sth
3. very thoroughly
4. to make certain of sth
5. to make a slight involuntary movement
6. very loyal and committed

● **b** Explain what the author refers to when she uses these words in the text.

5 Focus on analysis → S 8 → WB, p. 98

D1 I1 Self-check 1.1

a Sum up each paragraph. Say if it primarily describes what is happening or Roo's feelings.

b Examine how language is used to convey the action and Roo's feelings and thoughts.

c Explain which inner and outer conflicts the main character is facing. → ○ 3

d Analyse the effect the author's language has on the reader.

6 Writing a personal letter → S 6.4 → G 8

D10 I10 Self-check 3.3

a Research arguments for and against supplying everyone with the same wage. Take notes.

b Write a letter to Roo in which you comment on the situation she finds herself in. Include arguments for and against the government's decision to supply everybody with the same wage regardless of their job, and the restrictions on how people spend their money.

A STEP FURTHER

A45 7 Listening → S 2

D11 I11 Self-check 4.0

a Listen to the podcast "Forward Thinking: Universal basic incomes" and answer the following questions.

1. What is a universal basic income?
2. What does Meghan say about the distribution of wealth in the world?
3. Which three places have experimented with a basic income?

b Listen again and list the arguments for and against a universal basic income mentioned.

c In class, collect more arguments for both sides.

Talking about likes and dislikes → G 9.2 → WB, p. 99

A Identify the gerund constructions in the following sentences about trade unions.

1. Standing up for employees' rights is the core principal of trade unions.
2. Trade unions are very effective at bargaining with employers on behalf of their members.
3. Many people might think that workers in trade unions enjoy going on strike to make their grievances heard, but it is often necessary.
4. Time and again, trade unions have succeeded in improving working conditions in many different industries.
5. Trade unions do not spend all their time organising strikes and protests.
6. The majority of interaction between trade unions and employers does not involve strikes. Instead, they often talk about maintaining or improving the employment conditions at any given company.
7. However, union members are not afraid of taking drastic action if necessary. Currently, workers are striking all over the world in arguments over pay, discrimination and working conditions.
8. Some people, however, decide against joining a union and prefer to deal with their employer directly.

B Look at the sentences again and find examples of the following uses of the gerund.

- the gerund after a preposition
- the gerund after verbs of preference
- the gerund as a noun
- the gerund with the construction *verb + preposition + gerund*

C Complete the sentences by choosing the correct verb and transforming it into a gerund. There are two verbs you do not need.

originate | improve | demand | protect | employ | exploit | strike | take

1. Many companies deny (…) their workers.
2. Trade unions around the world are dedicated to (…) the rights and interests of their members.
3. Attempts at (…) working conditions and payment are often more successful when employees are part of a union.
4. (…) in Great Britain, trade unions became common in many countries during the Industrial Revolution.
5. Companies may not like their employees (…), but they are not able to stop them from (…) to the streets.

MK **D** Your English friend is interested in trade unions in Germany. Go online and research information about well-known German trade unions and their main tasks and concerns. Then write a short English text using at least five gerund constructions.

C Inequality at work

BEFORE YOU READ

1 Think – Pair – Share

a Make a list of challenges women may face in the world of work.

b Compare your list with a partner's and agree on the top three challenges.

c Share your list with another pair and decide on a final ranking.

Gender pay gap begins for students straight after university [...]

1 The gender pay gap in favour of men begins the moment students graduate from university, according to employment data published for the first time that also reveals black graduates are more likely to struggle in the labour market. Figures collected by universities from graduates entering the workforce found that men had already begun earning on average 10% more than women just 15 months after they left university, and that even among graduates with similar qualifications there remained a wide gap in pay.

2 The figures, published by the Higher Education Statistics Agency (Hesa), show that most 2018 graduates who gained their first degree and were in full-time paid UK employment were earning between £24,000 and £27,000 a year. But on average, men were better represented in the higher earning brackets. Only 16% of women graduates with a first degree earned more than £30,000 within 15 months, compared with 28% of men. In the highest bracket men had double the representation: 6% of men earned more than £39,000 a year after graduation, compared with 3% of women.

3 "No sooner than a year after young women have returned their graduation gowns, those who have a job find themselves worse off than their male counterparts," said Joe Levenson of the Young Women's Trust, an organisation advocating for economic justice for women aged 18 to 30.
"If these inequalities are to be tackled, we need to smash career stereotypes, which are leaving young women locked out of better-paid careers. Gender pay gap reporting – suspended by the government during the coronavirus outbreak – needs to be reinstated immediately to shine a light on the inequalities existing in employers across the country. More work also needs to be done to ensure employers are transparent about pay and progression."

4 Results from the inaugural graduate outcomes survey showed that 81% of graduates were in employment or unpaid work, with 76% of those living in the UK working in highly skilled occupations. But only half of black university graduates were in full-time employment more than a year after they left, compared with more than 60% of white students. And while only 3% of white graduates were unemployed 15 months after finishing their first degree, twice as many black graduates were, at 6%, as well as 7% of Asian graduates.

5 Chris Millward of the Office for Students, the higher education regulator for England, said the more detailed

23 **earning brackets** Gehaltsstufen
33 **gown** Umhang; Kleid
51 **inaugural** Eröffnungs-; Erst-

80 **MP** Abkürzung für *Member of Parliament*; Unterhausabgeordnete/-r (UK)
86 **GCSE (General Certificate of Secondary Education)** allgemeiner Abschluss der weiterführenden Schulen in GB
86 **A-level** Abschluss auf Abiturniveau in GB

responses from the data revealed that graduates felt their post-graduation work was meaningful and they were applying things they learned at university or college. "There is clearly more still to do to ensure that these benefits are felt equally across all student groups. It is concerning that black, Asian and minority ethnic graduates were more likely to be unemployed than their white peers, and that women are over-represented in lower pay bands," Millward said. [...]

6 A survey published by the Labour MP Afzal Khan found that 80% of pupils in England are concerned about the predicted grades they will receive this summer, with BAME students concerned that racial bias will influence the grades they are awarded in GCSEs or A-levels.

(526 words)

Richard Adams, *The Guardian*, 2020

WORKING WITH THE TEXT

2 Reading for gist → WB, p. 100/1

Come up with a heading for each of the paragraphs 1–6.

3 Reading for detail

a Explain the problem facing women after they leave university.

b Illustrate the difference between the average pay of men and women in the higher earning brackets. Include examples from the text.

c Describe the difference in situation between Black graduates and white graduates one year after having left university.

d Point out what BAME students are worried about regarding their exams.

4 Words matter → S 16.3

Explain the following words and expressions in your own words. Use a bilingual dictionary to help you.

1. a first degree (l. 19)
2. to be transparent (l. 49)
3. to ensure (l. 48)
4. counterparts (l. 35)
5. inaugural (l. 51)
6. to be over-represented (l. 78)
7. to advocate for sth (l. 37)
8. post-graduation (l. 69)

D1 I1
Self-check 1.1

5 Focus on analysis → S 8.2

a Point out the function of each of the paragraphs 1 to 6.

b Decide if the article is written in a more formal or informal style. Give reasons and line numbers.

c Analyse whether the author, Richard Adams, includes his opinion on the topic. Give reasons.

6 Working with an infographic → S 11.4

D6 I6
Self-check 1.6

Describe and analyse the infographic and discuss with a partner how it relates to the text.

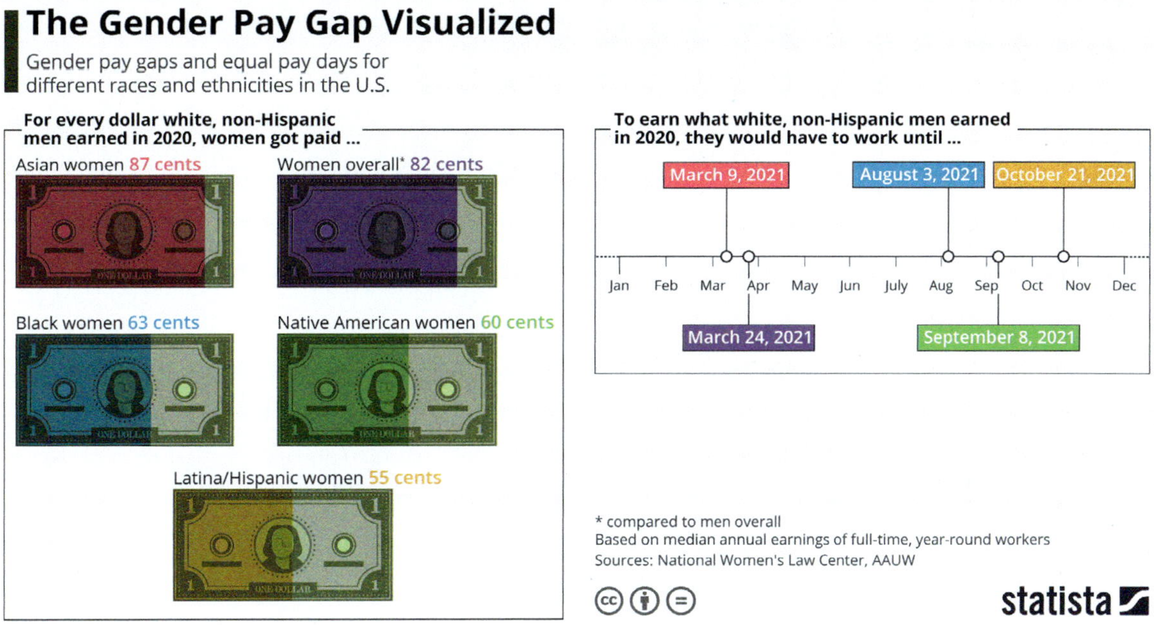

7 Writing an email → S 6.4 → ○ 4

D10 I10
Self-check 3.3

Write an email to the author in which you give your opinion on the issues raised in the article and make suggestions for what can be done to reduce the gender and ethnicity pay gap. Include information from the text and the statistics.

A STEP FURTHER

8 Online research

MK

Go online and try to find information about university graduates in Germany. How do male and female graduates compare in terms of entry-level wages? Make a 3–5-minute presentation about your findings.

9 Focus on grammar → G 9.2

Come up with your own ideas to complete these sentences and use a gerund.

1. This social affairs minister is a very interesting person. I always enjoy ...
2. I feel that my boss does not treat me fairly, but I don't dare ...
3. I'm afraid there aren't any open positions at our company at the moment. I suggest ...
4. It wasn't a well-paid job offer, so I decided against ...
5. The way women are looked down at in this company is shocking! I can't stop ...
6. My employer is very accommodating concerning my work schedule. I don't mind ...

D11 I11
Self-check 4.0

10 Listening → S2, S3 →WB, p.100/2

A46

You are going to listen to an excerpt from the podcast "More or Less" which deals with the topic of the 'gender pay gap'. While listening, answer the questions below. You don't need to write complete sentences.

1. What does the journalist Fraser Nelson claim?
2. What is the principle of 'equal pay'?
3. How many women work part-time compared to men?
4. What is the difference between full-time and part-time wages?
5. In which respect is Fraser Nelson's claim correct?
6. What are the IFS's (Institute for Fiscal Studies) findings?

D6 I6
Self-check 1.6

11 Working with a cartoon → S11.3

Describe and analyse the cartoon and explain how it relates to the podcast you have just heard.

D Workforce of the future

BEFORE YOU READ

1 Thinking about robots in the workforce

a Speculate on what Germany might learn from Japan in tackling changes in its demographic structure and workforce. Take notes and exchange your ideas with a partner.

b How could robots be helpful in the following fields of work? Create a mind map with your ideas. Discuss the results in class.

healthcare | education | administration | production

What the world can learn from Japan's robots

Japan is rolling out robots in nursing homes, offices and schools as its population ages and workforce shrinks. What can it teach other countries facing the same problems?

Japan is changing: a rapidly ageing society, a record-breaking influx of visitors from overseas, and more robots than ever. That's where the country's young people come in. *Gen J*, a new series by *BBC Worklife*, keeps you up to speed on how the nation's next generation is shaping the Japan of tomorrow.

At a sleek office building in Shinagawa, Tokyo, workers are strolling in and out for lunch. As they walk through the glass doors, they pass two security guards, each dutifully flanking the passage in stern silence. It all seems pretty unremarkable, until you realise one of those security guards is a robot. Standing up to five feet tall with wheels and a blue police cap, "his" name is Ugo. His battery lasts up to half a workday, and every two hours he'll do a routine patrol around the building – even summoning lifts by pushing the call button himself. His digital "face" – which usually displays two big blue cartoony eyes – is replaced with the Japanese text for "on duty".

"It's important for the robot to feel cute, so you're not intimidated," says Ken Matsui, CEO of Mira Robotics, the start-up behind Ugo. Right now, the police bot – whose built-in camera allows guards downstairs to see things from the robot's point of view – is one of only two prototypes in the country. But Matsui says companies in China and South Korea are interested in his company's work, which also includes cleaning robots for use in houses and schools.

In recent years, headlines, pundits and politicians have often warned that we're in the midst of a job-stealing robot revolution; but roboticists argue that their creations will complement, rather than replace, us. In Japan, the robots are already here – what's more, many are actively embracing the robot age, from suburban nursing homes to the highest levels of government, which announced an investment of 100bn yen ($100m) in robot development a few years ago. Some entities are even highlighting robotic colleagues as a selling point to young, new recruits. [...]

In Tokyo's Silver Wing nursing home, about two dozen seniors are sitting in the common area as pudding cups are distributed. In the middle of the room is a staff member and a humanoid robot named Pepper, who is leading the room in group games and exercises. [...] But it's not only in the common room that robotics is being employed. Upstairs, staff have access to robotic exoskeletons that fit

2 **to roll sth out** etw auf den Markt bringen
10 **to keep sb up to speed** jdn auf dem Laufenden halten
17 **to flank** flankieren
24 **routine patrol** Routinerundgang
25 **to summon a lift** einen Aufzug rufen
42 **pundit** Experte/Expertin
43 **to be in the midst of** mittendrin sein
54 **entity** Einheit
66 **exoskeleton** Außenskelett; tragbares Exoskelett

68 **body strain** körperliche Belastung
75 **fertility rate** Geburtenrate
88 **advisory firm** Beratungsfirma
99 **top vendor** Spitzenlieferant

around the waist and lower back: these apparatuses ease the severe body strain as they help their elderly clients get in and out of bed. (Some studies have shown that over 80% of nurses in Japan experience lower back problems.)

"Japan is facing major demographic challenges due to the elderly wave, low fertility rates and a shrinking population. This leads to a number of issues facing Japanese society which the West can learn from," says Roger A Søraa, robotics researcher at Centre for Technology and Society in Norway. "Elderly care facilities and hospitals see a severe lack of healthcare workers; there are not enough humans to do the tasks the way they used to be done." [...]

Still, whether Japan will lead a 'robots in the workforce' revolution remains unclear. Rian Whitton, senior robotics analyst at global tech market advisory firm ABI Research, says that robot deployment in places like nursing homes is low in practice and that Japan's recently eased rules for low-wage migrant workers show that the government knows widespread automation isn't yet possible. He also points out that China and the US, for example, are quickly catching up to Japan in areas like homecare robotics. "Ultimately, Japan is going to go from the top vendor for robotics globally, as it used to be, to being a relatively strong player alongside Germany, South Korea, Singapore and Taiwan," he says. "[Japan] will lose influence relative to the Chinese and American robotics ecosystems." [...]

Yet in Japan's favour is its very long history of embracing robots, not fearing them. In the West, pop culture and media often frame robots as job-stealing Terminators itching to start a revolution. [...]

(717 words)

Bryan Lufkin, *BBC*, website, 2020

WORKING WITH THE TEXT

2 Reading for gist

a Summarise each paragraph in one sentence.

b Find a caption for each paragraph. → ○ 5

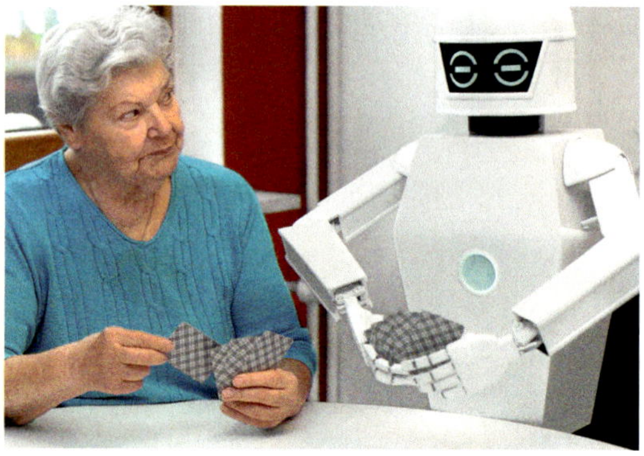

3 Reading for detail → WB, p. 101/1

a State the professional sectors robots are working in.

b Explain why robots should "feel cute" (l. 30) according to Ken Matsui.

c Outline Japan's demographic challenges and workforce revolution.

4 Words matter

a Write down ten important words from the text referring to robots in social life. Give line numbers.

b Compare your words with a partner and agree on 15 words. Give reasons.

c Compare your list with that of another pair. Agree on the 20 most important words and write them on index cards. Put the cards in a pile and take turns to pick a card. Talk for 30 seconds about the word in the context of the changing world of work.

5 Focus on analysis → S 8

D1 I1 Self-check 1.1

a Decide if the article is written in a more informal or formal style. Give reasons. → ○ 6

b Find examples in the text where the author addresses the reader directly.

c Analyse the language the author uses to establish a relationship with the reader and explain the effects stylistic devices used have on the reader. Include line numbers.

6 Writing an argumentative essay → S 6.3 → ○ 7

D8 I8 Self-check 3.1

"In the West, pop culture and media often frame robots as job-stealing Terminators itching to start a revolution." (ll. 106–109) Discuss whether German society is reluctant in embracing robot technology and include the message from the statement in your argumentative essay.

A STEP FURTHER

7 Giving a presentation → S 14.1

D12 Self-check 5.0

MK a Go online and research on a specific type of robot (e.g. chatbots, avatars, packbots) in a certain area of work (e.g. manufacturing, administration). Take notes on the robot's tasks and list both benefits and drawbacks this might have.

b Prepare and give your presentation. It should not be longer than five minutes. The audience gives feedback on content, language and style.

8 Discussion → G 8

Conduct a debate on the question "Should robots take care of elderly people?"

a Do a class survey on who is for and who is against robots working in healthcare. Note down the result.

b Team up in groups of four: two students are in favour of robots as health carers and two are against it. Make a list with arguments to support your point of view. Also counter-arguments, so you can react to them more easily in the discussion.

c Debate the question in your group presenting your pro and con arguments. After exchanging your arguments, make a list with the three strongest pro and con arguments. Share your findings in class.

d Do a second survey on who is now in favour of or against robots. Note down the result and compare it with the first survey. Discuss possible reasons for changes in opinion.

9 Working with a video

a Before you watch the video "The changing workforce", read the following short text by Capucine Yeomans. Then discuss with a partner how automation and robots could influence the types of jobs available to humans in the not-too-distant future. Report back to the class.

You'll still be working with robots

[Dreading] the day a robot replaces you? Fear not! There'll be plenty of jobs when our AI overlords take over, *Business Insider* predicts. Consider becoming a Voice UX Designer, [...] to make the machines sound more like us. As a "Joy Adjutant" you could coach fellow humans to appreciate that less is more. Bigger ambitions? Evidently companies will need a Chief Purpose Planner to "define and articulate their contribution to society." See? Nothing to worry about.

Capucine Yeomans, 2018

V9 **b** Now watch the video twice. While watching, note down the correct answer. There is only one correct answer to each question. → S 2

1. Surveys have shown that almost 40 % of people in the UK think that if their job didn't exist, it would ...
   A make no difference at all.
   B cause companies major problems.
   C save the government a lot of money.

2. According to Timandra, a profession that is being changed dramatically by robots is ...
   A care work.
   B education.
   C legal services.
3. David suggests that it would be better for society if everybody received ...
   A money according to the value their job has for society.
   B the same amount of money regardless of their job.
   C money according to their individual needs and family size.
4. According to Timandra, it is very important to make sure that computer algorithms don't ...
   A take away all the control from humans.
   B contain a bias against a certain group of people.
   C develop beyond what we humans can understand.
5. David thinks that the job of a tube driver should not become automated because ...
   A human employees need these kind of jobs to have a purpose in life.
   B there are too many lives at stake and the technology is not advanced enough yet.
   C they do not just drive trains but also look after the people they transport.
6. The purpose of this talk show was to discuss ...
   A the threats an increasing dependence on machines pose on societies all around the world.
   B the changes and possibilities arising in the world of work and in society as a result of automation.
   C the skills and qualifications that will be needed by humans in order to compete with robots in the future.

Designing a social media job advert

In many industrialised countries, including Germany, there is a shortage of skilled workers in various professions. One strategy to combat these shortages is trying to attract skilled workers from abroad. Many companies use social networks to get themselves noticed and to promote open positions.

MK

Step 1 Work in groups. Research fields of occupation for your local region in which skilled workers are needed. You can browse through your local newspapers or use online search engines. Choose one industry you would like to focus on and invent a company that operates in this field.

Step 2 Brainstorm ideas of what should be included in the social media post to attract skilled workers for this particular industry. Consider the following aspects:

company profile | job requirements and qualifications | perks and benefits

Step 3 Create a short social media post to be published on various social media networks. Your post should contain:

- a simple, attention-grabbing heading
- a clear structure
- (a) visual element(s)
- a strong closing message

You can use the example below to help you complete the task.

Interior Intelligence / Audio Systems Engineer

Are you ready to shape the future of the car? Become part of the Interior Intelligence team and help revolutionise the experience of driving!

THE POSITION
- Analysis of customer requirements for audio systems
- Development of in-car acoustic systems based on customer requirements
- Design and construction of prototypes
- Testing of new components and systems
- Presentation of development and test results

THE PERSON
- Degree in electrical or communications engineering or equivalent qualification
- 2–3 years of professional experience desirable
- Knowledge of technical acoustics and the development of automotive electronics
- High level of initiative and commitment, communication and team skills
- A strong desire to find solutions
- Driving licence
- Good knowledge of German and English

Like the way this sounds? Click here to find out more and apply.

Step 4 Present your post to the other groups. Give each other feedback on whether or not the material could be successful in attracting skilled employees and how it might be improved.

12 **commute** Strecke zur Arbeit
15 **to be rewarded** ausgezeichnet werden; belohnt werden
16 **sole** einzige/-r; alleinige/-r
28 **extended** ausgedehnt

The world of work now and then

Following her interview on the *Forward Thinking* podcast, sociologist Melanie Bishop and her father Oscar talk more about changes in the world of work.

Oscar: Things have certainly changed a lot throughout my career. I've been with the company for over 30 years now and I've worked hard to become one of the managing directors. I'm proud of my achievements but they came at the cost of my private life. Without the support of my wife, I would never have been able to give 100 % for the company. When Melanie and her two brothers were growing up, I wasn't around very much. Leaving early, two-hour commutes and arriving home after the kids were already in bed was normal for me. My colleagues and I regularly clocked up 50–60 hours a week and the idea of a **work-life balance** simply did not exist. Many of the people I worked with were prepared to invest a lot of time and energy into the company, hoping to be rewarded with **promotions** and **financial security**. As a father of three and the sole breadwinner, the idea of a **job for life** was very appealing. My wife took care of things at home and I tried to provide for the family. It may sound old-fashioned, and even outdated now, but that is just the way it was – in the earlier days, anyway. Over the last decade or so, I've also seen many changes, mostly for the good. We not only have to prepare ourselves for widespread **automation** and developments in **artificial intelligence**, but also in terms of our workforce.

One positive development has been the number of **women in higher positions**, which has given a sense of balance to our company. Our company also prides itself on having a **diverse workforce** and we're constantly looking at ways to attract and keep talented workers. At a management level, we've had many discussions recently about new ways of working, such as **remote working**, a more flexible approach to working hours and increased opportunities to take extended **periods of leave**. I don't want our employees to miss out as I did for so many years.

Where Do Employees Work Longer Than 9 To 5?

*% of employees working more than 50 hours per week on average in selected countries**

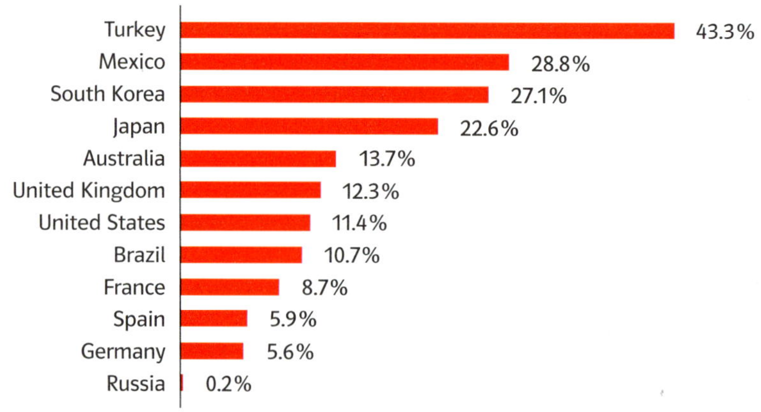

*Latest available year

Source: OECD

Melanie: It is not enough to say that things have changed. The world of work has to constantly develop and **move with the times**. For example, it may be true that many companies are looking to promote diversification among their employees, but in the UK, there is still not enough support in terms of **trade unions** and **BAME employees**. And even though many companies are doing more to recruit and promote women to positions of authority, we're still a long way behind other countries. If you ask me, one major obstacle is that we place too much **emphasis on experience**, and not enough on **talent** and **potential**. The idea that only people that have had decades on the job can make key decisions automatically puts many women at a disadvantage. Regardless of gender and background, many people now want different things from their job. Of course, money and financial security will always be an important factor, but nowadays many people are **not committed to one employer** as they were in my father's generation and before him. In fact, a recent study suggested that there are a number of benefits to changing your job every few years. For example, you can learn **new skills** by challenging yourself and leaving your **comfort zone**. Furthermore, by switching employers you can develop new relationships, take control of your own career and even earn more money. However, it's also important to say that **job security** is not as prevalent with more people working on **short-term** or **freelance agreements**, or even **zero-hour contracts** where the employer is not obliged to provide the employee a minimum number of working hours.

Many young people are thinking not only about what they want to do, but also whom they want to work for. Companies that operate in a **sustainable**, **ethical** and **environmentally friendly** manner are becoming very attractive employers. How we choose to live our life, what we stand for and what we do for a living can no longer be separated. One thing is clear though: Employees of the future need to be adaptable, multi-skilled and willing to learn.

33 **to promote** fördern; unterstützen; voranbringen
49 **prevalent** weit verbreitet
50 **to be obliged to** verpflichtet sein, etw zu tun; müssen

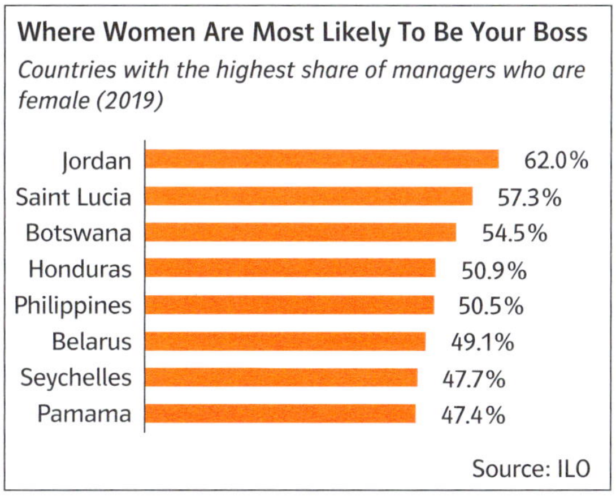

1 Work with a partner and discuss the pros and cons of the world of work at the time when Oscar began his career.

2 Team up with another pair and compare your pros and cons.

3 Choose one of the graphs, describe it and analyse it in relation to the text.

Outlook: For further discussion, consider the following questions:
- What can be done to help young people choose which career path to take?
- Which advantages and disadvantages do you see with more employees working remotely?
- What do you think will be major changes in the world of work in the next 5–10 years and how might they affect your generation?

1 Lesen und Schreiben

Forget stereotypes ... how to recruit talented, neurodiverse employees

By improving workplaces and recruitment, firms can attract neurodiverse talent. Entrepreneurs and workers with autism and dyspraxia offer advice.

James Neely used to work in an open-plan office. His journey to work included busy, stressful train journeys. "I tended to isolate myself from people, so I had my headphones on and turned up all day and I wore a cap to limit my peripheral vision and reduce the light," he says.

However, the 33-year-old data analyst struggled to find the quiet he needed at work. Eventually he had a breakdown. During subsequent treatment for anxiety and depression he was diagnosed with an autistic spectrum condition.

Neely now works for Auticon, a company that employs 15 full time IT consultants who have autism. They work on projects at major companies in the UK, including Experian and GlaxoSmithKline. Neely's found comfort in his new role. "We have back-office support from project managers and job coaches," he says. This takes off some of the pressure if a difficult situation arises.

The job coaches encourage Auticon's consultants to take regular time off, which, Neely says, helps to "avoid the build up of anxiety or sensory overload". They also assist them with prioritising tasks and ensure the workplace environment is comfortable.

In the UK, just 16 % of autistic adults are in full time employment, according to the National Autistic Society. And yet research has shown autistic traits can be associated with high numbers of unusual responses on divergent thinking tasks; a mark of creativity, which is sought after by ambitious startups. Meanwhile, research from University of Montreal suggests that people with autism are up to 40 % better at problem solving.

Ray Coyle, Auticon's CEO, says there's a strong business case for employing neurodiverse people. One of Auticon's clients, Siemens, say the two Auticon consultants who were working for them increased the team's product testing efficiency by 50 % within their first week. Coyle adds: "The fact that Auticon is profitable [revenues have grown by around 50 % each year since 2014] shows that our business model is sound and reflects the quality of our workforce."

Dr Linda Buchan is director of Cheshire-based Axia-ASD Ltd, which offers assessment services, including for autism spectrum disorders. She says while running a small business with neurodiverse staff can bring particular challenges, the benefits are clear. Buchan has dyspraxia. She says many people assume dyspraxia just affects coordination, but it goes much further. "Dyspraxia can affect any muscle groupings in the body, it can affect your sense of time, distance and visual tracking too."

For Buchan, who employs 11 people, dyspraxia affects her ability to do admin; she struggles with dates and finds writing difficult. To stay organised, she relies on lists. But she also notes the positive sides. "Dyspraxic people can go off on tangents and that can take you to a really interesting place. We're good at noticing detail and we can be good at innovating and coming up with off-the-wall ideas." [...]

Sarah Hendrickx, an autism consultant and trainer, suggests that simple changes can make a huge difference to neurodiverse people's experience of work. "[For example, neurodiverse] people can find it difficult to take in a lot of information from multiple sources at once." This can make group meetings a challenge, and so Hendrickx recommends providing an agenda in plenty of time, that minutes are taken and that clear action points are emailed to attendees afterwards.

The recruitment process could be better streamlined too, adds Hendrickx. She is autistic, dyslexic and has Tourette syndrome, and was diagnosed as an adult: "Some highly talented, unusual thinkers may have struggled for many years to find their niche, and [might] not look great on paper." [...] (621 words)

Hazel Davis, *The Guardian*, 2017

ASSIGNMENTS → WB, pp. 103–104/1–4

1. Outline the situation of autistic adults in the workforce in the UK.
2. Analyse the structure of the text. Consider how difficulties and support for neurodiverse employees are presented in order to get the central message across.
3. Choose one of the following tasks:

3.1 Discuss which opportunities and challenges companies might be faced with when employing people with physical disabilities or neurodiverse people. Make use of the text, definition and the quote below.

Inclusion in the world of work refers to a concept wherein people with physical or mental disabilities work together with people without disabilities. In an inclusive work environment, employees with special needs are provided with the necessary equipment, a working atmosphere and changes in work processes that help them fulfil their tasks. It makes people feel welcome and valued.

"I have Aspergers and that means I'm sometimes a bit different from the norm. And – given the right circumstances – being different is a superpower."

Greta Thunberg, Swedish climate activist

Or:

3.2 You are doing an internship at an international insurance company which has only a small percentage of employees with disabilities. As a member of the youth and trainee council you are asked to prepare a speech for the next staff meeting in which you point out the advantages of having people with disabilities as colleagues and employees. Write the speech.

2 Hörverstehen

ASSIGNMENTS → WB, pp. 104–105/1–2

A47 You will hear a podcast about stay-at-home dads and the challenges they face. While listening, answer the questions below. You do not need to write complete sentences.

1. What is the governmental scheme "shared parental leave" criticised for?
2. What experience are stay-at-home dads often faced with? Give an example.
3. After having cared for his children for 14 years, what did Ian Blithe decide to do? Give a reason.
4. What happened to him during a photo shoot in the forest?
5. What increased his feeling of loneliness?
6. Why did Ian receive many comments like "giving mum a break, are you?" when he went shopping with his children?

3 Kommunikation

Monologue

You are a guest on a talk show that is discussing the attitude about work and what young people can bring to the workplace. Give a 5-minute presentation on work attitudes based on the following quotation, the cartoon and the diagram.

Quotation

"Developing a good work ethic is key. Apply yourself at whatever you do, whether you're a janitor or taking your first summer job because that work ethic will be reflected in everything you do in life."

Tyler Perry, US actor and director

Cartoon

Describe and analyse the cartoon and refer it to the quotation.

Diagram

Describe and analyse the diagram. Relate it to the cartoon and the quote.

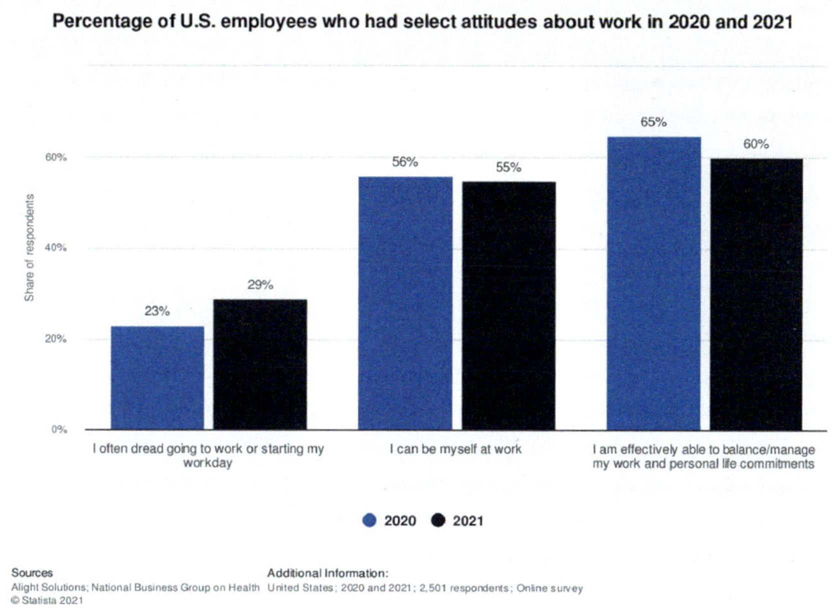

Dialogue → WB, p.105

In the talk show, other topics are brought up. Be prepared to discuss the positive and negative effects of teleworking and automation on the world of work.

D7 I7
Self-check 2

Social change in consumption

Shopping habits are important economic indicators which is why many companies commission surveys on them. You are a trainee at an international social research institute. Your trainer asks you to write a business email to Mr Blacksmith, who plans a research project on changing consumer behaviour. To complete the task, you are given an article and you are asked to inform Mr Blacksmith about changing consumer behaviour in Germany.

Die Generation Z entdeckt den stationären Handel

Um die junge und kaufstarke Generation anzusprechen, sollten Händler nicht nur in E-Commerce investieren, sondern auch stationäre Filialen aufpeppen. Denn die Gen Z schätzt den Ladenbummel.

Was motiviert die Generation Z zum Kauf und welche Anforderungen hat die junge Zielgruppe an den Handel? Welche Rolle spielen Smartphones und soziale Netzwerke für ihr Einkaufsverhalten? Und welche Bedeutung hat der stationäre Handel für die Gen Z?

Diesen Fragen geht eine Studie des Commerce-Marketing-Dienstleisters Criteo nach. Der *Gen-Z-Report* [...] analysiert das Einkaufsverhalten der kaufstarken jungen Generation (Jahrgang ca. 1995 bis 2010). Befragt wurden 940 Personen in den USA, Großbritannien, Frankreich, Deutschland, Brasilien und Japan.
„Zehn Prozent der deutschen Bevölkerung gehören der Generation Z an; das entspricht acht Millionen potenziellen Käufern und damit immensen Möglichkeiten für Händler und Marketingtreibende", sagt Alexander Gösswein, Regional Managing Director [...] bei Criteo.

Bummeln beliebt

Ein Fazit der Studie sollte stationäre Händler aufhorchen lassen: Nicht nur E-Commerce ist wichtig, die jungen Käufer lieben auch den Ladenbummel. Und wollen dort entsprechend angesprochen werden. „Was bei den Millennials noch die Regel war, gilt nicht uneingeschränkt auch für die Gen Z, denn: Diese Generation hat trotz des omnipräsenten Smartphones das stationäre Einkaufen wieder für sich entdeckt", erklärt Gösswein. „Für Händler ergeben sich daraus zwei Schlussfolgerungen: Einerseits gilt es, diese mobile-fokussierte Generation mit einem hohen Grad an Personalisierung anzusprechen, was auch Ads und Apps beinhaltet. Andererseits gewinnen überzeugende Omnichannel-Konzepte zusätzlich an Bedeutung."
Die Gen Z ist jung und mobil, will Neuheiten und Erfahrungen – auch im Handel. Die Instagram-Generation lebe von Visuals und erwarte dies auch von Händlern: coole und ästhetische Online-Erfahrungen mit perfekt in Szene gesetzten Produkten. Criteo rät deshalb, dass Händler nicht nur ihre Online-Shops, sondern auch die stationären Geschäfte in Sachen Präsentation und Design auf das nächste Level heben. „Händler und Brands, die die Gen Z und ihre Bedürfnisse wertschätzen, gewinnen ihre Loyalität – durch personalisierte Erlebnisse, z.B. Limited Editions bestimmter Produkte, durch außergewöhnliche und besondere Angebote und durch auffällige Stores", so die Experten.

Die wichtigsten Erkenntnisse des Gen Z Reports:

Enorme Kaufkraft: Sowohl online als auch offline verfügt Gen Z über eine signifikante Kaufkraft. Durchschnittlich geben sie dabei online 220 USD (offline: 169 USD) für Unterhaltungselektronik aus, für Kleidung online 188 USD (offline 177 USD) [...], gerechnet auf einen Zeitraum von sechs Monaten.

Mobile First: Keine andere Generation verbringt mehr Zeit an Mobilgeräten: Mit 11 Stunden durchschnittlicher Online-Zeit pro Woche – ohne Arbeit und Mails – ist Gen Z absoluter Spitzenreiter in Sachen Mobile.
Neuere Soziale Netzwerke: 49 Prozent der befragten Gen Z nutzen mehrmals täglich Instagram, bei Snapchat sind es 43 Prozent. Überraschend ungeschlagen ist jedoch Facebook, das von 59 Prozent der Befragten mehrmals genutzt wird. Von geringerer Relevanz ist Twitter mit 23 Prozent.
I'm a Streamer, Baby: Ob Fernsehserien, Musikvideos oder Podcasts. Die Generation Z liebt es, Content online zu streamen. Durchschnittlich verbringen die 16- bis 24-Jährigen insgesamt 22 Stunden mit Online-Video-Content pro Woche.
Stationärer Handel weiterhin wichtig: Gen Z liebt neben Technologie auch die Haptik: Sie wollen Produkte erleben und fühlen, bevor sie sich für den eigentlichen Kauf entscheiden. Während 77 Prozent angaben, so viel wie möglich online zu shoppen, gehen 80 Prozent gerne im stationären Handel einkaufen, wenn es ihre Zeit zulässt.
Retail Websites und Apps sind einflussreich: Über 50 Prozent der Gen Z gaben an, dass Händlerwebsites und -apps mehr Einfluss auf ihr Kaufverhalten haben als Search, Fernsehwerbung oder auch Online-Ads.
Vorbereiteter denn je: Webrooming ist bei der Gen Z populärer als Showrooming. 34 Prozent gaben an, dass sie sich Produkte zuerst gerne online ansehen, bevor sie sie anschließend im Laden kaufen. Im Laden angesehene Ware kaufen dagegen nur 23 Prozent später online.
Alles personalisiert: Gen Z will alles personalisiert haben, auch Anzeigen. 63 Prozent sagen, dass sie Anzeigen mögen, die einen Mehrwert für sie bieten.
(622 Wörter)

Frauke Schobelt, *Verlag Werben & Verkaufen GmbH*, 2018

1 Words matter

a Find English equivalents for the expressions from the text. Use a dictionary.

1. kaufstarke Generation (l. 2)
2. stationäre Filialen aufpeppen (l. 5)
3. Händler aufhorchen lassen (l. 31)
4. perfekt in Szene gesetzt (l. 55)
5. absoluter Spitzenreiter sein (l. 81)
6. einen Mehrwert bieten (l. 122)

b Look at the compound nouns from the text and express them in English.

Ladenbummel | Einkaufsverhalten | Marketingtreibende | Unterhaltungselektronik | Mobilgeräte | Händlerwebsite

2 Writing a business email → S 13.2

D 10 I 10
Self-check 3.3

a List the examples of changing shopping habits given in the text.

b Find arguments that could convince Mr Blacksmith to start his project.

c Write a formal email to Mr Blacksmith informing him about changing consumer behaviour in Germany and recommending to start the research project.

USEFUL PHRASES

I am writing to inform you that …
In addition, I would like to …
If I can be of any further assistance, please let me know.
For further details …

D 7 I 7
Self-check 2

The British history you may not know about

You are doing an internship at a musem in the UK. The museum is preparing an exhibition of photographs and artefacts documenting the horrors of slavery. You have been asked to write an informative handout which will be given out at the exhibition, explaining how Britain is facing up to its hidden history of slavery. You have found the following article as a source for your handout.

Großbritannien und der lange Schatten der Sklaverei

Das patriotische Lied „Rule Britannia" versprach den Briten, sie würden „niemals Sklaven sein". Viele Nicht-Briten konnten davon nur träumen. Ein Blick auf eine aktuelle Debatte im Vereinigten Königreich.

Das Interesse an den Ursprüngen und Auswirkungen des Sklavenhandels hat in Großbritannien sprunghaft zugenommen, seitdem im Zuge der US-Bewegung „Black Lives Matter" auch im Vereinigten Königreich Statuen niedergerissen werden. Das Land war im 17. und 18. Jahrhundert tief in den Sklavenhandel verstrickt. [...]

Nach Berechnungen des Historikers David Richardson haben britische Schiffe mindestens 3,4 Millionen gefangene Afrikaner nach Amerika transportiert. [...]

Profite durch Sklavenarbeit

Im Rahmen des „Atlantischen Dreieckshandels" segelten mit Waren beladene Schiffe von Großbritannien zur Küste Westafrikas und tauschten die Waren gegen Sklaven, die lokale Herrscher gefangengenommen hatten. Die Sklaven wurden über den Atlantik transportiert und zur Arbeit auf Plantagen gezwungen. Die Produkte dieser Sklavenarbeit – für den Export bestimmte Pflanzen, Zucker oder Rum, wurden dann von den Schiffen zurück nach Großbritannien gebracht.

Vor allem Zuckerplantagen machten britische Kolonien besonders wertvoll. Und auf britischer Seite entwickelten sich Bristol, Glasgow und Liverpool durch den Handel bis Ende des 18. Jahrhunderts zu bedeutenden Hafenstädten.

„Großbritanniens Sklavenwirtschaft war riesig und äußerst komplex", so Ryan Hanley, Geschichtsdozent an der Universität Exeter, zur DW. „Es ist zwar nicht möglich, die britischen Gewinne aus der Sklaverei genau zu beziffern. Sicher ist aber, dass die Wirtschaft von der Ausbeutung afrikanischer Sklaven in der Karibik enorm profitiert hat." [...]

„Sklaverei und Kolonialismus waren zudem eng verbunden mit der Entwicklung der Finanzinfrastruktur, die Großbritannien in die Lage versetzte, sich als wirtschaftliches und imperiales globales Kraftzentrum des 19. Jahrhunderts zu etablieren", so Hanley. [...]

„Der Bau der Eisenbahnstrecken, jenes Symbols des industriellen Fortschrittes im viktorianischen Zeitalter, wurde zu einem Großteil durch Mittel finanziert, die Sklavenhalter nach Abschaffung der Sklaverei als Entschädigungszahlung erhalten hatten", sagt Hanley.

Einige Historiker bezweifeln jedoch, dass der Sklavenhandel die britische Alltagswirtschaft so grundlegend durchdrungen hat. „Wenn es um Ernährung, Kleidung und Unterkunft ging, dann hat so gut wie niemand auf Produkte zurückgegriffen, die durch Sklavenarbeit entstanden sind", sagt David Eltis, britischer Professor für Geschichte an der Emory University im US-Bundesstaat Georgia, der auch die Website slavevoyages.org betreibt. „Zucker, Kaffee und Rum spielten in der britischen Ernährung damals kaum eine Rolle", so Eltis zur DW. Auch eine angebliche Verbindung zwischen Sklaverei und

Industrialisierung sieht er kritisch und verweist darauf, dass die größten Sklavenhändler auf dem amerikanischen Kontinent die Portugiesen waren, und Brasilien das Land mit den meisten Sklaven. [...]

Abschaffung und Entschädigung

Erst mit dem Slavery Abolition Act von 1833 wurde die Sklaverei im britischen Empire endgültig abgeschafft. Sklavenbesitzer auf den British West Indies in der Karibik erhielten Entschädigungen von insgesamt 20 Millionen Pfund. Schätzungen zufolge wäre das heute eine Summe von 20 Milliarden Pfund.

Damals entsprach der Betrag rund 40 Prozent des britischen Staatshaushalts. In der britischen Geschichte war es die größte Auszahlung durch den Staat vor der Bankenkrise ab 2008, als Finanzinstitute mit Milliardensummen gerettet wurden. [...]

„Nach der Abschaffung der Sklaverei wurde ein großes Unrecht begangen, denn nicht die Versklavten wurden entschädigt, sondern die Sklavenhalter", sagt Historiker Richard Toye.

Selektive Erinnerungen

„Wir sollten jetzt nicht versuchen, unsere Vergangenheit zu umschreiben oder zu zensieren", sagte der britische Premierminister Boris Johnson in der vergangenen Woche. Als Kolumnist für die Zeitschrift *The Spectator* hatte Johnson im Jahr 2002 geschrieben, die britische Kolonialgeschichte in Afrika sei „kein Schandfleck auf unserem Gewissen. (...) Das Problem ist nicht, dass wir einmal das Sagen hatten, sondern dass wir das Sagen nicht mehr haben".

Catherine Hall, die an der Universität London ein Forschungsprojekt über Sklaverei leitet, ist der Ansicht, das Thema werde im britischen Geschichtsbewusstsein einfach ausgeblendet. „Man erinnert sich eher an die Abschaffung als an den Sklavenhandel, und außerordentlich viele Menschen wissen nichts über Großbritanniens koloniale Vergangenheit im Zusammenhang mit der Sklaverei", sagte sie im BBC Radio.

Der Historiker David Olusoga schrieb in der Zeitung The Guardian, das britische Bildungssystem habe jahrzehntelang „Bitten und Forderungen abgelehnt", schwarze Geschichte zu einem zentralen Bestandteil des nationalen Lehrplans zu machen.

„Und so gibt es einen nationalen blinden Fleck, eine Lücke in unserem kollektiven Wissen, die uns alle betrifft – schwarz und weiß", schrieb Olusoga. [...] (686 Wörter)

Jo Harper, *dw.com*, 2020

1 Preparing a handout

a Look at the structure of the text. Come up with a suitable English heading for each of the main sections. Use the words and phrases from the word bank to help you.

abolition of slavery | Britain's approach | Britain's involvement | look to the future | history of the slave trade | compensation

b Identify important dates, facts and statistics from the text and look for additional keywords and phrases to include in your handout. Mediate them into English.

2 Writing an informative handout → S 6.7

D 9 I 9
Self-check 3.2

a Decide on a suitable structure for your informative handout.

b Write an informative handout for the exhibition summing up Britain's historical involvement in the slave trade and how the issue is dealt with today. Include dates, facts and statistics from the text.

D7 I7
Self-check 2

Global strategies for modern management

Your college is taking part in a workshop about leadership strategies in a globalised world. Students from 15 European vocational colleges, entrepreneurs and communication experts will discuss the role of cross-cultural communication in management. Each participant has to deliver a speech at the workshop, including key ideas on cross-cultural communication in successful international collaboration and their opinion on the topic. Use the following text as a basis for the manuscript of your speech.

Unternehmenskulturen in globaler Interaktion

Führung und Verantwortung in einer globalen Welt: Menschen integrieren – Kulturen respektieren

Führungskräfte und Mitarbeiter stehen heute vor Herausforderungen, deren Ausmaß wir uns noch vor Jahrzehnten kaum vorstellen konnten. Neben der Entwicklung neuer Technologien hat insbesondere die Globalisierung gravierende Umbrüche in Wirtschaft und Gesellschaft in Industrie- und Schwellenländern mit sich gebracht.

Wir leben daher weder in einem europäischen oder amerikanischen und auch nicht in einem asiatischen Jahrhundert – wir leben in einem globalen Jahrhundert! Die Konsequenz: Internationaler Wettbewerbsdruck, dynamische Umweltbedingungen und hoch komplexe Verflechtungen in Wirtschaft und Gesellschaft sowie sich ständig wandelnde Arbeitsformen erfordern neue Kompetenzen – nicht nur auf der Führungsebene, sondern im gesamten Unternehmen.

Wie aber können Unternehmen und ihre Mitarbeiter diesen Herausforderungen gerecht werden? Welche Strategien werden zukünftig im globalen Wettbewerb bestehen? Welche Konsequenzen ergeben sich für Standortentscheidungen und die Zusammenarbeit unterschiedlicher Kulturen? Wie können wir Mitarbeiter an die Flexibilität und Mobilität einer modernen Arbeitswelt heranführen, in der die Kolleginnen und Kollegen in Bombay, New York, Hongkong oder Rio de Janeiro sitzen?

Unternehmen reagieren in der Regel bis heute mit Fusionen und Akquisitionen, um schnelles Wachstum zu ermöglichen, Synergie- und Wettbewerbsvorteile zu erzielen und neue Märkte zu erschließen. Zukünftig werden aber auch Kooperationen mit Partnerunternehmen und die Nutzung internationaler Netzwerke, in denen Synergien je nach Produkt, Kunde oder Markt bedarfsgerecht und temporär ausgeschöpft werden, zunehmend an Bedeutung gewinnen. Innovative Technologien und Kommunikationsformen werden diesen Prozess noch unterstützen und die Entwicklungen beschleunigen! Sie erleichtern aber nicht nur die internationale Zusammenarbeit und vereinen Kollegen rund um den Globus – es führt auch dazu, dass viele Menschen angesichts der Schnelligkeit und des Umfangs der Veränderungen zunehmend Unsicherheiten und sogar Ängste spüren. Nimmt man die heute oft beschworene Forderung nach der gesellschaftlichen Verantwortung eines Unternehmens wörtlich, dann mündet dies im globalen Kontext in die Aufforderung: Menschen integrieren und Kulturen nicht entwurzeln.

Wie erfolgreich ein Unternehmen mit diesen und den noch zu entwickelnden Maßnahmen in der globalen Wirtschaft sein wird, liegt nicht nur an der Unternehmensführung, die über Strategie, Struktur und Prozesse entscheidet – der Erfolg wird von jedem einzelnen Mitarbeiter mitgetragen. Die Verpflichtung auf ein transparentes, nachvollziehbares Leitbild wird auch für global agierende Unternehmen zu einem Muss! Dabei wird man Grundwerte des gemeinsamen Umgangsmiteinander definieren können – aber diese Werte müssen immer auch den lokalen Gegebenheiten, Traditionen und Kulturen angepasst werden.

Der Vorbildfunktion der Führung kommt hier eine zentrale Bedeutung zu – auch die Gestaltung einer Unternehmenskultur ist „Chefsache"! Die globale Ausrichtung eines Unternehmens sollte aber nicht nur auf Führungsebene gestaltet und gelebt werden, sondern sie muss im Idealfall die gesamte Organisation und die Denkweise jedes Mitarbeiters erfassen. Es sind nicht allein Unternehmen, Divisionen oder Abteilungen, die international zusammenarbeiten – es sind in erster Linie die Menschen aus unterschiedlichen Kulturen.

Um sich gegenseitig zu verstehen, die Werte und Überzeugungen des anderen zu respektieren, mit ihm umzugehen und erfolgreich zusammenzuarbeiten, bedarf es einer besonderen Sensibilität, Toleranz, Achtung und Bescheidenheit. Diese interkulturelle Kompetenz wird mit der Globalisierung von Wirtschaft und Gesellschaft immer wichtiger. Denn wir stehen erst am Anfang einer Entwicklung, bei der immer mehr Menschen am Geschehen in einer globalen Welt teilhaben werden.

Die Globalisierung ist als Chance zu begreifen, die wir gemeinsam gestalten können. Unternehmen können sich nicht den internationalen Handelsbeziehungen entziehen – im Gegenteil: Sie sind für ihren unternehmerischen Erfolg darauf angewiesen. Sie benötigen dafür motivierte und kreative, leistungs- und veränderungsbereite Mitarbeiter, die sich mit dem Unternehmen und seinen Zielen, aber auch ihren Aufgaben identifizieren – unabhängig vom Standort und Land! Ein wichtiger Baustein ist die Schaffung einer partnerschaftlichen Unternehmenskultur, die von interkulturellem Denken und Handeln geprägt ist und weltweit zu Leistung und Innovation anregt. So gelingt es, eine Brücke über Sprachen und Grenzen hinweg zwischen den Menschen auch in der Arbeitswelt zu schlagen. Fachliche Fähigkeiten werden daher nicht mehr allein ausschlaggebend sein – sie müssen ergänzt werden durch soziale, emotionale und interkulturelle Kompetenzen! [...]

(628 Wörter)

Liz Mohn, *Bertelsmann Stiftung*, 2008

1 Preparing a speech

a Read the article and summarise each paragraph in a few words in German.

b Cluster all relevant points related to the message as expressed in the heading.

c Write short English sentences expressing the key ideas of the text.

d Decide on aspects to add which state your opinion about cross-cultural communication.

2 Writing a speech → S 6.6

a Decide on the structure and order of the information in your speech.

b Write the speech and choose suitable language considering the purpose and target group for the speech. Make sure that your style, tone and register are appropriate.

D 8 I 8
Self-check 3.1

USEFUL PHRASES

The first thing that needs to be said is …
We should all be aware that …
The majority of you might ask yourselves …
The other side of the coin is, however, that …
It's important to point out that …
Where does this lead us?
A good idea would be to …
In conclusion, …

The most important instructions (= *Operatoren*) that you will meet in this book and in your exam are listed below with their definitions and with sample sentences. The Roman numerals refer to the type of exercise involved: I = comprehension; II = analysis; III = comment.

Operatoren	Definitionen	Beispiele
analyse, examine II	describe and explain in detail certain aspects and/or features of the text	Analyse the opposing views on class held by the two protagonists. Examine the author's use of language.
assess III	consider in a balanced way the points for and against sth	Assess the importance of standards in education.
characterise II	describe and examine the way in which the character/s is/are presented	Characterise/Write a characterisation of the principal figures in the play.
comment III	to clearly express one's opinion and to give evidence in order to support one's view	Comment on the suggestion made in the text that a "lack of women in the armed forces demonstrates a weakness in the role of women in society".
compare II–III	point out similarities and differences	Compare X's and Y's views on education.
contrast II	emphasise the differences between two or more things	Contrast the author's idea of human aggression with the theories of aggression you have read about.
describe I–II	give a detailed account of sth	Describe the soldier's appearance. (I) Describe the way the author creates an atmosphere of suspense. (II)
discuss III	to consider different ideas or opinions (reasons for and against) about a topic and to eventually decide something	Discuss the implications of globalisation as presented in this text.
examine II	see "analyse"	
explain II	describe and define in detail	Explain the protagonist's obsession with money.
illustrate II	use examples to explain or make clear	Illustrate the author's use of metaphorical language.
interpret II–III	make clear the meaning of sth and give your own views on it	Interpret the message the author wishes to convey.
point out I–II	to find and present certain aspects	Point out the main reasons given for climate change in the text.
state I	specify clearly	State briefly the main developments in the family described in the text.
summarise, write a summary outline I	give a concise account of the main points give the main features or general principles of a topic, leaving out minor details	Summarise the information given in the text about the hazards of cloning. Outline the author's views on love, marriage and divorce.
present I	to find and show certain aspects in a structured way	Present the arguments in a coherent way.
Write (an email / a letter / a blog post etc.) III	to write a text in your own words according to the text type requested	Write a blog post commenting on your behaviour as a consumer.

Topic 1

GETTING STARTED

1 Working with an infographic → SB, p. 12, exercise 3

Consider these factors to explain the differences in the dates in the infographic.

- the country's population (e.g. size of the population, population density)
- the wealth and consumption patterns of a country's population
- the climate in the country
- the natural resources found in a country

2 Discussion → SB, p. 13, exercise 5

Discuss the following aspects that make up the ecological footprint of a person.

- food
- housing (e.g. appliances, materials, insulation)
- energy (e.g. transport, heating, light, warm water, use by appliances)
- clothes (e.g. production, disposal)
- consumption of goods
- packaging
- dealing with waste (e.g. avoiding, recycling, composting)

TEXT WORKSHOP B

3 Reading for gist → SB, p. 22, exercise 3

Use the following hints to match the correct subheadings with paragraphs 1–6.

A Why are Dutch courts leading on climate?
Look out for rules and clauses that make the Dutch system special.
B Which grounds for appeal does *Shell* have?
Search for the law which is violated by *Shell*.
C What was the *Shell* verdict?
Find the section which deals with a court ruling.
D How could *Shell* comply with the court?
Look for information on what *Shell* would have to do to follow the court ruling.
E What about *Shell's* longer-term targets?
Find details on *Shell's* plans.
F What does it mean for other companies?
Search for an answer to the question as to whether other companies can be treated in a similar way.

4 Focus on analysis → SB, p. 22, exercise 5

An argument is typically made up of the elements listed below. Copy the table and fill in examples of these elements in the text to help you analyse the structure of the arguments.

Statement	Explanation	Evidence (e.g. statistics, quotes, experience)	Examples	Critique / Counter-arguments (optional)
...	...	...	...	...

5 Writing a speech → SB, p. 22, exercise 6

You could address the following aspects and use these quotations to help you write your speech.

1. Shared responsibilities: Governments, companies and individuals

   Possible aspects:
   - the *Shell* case as a precedent
   - large corporations to be held responsible for the effects their actions have on the environment
   - profit versus responsibility
   - interpretation of human rights linked with responsibility for the environment
   - governments equally responsible (e.g. Paris Agreement)
   - individuals have power through elections, demonstrations etc.

   Possible quotations:
   - "[...] the oil giant is violating human rights by contributing to global warming." (ll. 6–8)
   - "[...] a 'duty of care' clause in the Dutch system which provided judges some liberty to interpret unwritten rules and consider links to human rights and the effect climate change has on the right to a healthy environment." (ll. 100–105)

2. Avoiding or offsetting? – how best to reduce CO_2 emissions

   Possible aspects:
   - websites that calculate prices to offset flights, bus trips etc.
   - 'net-zero' companies offset their carbon output
   - issues concerning efficiency
   - question if companies and individuals just try to buy a clean conscience and avoid more painful consequences
   - possibilities for companies to avoid carbon emissions in the best way
   - ways of reducing carbon emissions as individuals

   Possible quotations:
   - "[...] companies should focus first on cutting emissions and offset only those that can't be eliminated." (ll. 32–34)
   - "In *Shell's* case, opponents say it would have to plant an improbably large number of trees." (ll. 34–36)

TEXT WORKSHOP C

6 Reading for detail → SB, p. 27, exercise 4

To help you complete the tasks, read the headings (in bold) and the following excerpts from the text, underlining key information as in the example below.

The Great Pacific Garbage Patch
- "The Great Pacific Garbage Patch is the most well known of these trash vortices – it's double the size of Texas and now holds 79,000 tons of trash." (ll. 32–35)
- "'It's not a big floating island,' he said. Rather, it's an area of the ocean where the current conditions usher in trash." (ll. 73–76)
- "'There is much more plastic debris floating here in the Great Pacific Garbage Patch than anywhere that I ever swam,' Lecomte said." (ll. 77–80)
- "In addition to plastic bags and big pieces of trash, Lecomte also comes into contact with a lot of small particles in the water." (ll. 81–83)

Ben Lecomte's motive
- "'I'm not trying to go for any record,' Lecomte told *Business Insider* from the sailboat that's following him as he swims. 'It's a unique opportunity to show exactly what is under the surface.'" (ll. 15–19)
- "He wants the effort to bring more awareness to the issue of plastic consumption and show people what the garbage patch really looks like. 'I want to share what it is through swimming and bring people with me,' he said." (ll. 37–43)

Support
- "In June, Lecomte set out from Hawaii in a 67-foot yacht, headed toward the patch. He's traveling with nine other crew members." (ll. 51–54)
- "When Lecomte starts swimming each day, a support dinghy follows him, making sure he doesn't get lost and feeding him soup and bread every two or three hours." (ll. 66–69)
- "On board the ship, scientists periodically drop a net in the water to capture and count microplastics in the patch. They leave the net in the waves for a half hour at a time, and Lecomte said the crew captures around 36 plastic pieces every minute." (ll. 85–91)

7 Words matter → SB, p. 27, exercise 5

Complete the word web by adding words and expressions from the list below to the appropriate fields in the web.

bag | bin | clear (out) | collect | collection | disposal | dispose of | dump | hazardous | household | junk | piece (of) | pile | recycle | refuse | remove | skip | take away | throw (away/out) | tip | ton (of) | truck | rubbish | waste

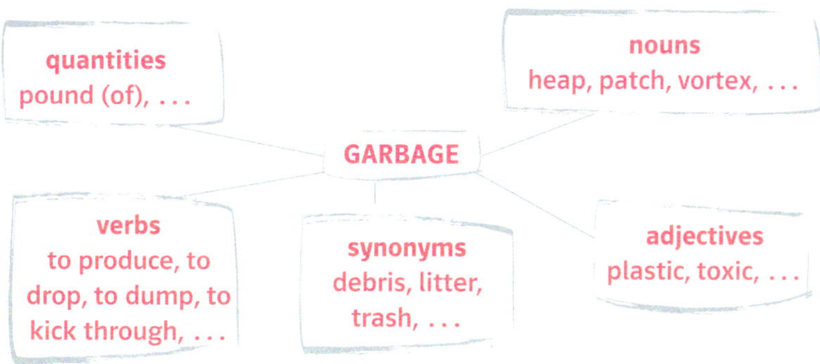

Topic 2

TEXT WORKSHOP A

1 Reading for detail → SB, p. 41, exercise 3

The following steps may help you complete the task.

Step 1 First, note down the devices and apps mentioned in the text and collect relevant information about them.
Step 2 Then put them into two groups:
- what the author uses for his own comfort and benefit
- what is used to record the author's information for other purposes

Step 3 Now compare the devices and apps by finding out what they have in common and where they are different.

2 Focus on analysis → SB, p. 41, exercise 4

The following three categories with examples from the text might help you complete the tasks.

Word fields
Private life: alarm, cup of coffee, way to work, ...
Consumer/Customer: electricity provider, mobile phone carrier, local government, bank account, ...

Technical terms
Data analytics: GPS receiver, accelerometer, phone signal, ...
Devices: to track, to log, to register, to detect, to pick up a signal, ...

Sentence structure
At 6:45 a.m., the alarm on my mobile phone wakes me up.
After breakfast, I'm ready to make my way to Stanford University.

TEXT WORKSHOP B

3 Writing a comment → SB, p. 45, exercise 6

The following arguments might help you get started.

Pros
- Access to healthcare will be improved.
- Companies will track a lot of information.
- Personal information and data will get people loans.
- Corruption and fraud will be reduced.

Cons
- People know very little about data protection.
- Traditional privacy will be lost.
- Who can guarantee data security?

TEXT WORKSHOP C

4 Talking about genetic engineering → SB, p. 50, exercise 2

Match the English words with their German equivalents. Then use these words to describe the pictures.

1. clipboard	A DNA Strang
2. DNA strand	B erforschen
3. injection	C Forscher/in
4. magnifying glass	D Injektion
5. petri dish	E injizieren, spritzen
6. reagent liquid	F Klemmbrett, Manuskripthalter
7. researcher	G Lupe, Vergrößerungsglas
8. scientist	H Petrischale
9. syringe	I Reagenzflüssigkeit
10. test tube	J Reagenzglas
11. to inject	K Spritze
12. to research	L Wissenschaftler/in

5 Reading for gist → SB, p. 52, exercise 3

Match these headings with the corresponding nine paragraphs of the text. There is one heading you do not need.

A Ethical questions
B The power to heal
C Start the discussion now
D More fiction than science
E The power to change the world
F Making the future possible, now
G The speed of scientific progress
H An important time for humankind
I Technology still too expensive and too dangerous
J Living in a society influenced by science and technology

6 Focus on analysis → SB, p. 52, exercise 5

When analysing the text to find the structural features used by the author, look out for the following aspects.

- Where does the author try to show a contrast? Look out for words like "but", "on the other hand", "then / in the past ... now".
- Where does the author make a comparison? Look out for words like "as likely as", "like", "then ... now".
- Where can you find sentence parts or words that are repeated several times in one paragraph to establish a pattern?
- Where does the author start to shift his focus away from himself towards the readers?
- Where can you find a cause-and-effect relationship in the text? Look out for the phrase "this is why ..."

7 Words matter → SB, p. 53, exercise 9

You may start your word web like this:

TEXT WORKSHOP D

8 Focus on analysis → SB, p. 56, exercise 6

Decide which of these descriptions fit George and his behaviour, and which ones could be attributed to Helen. Copy the table and fill it in. Sometimes the descriptions may fit both characters. Add your own ideas too.

angry | demanding | exhausted | feels bitter | feels helpless | feels let down | feels patronised by the government | feels sad and lonely | feels trapped by the situation | frustrated | hard-working | impatient | outspoken | resents the other person | uncommunicative | withdrawn

	characteristics
George	...
Helen	...

Topic 3

TEXT WORKSHOP A

1 Replying to readers' reactions → SB, p. 68, exercise 4

You can start your reply to one of the reader's comments like this:

→ Reply to Matt_77
Hello Matt. If it were that easy, I wouldn't have written this article. I wanted to share my story to help others and ...

→ Reply to EddieM
Hi Eddie. Thanks for your understanding. I know what you mean about the sales. It seems like there is always a special offer on something, and it always made me ...

→ Reply to Natalie
Hi Natalie. You're absolutely right. Admitting to yourself that you have a problem, whatever it might be, is the hardest step. After that ...

TEXT WORKSHOP B

2 Writing an email → SB, p.72, exercise 8

The following structure and phrases may help you write your email.

Starting the email
Dear Aja,
I am writing to you because I read your article about …

Main part
Give your opinion on the content of the article:
I found / didn't find the article interesting because …

Talk about your own attitude towards sustainable consumption and your shopping habits:
When I buy clothes, I pay attention to …
I used to buy …, but now I …
However, it is difficult to know …
I think fashion companies and brands should …

Finishing the email
Thank you for talking about this important topic.
I hope …
I will try …
Best wishes,

TEXT WORKSHOP C

3 Reading for gist → SB, p.74, exercise 2

Copy the table and fill in the correct information about the characters from *Copygirl*. Some of the information matches more than one character.

bullied by Johnjoshjay | bully Kay | copywriters | creates images for the adverts | creative director | dress like hipsters | in love with Ben | lives with Ben | lives with Kay | male colleagues | responsible for all the accounts | responsible for Little Kitty account | uses intimidating behaviour to motivate his employees

Kay	Elliot	Johnjoshjay	Ben
…	…	…	…

TEXT WORKSHOP D

4 Think – pair – share → SB, p. 78, exercise 1

Follow these steps to help you complete the task.

Step 1 First of all, explain what you can see, including the drawing, the positioning of the keywords and how they are explained in more depth. Start with "The infographic shows …" and use phrases such as "on the left/right there is …"
Step 2 Once you have described what you can see, think about what the key message is. Explain what is said, but don't just copy the text word for word. Start with "The message of the infographic is …" and then say in your own words what it is about.
Step 3 Afterwards, identify the most important terms you have used for your description and use them to form one sentence summarising the overall message.

5 Reading for detail → SB, p. 80, exercise 3

Complete the following example solution with the correct words and phrases.

aims | Black Friday | examples | explains | importance | make money | majority | priority | publicity | purpose

The infographic shows the 1 of organisations, and how and why they do what they do. It depicts the level of 2 placed on what, how and why companies make or do what they do. The infographic 3 that all companies know what they do, as they have chosen to do so for some reason, generally to 4. The 5 of companies also know how they produce or carry out their products or services. However, not many companies have a real sense of the 6 or belief behind their existence and daily business. The two companies in the text are 7 of the opposite. For these companies, the purpose behind their actions is a 8. Although they make money and create 9 with their actions, such as closing on 10, profit is not the main goal.

Topic 4

GETTING STARTED

1 Working with a video → SB, p. 89, exercise 4

When preparing to sum up the gist of the message of Gorman's poem, take notes of what she says about the following topics. Then summarise your notes in two or three sentences.

- the nation: e.g. broken, …
- the country: e.g. bruised but whole, …
- democracy: e.g. temporarily delayed, …
- the past: e.g. repair it, …
- the future: e.g. move to what shall be, …

TEXT WORKSHOP A

2 Reading for detail → SB, p. 92, exercise 5

To help you complete the tasks, look at the following sections of the text, making a note of key information.

- To summarise what motivated Alexander Hamilton, look at ll. 77–82.
- To outline why colonial Americans thought that ambition was dangerous, look at ll. 84–110.
- To explain how ambition came to be seen as a national virtue, look at ll. 111–131.

3 Writing a comment → SB, p. 92, exercise 7

Follow these steps to help you write your comment.

Step 1 Start your comment by rephrasing what is said in the quotation. Include the important information on the article, i.e. author, title, source, year of publication.
Step 2 Explain what the statement means considering the role of extraordinary people and ordinary people in history.
Step 3 Find examples in history of outstanding personalities and the role of ordinary people in making extraordinary events possible.
Step 4 Draw a conclusion about whether or not we should tell the story of extraordinary people any more.

You can use the following phrases in your comment.

Author J. M. Opal concludes his article … published in … in the year … by pointing out that …
What this means is …
History has shown again and again …
While it takes extraordinary people … they would not achieve this without …
To conclude, I would say that …

4 Creating a timeline of US history → SB, p. 93, exercise 9

Follow these steps to create a timeline of US history.

Step 1 To prepare your timeline, use a thick marker and draw a line from left to right that is placed roughly in the middle of a large sheet of paper.
Step 2 Mark the centuries from 1776 to the present.
Step 3 Add significant dates in US history, e.g.:
1776 Declaration of Independence
1783 End of Revolutionary War; independence established
1787 Constitution adopted
1789 George Washington first president of the USA
…
2021 Joe Biden becomes 46th president of the USA
Step 4 Fill in the dates of events for the topic that you have worked on to complete the timeline with your cards.

TEXT WORKSHOP C

5 Writing a letter → SB, p.101, exercise 5

You can structure your letter as follows:

Salutation

Main part of the letter
- state how you heard of the programme
- express your interest in the programme
- describe the importance of space travel for the world
- give examples for the realms of ...
  - → technological advances and innovations
  - → politics and international cooperation
  - → research (e.g. weather, climate change, health)
  - → economic issues (e.g. space mining)
  - → future colonisation
- express hope that you will be considered

Complimentary clause

TEXT WORKSHOP D

6 Talking about the United States → SB, p.102, exercise 1

You may want to consider the following aspects in your discussion. If necessary, use the internet to find information on possible changes in recent years.

- the USA's attitude to free trade
- the USA's relationship with China (e.g. trade relations, questions of democracy)
- the Iran nuclear deal
- the USA's involvement in Afghanistan
- the USA's participation in the Paris Agreement

7 Reading for detail → SB, p.104, exercise 4

Concentrate on the following parts of the text to complete the tasks.

- To explain how Joe Biden intends to restore a positive image of the USA in the world, look at ll. 68–78.
- To outline three pressing issues that the USA is planning to confront, look at ll. 79–93, ll. 95–103 and ll. 104–118.
- To describe how Biden sees the mutual influence of US foreign and domestic affairs on each other, look at ll. 119–139.

Topic 5

GETTING STARTED

1 Discussion → SB, p.113, exercise 5

The following keywords and phrases might help you to talk about how united (or unified) you think Germany is.

History
- the influence of living four decades under fundamentally different political and social systems
- the impact of German reunification
- hopes and disappointments about reunification

Standard of living
- the prosperous south versus the relatively poor former east
- wealth gap
- lower/higher average household incomes and wages

Politics
- rise of right-wing extremist parties, especially in the former east
- Green movement
- conservativism

Dialects
- standard German (*Hochdeutsch*)
- regional accents and dialects
- differences in vocabulary, grammar and pronunciation

Prejudice
- xenophobia
- racism
- east-west divide

TEXT WORKSHOP A

2 Focus on analysis → SB, p.116, exercise 5

To help you get started, you may use the following examples and underlined words from the text that illustrate the author's attitude to regional varieties of English.

- "linguistic ingenuity" (l.3)
- "the delicious word 'jibbons'" (ll.11–12)
- "That the wise custodians of the English language are actively embracing regional variation is pleasing for many reasons." (ll.23–25)
- "cute accents" (l. 54)
- "It feels reassuring to learn that, linguistically at least, Britain is embracing difference and change." (ll.74–76)
- "I'm […] a fan of a neat phrase" (l.104)
- "the diverse glory of British English" (ll.106–107)
- "I for one am all in favour of upspeak, variety, linguistic inventiveness and chuddies." (ll.111–113)

TEXT WORKSHOP B

3 Working with videos → SB, p.119, exercise 5

The following definitions and examples may help you identify the types of humour used in the clips.

banter	= a jokey conversation that involves good-natured teasing, e.g.: Mark: My burgers are way better than Lottie's. Burger off, Lottie. Lottie: No, you burger off!
innuendo	= a remark that suggests sth sexual but does not refer to it directly, e.g.: I remember worrying a bit about your very large nuts.
pulling faces	= to produce an expression on your face in order to make sb laugh
sarcasm	= using words that are the opposite of what you mean for a humorous effect
self-depreciation	= making your own achievements or abilities seem unimportant
the absurd	= extremely silly, ridiculous or surreal, e.g.: Bakers, you have one hour remaining, and if you don't finish, Mr Spoon's going to be angry.
understatement	= a statement that makes sth seem less important or serious than it really is

4 Writing a blog post → SB, p.120, exercise 6

The following sentence beginnings may help you write your blog post.

- I'd like to comment on ...
- In contrast to ... / Compared with ...
- On the one hand ..., on the other ...
- There's a clear difference in the way ...
- However, ...
- Considering the fact that ...
- As you can imagine ...
- As everyone knows ...
- Here's the interesting part ...

TEXT WORKSHOP C

5 Words matter → SB, p.125, exercise 4

Look at these sections of the text to find the words or phrases that match the definitions.

1. a person who is not in a place where he or she was expected to be: ll.3–6
2. a person who is against the abolition of slavery: ll.6–7
3. to risk losing one's life: ll.18–21
4. in this case: a block of wood on which a person's head was cut off as a punishment: ll.18–21
5. a word used in parts of East Africa to address a man who has authority over you: ll.19–22
6. to steal something, especially something small or not very valuable: ll.23–27
7. the part of a business that always makes a profit and that provides money for the rest of the business: ll.28–33

Topic 6

TEXT WORKSHOP A

1 Reading for gist → SB, p.139, exercise 2

Use the following sentence beginnings to help you write the summary.

Stella's story starts in ...
Twice she is successful at ...
When she moves to New Orleans ...
She is very nervous about ...
After she gets the job ...
Blake makes her feel ...
Stella realises that becoming 'White' is ...
Desiree tells her that being 'White' ...

2 Writing a comment → SB, p.140, exercise 6

The following words and phrases to describe somebody's attitude may help you write the comment.

- to feel (over)confident
- her look was full of ...
- opportunistic in her every move
- selfish actions
- egotistical
- exaggerated
- to have a false sense of pride
- to see humbleness in her actions
- to have (no) scruples
- to have an arrogance about oneself

TEXT WORKSHOP C

3 Focus on analysis → SB, p.148, exercise 5

Use this background information on the 9/11 terrorist attacks to analyse Kumail's statement "We hate terrorists!" (l.18).

The 9/11 terrorist attacks
On 11th September 2001, Islamic Al-Qaeda terrorists hijacked four planes and flew two of them into the World Trade Center in New York City, one into the Pentagon near Washington, D.C., one crashed in a field. Almost 3,000 people were killed in total and more than 6,000 were injured. After the attacks, xenophobia (i.e. the fear and hatred of strangers and foreigners) became more prevalent in the United States.

TEXT WORKSHOP D

4 Focus on analysis → SB, p.152, exercise 5

The following phrases may help you analyse the intention of the text.

- The text aims to inform the reader by giving information/details about …
- The author describes how/where/what … This helps the reader to understand/imagine …
- It is the intention of the text to instruct the reader by educating/teaching him/her about …
- The author discusses/debates the topic of … thus arguing …
- The text intends to persuade the reader … by trying to convince him/her that …

Topic 7

TEXT WORKSHOP A

1 Focus on analysis → SB, p.164, exercise 4

Consider these aspects for your answer.

- Sunny is very direct to Arjun and wants to find out how much Arjun is lying.
- Arjun does not seem to be intimidated and answers in a very self-assured way.
- Sunny interrupts Arjun so that he cannot finish talking about his qualifications.
- When Sunny tells Arjun about his plans, he shows that he feels superior. He says that with his decisions, Arjun's life will start moving in a certain direction.
- Arjun accepts this role and shows his gratitude.

2 Writing an argumentative essay → SB, p.164, exercise 8

The following structure and questions might help you write your argumentative essay.

Introduction
- How do I define the issue that I am going to discuss?
- How can I get the reader's attention so that she/he becomes interested in the topic of outsourcing?

Main part
- Which arguments and examples do I know for both sides?
- How can I structure, explain and illustrate my arguments?
- How can I make the transition from one set of arguments to the other?

Conclusion
- What is my opinion on the topic?
- What is my strongest argument?
- How can I present the strongest argument again in a particularly convincing way?

TEXT WORKSHOP B

3 Focus on analysis → SB, p.169, exercise 6

You can use the following sentence beginnings to help you with your speculations.

When the Spanish executive arrived, he probably expected …
His US partners should have taken into account that …
It is typical in Spain to …
The two sides should have …
Not being personally welcomed by your business partners is …
It is better to ask than …
The meeting logistics were (not) …
It would have been better to hold the meeting …

TEXT WORKSHOP C

4 Reading for detail → SB, p.173, exercise 3

Skim the article and put these events into chronological order. Add dates from the article if possible.

A Camel-driven caravans
B Fiasco in the Suez Canal
C Triremes on the Mediterranean
D Size of container ships doubled
E Transferring loads required repacking
F Ships 50% larger than the Ever Given
G The very first beginnings of commerce
H Creation of the standardised cargo container
I 1.83 billion metric tons transferred in containers
J 102 million metric tons transferred in containers
K Realisation that standardised containers were easier to handle

TEXT WORKSHOP D

5 Focus on analysis → SB, p.177, exercise 6

Look at the sentences from the text and the underlined words. Decide which of the following intentions they match the best: to argue, to describe, to inform, to instruct or to persuade.

1. "The idea is based on an image that contains two rings." (ll.16–18) to describe
2. "The inner ring represents our social foundation and the outer ring represents our ecological ceiling." (ll.18–20)
3. "But we know that GDP growth and growth itself is not bringing all the wellbeing that we want in the world." (ll.39–42)
4. "[…] Raworth believes that we can structure our societies in a way that provides communities with the economic securities they need while maintaining a habitable planet." (ll.49–53)
5. "[…] the group created different working groups that focus on the different dimensions of bringing the doughnut model to California […]" (ll.114–118)
6. "That we can show other states and other places what is possible […]" (ll.123–124)

Topic 8

TEXT WORKSHOP A

1 Writing an email → SB, p. 190, exercise 6

The following structure and phrases may help you write your email.

Dear Robert and Edward,

In your blog you asked about the importance of a work-life balance, and this made me think.

In my opinion, it is very important to find a healthy balance between …
If people spend too much time working, they do not have enough time to …
Furthermore, overworking can lead to …
It can be hard to find a good work-life balance because …
Many people also work from home, which can make it difficult to …
For me personally, it is very important to …
In my opinion, companies should …
People also need to learn to …

Thank you for your interesting article and I look forward to …

Yours sincerely,

…

TEXT WORKSHOP B

2 Talking about financial security → SB, p. 191, exercise 1

Follow these steps to prepare and conduct the discussion with your partner.

Step 1 Write down what a person could do with an extra amount of money each month.
Step 2 Decide what you would do with the extra money.
Step 3 Look at the list of potential effects of receiving a fixed amount of money per month for life. Make a table and sort them into positive and negative effects.
- overconsumption
- more peace of mind
- higher standard of living
- taking things for granted
- less dependence on parents
- increased dependency on handouts
- lack of motivation to achieve good grades/high qualifications
- increased ability and willingness to support good causes
- potential to invest and build up capital from a young age
- opportunity to choose a profession based on interests rather than salary
- no need for part-time/holiday jobs while studying, therefore more focus on education

Step 4 Discuss your results of steps 1–3 with a partner. Add one more positive and negative effect to your tables.

3 Focus on analysis → SB, p. 193, exercise 5

Roo is faced with the following conflicts. Sort them into inner and outer conflict.

- Roo has the urge to save money, despite knowing it is illegal to do so.
- The government states everyone must spend the money they are allocated each month, but Roo does not want to.
- She is worried about the government finding out about her hoarding money but still decides to hide some money in her sofa.
- She has to find ways to spend her money, otherwise she will be found out.
- Roo wants her neighbour to leave her flat, as she is worried she will find the money she has hidden.
- Roo's neighbour thinks people who save money are evil, which makes Roo feel uncomfortable.

TEXT WORKSHOP C

4 Writing an email → SB, p. 197, exercise 7

For your email, you could use the following structure:

Dear Richard / Mr Adams,
I recently read your article on the gender pay gap and was quite shocked by … / not surprised by the information.

Although I was aware the gender pay gap exists, I did not know …
I was also intrigued / shocked / surprised to read that …
In my opinion, much more needs to be done. For example, …
Alternatively, low-paid, traditionally female jobs could be …
More could be done in schools to help …
National and local governments could …
All in all, more needs to be done to not only improve the rights and …

Thank you for highlighting this important issue in your article.

Yours sincerely, …

TEXT WORKSHOP D

5 Reading for gist → SB, p. 200, exercise 2

Match these captions with the correct paragraphs.

A Changing Japanese society
B Ugo, the robot security guard
C Robots in Japanese healthcare
D Japans's demographic challenges
E Matsui's view on the prospects of Mira Robotics
F Japan – robot embracing institutions and government
G The future role of Japan and other countries in robotics
H Different cultural preceptions of robots in Japan and the West

6 Focus on analysis → SB, p. 201, exercise 5

Look at the table and decide whether the text has more elements from the left or the right column. Find examples in the text and give line numbers.

formal language and style	informal language and style
– informative headline – use of formal language (e.g. long forms) – use of elaborate language – presentation of balanced facts and statistics – long and complex sentences – use of stylistic devices (e.g. metaphors, rhetorical questions)	– catchy, provocative headline – use of informal language (e.g. short forms) – use of colourful, strong adjectives – presentation of facts and statistics to support a one-sided perspective – short and simple sentences – use of stylistic devices (e.g. metaphors, vivid imagery, exaggerations)

7 Writing an argumentative essay → SB, p. 201, exercise 6

Use the following structure and phrases to help you write your argumentative essay.

Introduction
First refer to the quote and explain what it means.
The author of the text …, which was published in …, states that "In the West, …"
This means that …

Main part
To start with focus on arguments why German society might be "reluctant in embracing robot technology". Elaborate on at least two arguments by explaining and illustrating them with examples.
On the one hand, …
Secondly, …

Now move on to arguments for the opposite point of view. Explain and give at least two examples of how Germany has embraced new (robot) technology and/or AI.
On the other hand, …
Furthermore …

Conclusion
Finally, state your own point of view and come to a conclusion.
In my opinion, …
In conclusion, …

S 1 Language functions	**S 1** Mastering communication situations	236
S 2 Listening and viewing skills	**S 2** Dealing with listening/viewing tasks	238
S 3 Listening exams	**S 3** Preparing for a listening exam	238
S 4 Reading skills	**S 4.1** Dealing with reading tasks **S 4.2** Reading techniques	240
S 5 Writing skills	**S 5.1** Dealing with writing tasks **S 5.2** Improve your writing	241
S 6 Writing specific text types	**S 6.1** Writing a comment **S 6.2** Writing a blog post **S 6.3** Writing an argumentative essay **S 6.4** Writing a personal email or letter **S 6.5** Writing a letter to the editor **S 6.6** Writing a speech **S 6.7** Writing an informative handout **S 6.8** Writing a promotional text **S 6.9** Writing a summary **S 6.10** Writing a diary entry or interior monologue	242
S 7 Written exams	**S 7** Understanding writing tasks	248
S 8 Analysing language	**S 8.1** Stylistic devices **S 8.2** Style, tone and register	249
S 9 Analysing fictional texts	**S 9.1** Fictional text types **S 9.2** Analysing novels and short stories **S 9.3** Analysing poetry **S 9.4** Narrative perspectives **S 9.5** Narrative techniques **S 9.6** Characterisation	250
S 10 Analysing non-fictional texts	**S 10.1** Non-fictional text types **S 10.2** Structure of non-fictional texts **S 10.3** Analysing argumentative texts **S 10.4** Analysing newspaper articles	254
S 11 Describing and analysing visuals	**S 11.1** Describing and analysing pictures and paintings **S 11.2** Analysing films **S 11.3** Describing and analysing cartoons **S 11.4** Describing and analysing diagrams and statistics	258
S 12 Mediation skills	**S 12** Doing a mediation task	263
S 13 Business communication	**S 13.1** Writing business letters **S 13.2** Writing business emails **S 13.3** Writing a CV **S 13.4** Writing a letter of application	264
S 14 Speaking skills	**S 14.1** Giving a talk or presentation **S 14.2** Preparing for a job interview **S 14.3** Making phone calls	268
S 15 Oral exams *(Kommunikationsprüfung)*	**S 15** Preparing for an oral exam	273
S 16 Vocabulary skills	**S 16.1** Expanding your vocabulary **S 16.2** Guessing unkown words **S 16.3** Working with a dictionary	274
S 17 Making a video	**S 17** Making a video	277
S 18 References and sources	**S 18.1** Checking sources **S 18.2** Citing sources **S 18.3** Quoting	278

S1 Language functions

Mastering communication situations

Language has a huge variety of functions to offer: you can use it to make small talk, to have heated discussions, to write personal or business correspondence, to give instructions, to express feelings etc. The following phrases will help you to master key communication situations like these:

EXPRESSING OPINIONS

Stating your opinion

The point is … | Wouldn't you say that …? | If you ask me … | As I see it … | It seems to me that … | As far as I understand … | As far as I'm concerned … | In my opinion … | I am of the opinion that … | I take the view that … | From my point of view … | To my mind … | I would like to emphasise that … | I would like to mention/say that … | I'd like to point out that … | I strongly believe that … | I'm sure/convinced/certain that … | It is obvious that … | Obviously/Without a doubt, it is wrong/right to say that … | I reject the idea that … | It is completely/absolutely/totally wrong to argue that …

Expressing probability/predicting

Definitely: Of course, it'll … | It's going to … | There's no question that … | It's sure to say … | It's bound to …
Probably: It'll probably … | I expect it to … | I wouldn't be surprised if … | I bet it'll …
Perhaps: I guess it might … | There's a chance it'll …
Probably not: I doubt (if) it'll … | I don't think it'll …
Definitely not: Of course it won't … | There's no chance of it …-ing. | I'm absolutely sure it won't …

Emphasising

definitely | extremely | indeed | absolutely | positively | obviously | naturally | always | never | without a doubt | certainly

DISCUSSING

Persuading/objecting

That's a good idea, but … | That might be OK, but … | I really don't think so because … | Why don't you …? | I see what you mean, but … | That's true, but …

Giving reasons

because | since | therefore | consequently | accordingly | As there are … | As a result of … | Due to … | Because of …

Giving examples

for example | for instance | in another case | take the case of | to illustrate | as an illustration | to take another example | as shown by … | as illustrated by … | as expressed by …

Agreeing and disagreeing

Exactly. | I couldn't agree more. | That's just what I was thinking. | That's a good point. | I see where you're coming from, but … | I'm not sure if I agree … | Maybe, but don't you think that …?

Comparing and contrasting

Comparing: also | as well as | both | comparatively | in the same way | just as | like | similarly
Contrasting: although | besides | but | compared with | even though | however | in contrast to | instead | nevertheless | on the other hand | rather than | yet

Balancing pros and cons

On the one hand …, on the other hand … | although | however | We shouldn't forget that … | In contrast to … | On the contrary … | Weighing up the pros and cons …

STRUCTURING

Sequencing/structuring

I'm going to … | I would like to talk about … | I would like to point out/mention … | To begin with … | Now I want to describe … | There are three things to consider: Firstly … Secondly … Thirdly … | Finally …

Summarising/drawing a conclusion

All things considered … | Taking everything into account … | Briefly … | On the whole … | In short … | Finally … | That's why … | For this reason/these reasons … | Therefore … | As a result … | Consequently …

HANDLING CONVERSATIONS

Speaking politely
Could you please …? | Would you …? | May I …? | Maybe you could …? | I was wondering if …? | Excuse me, could you …? | Thank you.

Getting more information
Could you tell me some more about …? | Would you mind telling me more about …? | I'd like to know more about … | Something else I was wondering about was …

Hesitating
Um … | Well … | Well, let's see now … | You see … | You know … | The thing is … | How can I put it?

Repeating
As I have (already) said … | As I have pointed out / mentioned …

Checking understanding
OK so far? | Are you with me? | Is that clear? | Do you see what I mean?

Interrupting politely
If I could just come in here … | Sorry to interrupt, but … | The way I see it … | Um … (repeat until the speaker lets you speak)

Preventing and handling interruptions
There are three points I'd like to make clear … | Could I just finish my point? As I was saying …

MAKING SMALL TALK

Introducing oneself/introducing others
Hi, I'm … | Let me introduce myself … | I don't think we've met. My name is … | I'd like to introduce myself. My name's … | Nice to meet you. | It's a pleasure to meet you. | I'd like you to meet someone. This is … | I'd like to introduce you to … | There's someone I'd like you to meet …

Saying goodbye/closing
That's it for today. | That's all for now. | Bye for now! | Thanks for …

Talking about likes and dislikes
What I like doing is … | I really/especially/particularly like …-ing | One of my biggest hobbies is …-ing. | My favourite pastime is …-ing. | What I really dislike is … | What I am really not a fan of is …-ing. | I just hate …-ing.

ASKING FOR AND GIVING HELP

Asking questions
I was wondering if you could help me. I'd like to know … | I wonder if you could tell me … | Excuse me, do you know …? | I'm sorry to bother you, but … | There's something you could help me with.

Asking for a favour
Would/Could you do me a favour? | Would you mind …-ing …? | May I …? | Could you please …?

Asking for advice
What do you suggest/recommend? | What should I do? | What would you do if you were me?

Asking for permission
May I …? | Can I …? | Could I perhaps …? | Do you mind if I …? | Is it okay if …?

Refusing to help
I'm sorry, but … | I'd like to, but … | I'd really like to help you, but …

Making suggestions/giving advice
I was wondering if you have ever thought of … | I think it might be a good idea to … | Have you thought of …? | Don't you think it might be a good idea to …? | If I were you I'd perhaps … | Why don't you …?

EXPRESSING FEELINGS

Saying how you feel
I'm feeling … good | great | awesome | excited | fantastic | grateful | relaxed | happy | fantastic | awful | angry | annoyed | miserable | terrible | grumpy | upset | depressed | confused

Apologising
I'm sorry for … | I'm sorry that … | I would like to apologise for … | Please accept my apologies. | It was my fault.

Thanking
Thanks a lot. | Thank you for … | That's very kind of you. | You're welcome. / My pleasure. (when someone thanks you)

S 2 Listening and viewing skills

Dealing with listening/viewing tasks

Listening or viewing tasks assess your listening/viewing comprehension, which is your ability to listen to and understand what someone is saying. In everyday life, pure listening situations are limited to radio programmes, podcasts, radio plays and audiobooks. Videos can often be easier to understand thanks to visual clues. Images, the characters' body language and any cinematic devices used (e.g. lighting or camera angles) all give you further information.
Before you listen or watch, read through the assignments. It is often possible to predict what the speakers are going to talk about.

While listening/watching, follow these steps:

Listening/viewing for the 1st time: gist
- focus on the general topic
- get the overall picture
- identify the main points

Listening/viewing for the 2nd time: detail
- concentrate on specific details and relevant information

Listening/viewing for the 3rd time: further detail
- complete any missing information

TIP

As with all comprehension situations, it is important to first look out for keywords (e.g. names, times, numbers, places) and try to find out about the context (speakers, their situation and the type of conversation they are having).

MK Listen to English-speaking people as often as possible:
- The internet is a great source of free audio and video materials in English. Listen to audio clips or watch videos a couple of times. For video clips, turn on the subtitles if they are available.
- If you find an interesting online article, use a text-to-speech reader. Copy the article into the reader and have it read out loud to you.
- Listen to audiobooks.

S 3 Listening exams

Preparing for a listening exam

In your listening exam you are expected to do different types of tasks such as answering questions, multiple-/single-choice tasks, completion tasks and multiple matching tasks. You may be confronted with new information und unknown vocabulary and various elements such as accents or background noises.
By concentrating on what you already know about the topic and being well prepared for the different types of tasks, you can cope better with these challenges.

In your listening exam you might be asked to use these different listening strategies:

Listening for gist	– When you are listening for gist you try to grasp the main idea of the listening text. – Concentrate on the main content and keywords to form a general picture.
Listening for detail	– Listening for detail means you are collecting detailed information from the listening text. – Focus on relevant details (e.g. names, dates, numbers, times, places).
Selective listening	– Selective listening means you are directing your attention on specific information in the listening text. – Make sure you know what information you are required to select and concentrate on those aspects.
Making inferences	– When you are making inferences while listening you are using clues given in the text, the tone of the speaker(s) (e.g. positive/negative, sad/happy) and your prior knowledge about the topic to understand the listening text. – Pay attention to information you can infer from the setting and the language.

You should be familiar with these types of tasks in your listening exam:

Multiple choice	Pay attention to the instructions. Only one answer is correct. The tasks are always based solely on the information given in the text.
Multiple matching	Carefully read the headings and look out for keywords related to them while you listen. Check your answers by looking at the headings again and make sure that you matched them to the correct speakers.
Short answer questions	Use keywords to provide relevant information from the listening text to answer the questions. Note that the emphasis here is on the content.
Table completion	When completing a table, use keywords and/or numbers from the listening text to supply the relevant information.

Preparing	– Before you listen, note down the topic of the listening text and the text type (e.g. report, podcast). – Carefully read any information in the brief description and use your prior knowledge about the topic to predict the general message of the text. – Read through the task carefully. Make sure you know what type of task it is and what exactly you are expected to do.
Listening for the 1st time	– While you listen for the first time, write down your answers or keywords and phrases which sound important. Listen for stresses on words or the repetition of words which sometimes mark relevant information to find the answers. – Leave space between your first notes for more notes when you listen again.
Between listening times	– Read through your answers or notes and look at the task again. – Check what you easily understood to see if it still makes sense. – Decide which answers you are sure about and which ones you are not.
Listening for the 2nd time	– While you listen again, concentrate on the information that will help you answer the parts which you were not sure about the first time. – Listen for grammatical signals to help you understand the meaning (e.g. future/past tense, singular/plural). – Listen for connecting words (e.g. and, but, because, on the other hand) which help you to understand how the information is being used.

TIP

Don't panic if you don't hear or understand every word! You will probably still understand the most important information. Intonation patterns will help you to recognise a speaker's attitude or intention. Does what the speaker says sound like a question, criticism, suggestion, statement, agreement, ironic statement or a joke?

S 4 Reading skills

In order to improve your reading skills, read as much as possible. Focus on aspects you find interesting, from football news to the latest film and fashion gossip – make reading a discovery. While reading, be patient with yourself. Try not to read word for word, but instead focus on the introduction to the text, the headings and subheadings as well as the beginning and end of each paragraph. It is often enough to get a basic idea of a paragraph.
In the long run, make a habit of reading English texts. Maybe checking an English news site every day/week might be a good start?

S 4.1 Dealing with reading tasks

Reading tasks usually follow these three stages of the reading process:

pre-reading → while-reading → post-reading

Pre-reading	Before you start reading, ask yourself the following questions: – What will the text be about? – What does the title reveal? – Are there any subheadings or highlighted quotes? – What kind of text is it? – When was it published? – Are there any pictures/diagrams?
While-reading	– Read the assignments first. Find out what type of information you are looking for and then choose the appropriate reading technique. – Highlight the main ideas and make annotations. Marking and annotating a text helps you to focus while reading, as you are selecting and organising the most important information.
Post-reading	– Double-check your answers. – You might be asked to do further tasks related to the text you have just read to make sure you have understood it correctly, e. g. writing a summary or a comment.

TIP

Marking a text
Underline or highlight keywords, key phrases, examples etc. Use different styles:
- main ideas of the text
- key phrases
- author's opinion
- examples
- characterisation

Annotating a text
Make notes next to the text to help you find information quickly, e.g.
- defining vocabulary
- summarising/paraphrasing passages
- defining and understanding examples, quotes ...
- identifying important moments in the plot
- commenting on characters

S 4.2 Reading techniques

Skimming/reading for gist	– Skimming is reading a text quickly to get a general idea of the most important points. – Don't stop reading because you don't understand all the words. Just try to get an overall picture. – If possible, only read the headings and the first few paragraphs. – The last paragraphs in non-fictional texts (e.g. scientific research, newspaper articles) often summarise the main ideas of the article.
Scanning	– Scanning is reading in order to find specific information. – For a reading assignment, read the question(s) carefully and look for keywords and key phrases in the text.
Close reading/ reading for detail	– Sometimes it is necessary to understand a text in detail. Here, make sure you understand every word. – Look up unknown words in a dictionary and use the information you find on word category, register, collocation and usage to identify the word that best fits the context.

KWL: This technique is useful if you are reading a text to learn more about a certain topic.

Pre-reading
- **K** What I KNOW (What do I already know about the topic and the author?)
- **W** What I WANT to know (Why am I reading the text? What exactly do I want to find out?)

While-reading
- **L** What I have LEARNED (What are my findings?)

SQ3R:
- **S** SURVEY what you are asked to read. (What additional information about the text can I find if I survey the title, subheadings, images, charts …?)
- **Q** Ask yourself QUESTIONS about the text. (What exactly am I looking for?)
- **3R** READ the text and look for answers.
  RECITE what you have found out in your own words.
  REVIEW the text and your notes. (What am I going to do with my findings?)

S 5 Writing skills

S 5.1 Dealing with writing tasks

In order to improve the quality of your writing, consider following this step-by-step approach.

7. Proofread your text. Pay special attention to tenses, prepositions, word order and spelling.
6. Write a first draft of your text.
5. Your text should develop in a logical way. Use structuring devices and connectives. Pay attention to style and register.
4. Organise your ideas. Put your notes in a logical order and finalise them.
3. Brainstorm ideas and make notes.
2. Examine the material (e.g. text, quotation, cartoon, picture) that might be part of the assignment and that you need to refer to in your text. Make notes on how the message of that material can be integrated into your text.
1. Make sure you understand the assignment.

S 5.2 Improve your writing

Use connectives to make your writing more logical. They are used to illustrate a connection between certain aspects or ideas.

Adding ideas	*moreover, besides, furthermore, in addition to that*
Sequencing	*first of all, to begin with, next, then, finally*
Emphasising	*above all, in particular, especially, significantly, indeed*
Similarity	*in the same way, similarly, likewise*
Cause and effect	*therefore, thus, however, although, unless*
Illustrating	*for example, for instance, as revealed by, in the case of, nevertheless, despite, in spite of, on the contrary*
Contrasting	*instead of, alternatively, otherwise, unlike, on the one hand …, on the other hand*
Conclusion	*In conclusion …, Therefore …, All in all …, To sum up …*

TIP

Error log

Everytime you receive a text which has been corrected, analyse your mistakes according to the following categories:
- spelling mistakes
- use of tenses
- sentence structure
- style and register

When you write a text now, have a look at your error log in advance and try to avoid making these mistakes again.

S 6 Writing specific text types

In a written exam, you are asked to write a specific type of text. For each text type, you need to consider the typical structure, contents, purposes and writing style.

S 6.1 Writing a comment

In a written exam, you will often have to write a comment about a certain topic. You will usually have to deal with a controversial issue, a quote or a statement and give your personal opinion about it.

Structure your comment as follows:

Introduction
- Define the problem or topic.
- Get the reader's attention.
- Clearly state your opinion.

Main part
- Give reasons for your opinion.
- Support arguments with examples.
- Use connectives.

Conclusion
- Summarise the best argument.
- Restate your opinion.
- Give an outlook.

TIP

Before you start writing, read the quote or statement carefully and decide if you agree or disagree with it. Start with the weakest argument and end with the strongest. Write your comment in the simple present.

USEFUL PHRASES

Giving examples
for example | for instance | in another case | take the case of | to illustrate | as shown/expressed by …

Referring to a point already made
as I have already said/noted | as suggested above …

Emphasising your statements
definitely | indeed | extremely | absolutely | positively …

Balancing pros and cons
On the one hand …, on the other hand … | although | however | We shouldn't forget that … | In contrast to … | On the contrary … | Weighing up the pros and cons …

Drawing a conclusion
That's why … | For this reason/these reasons | therefore | as a result | consequently | Taking everything into account … | The arguments seem to indicate that … | It is clear therefore that … | Thus it could be concluded that … | The evidence seems to be strong that …

MK When writing a comment on a computer, run the spelling and grammar checker before you hand it in.

S 6.2 Writing a blog post

A well-structured blog post will catch the readers' attention and make them want to read on.

BLOG

Create blog entry

Choose an interesting, eye-catching headline

Structure
- Put the main point you are writing about in the first paragraph.
- All further details, explanations, examples etc. can go in the following paragraphs.
- End with a kind of conclusion, i.e. a final thought that summarises your main ideas.

Language and style
- Try to write in a friendly and informal style.
- Always be polite and respectful of other cultures and opinions.
- Use the first person 'I' and try to include examples/anecdotes from your own experience.
- Use interesting and varied language (e.g. adjectives, adverbs, connectives) and stylistic devices (e.g. rhetorical questions, exclamations, exaggerations). → S 8.1
- Think about your readers and what they might want to learn from what you are telling them.
- Use phrases and expressions that are suitable for expressing your opinion in a clear way.
- It might even be a good idea to directly invite your readers to join the discussion.
- In some blog posts it is common to add your username and the date of your post.

TIP

Never
- include links to commercial sites or resources or
- include links to inappropriate material.
- give specific names, places, addresses or contact details.

MK Have you ever thought about starting your own blog? You can find many free templates online.

S 6.3 Writing an argumentative essay

An argumentative essay presents a controversial topic from opposing points of view in a clear and logical way.

Preparing

- Collect ideas and information about the topic; note down arguments for and against it. Use tables or lists.
- Make an outline of what you are going to write and in which order.
- For the body of your essay choose a logical structure which fits the topic/task (e.g. present all of the negative points first, then the positive or alternate between arguments and counter-arguments for each aspect) and arrange points (e.g. from weakest to strongest).
- Decide if you want to persuade the reader to agree with you or if you want to remain neutral.

Writing

Introduction
Present the issue and attract the reader's attention by inserting a quotation or giving a suitable anecdote, for example using background facts about the problem and its relevance for the question(s) that you will give answers to in the essay.

Main part
Based on your outline, present each point in a separate paragraph. Support your points with evidence (examples, statistics, personal experience etc.).
You may use the hourglass method, i.e. start with the strongest argument that you disagree with and continue with the weaker ones. Then present the weakest argument in support of your opinion and continue with the stronger ones, ending with your strongest argument.

Conclusion
Give a short summary of what you have written, but do not introduce any new ideas here. Refer back to the question you posed initially. You may give an outlook on further consequences/future developments/possible solutions, state your own opinion/give a recommendation or appeal to the readers to reach their own conclusion.

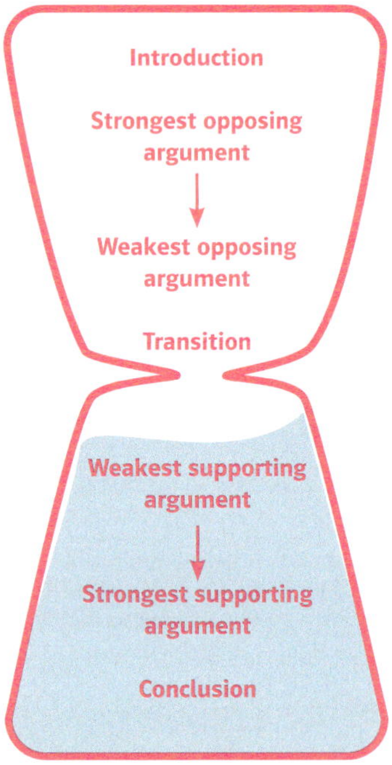

USEFUL PHRASES

Presenting aspects and examples
... consists of (two) aspects.
It is a ... rather than a ... problem/issue.
... should also be considered/mentioned.
... is relevant/completely irrelevant to ...
There are various reasons why ...
This also raises questions about ...
Some researchers say .../Studies show ...
Proponents/Opponents say/point out ...

Talking about developments and results
... can/will/should lead to/cause/result in ...
The main/short-term/long-term consequences are ...
... could have serious/far-reaching consequences for ...

Summing up/Concluding
Summing up .../Concluding ...
Therefore,/Consequently,/As a result, people should/might/must ...
In other words, ...
And here's what really (matters/happens/is at stake): ...

S 6.4 Writing a personal email or letter

In a personal email or letter, you directly and frequently address the person you are writing to.

EMAIL

Structure
- Use an appropriate salutation and a complimentary close.
- In personal letters also include the date.
- Very often, personal emails or letters start with stating the reason for writing.
- In the main part, go into more detail and focus on the purpose of your correspondence.
- You might want to end your email or letter by asking the person you are writing to a question, a favour etc.

Language and style
- Use the first-person perspective (1st person singular/1st person plural) in your text.
- The language you use very much depends on the topic you are writing about and on the relationship between you and the person reading your email or letter.
- Specific topics might require technical terms even in personal correspondence.

TIP

Before you send emails, always check for spelling and typing mistakes, and also for any sentences which could be misunderstood.

S 6.5 Writing a letter to the editor

If you want to share your opinion on an article in the newspaper or in a magazine, you can write a letter to the editor. You might want to either voice your anger or concern about a certain issue, express approval of an article, correct information in an article or try and persuade the public to share your point of view. Letters to the editor use emotive language and/or facts and are rarely longer than 250 words.

Structure your letter to the editor as follows:

Salutation and reference
- "To the Editor", "Dear (the) Editor" and "Dear Sir/Madam" are all appropriate to use as the salutation.
- Refer to the article that you are commenting on and say when it was published.

Content
- Try to catch the reader's attention in the opening sentence and clearly state your reason for writing.
- Explain why the issue is important.
- Give reasons for your point of view.
- Keep the letter brief and to the point.
- Be polite.

Close
- Sum up your arguments in one sentence.
- Suggest a solution to the problem.
- Do not use "Yours sincerely". Just give your name and the town/city where you live at the end of the letter.

TIP

Use the layout of a business letter. → S 13.1

USEFUL PHRASES

I am writing with reference to the article you published on/in … |
I am writing to express my support for/(dis)approval of the issues raised in the article … |
For these reasons, I completely agree/disagree with the author of the article … |
I would call on the government/politicians/all young people to … |
In my opinion, the most effective way of solving the problem is to …

S 6.6 Writing a speech

A speech is usually a formal talk on a chosen topic that a speaker gives to an audience. In your exam, you might be asked to write the **manuscript** for a speech. This means that you are expected to write down a speech which could in theory be held in front of an audience.

Here are some important aspects to consider:

Purpose and audience	– Check your purpose: Do you want to inform, explain or persuade? Should your speech be entertaining or serious or both? – Consider your audience: What do they already know about the topic? In which situation or scenario will the speech be held?
Structure	**Beginning** – State your topic and its importance. – Address the audience directly and create a link between them and your topic. – To catch your listeners' attention, you could start with a surprising fact, an eye-opening experience or a famous quotation. – Get your listeners engaged early. – State your aim and your key issue. – Outline the structure of your speech. **Main part** – Present your line of argumentation and supporting material in an organised way. – Develop your ideas step by step: either in chronological order, or from the least important to the most important idea, or first pros then cons, or by linking problems with their solutions. – Support your statements with facts, statistics or examples from personal experience. – Make clear, logical transitions from idea to idea. **Ending** – Round off your speech with a powerful conclusion, e.g. a rhetorical question, a quotation, a promise, an appeal, a vision of your topic in the future or a short summary. – Thank your audience for listening to what you had to say.
Language and style	– Keep in mind that your speech is meant to be presented orally, i.e. a clear language is important. – Address your audience directly. Using personal pronouns (often 1st person singular 'I' or 3rd person plural 'we') will establish a bond between you and the listeners. – Make sure that your line of thought is easy to follow. Use connectives for a clear and simple structure. – Include (rhetorical) questions to keep your audience interested. – Repetitions and exclamations are powerful rhetorical devices too. – Use logical appeals (i.e. presenting strong claims and evidence), ethical appeals (i.e. establishing the speaker as knowledgeable and trustworthy) and emotional appeals (i.e. creating an emotional connection with the audience).

TIP

A good speech only covers one topic. Use short sentences. Repeat and emphasise important ideas.

USEFUL PHRASES

Dealing with problems
… is a serious/pressing/urgent problem. | We can overcome this difficulty | settle the conflict | make a compromise | negotiate an agreement | promote reconciliation by …

Looking into the future
In the near future/short term/long term/long run, … | A short/long term solution would be to … | I am hopeful/confident that … | We should work towards …

Taking action
We have to ensure/see to it that … | We should take care not to … | I am prepared/determined to … | We should adopt a resolution to …

Special rhetorical devices for speeches
direct address | enumeration | anaphora | imagery | rhetorical questions | hyperbole | alliteration | contrast | repetition | appeal to the audience

S6.7 Writing an informative handout

In an informative handout you inform an interested group of people about facts, issues, events or a problem.

Structure

- Give your text a very clear, concise heading so that the readers know at a glance what your handout is about.
- Subheadings will provide a clear structure.

Language and style

- Depending on the situation or the topic you are writing about, you might consider addressing your readers directly.
- Use factual and objective language only; colloquial language is not suitable for an informative handout.
- Listing points or facts one by one will make your text easier to understand.
- Depending on the topic you are writing about, you will also be expected to use technical terms.

S 6.8 Writing a promotional text

This text type is written by an individual or an organisation to an individual, to a group of persons or to another organisation to promote an idea or to motivate the readers to take action.

Purpose

- You are addressing your target group because you want to raise awareness, e.g. for a cause or event.
- You want to get people to take action or want them to protest against an idea or a certain measure.
- Basically, you want to convince the readers to join you in your efforts, therefore your text very often is a call for action.
- For this reason, it is important that you manage to establish a personal tone in your text.

Structure

- Give your text a clear structure which is easy to follow.
- To grab the readers' attention, choose an interesting heading which is followed by a very straighforward introduction.
- Present your ideas to your readers and also outline why they should be concerned.
- Finish with an appeal which asks your readers to take action.

Language and style

- Establish a personal relationship by addressing your readers directly. Therefore use a personal style (1st person singular/1st person plural).
- Rhetorical questions are helpful because they involve the readers.
- Using repetitions, exclamations, appeals and enumerations will help to convince your readers of whatever idea you are promoting.
- Using figurative language (metaphors, similes etc.) might help too.
- Use short sentences and simple language, even though sometimes technical terms might be required.

S 6.9 Writing a summary

A summary sums up the main points of a text without adding a personal evaluation or opinion. A good summary will serve as a substitute for the actual text, as all the key arguments and conclusions are presented, including also information on the **title**, **author**, **source** and, if available, the **place and date** of publication. Your summary should be much shorter than the original, usually a quarter to a third of the length of the original text.

A good summary ...

- is **coherent** and **concise**
- is written in the **simple present tense**
- covers **all the essential elements** of the original text
- contains no information which is not included in the original text

S 6.10 Writing a diary entry or interior monologue

Diary entries are not normally meant to be read by anyone but the writer. Interior monologues usually appear in novels or short stories and allow the reader to get an insight into a character's most private thoughts and feelings. Typical contents of either text type are memories, feelings, fantasies, thoughts, emotions, recollections, daydreams or ideas, which can be connected with an experienced event.

A diary entry or interior monologue can be written from your own perspective or from the perspective of a fictional character in a story. When writing a diary entry or interior monologue for a character, follow the original style of the text and characters as much as possible.

S 7 Written exams

Understanding writing tasks

Questions on a text should be answered precisely and to the point. Try to use your own words as much as possible. Questions about fictional or non-fictional texts fall into three categories:

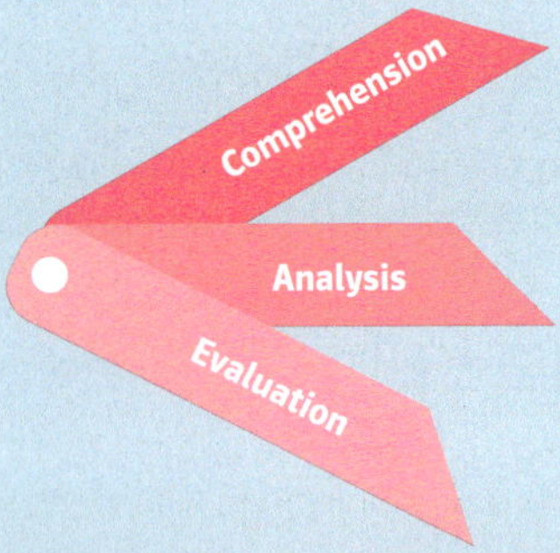

You are expected to answer questions about the contents of the text. Comprehension questions usually start with words like: show, outline, illustrate, summarise etc. The answer should usually be written in the simple present.

You are asked to concentrate on certain aspects of the text in detail. Analysis assignments typically start with words like: analyse, examine, explain, characterise etc.

You are asked to comment on certain aspects of the text, to look at the pros and cons and to give your own opinion. In these assignments you may also be asked to comment on a quote or to refer to the message of a picture or a cartoon. Evaluation assignments usually start with words like: comment, discuss, evaluate, interpret etc.

USEFUL PHRASES

Comprehension questions

The text is about … | deals with … | is an extract from … | describes … | is concerned with … |
The text was written by … / published in … |
In the text the author speaks about … | discusses … | expresses his/her view … | comments on … | gives his/her opinion on …

Analysis questions

The author highlights the aspect by using metaphors such as … | The author enhances his argument by repeating … | contrasting … | comparing … | The tone of the text is neutral … | optimistic … | aggressive …

Evaluation questions

From my point of view … | Weighing the pros and cons … | On the one hand, … | On the other hand … |
All aspects considered, … | In conclusion, … | Concluding, …

S 8 Analysing language

S 8.1 Stylistic devices

Whenever you are asked to analyse the language of a text, you have to mention the stylistic devices used by the author. It is equally important to explain their function. What might be the desired effect on the reader?

Stylistic device	Definition	Example
Alliteration	A series of words beginning with the same letter or sound.	*bold, bright and beautiful*
Anaphora	The first part of the sentence is repeated to create a certain effect.	*I didn't like his hairstyle. I didn't want to tell him.*
Ambiguity	When something can be understood in more than one possible way and therefore be unclear or confusing.	*Kids Make Nutritious Snack (a headline meaning either "Kids make good food" or "Eating kids is good for you")*
Appeal	A persuasive strategy directed at the emotions, values or beliefs of an audience.	*These children are starving – we are not. It's time to share!*
Comparison	When two or more people or things are compared with each other.	*She shines like the sun.*
Contrast	An obvious difference between two or more words.	*a fire-and-ice relationship*
Enumeration	Aspects are repeated step by step to create a list.	*old, grey, majestic*
Euphemism	Expressions that replace words that stand for something negative.	*"to pass away" instead of "to die"*
Exaggeration/Hyperbole	Ideas or opinions are made more important for the sake of effect.	*Her old mobile weighs a ton.*
Imagery	Words are used that create pictures in reader's minds.	*The song of the birds filled the woods.*
Irony	Words are used in such a way that the actual meaning differs from the intended meaning.	*That was clever! Now it's broken.*
Metaphor	A word or phrase comparing something to something else which shows that they are similar.	*a heart of gold*
Metonymy	Referring to something by the name of something else that is closely connected with it.	*Number 10 (referring to the British Prime Minister or government)*
Oxymoron	Two words with opposite meanings are joined together to create a strong effect.	*a deafening silence*
Paradox	A statement that appears to contradict itself.	*"I'm nobody," he said to introduce himself.*
Pun	A play on words that produces an often comical effect.	*"All she ever wanted was a camouflaged blouse, but she couldn't find one."*
Repetition	Enhances the importance of a particular aspect.	*Together, we are strong – strong and powerful.*
Rhetorical question	Does not expect a real answer. It is just asked to emphasise a certain point.	*Don't we all want to do our part to prevent the worst consequences of climate change?*
Sarcasm	Like irony, the literal meaning differs from the intended meaning. Often used to criticise or mock.	*"Wow, you're a genius!" (when someone made an obvious statement)*

S 8.2 Style, tone and register

When analysing a text, you might be asked to have a close look at the language used. Part of this is the analysis of style, tone and register:

Style is the typical way of writing or speaking used by a person; their choice of tone, grammar and narrative techniques.
Tone is the general mood, feeling or attitude being expressed. It is the emotional content of a text rather than the devices used.
Register is the choice of words, style and grammar used in a certain social context, usually reflecting the status of a speaker. Situations often have rules for appropriate register.

Situation	Features	Examples
Formal: in a formal speech or letter; adressing someone unknown or higher in a hierarchy	– respectful, neutral, detached style – complete and complex sentences – formal expressions – foreign/specialist words	*After analysing the evidence, the hypothesis was concluded to be correct.* *I would be grateful for your advice on this.*
Informal: used in spoken rather than written language, when speakers know each other well	– more personal and familiar style – simple sentences, can be incomplete or ungrammatical, dialect or slang – vivid, colloquial or vulgar expression	*Morning all! How's things? Fancy a cuppa? Gotta go get a donut. Ain't you got brains? C'mon, stupid.*
Literary: used mainly in written literary texts	– eloquent/elevated style – complex sentences – rich vocabulary – use of stylistic devices – can combine registers for various effects	*"So we went on in the quiet, and the twilight deepened into night. The clear blue of the distance faded, and one star after another came out." (Wells,* The Time Machine*)*

TIP

Style, tone and register are difficult to separate and are thus mainly considered together.
It is useful to note the way a character author/politician/expert speaks.
Don't forget: Form follows function. Comment on the way these devices are used to convey an impression.

S 9 Analysing fictional texts

S 9.1 Fictional text types

Fictional texts are made up, which means that they are based on imagination.
Non-fictional texts are based on facts and provide information and opinions about real-world issues.

Fictional texts	Novel	– a long, written, fictional prose narrative – has multiple characters, a plot and a narrator – is written in the past tense in most cases
	Short story	– same as novel but shorter – focuses on one major character and a turning point in their lives
	Graphic novel	– comic strip format published as a book – written for adults – texts can be fictional or non-fictional
	Play	– written to be performed on stage – consists of dialogues and monologues
	Poem	– artful arrangement of words to create rhythm – words are used to create images in the readers' mind

S 9.2 Analysing novels and short stories

A Characteristics of the novel

Function	– tells a fictional story, which transports the reader into a fictional world (which can be close to real life or fantastical) – to entertain and sometimes educate the reader
Focus	– able to give large amounts of detail because length is unlimited – can focus on any number of characters/protagonists and show developments over time – different narrative perspectives possible → S 9.4 – may cover several events or locations – can focus on a long period of time, sometimes over several generations – time settings could be historical, contemporary or futuristic
Structure	– long, informative introduction or direct start 'in the middle of things' (in medias res) – order of the plot can be chronological or written with narrative techniques such as frame story, flashbacks, back story or foreshadowing → S 9.5 – mainly separated into chapters – cliffhangers (exciting endings to chapters, making the reader want to read more) – ending can be closed, open, predictable or unexpected – effect created by the relationship between style and content
Language and style	– always in the genre of prose (following the flow of natural speech) – can be written in many different styles – contains descriptive sections, reported speech and direct speech

B Characteristics of the short story

Function	– gives a short glimpse of a life-changing event or revelation – captures an important moment or an important feeling
Focus	– single event, single setting, short time span – a limited number of characters
Structure	– direct beginning, little or no introduction – central turning point or surprising 'twist in the tale' near the end
Language and style	– often elliptical (details or sentence parts left out) – one distinctive language or style choice

S 9.3 Analysing poetry

Formal poetry types	– ballad, elegy, epic poem, haiku, ode, sonnet etc.
Free verse	– no rhyme or fixed rhythm pattern – sounds like natural speech – often used in the 20th and 21st century to express strong feelings or concentrate on unusual words/thoughts/associations
Enjambement (run-on line)	– connects lines and content – increases flow or tension
Style	– a poem can be lyrical, song-like, descriptive, narrative, comparative, humorous, reflective etc.
Title	– the title can be part of the poem
Metre (rhythm)	– pattern of accented or stressed (/) and unaccented (–) syllables
Rhyme	– words are labelled with letters to show the rhyme scheme

 SKILLS FILES

S 9.4 Narrative perspectives

The effect of a story is strongly influenced by the point of view, or perspective, from which it is told. Narrative types can be mixed and the point of view can sometimes change over the course of the story.

Third-person omniscient narrator This narrator does not play a part in the story. Although they are telling the story from the sidelines, they know everything about the characters' thoughts and feelings. This style of narration is mainly neutral and more distanced than others.	
Third-person limited narrator This narrator describes feelings and thoughts from the perspective of one particular character. It is often one of the main characters. This point of view enables us to feel quite close to this character.	
First-person narrator This narrator is a character who tells the story from his/her own perspective ('I'). We understand and sympathise easily with this type of narrator. Keep in mind that the first-person narrator is not the author unless the text is autobiographical.	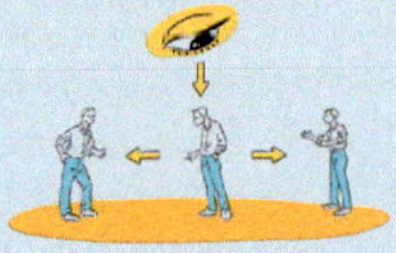
Objective narrator The objective point of view does not reveal any of the characters' feelings or thoughts. It is as if the narrator is watching the action and describing it objectively. This perspective usually does not create a sense of proximity to the characters.	

USEFUL PHRASES

Writing about narrative perspective

The story is told by a … narrator. | The narrator's views are very personal and subjective which can be seen … | The fact that the narrator is involved in the story leads to the effect that … | The narrator remains outside the plot. | The effect on the reader is … | The narrator describes the action and characters objectively.

S 9.5 Narrative techniques

When you analyse a fictional text, you should not only think about the story itself, but also about the ways in which it is told. These 'narrative techniques' influence the way the reader sees the story.

A Structure

The plot, i.e. the main events and the theme of a story, is usually structured in the following way:

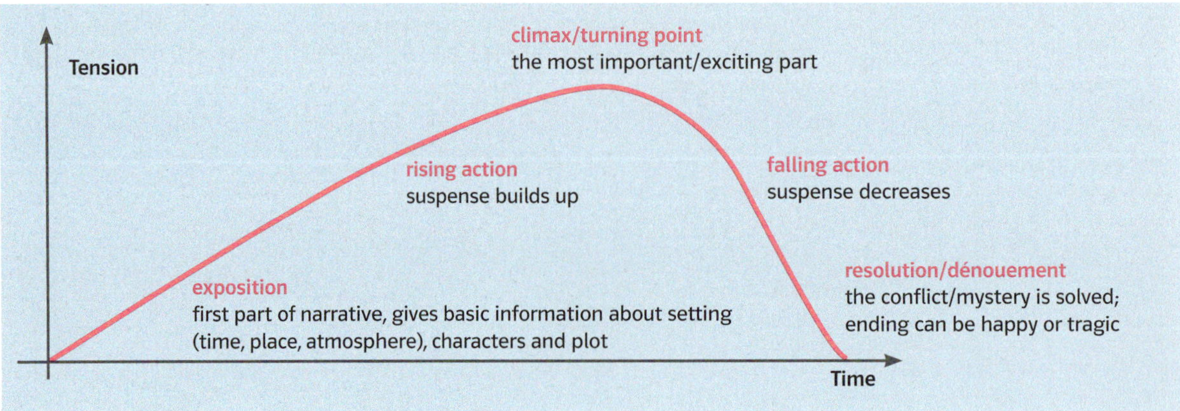

TIP

Tense as narrative technique
Tense influences the distance between readers and characters.
The use of **present tense** makes you feel closer to the action.
More distance is created when the narrator uses **indirect speech**.

B Chronology

Authors use different possibilities of relating the events in a story.

Back story	gives the history of characters, objects, places or events in the story
Flashback	the narrative is taken back in time
Flash-forward	future events are revealed
Foreshadowing	clues in the story that hint at a future development

C Narrative situation

Point of view	the narrator shows his/her attitude to the characters and can limit what the reader knows
Suspense	created by not giving away too much information; typical of crime or adventure stories
Tense	influences the distance between reader and characters (e.g. if the narrator uses present tense, you feel close to the action)
Irony	can be used as a distancing effect by the narrator
Narration	can vary between dialogues (direct speech), description and comments

S 9.6 Characterisation

When dealing with a novel, film or play, you will often be asked to analyse a certain character and his/her behaviour. In general there is a main character (protagonist, hero/heroine) and an antagonist (another important character who is in conflict with the protagonist).

Types of characters

Static/flat character
- shows no development
- has no depth

Round character
- complex
- shows inner conflict
- is presented in detail

Dynamic character
- changes over time
- shows development

How to analyse a character:

Preparing	– Collect any relevant information from the text about the character (personal details, appearance, behaviour, what he/she says and what others say about him/her). – Collect these facts as quotations and include line references.
Writing	1. Briefly present the character (personal details). Say what his/her function in the story is and how he/she relates to the other characters. 2. Describe the character's personality and behaviour. 3. Sum up their most important traits.

TIP

Direct characterisation
The narrator or a character tells the reader explicitly what a character is like.

Indirect characterisation
It is the reader's job to interpret a character through what the character thinks, does or says.

USEFUL PHRASES

Personal details
The protagonist is young/middle-aged/single/married …

Outward appearance
He/She is described as being tall/small/good-looking …

Positive character traits
He/She is/seems to be friendly/cheerful/good-natured/attentive/observant, intelligent/honest/trustworthy/sensitive/brave/generous/optimistic/polite …

Negative character traits
He/She seems to be bad-tempered/rude/violent/unreliable/pessimistic/dishonest/untrustworthy/mean/selfish/foolish/careless/ignorant …

Drawing conclusions about a character
The plot reveals that … |
His/Her statement "…" (line …) shows/proves that … |
He/She appears to be portrayed as … |
His/Her behaviour clearly indicates that … |
The character is described/presented/portrayed as …

Talking about relationships
to build up/to continue/to break off a relationship

S 10 Analysing non-fictional texts

S 10.1 Non-fictional text types

Non-fictional texts can be categorised according to their **intention**, i.e. what effect they want to have on the reader:

intentions of non-fictional texts

- to inform: newspaper/magazine article, summary/abstract, information brochure/informative handout, report, business letter, invoice
- to instruct: recipe, manual
- to make a request: business letter, business email
- to argue: speech, comment, letter to the editor
- to persuade/to appeal: argumentative/promotional text, political speech, advertisement
- to describe: technical description, description of a painting, biography

TIP

Remember that non-fictional texts, like newspaper and magazine articles, may have several different intentions.

S 10.2 Structure of non-fictional texts

One of the key steps in dealing with non-fictional texts is to analyse the text structure. How is the information generally organised and presented?

Structural feature	Intention	Analysis
opening	to spark interest in the reader	How does the writer introduce ideas/questions? e.g. *The writer begins with … In l. xx he/she introduces/asks … This highlights that …*
shifts	to give a different viewpoint or angle	What effect does the change of perspective have on the reader? e.g. *In l. xx the author offers a different viewpoint on the topic of … This makes the reader …*
repetition or patterns	to emphasise or highlight an idea/a problem/a question	What do these repetitions/patterns stress? e.g. *In l. xx, repetitions/patterns of … are used. This stresses/reinforces development/lack of change/… By doing so, the writer places emphasis on/calls attention to/brings the focus on/to …*
direct speech and quotes	to show different points of view, to give the text more credibility or to add to the importance of issues raised	Are these elements used to give examples, to emphasise or to introduce points of view? e.g. *In l. xx the author makes use of a strong direct quote by … This has the effect that …*
pace	to use speed to prompt a particular response or feeling in the reader	How does the pace of the text build excitement, tension, curiosity etc.? e.g. *The pace of the text is slowly/suddenly increased/sped up by … which helps to build up a sense of excitement/tension about … The pace of the text is decreased/slowed down by … which prompts the reader to …*
temporal references	to refer to time	Does the writer make reference to time to change the pace of the text? e.g. *In l. xx the author refers to the present/past/future which increases/reduces the pace of the text … In l. xx he/she jumps/travels forward/backwards in time, which brings a new perspective/setting/tone/atmosphere.*
sentence structure	to influence the flow of a text	How do different sentence types affect the flow of the text? e.g. *The writer uses (very) complex/simple sentences in l. xx. The flow of the text is thereby interrupted/eased/… Therefore, the text has quite a smooth/fragmented feel to it …*
order of events	to put the events in a sequence e.g. *first, then, next, finally*	Are the events presented in (chronological) order or not? How are key ideas/events presented and what effect does this have? e.g. *The author (doesn't) present the events in chronological order. He/she presents his/her main ideas … Ideas/events are coherent/easy to follow/hard to follow. This has the effect that …*
cause and effect	to describe the cause of an event and the consequences e.g. *is caused by …, as a result, for this reason, therefore, leads to …*	Does the writer use cause-and-effect relationships to get his/her message across? e.g. *By using a cause-and-effect relationship in l. xx, the author expresses her/his opinion on … He/she portrays … as significant/important/serious/… in the series of events.*
comparison and/or contrast	to show difference or similarity e.g. *Different from/to …, Same as …, Similar to …, As opposed to …, Instead of …, Compared with/to …, although, however, but, yet*	What effect does the use of comparisons and contrasts have on the text and the reader? e.g. *In l. xx, contrast is used to make the reader aware of … Contrast is used in l. xx to emphasise … on the background of … A comparison is presented in l. xx, where the author wants to raise the issue of … from a perspective of its relationship with …*
problem and solution	to describe a problem and present possible solutions e.g. *The problem/question is …, A solution might be …, One answer is …*	Does the writer focus on problems, solutions or both? What effect does this have? e.g. *The author focuses on the problem of … in l. xx but also offers a solution straight away. This gives the reader the impression that …*
description	to describe ideas, concepts, events or emotions in detail e.g. *for instance, for example, such as, to illustrate, to show*	What effect does this descriptive language have on the reader? e.g. *By using a very descriptive/elaborate language the author creates … This makes the reader/brings the reader closer to the text by appealing to the sense of …*

visual elements	to give more details, to present evidence or to convince the reader	How do visual elements influence the text and affect the reader? e.g. *The author uses an illustration/a photo/a diagram which shows … The visual element complements the text in that it … This convinces the reader of …*
closing	to give the reader some food for thought, to make a final statement or to build a bridge to the beginning	How does the text end? Is the reader provided with answers or left with open questions? How does the end relate to the beginning? e.g. *The article ends with …, leaving the reader thinking … It relates to the beginning in that …*

S 10.3 Analysing argumentative texts

A Types of arguments

Argumentative texts offer a lot of claims and theses, each of which is or should be supported by logical arguments as well as ethical and emotional appeals. In order to analyse an argumentative text, find out which types of arguments are used.

Practical argument	Refers to widely known facts and common experience in order to appear logical.	*Humans need oxygen to survive and plants produce oxygen – that's why it is important to protect the environment.*
Argument by illustration	Uses examples to support and illustrate a claim.	*The death penalty should be abolished because innocent people may be put to death. In 1990, for example, a man was executed in Florida for the murders of two police officers. Two years later he was found innocent.*
Argument by authority	Uses the opinion of experts and the results of statistics to prove a point.	*Recent studies show that very frequent use of social media affects mental health.*
Normative argument	Refers to accepted norms and values. Often based on common sense.	*To save our planet we will have to drastically reduce water and air pollution.*
Argument by analogy	The reader can easily draw parallels to other areas of life.	*In sports as well as in business, we can see globalisation, monopolies and illegal actions to "win at all costs" increasing. Sport is more and more heavily regulated to ensure that competition is fair and equal, thus business should be too.*

B Line of argumentation

Analysing the line of argumentation in a text includes describing and explaining how the argumentation is being developed throughout the text. How are the various parts of the text connected? What is the function of each individual paragraph?

S 10.4 Analysing newspaper articles

If you are asked to analyse a newspaper article, you need to identify the topic and the main points in the text. You will also have to identify and explain the type of article and its intention, as well as the article's structure.

A Types of articles

Reports/ News articles	– discuss current or recent news of general interest or on a specific topic – are formal and objective – focus only on the facts – answer general questions like Who? What? When? Where? Why? How? – may contain photographs, personal accounts, statistics, graphs, polls etc. – are often written in the simple past tense
Feature articles	– deal in depth with a topic, person or event by providing a great deal of a background information – analyse a series of events or a development that is of human interest – have a storyline and are entertaining – may contain quotations, personal interviews and descriptions
Editorials	– are written by the editor of the paper or magazine – focus on current events – include the writer's opinion – are usually run all together on a specific page of the paper or magazine (editorial page)

TIP

Quality of news reports
News reports are supposed to inform the public about interesting and important events in an unbiased way. However, their quality and neutrality differ depending on the newspaper or magazine.

B Structure of articles

Newspaper articles are often structured like an inverted pyramid with the most important aspect at the top. More facts and additional details follow, with the least important ones at the end, so readers can stop reading when they feel they have enough information. The typical parts of a newspaper article are explained in the following example:

British backpacker Sam Woodhead missing in Australian outback

The **headline** catches the reader's attention.

A British backpacker has disappeared after he set out on a run in the Australian outback.

The last picture Sam Woodhead posted, two days before he went missing .

Pictures often have a **caption**.

The **lead paragraph** introduces the news story by telling the most important facts (who, what, when, where, why, how).

Sam Woodhead was reported missing from a cattle station after he failed to return from a jog two days ago.

Local authorities launched a hunt for him amid fears he may have lost his way in a hot, isolated region of central Queensland. His mother is understood to have urged police to widen the search on the grounds that her son, an experienced long-distance runner, could have travelled some way from his base, near the town of Longreach.

Sister uses social media to reach out

His sister, Rebecca, issued an anxious plea for news on her social media. "If anyone hears from my brother, please contact me ASAP" she posted. In another posting, she added: "Thanks so much for all your messages regarding Sam. Still no further news but we have the helicopter going out again in the morning, Aus time, and hundreds of people going on voluntary search party. Will keep you all posted."

Subheadings are used to split articles into sections.

Newspaper articles are usually written in **columns**.

S 11 Describing and analysing visuals

There are four main types of visuals:

- pictures and paintings
- films
- cartoons
- diagrams

S 11.1 Describing and analysing pictures and paintings

Introduction	– Give information about the type of picture and the artist/photographer. – Say when the painting/photo was most likely painted/taken.
Description	– Give a general description of what is in the picture and what you can see. – Then describe the painting/photo in greater detail, including its structure (foreground/background, top/bottom, right/left/middle).
Analysis	– Describe the message conveyed by the picture and how this message is communicated. – Consider aspects like colour, contrast, tone, composition, focus, light and perspective. – If you think the picture is intended to have a certain effect on the viewer, describe how this is achieved.
Evaluation	– Based on the results of your analysis, state whether the picture is effective and which elements are responsible for it being successful or unsuccessful. – Give your personal opinion (if asked) or your thoughts on what topic the picture represents.

TIP

Use the **present progressive** to describe what people are doing.
Use the **simple present** to describe objects and the setting.

USEFUL PHRASES

Introduction
The photo/sketch/portrait/still life/oil painting was taken/drawn/painted by … and published in (year) … | The main focus is … | The picture illustrates …

Description
The picture/painting/photo depicts/shows a scene from … | On the left/right we can see … | In the foreground/background/middle/centre there is/are … | In the top/bottom left-/right-hand corner there are … | The light/colour/position of … creates an atmosphere of/gives an impression of …

Analysis
The artist/photographer (probably) wants to express/show/criticise … | The artist presents … | The light/colours of … create an … atmosphere/give an impression of/contribute to … | The position of …

Evaluation
The overall effect of the picture is … because … | In my opinion, the painting/photo only shows one aspect of/idealises/… | The picture reminds me of … because … | It is effective/moves me deeply because …

S 11.2 Analysing films

Writing an analysis of a film is quite similar to writing an analysis of a fictional text. Depending on the assignment, your film analysis may consist of the following parts:

1. Short summary of the scene
- What is happening (plot) and where (setting)?
- When does the scene happen?
- Which characters are involved?

2. Characterisation
- How are the main characters presented in this scene?
- How do they act?

3. Analysis of cinematic devices
- Which camera techniques are used?
- What effect do they have on the scene/the audience?

4. Analysis of the atmosphere
- How are sound, music and light used to create a certain atmosphere/special effects in the film?
- Do these effects enhance/complement those created by the camera techniques used?

TIP

Viewing table
Make a viewing table for your notes with spaces for details like action/story, characters/body language, space/setting, sound/music, camera techniques, editing/special effects, colours/lighting and language. Watch the scene your are analysing several times.

When writing a film analysis, you should name the cinematic devices (camera techniques) used in the scene/film and explain their functions and effects. When analysing the camera techniques used in a scene/film, focus on the following camera operations:

A Camera shots

An extreme close-up shot shows just one part of an object or a character's face and it concentrates on a single, important detail. If it shows a part of a character, then the viewer can see his/her emotions and facial expressions more clearly.

A close-up shot shows only part of a subject or, with people, the body from the waist up. This shot emphasises action and interaction.

A medium shot provides a complete view of the whole body or subject. It is often used during dialogues and conveys emotions by showing the characters' body language.

A full shot shows a complete view of all the characters in a scene, showing nothing or next to nothing of their surroundings.

A long shot shows a character or characters from top to bottom, including their surroundings. These shots establish a scene and give a general idea of the situation.

An extreme long shot usually shows a landscape. It is often used at the beginning of a film or scene to establish either the location (setting) of the scene or the general atmosphere/mood.

B Camera angles

Camera angle	Explanation	Effect
Bird's eye angle	Looks directly down on a scene.	- Often used to establish the setting. - Makes people look smaller and less significant.
Eye-level angle	Puts an audience on an equal footing with the character(s).	- Natural viewpoint which makes the viewer comfortable with the characters. - This is the most commonly used angle in films.
Low angle	Looks up at a character.	- Makes a character look more powerful.
High angle	Looks down on a character.	- Makes a character look vulnerable or small.
Over-the-shoulder shot	Shows a character from behind the shoulder of another character.	- Often used in scenes where a conversation takes place to show the interaction between the speakers.

USEFUL PHRASES

Analysing cinematic devices

to show someone in an establishing/extreme long … shot | to use a medium/close shot | to present someone from a low angle/from a high angle | to shoot something from a … perspective | to change/switch perspective

C Camera movement

Panning shot
- the camera moves horizontally from a fixed position to either follow a moving object or to give a panoramic view of the setting

Tracking shot/Dolly shot
- the camera is mounted on a "dolly" (a camera wagon) which moves on tracks or wheels
- is used to follow a character or another subject
- allows the viewer to feel part of the action

Tilting shot
- the camera moves vertically from a fixed position
- is often used to reveal someone's identity or to establish a scene

Crane shot/Booming
- taken by a camera on a moving crane
- is used to show characters from above, or to move up and then away from them at the end of a film

USEFUL PHRASES

Camera movements
to fade in/out | to zoom in/out | The camera pans from left to right/top to bottom. | The tracking shot follows the movement of …

S 11.3 Describing and analysing cartoons

A cartoon usually combines a drawing with a text and/or a caption. Cartoons often pick up on current events and criticise people, institutions or developments in society and politics. Some cartoons are just intended to be entertaining, e.g. making fun of a public figure. On the other hand, others can make a serious and important critical point, simply by using visual means.

Introduction	– Give information on the context (artist, date of publication and source). – Briefly say what the cartoon is about (a topic, an event, a person etc.).
Description	– Describe the cartoon in detail. – Use the present progressive to describe what people are doing in the picture, and the simple present to describe objects and the setting. – Include the contents of the text, captions, speech bubbles etc. and their relationship to the picture.
Analysis	– Examine each important element (people, objects, text) and explain the message they convey. – Pay attention to the function of the characters (Do they represent well-known people or a particular group of people?) and typical techniques (see tip box).
Evaluation	– State whether you think the cartoon is effective and which elements are responsible for it being successful/unsuccessful. – Give your personal opinion (if asked) or your thoughts on the topic presented in the cartoon.

TIP

Typical techniques used by cartoonists
- caricature (exaggerating certain striking characteristics)
- irony (depicting the opposite of what is really meant)
- exposing inconsistencies (e.g. contrasting a statement with a picture showing the exact opposite) emphasising stereotypes
- using wordplay and symbolism

USEFUL PHRASES

Introduction
The cartoon was drawn by … and was published/appeared in (source) on (date). | It was created in response to … | It shows/deals with/refers to/comments on … | The cartoonist makes fun of …/criticises … for (doing sth).

Description
The cartoon consists of/is made up of (several) …/is divided into … | There is a (short/an ironic) caption/speech bubble/thought bubble in/on/ next to … | The caption says/states that …/is a comment by … |
On the left-hand/right-hand side you can see … |
In the foreground/background/middle/centre there is … |
In the top/bottom left-/right-hand corner …

Analysis
The cartoon satirises/represents/is a caricature of … |
This figure is a stereotype of …/is exaggerated/supposed to represent …/supports the message of … |
The cartoonist is making fun of … | It is obvious that the artist wants to criticise/express/show …

Evaluation
The cartoon (only partly) achieves its aim of (doing sth). |
I (do not) think the cartoon is funny/easy to understand because … | In my opinion, the cartoonist is (not) successful in presenting/criticising … because … |
I (do not) like the cartoon because … |
The cartoon appeals/does not appeal to me. |
In my opinion, it is convincing/confusing/unfair/…

S 11.4 Describing and analysing diagrams and statistics

Diagrams visualise statistics and make them much easier to understand.
Data can be graphically presented in different ways:

Bar chart

Bar charts present data in coloured bars so as to make it easier to compare figures directly.

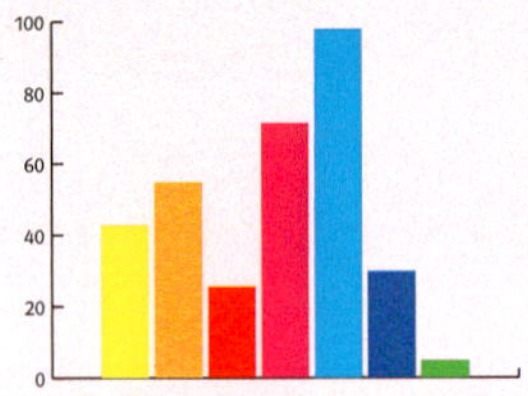

Pie chart

A pie chart is usually used to illustrate percentages or proportions.
The entire circle represents 100%. Each segment shows a percentage of the whole.

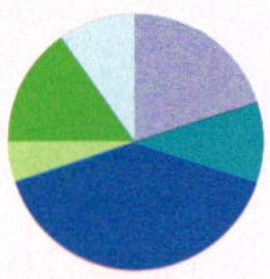

Line graph

A line graph shows a change/development over a certain period of time.

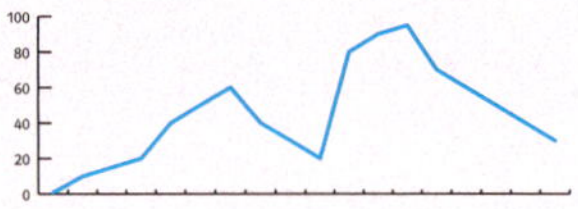

Flow chart

A flow chart shows the links between elements and their influence on each other.
It is best used to describe processes that contain decisions at certain points and where alternatives need to be shown.

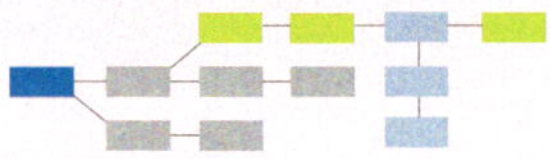

MK If you want to practise describing and analysing diagrams, you can search online for:
- Eurostat, the European Union statistical office
- ONS, the Office for National Statistics in the UK
- US data and statistics
- UNSD, the United Nations Statistics Division

USEFUL PHRASES

Bar chart
The vertical/horizontal axis shows/represents … |
The chart indicates/makes clear that … | The number of … is far greater than/is significant in comparison to …

Line graph
The line graph of … shows the development of … from … to … | The vertical axis shows the number/percentage/amount of … | The horizontal axis shows the time from … to … | The number of … increased/rose/remained constant/decreased/fell (gradually/steadily/rapidly/steeply/significantly) until … |
This change was possibly caused by …

Pie chart
The chart is divided into … segments. | The pie chart shows/represents … | The segments compare … | As you can see from the pie chart …

Flow chart
The process is divided into … stages/phases. | The first stage of the process is … | The process starts with/by … |
In this phase … | First/Second/Third … | Then … | After that … | Before that … | Following … | This is followed by … |
The next step is … | Alternatively … | There are then two possibilities … | Having completed … the … moves onto … |
Finally … | The process concludes with …

S 12 Mediation skills

Doing a mediation task

Mediation means providing a link between two languages and usually also between different text types or (cultural) situations.
In the mediation task, you are given a **scenario** which includes a particular context, a specific text type and an addressee. For your target text, you should pick out particular information from the source text and 'repackage' it for this scenario. Sometimes you need to summarise all of the important points, but more often you should go through the whole text to find all of the information on just one or more aspects (e.g. all of the reasons for something). Certain terms and cultural concepts may need explanation (e.g. political parties, institutions).
Sometimes you need to add some suitable text before or after, e.g. if you have to write an email, you should greet the reader, say why you are giving him/her this information and end the email formally or informally, depending on the situation.

Checking the task	Look carefully at the task and check: – who will be your addressee; depending on who it is, you will have to adapt the register/style in your target text – which information the addressee needs and why – which text type you are being asked to produce
Reading for gist	Read the source text once for gist. Note the title, the text type and the purpose, and if necessary, the author's name, intention and tone, in order to pass the information on correctly.
Preparing the mediation	Check the scenario and make sure you know: – the text type of your target text – the addressee – the purpose of the target text – the relationship between you and the addressee Mark only keywords in the source text which are relevant to the task. Take notes. Don't stop after finding one point you need. Check for more in the rest of the text. Only include information from the source text, not your personal opinion. Leave out any information you don't need. Sum up relevant points in your own words in English – do not translate word for word.
Writing the target text	Use suitable language and sentences for the target text. Rearrange the order of the information for your purpose. Paraphrase unknown words and explain anything your addressee might not understand. Think about the appropriate style, tone and register depending on the type of text you have to write. → S 8.2
Proofreading	Check for false friends, incorrect tense, spelling, prepositions, word order and style. Make sure that your text sounds natural.

S 13 Business communication

S 13.1 Writing business letters

A business letter is a type of written communication between two companies, or between a company and an individual. There are various different ways of setting out a business letter. The model letter below is set out in "block form" which is the best layout to use as it is universally accepted. Business letters are written in a polite and formal style. Therefore, use suitable forms of politeness and appropriate modal verbs. Make sure that your salutation and complimentary close corresponds with your relationship with the person you are writing to. Depending on the topic you are writing about, you will need to use technical terms too.
Business letters contain a date, a salutation, a subject line, a complimentary close and the signature/name of the person writing the letter. The text itself should have a clear structure and consist of short paragraphs only.

Sit in style Ltd.
14-20 Beccle Drive
Lowestoft
Suffolk
NR32 4LA
Phone: ...
Email: ...
www...

Monika Schwerberg
Presselstr. 123
75417 Mühlacker
Germany

Your ref:
Our ref: FS

20th May 20...

Dear Mrs Schwerberg

RE: The Broads leather sofas

Thank you very much for your letter from 10th May 20 ... regarding the sofas supplied by our company.

We are sorry to hear that the sofas which you ordered did not arrive in the shade of brown you had expected.
As you will surely have noticed, our sofas are handmade. The leather which we use for our sofas is a natural, breathable material which gets darker and more attractive with age.
Therefore, we are confident that you will soon be as fond of your sofas as you were when you visited our showroom in Lowestoft.
Should you however decide that the sofas do not come up to your expectations, you can still return them at your own expense within the next 14 days. We will then give you a refund for the sofas.
Please let us know of your decision. We sincerely hope that you will be as satisfied with the look and comfort of our sofas as many of our customers are.

Yours sincerely

Fiona Stewart

Fiona Stewart
Sales manager

Enc.

Writer's address: In commercial correspondence you should include the company's name, phone number, email address and website.

Include **references**: "Our ref:" is usually the initials of the person who wrote the letter (FS = Fiona Stewart).

Date: The British write day, month, year (20.5.20…). Americans write month, day, year (5.20.20…). Write the date in full or use the international date format year-month-date (20...-05-20) to avoid confusion.

Include a **subject line** beginning "RE:".

Main part: State your reason for writing in formal, polite language. Group your points in paragraphs.

Complimentary close

Signature

Name in full

Writer's position in the company

Enc(s). = Enclosed: Indicates that additional material is being sent with the letter.

USEFUL PHRASES

Explaining the purpose of your letter
We are writing / I am writing to tell you that … / … to let you know… / … in connection with … / … to confirm … / … to ask you… / … to inform you…

Stating a reference
Thank you for your email / letter … | Referring to your recent letter / email / phone call / enquiry … | Further to our telephone conversation … | I came across/saw your job offer/advert …

Giving good news
I am delighted to tell you that… | You will be pleased to hear that …

Giving bad news
We regret to inform you that … | I'm afraid that … | Unfortunately we are unable to …

Making a request
Could you please / possibly… | We would be grateful if you would / could … | We would appreciate if you could …

Enclosing documents
I am enclosing … | Please find enclosed / attached …

Thanking
Thank you for sending us … | Many thanks for your …

Closing remarks
If you have any questions, please don't hesitate to call/ to contact us on … | Please feel free to contact us with any questions you might have. | We look forward to hearing from you soon. | Please find enclosed a copy of …

TIP

Run the spelling and grammar checker on your computer before you send any important documents.

S 13.2 Writing business emails

A great deal of today's business communication is done via email because it is one of the most efficient means of communication: it is quick, convenient and easily traceable. However, emails can only be efficient if they are written correctly. Business emails are often less formal than business letters. Business emails are written in a polite and formal style. Therefore, use suitable forms of politeness and appropriate modal verbs. Make sure that your salutation and complimentary close corresponds with your relationship with the person you are writing to. Depending on the topic you are writing about, you will need to use technical terms too.
Business emails contain a salutation, a subject line, a complimentary close and the name of the person writing the email. The text itself should have clear structure and consist of short paragraphs only.

From: lhamilton@mail.uk Sent: 04.06. … 10:06
To: jwise@radiosouthwest.uk
CC:
Subject: Work placement at Radio SouthWest
Attachments: Louise_Hamilton_CV.docx

Dear Mr Wise,

With reference to the work experience advert on your website I would like to be considered for the position …

…

Best regards,
Louise Hamilton

Sender

Recipient

Attachments: Be sure to name the attached files clearly.

Salutation: Start with "Dear …," or just "Hello/Hi," if you know the adressee well.

Complimentary close: Close your email with "Kind / Best regards" or "Best wishes".

Date and time: These details will appear automatically.

CC = carbon copy (*Kopie an …*): Add the email addresses of others who are also concerned by the subject.

Subject line: Always mention the precise subject matter to help the recipient best deal with your email.

Body: Start your email with a capital letter.

Signature block: If you are writing an email from one company to another, include your position and/or department below your name.

TIP

Email etiquette
- Limit your email to one subject only, be precise and clear.
- Make sure your email has a clear structure.
- Even though emails tend to be less formal than letters, remain polite.
- Do not use colloquial language or emoticons.
- Proofread your emails (grammar, spelling, punctuation, choice of words …).

S 13.3 Writing a CV

CV is short for "curriculum vitae" which is Latin for "the course of your life".
Use the following Dos and Don'ts and the model CV below as a guide for writing a CV in English:

Dos	Don'ts
- include skills and interests which are relevant to the job	- write more than one page
- give the English equivalents of German terms, if possible	- include a photo, unless asked to
	- sign your name at the end

Curriculum Vitae

Name	Tizian Baumann
Address	Schmidstr. 119, 73430 Aalen, Germany
Phone	+49 123 456 7890
Email	t.baumann@email… .de
Date of birth	6th May 2002
Nationality	German
Personal statement	I am a student at a vocational college who is looking for a work placement in a hotel with a good reputation. I enjoy working in a team and I am interested in gaining experience in the hospitality sector. I am also looking for a challenge where I can use and improve my skills.
Education	2019 – 2021: KKS Aalen (vocational college) Abitur (A-levels): English A, Business Studies B, Mathematics B, Social Studies A 2012 – 2019: Luise-Hensel Realschule (intermediate secondary school) Realschulabschluss (secondary school certificate comparable to GCSEs) in 2019
Work experience	Summer job at the Regency Hotel in Cologne Reception desk and maintenance
Interests	Sports: I am an active basketball player and I also enjoy skiing. Leadership: I train a 4 – 6-year-old football team at my local sports club.
Skills	Language: Fluent English and a working knowledge of Spanish Computing: Good computer skills (MS Office) Driving: Full driving license

S 13.4 Writing a letter of application

A letter of application (or cover letter) is often your first form of contact with a prospective employer. It is supposed to complement the CV that you send with it. In a cover letter, you should introduce yourself to the organisation, demonstrate your interest in the company and job, explain why you are qualified for the position you are applying for and persuade the reader to interview you.
The job advert itself will usually provide a list of requirements, i.e. "desirable" skills and experience. Ideally, your letter of application will respond to the majority of these requirements.

Nils Borchert
Oberfeldstrasse 20
74564 Crailsheim
Germany

Ms L. Johnson
Creative Concepts Ltd.
London WC5 10B
England
UK

19th February 20 ...

Dear Ms Johnson

Application for a work placement

With regards to the advertisement on your homepage, I would like to apply for ...
I am currently a pupil at a vocational college in ...

As you will see from the enclosed CV, I have ...

I am particularly interested in working at your company because ...

My computer skills would be an asset to your company, as I ...

I believe that I would make a valuable contribution to your company. I look forward to hearing from you.

Yours sincerely

Nils Borchert
Nils Borchert
Enc.: CV

Include a subject line to show what you are applying for.
Careful: BE = work placement, AE = internship

Who are you?
Say why you are writing the letter and introduce yourself in the first paragraph.

What have you done so far?
In the second paragraph, mention important points from your CV.

Why are you interested in the vacancy?
Say why you want the job and what you know about it.

Why are you the best candidate for the job?
Explain what you think you can bring to the company and job.

End with a friendly sentence which looks forward to a reply.

Print your name under the signature and mention what you are enclosing.

TIP

Dos and don'ts: Letter of application
- Choose an email address that creates a professional impression.
- Double-check: grammar, spelling and also dates, numbers, facts etc.
- Don't mention any of your other job applications.
- Limit your letter of application to one page.
- Avoid overusing the word 'I'. Try rephrasing your sentences.

USEFUL PHRASES

Applying for a job
As you can see from my CV, my qualifications and work experience pefectly match your requirements/ make me a suitable candidate for this job. | My negotiating skills / computer skills /language skills /... would be an asset to your company. | I have considerable experience in ... | I have gained valuable experience in ... | I am fully proficient in MS Office /programming /... | During my work placement with ... I gained further experience in / knowledge about ...

S 14 Speaking skills

S 14.1 Giving a talk or presentation

The key to giving a good talk or presentation is to prepare well in advance. Think of a good structure for your talk or presentation and prepare prompt cards with keywords. Then you'll be ready to go!

A Preparing a talk or presentation

4

Prepare your introduction and conclusion
- Catch the listener's attention by starting with an interesting question or fact, a quote, a picture or a cartoon.
- Write a prompt card featuring your main points so you can give a brief outline of your talk or presentation at the beginning.
- Choose a final quote or example you'd like to use.
- Make a prompt card with the points you want to emphasise or summarise again.

3

Arrange your prompt cards in a logical order
Choose how you want to present your points:
- chronologically (presenting a person or historical events)
- contrasting (comparing different approaches or arguments)
- from least important to most important important or vice versa (arguing for or against something)

2

Choose the points you want to talk about and make prompt cards
- Choose three main points or arguments for the main part of your talk/presentation.
- Prepare a prompt card with keywords and useful phrases for each part of your talk or presentation.
- Note down any examples or quotations.

1

Gather material on your topic
- Brainstorm ideas and organise them in a word web.
- Do research and collect information from relevant sources (online, library, newspapers, ...).

Prompt cards

1 Introduction
- note down main points of talk
- keywords for initial joke/ quote/example ...
- note useful phrases

2 Main point 1
- one argument / point per card
- note keywords
- note useful phrases

3 Main point 2

4 Main point 3

5 Conclusion
- note down main points of talk
- keywords for final quote/ example
- note useful phrases

TIP

Before your talk
- Practise your talk or presentation out loud in front of a mirror.
- Ask a friend/relative to listen to you and give feedback.
- Prepare a handout for your audience which briefly lists your main points or arguments.
- Use keywords and make sure you include your sources on the handout.
- Test any equipment you need (laptop/tablet/ projector/speakers ...) as early as possible.

B Speaking in front of other people

Follow these Dos to make your talk or presentation as successful as possible for both you and your audience:

Dos for giving a talk or presentation

- Speak slowly and clearly.
- Use short, clear sentences.
- Use vocabulary that is known to your audience.
- Explain unknown terms or phrases.
- Vary your intonation so that you don't sound boring.
- For example, you could emphasise particularly important points by speaking a little more loudly.
- Look at your audience as often as possible and speak freely.
- Smile! (But don't laugh nervously!)
- Start by introducing yourself (if necessary) and your topic.
- Finish by thanking your audience for listening and asking if anyone has any questions.

USEFUL PHRASES

Introduction
Good morning/afternoon, (my name is …).
My topic today is … / The title of my talk today is: …
In my presentation today I want to talk about …
I will begin by explaining/describing … and continue with … Finally, I will …

Main part/structuring ideas
Have you ever thought about …
Did you know that …?
I would like to cover three aspects in my talk: …
First of all … / Secondly … / Finally …
Moving on to the next point, I would like to talk about …
For this reason/Therefore, we can assume that …

Examples/quotes
In the words of … (name of person) "…" (quote).
This example proves that …
X once said that … / According to X …

Commenting on visuals
As we can see from the cartoon/photo …
The statistics clearly show that a minority / a majority of …

Conclusion
I think we can safely say that …
So in conclusion, I would like to sum up by …
Thank you for listening. Are there any questions?

S 14.2 Preparing for a job interview

Your aim at a job interview is to show that your skills, work experience and attitude make you a good choice for the position.
Job interviews differ depending on the company, the interviewers and the position. That being said, you can still prepare yourself in some ways.

If you are invited to a job interview, make sure to do the following things beforehand:

Preparation for a job interview

- Find out about the business or institution.
- Think of questions that you might want to ask the interviewer about the business or institution.
- Think of questions that you might be asked and prepare suitable answers.
- Practise the interview with a friend. Ask for feedback.
- On the day of the interview, dress appropriately, be polite, friendly, communicative and on time.

Be prepared for the following phases and questions which are likely to be part of a job interview:

	Interviewer	Ideas for your answers
Breaking the ice	How are you? How was your journey?	Tell them about how you are feeling right now and how you got there.
Getting to know each other	Let me tell you something about us … Tell us about yourself.	Say what you are doing at the moment (school, internship etc.). Say when you will finish and what qualification you will then have.
Talking about the company and the job	Why do you want to work for us?	Explain what interests you about the company and its products/services.
Work experience	What have you done so far?	Talk about experiences that are relevant to the job (internships, volunteer work etc.).

Strengths and weaknesses	What are your strengths and weaknesses?	Explain what you are good at: – school subjects you are good at and that are relevant to the position – hobbies that have taught you a life skill (as a team player/coach, in first-aid etc.) – characteristics that your friends like about you Explain what you'd like to improve: – tell about one of your flaws and say how you are trying to work on/overcome it
Career goals	Where do you see yourself in 2–5 years?	Say what you want to achieve professionally.
Closing the interview	Do you have any questions?	You could ask questions about: – the starting/finishing date – working hours, working at weekends, overtime – who you would be working with – …

A short while after your interview, send a brief follow-up email thanking your interviewer and expressing interest in the position again. If you haven't been told when the decision will be made, ask politely when you can expect a reply. If you don't get the job, don't worry! Think about what you can do better next time, and work on these points. As with any other skill, the more interviews you do, the better you will get!

TIP

Privacy matters

Interviewers are not allowed to ask everything. Questions have to be strictly related to the job. No-gos are, for example, questions about your religion or your private plans for the future like having children.

USEFUL PHRASES

Breaking the ice / small talk

I had a very short/long/pleasant / … journey here. | I'm a little bit nervous but I'm looking forward to the interview.

Introducing yourself

I graduated / will be graduating from school in … | I have always been interested in science / languages … | I have a passion for …

Talking about the company and the job

Your company is of particular interest to me because … | I have always wanted to work for … | I would welcome the opportunity to work at your company because … | I'm well qualified for the position because …

Work experience

As you can see from my CV … | I trained in … | I did an intership at/with … | I have a part-time job as … | I did work experience as …

Strengths and skills

I'm able to work under pressure / to work independently | I'm hard-working | patient | polite | well-organised | a team player | creative | flexible …

Career goals

In five years' time I would like to be …

Questions about the company or the job

When will the job start? | How long will the internship/ job / training … be? | What are the usual working hours? | Am I expected to work on weekends? | How big is the team / department …? | How many employees work here?

S 14.3 Making phone calls

The key to making a phone call is good preparation. Think about what you want to say and then prepare how you are going to say it.

Preparation

- Make a list of things you want to say / ask in English.
- Choose a suitable greeting and close (see "Useful phrases"). Add them to your list.
- Collect phrases you could use if the person is not there and you need to leave or pass on a message.

Making the phone call

- Give your name and, if it is a business call, the name of your company.
- Be as polite as possible and speak clearly.
- Do not just answer questions with "Yes" or "No". Give more information.
- If you miss some information or can't understand/hear the caller, ask them to repeat themselves.

Closing

- Tell the caller what action you are going to take.
- Thank the person for calling and say goodbye politely.

TIP

Spelling alphabet

Use the international spelling alphabet to spell names, addresses etc.:

A	Alpha	H	Hotel	O	Oscar	V	Victor
B	Bravo	I	India	P	Papa	W	Whiskey
C	Charlie	J	Juliet	Q	Quebec	X	X-ray
D	Delta	K	Kilo	R	Romeo	Y	Yankee
E	Echo	L	Lima	S	Sierra	Z	Zulu
F	Foxtrot	M	Mike	T	Tango		
G	Golf	N	November	U	Uniform		

USEFUL PHRASES

Spelling

A for Alpha, B for Bravo …
a umlaut/ä, that's an 'a' with two dots on top.
I come from Kehl, that's K-E-H-L.
My email address is C-H-A-L-L-E-N-G-E-at-E-N-G-L-I-S-H-dot-D-E.

Greeting

Hello, this is / my name is …
Good morning, … speaking.
I'm a student at … | I'm calling about …
I just wanted to know/ask …

Asking to speak to someone

Could I speak to … please?
Could you put me through to …, please?
May I speak to …?

Leaving a message

Would you mind taking a message for …?
Could you please tell … that I called and ask him/her to call me back?

Checking information

I'm sorry. What did you say your name was?
I'm afraid I didn't get your name/number …
Sorry, I didn't quite get/catch that.
Could you give me your name / number… again?
Could you repeat …?
Could you spell …?

Closing

Thank you for your help/time.
Thanks for calling. Goodbye.

S 15 Oral exams (*Kommunikationsprüfung*)

Preparing for an oral exam

The *Kommunikationsprüfung* is an oral exam which you do with one other classmate or with your teacher. You will be given marks for the points you make, your vocabulary, grammar and pronunciation, and how you interact with your classmate or your teacher. The exam consists of two parts:

Part 1: monologue

- You give a short talk based on a prompt (a cartoon, an advert, a diagram, a picture, a quote etc.).
- To prepare, look carefully at the following skills: → S 11, S 14

Part 2: dialogue

- You have a conversation with your classmate or your teacher.

USEFUL PHRASES

Introducing yourself
Good morning. I'm … | Let me introduce myself. I'm … | I'd like to introduce myself. My name's …

Structuring a talk
I'm going to look at … | I'd like to talk about / point out / mention … | There are three things to consider. Firstly … Secondly … Thirdly … | One point is … Another aspect is … | To begin with … | Now I want to describe … | Finally I'd like to …

Getting more information
Could you tell me more about …? | I'd like to know more about … | Something else I was wondering about was …

Agreeing and disagreeing
Exactly. I couldn't agree more. | That's just what I was thinking. | That's a good point. | I see what you mean, but isn't it also true that …? | I'm not sure if I agree with you about …

Asking questions
What I'd like to know is who / what …? | Why do you think that …? | Could you explain what you mean by …?

Checking that someone has understood you
Are you with me? | Do you see what I mean?

Hesitating
Well, let me see now … | How can I put it?

Interrupting / being interrupted
I'm sorry to interrupt you, but … | Could I just finish my point? As I was saying …

Giving opinions
Well, if you ask me … | The point is … | As I see it … | I'd like to point out the fact that …

Giving reasons
As a result (of) … | Because (of) / due to … | Therefore… | Consequently …

Making suggestions
I think it might be a good idea to … | Why don't we all …? | Don't you think it would be a good idea to …?

Persuading / objecting
That's a good idea, but … | I really don't think so because … | I see what you mean but … | That's true but …

Summarising / drawing a conclusion
All things considered … | On the whole … | For this reason / these reasons … | Taking everything into account, we can say that …

S 16 Vocabulary skills

S 16.1 Expanding your vocabulary

Word webs are a great tool to cluster and organise new vocabulary which makes it easier to learn new words. You can either make a word web for each new word you want to learn or you can collect vocabulary that relates to a specific topic.

A Learning new words

increase

- word class: noun
- sample sentence: There was an increase in the number of college students last year.
- meaning: a rise in the size or number of something
- word family: to increase, increasing
- synonyms: rise, growth
- antonyms: decrease, drop

TIP

antonym = a word with the opposite meaning
synonym = a word with a similar or the same meaning

B Collecting topic vocabulary

Young people's style

- self-expression
- self-comparison
- poor self-esteem
- social media influencers
- to wear what you want
- to blend in with the crowd
- a unique sense of style
- to compromise who you are
- personal style

S 16.2 Guessing unknown words

There is no need to be afraid of texts containing new words. You already know many different ways of guessing their meanings. After applying your guessing technique, it is likely that there are still some words you don't know the meaning of, but you will probably understand the most important points in the text.

Guessable words	Examples
Words that are also used in a German context	*bestseller, boycott, clown, laptop, track, …*
Words that are similar to German words → watch out for false friends!	*individuality, install, parallel, to wander, …*
Words that are similar to words you know from another foreign language (e.g. French, Latin, Spanish, Italian) → watch out for false friends!	*academic, announcement, artificial, descendant, dignity, individuality, junior, minor, pasta, phase, …*
Compounds of words you already know	*handwriting, heartfelt, mixed ability, single-sex, washing machine, whole-heartedly, …*
Words from a word family you already know	*adventurous, announcement, to mirror, nationalism, relevance, …*
Words with prefixes or suffixes whose root you already know	*to dislike, impatient, to rewrite, profitable, paperless, …*
Words you already know, but with a different meaning – the new meaning may be guessed from the context	*to admit, light, plain, pretty, to report sb, …*
Words whose meaning you can guess from the context	*(he) dozed off (in his chair); (it's old-fashioned) out of date; …*

TIP

prefix = an element placed before a word that changes its meaning (*dis*like, *im*patient)
suffix = an element placed after a word that changes its meaning or word class (profit*able*, paper*less*)

S 16.3 Working with a dictionary

When you cannot guess a word from its context in the text, you can look it up in a dictionary. Using a dictionary takes time however, so decide if you really need to know the meaning of the word in order to understand the sentence or text.

A English-German, German-English (bilingual)

This type of dictionary is best used for translating or finding the meaning of new words quickly. You can use a bilingual dictionary to do mediation exercises.

Check the following information in your dictionary:

- Which word class does the word belong to?
- Which words does it often go together with?
- What topic or word field does it belong to?
- How is it pronounced?
- Are there irregular forms?
- What translations are given?
- Which of the translations can only be used in a limited context (AE, formal, slang etc.)?
- Which of the translations fits the context?

Example

fo·cus['fəʊkəs] <pl focuses, foci> [pl 'fəʊsaɪ] s ❶ (MATH OPT) Brennpunkt m ❷ (fig) Brennpunkt, Herd m, Zentrum nt; ~ (un)scharf eingestellt; ~ scharf einstellen vt ❶ (OPT PHOT) einstellen (on auf) ❷ (fig) konzentrieren (on auf);
focus group s (in marketing) [ausgewählte]

B English-English (monolingual)

This type of dictionary is best used for writing an English text when you are not quite sure which is the best word to choose in a given context.

An English-English dictionary provides you with the following information:

- What part of speech is the word?
- Which words does it often go together with?
- What topic or word field does it belong to?
- How is it pronounced?
- Are there irregular forms?
- What synonyms and/or definitions are given?
- Which of the given meanings fits the context?
- Examples show how the word is typically used.

TIP

- Before looking up a word, identify whether it is a verb, noun, adjective, adverb etc.
- When you have found the entry for the word, make sure you look at the meaning for the correct word class.
- Read any additional information which the dictionary gives you about the word.
- Take your time to read the entry carefully.
- Make sure you find the entry which matches the use of the word in the given context.

Example

different uses of "air"

pronunciation in British and American English

intransitive or transitive verb

word class

noun without a plural form

other usages and where to find them

examples to show typical contexts

air [GAS] / eəʳ / (US) / er / *noun* [U] the mixture of gases which surrounds the earth and which we breathe: *I went outside to get some* **fresh** *air.* ' *You should put some air in your tyres – they look flat to me.*
➲ See also **airy** LIGHT; **airy** NOT SERIOUS; **airy** DELICATE.
• be walking/floating on air, to be very happy and excited because something very pleasant has happend to you: *Ever since she met Mark, she has been walking on air.*

air [MANNER] / eəʳ / (US) / er / noun [S] manner or appearance: *She has* **an** *air* **of** *confidence about her.*
• airs and graces, false ways of behaving that are intended to make other people feel that you are important and belong to a high social class.
• put on airs (and graces) (ALSO give yourself airs (and graces)), DISAPPROVING to behave as if you are more important than you really are.

air [DRY] / eəʳ / (US) / er / *verb* [I *or* T] to become try and/or fresh, or to cause to become try and/or fresh: *My mother always airs the sheets before she makes the beds.* ' *Leave the window open to let the room air a bit.*

S 17 Making a video

Preparing a video

Preparation
- find suitable actors, location(s) and setting
- decide on the use of light (e.g. bright, fading), colours (e.g. dark, warm), space (e.g. interior or exterior, wide or narrow) and cinematic devices → S 11.2
- produce a film script and a storyboard

Filming
- follow your storyboard
- repeat takes if necessary

Editing
- use suitable editing techniques (e.g. cut, fade in, fade out, slow motion, fast motion)
- add sound (e.g. music, dubbing, silence, voiceover, effects)
- include still images or signs

Example of a script (adaptation of the first scene from *The White Tiger* by Aravind Adiga)

```
1 EXT. Beijing, Great Hall of the People -- DAY
    Fade-in to time lapse of PEOPLE of all kinds walking across Tiananmen Square past
    the façade, including businessmen and street vendors. Chinese music.

2 INT. Beijing, Premier Wen Jiabao's office -- SAME TIME
    Crosscut to Chinese PREMIER at desk, leaning back in chair, reading a printout
    letter (several pages). Secretary, nervous, stands waiting for reaction. Silence.
                   PREMIER
    (annoyed, irritated; speaks in Chinese. Subtitle; subtitle in English appears)
              It's in English.
                   VOICEOVER BALRAM
    (Balram, speaking in English with an Indian accent)
              Mr Premier, Sir.
              Neither you nor I can speak English, but there are some things
              that can be said only in English.

3 INT. Bangalore, India, huge and shabby room, nearly empty, one large 70's chandelier;
  fan above, splitting up the light; radio -- NIGHT
    Fade-in to Balram cross-legged on floor with a silver laptop but talking, not
    typing. Dreamy look on his face.
                   BALRAM
              … and at 11:32 p.m. today, which was about ten minutes ago, when
              the lady on All India Radio announced, "Premier Jiabao is coming
              to Bangalore next week", I said that thing at once.
```

Example of a storyboard (shot 3 from the film above)

Audio	Near silence, voice fades in	Radio background: Indian music	Fade out radio, Balram louder
Video			
Shot	Fade-in establishing shot: bird's eye view, chandelier to left, Balram small, centre	Move: slow crane zoom round back of Balram to front close-up at "announced"	Stop at: close-up frontal shot Balram, from "I said that thing at once."

S 18 References and sources

S 18.1 Checking sources

You will often have to research a topic before you can talk or write about it. There are many different ways of finding out information: by researching online, by going to a library and looking in books, newspapers or magazines or by talking to an expert. However, sources differ in quality and reliability, especially online. Therefore, it is absolutely vital that you check your sources before using them. Here is how you distinguish between reliable and unreliable sources:

Reliable	**Unreliable**
– written by respectable journalists, professors, experts or institutions	– without a named author – written by hobby "experts" – from the popular press
– up to date	– too old to be useful
– neutral and objective	– expressing a biased opinion
– covering both sides of a controversial topic	– offering one-sided information only
– with expert proof or personal experience	– just hearsay
– correct grammar and spelling	– many grammar and spelling mistakes

TIP

Don't believe everything you read! Anyone can publish anything on the internet. Printed articles and books have normally been more carefully chosen and edited, but these can also be biased or too generalised and simple.

MK If you are unsure about certain news or facts, use a fact check website to validate your source.

S 18.2 Citing sources

You must document all the sources (texts, pictures, statistics, videos etc.) you have used in a presentation or written text. There are different citing styles, for example MLA, APA, Harvard or Chicago. The examples below are in MLA style since this is the most commonly used style.

A Citing in the text

Within your text, you can either cite your sources in a footnote or in brackets within the text. Add the footnote or brackets at the end of the sentence or paragraph in which you reference or use the source.

Bill Smith analyses migration problems in Britain. He writes that real life is about integration.[1]

[1] Smith, Bill. *Real Life in the UK*. London, Brown, 2014, p. 23.

Bill Smith analyses migration problems in Britain. He writes that real life is about integration (Smith 23).

B Creating a list of references

For each of the sources that you have used and referenced in your text, include the following details in your list of references:
Author's name, Author's surname. *Title*. Place of publication, Publishing house, Year of publication.

References/Bibliography

Books:

Egger, Dave. *The Circle*. New York, Knopf, 2013.

Smith, Bill. *Real Life in the UK*. London, Brown, 2014.

Articles:

Jones, Owen. "London riots – one year on." *The Independent*, 24 July 2012.

Online sources:

Darzi, Ara. "Great communication in healthcare can save lives." *The Guardian* online, 18 November 2015, theguardian.com/healthcare-network/2015/nov/18/nhs-great-communication-healthcare-save-lives-behavioural-insight-nudge. Accessed 5 June 2019.

TIP

Copyrighted material

It is important to check whether the material you are including is copyrighted, i.e. it can only be used with the permission of the author. You can include copyrighted material in your presentation in class if you cite it correctly, but you are not allowed to publish or upload it online. Check the material for a copyright notice: the symbol "©" or the word "copyright" followed by the date of publication and the author's name. Pictures may have a watermark to show that they are copyrighted.

S 18.3 Quoting

Always make a clear difference between text you wrote yourself and text or facts written by others. You can cite a text in different ways:

Direct quotation: Copy the exact words of the source text and cite them with quotation marks. If you cite a whole sentence, add a colon (…: "…").

Indirect quotation: Paraphrase the source using your own words.

In her article "Great communication in healthcare can save lives", Ara Darzi states: "More than one in 15 hospital prescriptions contains some kind of error […]". She argues that "the most frequent cause of avoidable harm to patients in hospital" is that prescriptions are not written clearly and do not contain all the necessary information (Darzi, *The Guardian.com*).

TIP

Symbols and abbreviations

[…]	to add to or leave words out of a direct quote
l./ll.	to indicate the line or lines you are quoting (e.g. in a poem or newspaper article)
p.	to indicate the page you are quoting from
ff.	to indicate the page on which the quote starts (ff. stands for "and the following pages")
'…'	to mark direct speech in a quote
/	to mark the beginning of a new line in a quoted poem

USEFUL PHRASES

Direct quotation (whole sentence)
In his/her book/article …, X states: "…" (p. 7ff.).

Direct quotation (built into your sentence)
X claims/argues/assumes/concludes that "…" (l. 6). | X presents … as "…", which … (p. 12).

Indirect quotation (paraphrasing)
X claims/reports/writes in … that… | According to X, … is/has/was/could … (ll. 7–9). | In X's article, he/she describes …, which is based on/gives reasons for/explains why … (l. 4). | While X argues that …, Y gives reasons for … (l. 23ff.; l. 76ff.).

G1	**Tenses**	281
G1.1	Simple present	281
G1.2	Present progressive	281
G1.3	Simple past	282
G1.4	Past progressive	282
G1.5	Present perfect simple	283
G1.6	Present perfect progressive	283
G1.7	Past perfect simple	284
G1.8	Past perfect progressive	284
G1.9	Going to-future	285
G1.10	Future simple (will-future)	285
G1.11	Future progressive	286
G1.12	Future perfect simple	286
G1.13	Future perfect progressive	287
G1.14	Conditional I	287
G1.15	Conditional II	288
G2	**If-clauses**	288
G2.1	Type 1	288
G2.2	Type 2	289
G2.3	Type 3	289
G3	**The passive**	290
G4	**Relative clauses**	291
G4.1	Defining relative clauses	291
G4.2	Non-defining relative clauses	291
G5	**Adjectives**	291
G6	**Adverbs**	292
G7	**Question tags**	293
G8	**Modal auxiliaries**	293
G9	**-ing forms**	294
G9.1	The present participle	294
G9.2	The gerund	294
G10	**Reported speech**	295
G11	**Word order**	296
G11.1	Statements	296
G11.2	Questions	296
G11.3	Negated statements	296
Übersicht Grammatik-Erklärfilme und interaktive Übungen		297

G1 Tenses

G1.1 Simple present

V10 I12
Talking about the present

Positive sentences	Negative sentences	Questions
I use social media. You use social media. He/she/it uses social media. We use social media. You use social media. They use social media.	I don't use social media. You don't use social media. He/she/it doesn't use social media. We don't use social media. You don't use social media. They don't use social media.	Do I use social media? Do you use social media? Does he/she/it use social media? Do we use social media? Do you use social media? Do they use social media? Questions with a question word: Why do I use social media? Why do you use social media? Why does he/she/it use social media? Why do we use social media? Why do you use social media? Why do they use social media?

! Be careful with these verbs: be, have.

Examples of typical use:

- Facts and general statements: The cartoon shows a family.
- Everyday activities or habits: Justin listens to podcasts on the bus.
  Tense markers: always, often, sometimes, never, usually, every day/week/month/year, on Mondays/Tuesdays…, at 7 o'clock/11 o'clock…
- A set sequence of events or actions: Young people spend too much time on their phones, get very little sleep and are tired the next day at school.
- For scheduled future events with an adverbial phrase of time: The programme finishes at ten o'clock.

G1.2 Present progressive

V11 I13
Talking about the present

Positive sentences	Negative sentences	Questions
I am studying. You are studying. He/she/it is studying. We are studying. You are studying. They are studying.	I'm not studying. You aren't studying. He/she/it isn't studying. We aren't studying. You aren't studying. They aren't studying.	Am I studying? Are you studying? Is he/she/it studying? Are we studying? Are you studying? Are they studying? Questions with a question word: What am I studying? What are you studying? What is he/she/it studying? What are we studying? What are you studying? What are they studying?

! Some verbs are never used in the progressive form, especially those which express feelings or a belief: believe, love, hate, seem, have (in the sense of own), can, mean, want to, feel, notice, realise.

Examples of typical use:
- An activity that is going on right now and will continue for a limited period of time: Reese is giving an interview (now).
  Tense markers: now, just now, at the moment
- Planned future events with an adverbial phrase of time: Reese is flying to London next week.

V12 I14
Talking about the past

G1.3 Simple past

Positive sentences	Negative sentences	Questions
I played a video game. You played a video game. He/she/it played a video game. We played a video game. You played a video game. They played a video game.	I didn't play a video game. You didn't play a video game. He/she/it didn't play a video game. We didn't play a video game. You didn't play a video game. They didn't play a video game.	Did I play a video game? Did you play a video game? Did he/she/it play a video game? Did we play a video game? Did you play a video game? Did they play a video game? Questions with a question word: Why did I play a video game? Why did you play a video game? Why did he/she/it play a video game? Why did we play a video game? Why did you play a video game? Why did they play a video game?

! Be careful with irregular verbs.

Examples of typical use:
- For activities that began and ended at a specific time in the past: The technical team tested the device last week.
  Tense markers: yesterday, ago, last week/month/year, in 2017/…, on Tuesday/…
- For a series of events in the past, as in a story, often called the 'narrative past':
  As Kate didn't have a job, she went to Australia. Her aunt found her a job there and one thing led to another. After six months, Kate had a permanent job.

V12 I14
Talking about the past

G1.4 Past progressive

Positive sentences	Negative sentences	Questions
I was thinking. You were thinking. He/she/it was thinking. We were thinking. You were thinking. They were thinking.	I wasn't thinking. You weren't thinking. He/she/it wasn't thinking. We weren't thinking. You weren't thinking. They weren't thinking.	Was I thinking? Were you thinking? Was he/she/it thinking? Were we thinking? Were you thinking? Were they thinking? Questions with a question word: What was I thinking? What were you thinking? What was he/she/it thinking? What were we thinking? What were you thinking? What were they thinking?

Examples of typical use:
- An activity in the past that was already in progress when something else happened: Kate was working in a bar when she heard about the job in a bank.
- Several activities or events that were happening at the same time in the past: While Kate was living in England, she only had temporary jobs.

G1.5 Present perfect simple

V14 I16
Talking about the present perfect

Positive sentences	Negative sentences	Questions
I have finished. You have finished. He/she/it has finished. We have finished. You have finished. They have finished.	I haven't finished. You haven't finished. He/she/it hasn't finished. We haven't finished. You haven't finished. They haven't finished.	Have I finished? Have you finished? Has he/she/it finished? Have we finished? Have you finished? Have they finished? Questions with a question word: What have I finished? What have you finished? What has he/she/it finished? What have we finished? What have you finished? What have they finished?

! Be careful with irregular verbs.

! With the present perfect simple the result of the action is usually more important than the action itself. Never use the present perfect with adverbs of past time, e.g. yesterday, last week, three years ago, in 2017…

Examples of typical use:
- Activities that happened recently and whose effects are still being felt in the present: Kate has moved to Australia and she is still getting used to the different accent there.
- With certain adverbs: just, so far, ever, never, recently, lately, today, this week, already, (not) yet He has listed all his work experience so far. – Has he ever worked abroad?
- With for and since, for activities that started in the past and are continuing: Lisa hasn't checked her emails for two days. – She has received 20 emails since Tuesday.

G1.6 Present perfect progressive

V13 I15
Talking about the present perfect

Positive sentences	Negative sentences	Questions
I have been waiting. You have been waiting. He/she/it has been waiting. We have been waiting. You have been waiting. They have been waiting.	I haven't been waiting. You haven't been waiting. He/she/it hasn't been waiting. We haven't been waiting. You haven't been waiting. They haven't been waiting.	Have I been waiting? Have you been waiting? Has he/she/it been waiting? Have we been waiting? Have you been waiting? Have they been waiting? Questions with a question word: Why have I been waiting? Why have you been waiting? Why has he/she/it been waiting? Why have we been waiting? Why have you been waiting? Why have they been waiting?

Examples of typical use:

- Activities that have been going on either continuously or at intervals up to the present, often with adverbials of time such as all day, for a week, etc.: We have been looking at job adverts all evening.
- There is no mention of time but the activity has taken place very recently and the result is still visible: It has been raining.

G1.7 Past perfect simple

Positive sentences	Negative sentences	Questions
I had finished. You had finished. He/she/it had finished. We had finished. You had finished. They had finished.	I hadn't finished. You hadn't finished. He/she/it hadn't finished. We hadn't finished. You hadn't finished. They hadn't finished.	Had I finished? Had you finished? Had he/she/it finished? Had we finished? Had you finished? Had they finished? Questions with a question word: What had I finished? What had you finished? What had he/she/it finished? What had we finished? What had you finished? What had they finished?

! Be careful with irregular verbs.

Examples of typical use:

- An activity that happened before another activity in the past, showing the connection between the two activities:
  When I arrived at college, the lesson had already started.
  After I had finished my homework, I decided to go out.
- In reported speech, when the original statement is in the past or present perfect:
  Jane said that she had forgotten to do her homework.

G1.8 Past perfect progressive

Positive sentences	Negative sentences	Questions
I had been waiting. You had been waiting. He/she/it had been waiting. We had been waiting. You had been waiting. They had been waiting.	I hadn't been waiting. You hadn't been waiting. He/she/it hadn't been waiting. We hadn't been waiting. You hadn't been waiting. They hadn't been waiting.	Had I been waiting? Had you been waiting? Had he/she/it been waiting? Had we been waiting? Had you been waiting? Had they been waiting? Questions with a question word: Why had I been waiting? Why had you been waiting? Why had he/she/it been waiting? Why had we been waiting? Why had you been waiting? Why had they been waiting?

Examples of typical use:
- An activity that occurred over a period of time, and before another activity, in the past. The two activities are directly related: He was tired because he had been working so hard.
- In reported speech, when the original statement is in the present perfect progressive: He said that he had been working hard.

G1.9 Going to-future

V15 I17 Talking about the future

Positive sentences	Negative sentences	Questions
I am going to leave early. You are going to leave early. He/she/it is going to leave early. We are going to leave early You are going to leave early. They are going to leave early.	I'm not going to leave early. You're not going to leave early. He/she/it's not going to leave early. We're not going to leave early. You're not going to leave early. They're not going to leave early.	Am I going to leave early? Are you going to leave early? Is he/she/it going to leave early? Are we going to leave early? Are you going to leave early? Are they going to leave early?

Examples of typical use:
- For an action in the future that has already been planned or prepared: They're going to buy new tablets for the whole school.
- For a prediction about the future, when you can see that something is about to happen: Look at those clouds. It's going to rain soon.

G1.10 Future simple (will-future)

V15 I17 Talking about the future

Positive sentences	Negative sentences	Questions
I will finish college. You will finish college. He/she/it will finish college. We will finish college. You will finish college. They will finish college.	I won't finish college. You won't finish college. He/she/it won't finish college. We won't finish college. You won't finish college. They won't finish college.	Will I finish college? Will you finish college? Will he/she/it finish college? Will we finish college? Will you finish college? Will they finish college? Questions with a question word: When will I finish college? When will you finish college? When will he/she/it finish college? When will we finish college? When will you finish college? When will they finish college?

! English will = German werden
English want = German wollen

Examples of typical use:
- Things that are likely to happen at a defined or undefined time in the future: You'll be a great business person one day.
- For forecasts, such as the weather forecast: On Saturday, it will rain for most of the day.
- In if-clauses Type 1 – future situations that are probable/possible: If the weather is nice, I'll revise for my test in the park.

G1.11 Future progressive

Positive sentences	Negative sentences	Questions
I will be learning. You will be learning. He/she/it will be learning. We will be learning. You will be learning. They will be learning.	I won't be learning. You won't be learning. He/she/it won't be learning. We won't be learning. You won't be learning. They won't be learning.	Will I be learning? Will you be learning? Will he/she/it be learning? Will we be learning? Will you be learning? Will they be learning? Questions with a question word: What will I be learning? What will you be learning? What will he/she/it be learning? What will we be learning? What will you be learning? What will they be learning?

Example of typical use:
- Events – which are often planned – that will be going on at a certain time in the future when another event occurs: You will be sleeping by the time I get home.

G1.12 Future perfect simple

Positive sentences	Negative sentences	Questions
I will have finished. You will have finished. He/she/it will have finished. We will have finished. You will have finished. They will have finished.	I won't have finished. You won't have finished. He/she/it won't have finished. We won't have finished. You won't have finished. They won't have finished.	Will I have finished? Will you have finished? Will he/she/it have finished? Will we have finished? Will you have finished? Will they have finished? Questions with a question word: When will I have finished? When will you have finished? When will he/she/it have finished? When will we have finished? When will you have finished? When will they have finished?

! Be careful with irregular verbs.

Example of typical use:
- For an activity in the future that takes place before a second activity, to show the relation between them. The second activity is in the present tense:
  Joanna will have finished the college course by the time she is 20.

G1.13 Future perfect progressive

Positive sentences	Negative sentences	Questions
I will have been waiting. You will have been waiting. He/she/it will have been waiting. We will have been waiting. You will have been waiting. They will have been waiting.	I won't have been waiting. You won't have been waiting. He/she/it won't have been waiting. We won't have been waiting. You won't have been waiting. They won't have been waiting.	Will I have been waiting? Will you have been waiting? Will he/she/it have been waiting? Will we have been waiting? Will you have been waiting? Will they have been waiting?

Example of typical use:

- Used in the same way as the future perfect simple, but it places more emphasis on the length of time the activity is expected to take:
  They will have been studying English for eight years by the time they take the exam.

G1.14 Conditional I

V21 I23
Talking about conditions

Positive sentences	Negative sentences	Questions
I would take a gap year. You would take a gap year. He/she/it would take a gap year. We would take a gap year. You would take a gap year. They would take a gap year.	I wouldn't take a gap year. You wouldn't take a gap year. He/she/it wouldn't take a gap year. We wouldn't take a gap year. You wouldn't take a gap year. They wouldn't take a gap year.	Would I take a gap year? Would you take a gap year? Would he/she/it take a gap year? Would we take a gap year? Would you take a gap year? Would they take a gap year? Questions with a question word: Why would I take a gap year? Why would you take a gap year? Why would he/she/it take a gap year? Why would we take a gap year? Why would you take a gap year? Why would they take a gap year?

Examples of typical use:

- For suggestions, polite questions and requests:
  Which country would you visit? – Well, I would visit Australia.
  Would you like a drink?
  Would you help me, please?
- In if-clauses Type 2 – future situations that are improbable/unlikely:
  If I had enough money, I would start my own company.

V21 I23
Talking about conditions

G1.15 Conditional II

Positive sentences	Negative sentences	Questions
I would have applied for the job. You would have applied for the job. He/she/it would have applied for the job. We would have applied for the job. You would have applied for the job. They would have applied for the job.	I wouldn't have applied for the job. You wouldn't have applied for the job. He/she/it wouldn't have applied for the job. We wouldn't have applied for the job. You wouldn't have applied for the job. They wouldn't have applied for the job.	Would I have applied for the job? Would you have applied for the job? Would he/she/it have applied for the job? Would we have applied for the job? Would you have applied for the job? Would they have applied for the job? Questions with a question word: Why would I have applied for the job? Why would you have applied for the job? Why would he/she/it have applied for the job? Why would we have applied for the job? Why would you have applied for the job? Why would they have applied for the job?

! Be careful with irregular verbs.

Example of typical use:
- In if-clauses Type 3 – past situations that are unreal/impossible/hypothetical:
  If you had prepared before the interview, they would have given you the job.

V21 I23
Talking about conditions

G2 If-clauses

There are three main types of if-clauses (or conditional sentences) in English. They are basically used in the same way as conditional sentences in German. You can put the if-clause at the beginning or at the end of the sentence.

G2.1 Type 1 – Future situations (probable/possible)

a) if-clause: simple present – main clause: will-future
   If you study hard, you will pass the exam.
   Wenn du fleißig lernst, wirst du die Prüfung bestehen.

b) if-clause: present perfect – main clause: will-future
   If you have studied hard, you will pass the exam.
   Wenn du fleißig gelernt hast, wirst du die Prüfung bestehen.

c) if-clause: simple present – main clause: can + infinitive
   If you study hard, you can pass the exam.
   Wenn du fleißig lernst, kannst du die Prüfung bestehen.

d) if-clause: simple present – main clause: might + infinitive
   If you study hard, you might pass the exam.
   Wenn du fleißig lernst, wirst du eventuell die Prüfung bestehen.

G2.2 Type 2 – Future situations (improbable/unlikely)

a) if-clause: simple past – main clause: conditional I (would + infinitive)
If you studied hard, you would pass the exam.
Wenn du fleißig lernen würdest, würdest du die Prüfung bestehen.

b) if-clause: simple past – main clause: could + infinitive
If you studied hard, you could pass the exam.
Wenn du fleißig lernen würdest, könntest du die Prüfung bestehen.

G2.3 Type 3 – Past situations (unreal/impossible/hypothetical)

a) if-clause: past perfect – main clause: conditional II (would + have + past participle)
If you had studied hard, you would have passed the exam.
Wenn du fleißig gelernt hättest, hättest du die Prüfung bestanden.

b) if-clause: past perfect – main clause: could + have + past participle
If you had studied hard, you could have passed the exam.
Wenn du fleißig gelernt hättest, hättest du die Prüfung bestehen können.

c) if-clause: past perfect – main clause: might + have + past participle
If you had studied hard, you might have passed the exam.
Wenn du fleißig gelernt hättest, hättest du eventuell die Prüfung bestanden.

! Exceptions to the rules:

- The present tense is used in both clauses in general statements and for repeated activities or habits:
If plants don't get enough water, they die. – If she has time, she goes to the gym.
- For recommendations and advice use 'were' in the if-clause and conditional I in the main clause: If I were you, I would study a bit harder.
- 'If' can be left out when the order of the verb and subject are reversed:
Had I studied harder, I would have passed the exam.

! Be careful!

- If you start a sentence with an if-clause, use a comma. Don't use a comma if you start with the main clause:
If you study hard, you will pass the exam.
You will pass the exam if you study hard.
- Don't use 'will' in the if-clause, except to express willingness:
They can come to Britain if they'll work.
- Don't use 'would' in the if-clause except when you are making a polite request:
I would be grateful if you would hand in your homework on time in future.

V23 I25
Talking about processes

G3 The passive

The passive is often used when the action is more important than who or what performed it. The passive is frequently used in scientific and technical writing. The passive can be formed with or without an 'agent'. The 'agent' is the person or thing that causes an action to occur.

Form the passive using a form of 'to be' + past participle (+ by + agent)

The Youth Agency carries out research projects.

Research projects are carried out by the Youth Agency.

Simple present	Present progressive
I am invited for an interview. You are invited for an interview. He/she/it is invited for an interview. We are invited for an interview. You are invited for an interview. They are invited for an interview.	I am being interviewed for a survey. You are being interviewed for a survey. He/she/it is being interviewed for a survey. We are being interviewed for a survey. You are being interviewed for a survey. They are being interviewed for a survey.
Simple past	**Past progressive**
I was invited for an interview. You were invited for an interview. He/she/it was invited for an interview. We were invited for an interview. You were invited for an interview. They were invited for an interview.	I was being interviewed for a survey. You were being interviewed for a survey. He/she/it was being interviewed for a survey. We were being interviewed for a survey. You were being interviewed for a survey. They were being interviewed for a survey.
Present perfect	**Modal verbs**
I have been invited for an interview. You have been invited for an interview. He/she/it has been invited for an interview. We have been invited for an interview. You have been invited for an interview. They have been invited for an interview.	I can be contacted online. You must be contacted online. He/she/it mustn't be contacted online. We needn't be contacted online. You ought to be contacted online. They should be contacted online.
Future	**Future perfect**
I will be invited for an interview. You will be invited for an interview. He/she/it will be invited for an interview. We will be invited for an interview. You will be invited for an interview. They will be invited for an interview.	I will have been invited for an interview. You will have been invited for an interview. He/she/it will have been invited for an interview. We will have been invited for an interview. You will have been invited for an interview. They will have been invited for an interview.

! Be careful with irregular verbs.

G4 Relative clauses

V20 I22
Talking about describing people or things in more detail

Relative clauses are used to describe people or things. A relative clause usually begins with a relative pronoun.

Relative pronoun	refers to
who	people (subject or object)
whom	people (object), formal English
which	things
that	people or things (subject or object)
whose	possessions

G4.1 Defining relative clauses

- A defining relative clause is important for the meaning of the sentence. Without the relative clause the sentence would not make any sense. Defining relative clauses are not separated from the rest of the sentence by commas:
  The text message that/which you sent me didn't arrive.
  This is the woman who(m) I emailed yesterday.
  This is the boy whose smartphone was stolen.
- The pronouns 'that', 'which' and 'who(m)' can be left out if the pronoun is the object of the relative clause. This type of relative clause is known as a 'contact' clause:
  The apps we use are all free.
  This is the woman I emailed yesterday.

G4.2 Non-defining relative clauses

- The information in non-defining relative clauses is additional and descriptive. Even without the relative clause the sentence is clear. Non-defining relative clauses are separated from the rest of the sentence by commas:
  Aiden, who is still a teenager, runs a successful online business.

G5 Adjectives

V17 I19
Talking about qualities

Adjectives describe people and things: the tall man – bright lights

- The present participle (-ing form) and past participle of verbs can often be used as adjectives:
  an interesting book – the finished report
- Verbs are usually followed by adverbs, however some verbs are followed by adjectives:

to be	The laptop is heavy.
to become	Anne became nervous before the interview.
to feel	Thomas felt excited about his new job.
to get	Her smartphone got broken.
to look	The office block looks modern.
to seem	My new colleagues seem nice.

- Adjectives can be used as collective nouns. In such cases, the + adjective refers to a particular group of people as a whole:
  It is important to help the unemployed to find work.
  The very young and the very old are particularly at risk.

- The comparison of adjectives:

Positive form	Comparative form	Superlative form
cold hot funny modern	colder hotter funnier more modern	the coldest the hottest the funniest the most modern

! Remember the irregular forms: good – better – the best
much – more – the most
bad – worse – the worst
far – further – the furthest

Use more/-er than, as … as and not as … as to make comparisons:
An email is more modern than a letter.
My smartphone is newer than yours.
Tablets are just as popular as laptops.
The internet at school is not as fast as the internet at home.

V18 I20
Talking about qualities

G6 Adverbs

Adverbs are formed by adding -ly/-ily to an adjective:

Adjective	Adverb
safe happy real reasonable	safely happily really reasonably

! Remember the irregular forms: good – well
fast – fast
hard – hard

- Adverbs describe actions (verbs): He walked quickly. She spoke slowly.
- Adverbs before other adjectives: This is an extremely good essay.
- Adverbs before other adverbs: He was driving incredibly fast.
- Adverbs before past participles: Credit cards are frequently accepted.
- Some useful adverbs: always, usually, often, frequently, sometimes, seldom, rarely, never, recently, soon, lately, in the past, in the future, largely, for the most part, partly, probably, possibly, hardly, definitely, obviously, clearly, basically, consequently, as a result
- The comparison of adverbs:

Positive form	Comparative form	Superlative form
fluently	more fluently	the most fluently

! Remember the irregular forms: well – better – the best
badly – worse – the worst
fast – faster – the fastest

G7 Question tags

A question tag is added to the end of a sentence to turn it into a question. In German you use expressions like '..., *nicht wahr?*' and '..., *oder?*' in a similar way.

- If the statement is positive, the question tag is negative:
  He uses social media, doesn't he?
- If the statement is negative, the question tag is positive:
  He doesn't use social media, does he?
- The subject of the sentence is also the subject of the question tag:
  Lisa never turns off her smartphone, does she?
- If the statement is in the simple present, the question tag is formed with 'is/are' or 'isn't/aren't', 'do/does' or 'don't/doesn't':
  He likes video games, doesn't he?
- For statements in the simple past, the question tag is formed with 'was/were' or 'wasn't/weren't' or 'did/didn't':
  He took a gap year, didn't he?
- If the statement uses an auxiliary verb (to be, to have, will, etc.) or a modal (can, must, etc.), use the modal or auxiliary in the same tense in the tag:
  Tom is here, isn't he?
  Roger has bought a new laptop, hasn't he?
  Jill will be at the interview, won't she?
  You can contact me by email, can't you?

G8 Modal auxiliaries

V19 I21
Talking about ability, permission and necessity

- Will/would/can/could/may:

  Asking someone to do something:
  Will/Would/Can/Could you do me a favour?

  Asking for permission/giving permission:
  May I use your phone? – Yes, of course, you may.

  Talking about abilities:
  She can speak English.

- Must/mustn't/needn't:

  Instructing someone to do something or not to do something:
  You must prepare before an interview.
  You mustn't tell lies at an interview.

  Talking about a necessity or duty:
  I must send in my job application by Friday.
  You needn't be nervous before the interview.

- May/might/could/must/will:

  Expressing a possibility or probability:
  It may/might/could/will rain.
  You must be Mr Jones.

  Making a suggestion:
  We could look for typical interview questions online.

- Should/ought to/shouldn't/ought not to:

  Giving advice:
  You should/ought to use a dictionary.
  You shouldn't/ought not to arrive late for the interview.

- Modal auxiliaries only have a present and/or past tense form. Substitutes are used for other tenses:

Modal auxiliary	Substitutes	Examples
can/could	be able to	He won't be able to to work under pressure.
may/mustn't	be allowed to not be allowed to	We were allowed to use our smartphones in class. We weren't allowed to play music.
must/needn't	have to not have to	She will have to work this weekend. We didn't have to work late.

V22 I24
Talking about likes and dislikes

G9 -ing forms

An -ing form can be either a present participle or a gerund.

G9.1 The present participle

- The present participle is used in the progressive tenses (present progressive, past progressive, etc.):
  Mary is checking her emails. – The class was discussing the topic 'Take a gap year or find a job?'.
- The present participle can be used as an adjective: the winning party – a growing child
- The present participle can be used to shorten clauses, often after a conjunction, e.g: after, while, before, when
  I was riding my bike to work when I saw her. → While riding my bike to work, I saw her.
  The class listened to the entrepreneur who was talking about start-ups. → The class listened to the entrepreneur talking about start-ups.
  After we had collected ideas in a word web, we discussed them. → After collecting ideas in a word web we discussed them.
  Read the text before you answer the questions. → Read the text before answering the questions.

G9.2 The gerund

- The gerund is used after prepositions: You're very good at speaking English.
- The gerund is often used after certain verbs: like, hate, enjoy, love, mind, prefer
  I don't mind watching TV but I prefer reading and I also enjoy playing computer games.
- The gerund can be used as a noun: Laughing is good for you. – Studying is very important.
- Some verbs have the construction verb + preposition + gerund:
  to be afraid of, to look forward to, to feel like, to talk about, to insist on, to decide against, to think about/of, to succeed in, to apologise for
  I'm afraid of flying.
- When the following expressions are followed by a verb, use the gerund:
  There's no point in waiting any longer.
  It's not worth going to see the new James Bond film.
  A waste of money/time: It's a waste of time talking to you.
  To spend/to waste time/money: He spends all of his time sitting in front of a computer.

G10 Reported speech

V24 126
Talking about passing on information

Reported speech (or indirect speech) is used to report what someone has said without quoting them.

- Start the reported speech with a reporting verb:
  a) Statements: say (that), tell sb. (that), answer, mention, explain, reply, etc.
     "I'm tired." → She says (that) she's tired.
  b) Questions: ask, want to know
     "Are you hungry?" → She asks me if I'm hungry.
     "Where do you go to school?" → She wants to know where I go to school.
  c) Commands: tell sb. to + infinitive
     "Leave me alone!" → She told me to leave her alone.

- If the reporting verb is in the present, present perfect or future tense, the tense stays the same:
  "Spending hours on social media is bad for you".
  → Mr Jones says spending hours on social media is bad for you.
  → Mr Jones has said spending hours on social media is bad for you.
  → Mr Jones will say spending hours on social media is bad for you.

- If the reporting verb is in the past tense, the tense of the reported speech changes:

simple present "I text my best friend every day."	→	simple past She said she texted her best friend every day.
present progressive "I am texting my best friend."	→	past progressive She said she was texting her best friend..
simple past "I texted my best friend last night."	→	past perfect She said she had texted her best friend the night before.
past progressive "I was texting my best friend."	→	past perfect progressive She said she had been texting her best friend.
present perfect "I have texted my best friend."	→	past perfect She said she had texted her best friend.
present perfect progressive "I have been texting my best friend."	→	past perfect progressive She said she had been texting her best friend.
past perfect "I had texted my best friend."	→	past perfect She said she had texted her best friend.
past perfect progressive "I had been texting my best friend."	→	past perfect progressive She said she had been texting her best friend.
will-future I will text my best friend every day."	→	conditional I She said she would text her best friend every day.

- Questions follow the same tense changes as statements:
  "How many jobs have you applied for?" → My friend asked me how many jobs I had applied for.

- Some adverbs of time also change in reported speech, for example:

now	→	then
yesterday	→	the day before/the previous day
here	→	there
last year	→	the year before/the previous year
today	→	that day
tomorrow	→	the next day

- Statements involving truths and facts do not have to change in reported speech:
  "The novel is by Zadie Smith." → The teacher said that the novel is by Zadie Smith.

V16 I18
Talking about quantities

G11 Word order

Generally, the word order in English sentences is subject – verb – object.
This is the case in main clauses and subordinate clauses:
We live in a world that is heavily influenced by the media.
I like Las Vegas because it has something for everyone.

G11.1 Statements

- Normally, place comes before time:
  I went to school yesterday.
  I've wanted to visit the UK for years.
- The adverbs in a sentence generally follow the sequence: adverb of manner – adverb of place – adverb of time:
  I was waiting patiently for tickets outside the stadium all morning.
  I will be working hard in London this summer.
- In English, adverbs of frequency (never, sometimes, often, always, etc.) are directly in front of the verb:
  I usually check my phone as soon as I wake up.
  I never leave home without my phone.

! But be careful – there is an exception when you use the verb to be:
I'm always in the gym on Fridays.

G11.2 Questions

- Questions never begin with a main verb:
  Do you like British food?
  Did you get my message last night?

! But be careful – there is an exception when you use the verb to be:
Are you thinking of taking a gap year?
Am I the first person to arrive?

- Negative questions do not end with a main verb like they do in German:
  Aren't you going to miss German food?

G11.3 Negated statements

- The negation of don't/doesn't comes before the main verb, unlike in German:
  I don't have school on Friday afternoons.
  I don't use my mobile phone during lessons.

Grammatik-Erklärvideos und interaktive Übungen

Mit Hilfe von Grammatik-Erklärvideos und interaktiven Übungen können grammatische Phänomene wiederholt und gefestigt werden.
Die Videos sowie die Übungen finden Sie in den Medien zum Schulbuch und im eBook.

Talking about the present	– simple present, present progressive – questions and negative sentences
Talking about the past	– simple past, past progressive
Talking about the present perfect	– present perfect simple, present perfect progressive – present perfect, simple past
Talking about the future	– will-future, going to-future, present with future meaning
Talking about quantities	– some, any, every, no and their compounds
Talking about qualities	– adjectives, adverbs – comparison of adjectives and adverbs, exceptions
Talking about ability, permission and necessity	– modal auxiliaries and their substitutes
Talking about describing people or things in more detail	– relative clauses: who, which, that, whose
Talking about conditions	– if-clauses
Talking about likes and dislikes	– the gerund
Talking about processes	– the passive: present, past, future
Talking about passing on information	– reported speech

Das "Vocabulary" enthält die zu lernenden Vokabeln der Topics in chronologischer Reihenfolge.

Die blau gedruckten Vokabeln stammen aus den Audio- und Videotexten.

D22 Alphabetische Wortliste

Symbole und Abkürzungen:
Vok ↔ ist das Gegenteil von
Vok → ist verwandt mit
Vok = entspricht
= Definition
sth something
sb somebody
(AE) Amerikanisches Englisch
(BE) Britisches Englisch
(sg) Einzahl (Singular)
(pl) Mehrzahl (Plural)
etw etwas
jdn jemanden
jdm jemandem
Achtung: Aussprache

Topic 1 Ecological issues

Getting started

growth [grəʊθ]	Wachstum	**growth** → to grow
to occur [ə'kɜː]	vorkommen; auftreten	**to occur** = to happen
arable land [ˌærəbl 'lænd]	Ackerland; landwirtschaftliche Nutzfläche	= land suitable for growing crops
to estimate ['estɪmeɪt]	schätzen	Can you **estimate** how long it will take?
to exceed [ɪk'siːd]	übersteigen; übertreffen	**to exceed** = to surpass; to outperform; to top
to counter sth ['kaʊntə]	etw entgegenwirken	= to oppose sth or defend against sth
destruction [dɪ'strʌkʃn]	Zerstörung	**destruction** → to destroy
urban ['ɜːbn]	städtisch; Stadt-	**urban** ↔ rural
aim [eɪm]	Ziel; Absicht	**aim** = goal
catastrophe [kə'tæstrəfi]	Katastrophe	**catastrophe** → catastrophic
extreme weather [ɪkˌstriːm 'weðə]	Extremwetter	We are seeing more and more **extreme weather** all over the world.
man-made [ˌmæn'meɪd]	menschengemacht; hausgemacht	**man-made** ↔ natural
harmful ['hɑːmfl]	schädlich	**harmful** → to harm
to adopt [ə'dɒpt]	annehmen; übernehmen	= to formally accept a suggestion or policy
to compost ['kɒmpɒst]	kompostieren	We **compost** nearly all of our kitchen leftovers.
landfill ['lænfɪl]	Mülldeponie	**landfill** = dump
mandatory ['mændətri]	verpflichtend	**mandatory** = compulsory
alike [ə'laɪk]	gleichermaßen	= in the same way
rubbish collection rate [ˌrʌbɪʃ kə'lekʃn ˌreɪt]	Müllgebühr	= the amount you pay to have sb pick up your rubbish and take it away
nudge [nʌdʒ]	Stupser; Anstoß	= a gentle push
vertical ['vɜːtɪkl]	senkrecht; vertikal	**vertical** ↔ horizontal
to flourish ['flʌrɪʃ]	großen Erfolg haben; florieren	Their new business struggled for two years before it really began **to flourish**.
extensive [ɪk'stensɪv]	großflächig; umfangreich	**extensive** → to extend
to lower ['ləʊə]	senken	**Lowering** taxes is a good way to get votes.
to adhere to sth [əd'hɪə tə ˌsʌmθɪŋ]	etw einhalten *(z. B. eine Regel)*	**to adhere to** = to comply with
to follow suit [ˌfɒləʊ 'suːt]	dem Beispiel folgen	= to do sth the same way as sb else
organic [ɔː'gænɪk]	biologisch; Bio-	Tom prefers **organic** food to conventional food.

Text workshop A - How to feed the world

food production ['fu:d prəˌdʌkʃn]	**Lebensmittelproduktion**	**production** → to produce
to stick to sth ['stɪk tə]	**sich an etw halten**	= to continue doing what you have planned to do, even though it might be difficult
dairy ['deəri]	**Milch-**	**Dairy** products are food stuffs that are made from milk.
cropland ['krɒplænd]	**Anbaufläche** (für Nutzpflanzen)	= the land where plants are cultivated
pasture ['pɑ:stʃə]	**Weideland**	That farmer has about 20 ha of cropland plus about 50 ha of **pasture** for the cows and horses.
nutritional requirements [nju:ˌtrɪʃnl rɪ'kwaɪəmənts]	**Ernährungsbedarf; Nährstoffbedarf**	**nutritional** → nutrients
to switch [swɪtʃ]	**wechseln; tauschen**	We **switched** providers in order to save money.
equivalent to [ɪ'kwɪvlənt tə]	**entsprechend**	1 yard is **equivalent to** 3 feet or 36 inches.
alongside [əˌlɒŋ'saɪd]	**neben; daneben**	**alongside** = next to; in addition to
greenhouse gas emissions *(pl)* [ˌgri:nhaʊs 'gæs‿ɪˌmɪʃn]	**Treibhausgasausstoß**	The factory installed new filters to reduce its **greenhouse gas emissions**.
carbon ['kɑ:bn]	**Kohlenstoff;** *hier:* **Kohlendioxid**	**Carbon** is a component of two important greenhouse gases: carbon dioxide and methane.
in the absence of [ɪn ði‿'æbsns‿əv]	**bei Fehlen von; aus Mangel an**	= for lack of
comprehensive [ˌkɒmprɪ'hensɪv]	**umfassend**	= including all the necessary aspects
to date [tʊ 'deɪt]	**bislang; bis heute**	I have seen a lot of her music videos, but this was the best one **to date**.
to supply [sə'plaɪ]	**versorgen**	= to provide sb/sth with sth that they need
overwhelming [ˌəʊvə'welmɪŋ]	**überwältigend**	**overwhelming** = stunning, great
to emit [ɪ'mɪt]	**ausstoßen; emittieren**	**to emit** → emission
to generate ['dʒenreɪt]	**erzeugen; generieren**	**to generate** → generator
anticipated [æn'tɪsɪpeɪtɪd]	**voraussichtlich; erwartet**	**anticipated** → to anticipate → anticipation
demand [dɪ'mɑ:nd]	**Bedarf**	= a request or need for sth
to occupy ['ɒkjəpaɪ]	**einnehmen; füllen**	Industrial agriculture has **occupied** the best position for years.
sufficient [sə'fɪʃnt]	**genug; genügend; ausreichend**	My grades are **sufficient** to get into college.
to fulfil [fʊl'fɪl]	**erfüllen**	Well, you **fulfil** all our requirements, so when can you start?
to create a stir [kriˌeɪt‿ə 'stɜ:]	**einen Aufruhr verursachen**	= to make people excited or upset
suggestion [sə'dʒestʃn]	**Vorschlag; Anregung**	**suggestion** → to suggest
to cause harm to sth/sb [ˌkɔ:z 'hɑ:m tə ˌsʌmθɪŋ/ˌsʌmbədi]	**etw/jdn Schaden zufügen**	**to cause harm to** = to do damage to
to raise [reɪz]	**aufziehen;** *hier:* **züchten**	They have a small farm where they **raise** pigs and chickens.
to chop down [ˌtʃɒp 'daʊn]	**abholzen**	The city **chopped down** all the trees to build a car park.
global warming [ˌgləʊbl 'wɔ:mɪŋ]	**Erderwärmung**	**Global warming** is already having a negative influence on our environment.
to consume sth [kən'sju:m]	**etw konsumieren; etw verbrauchen**	**to consume sth** → consumer → consumption
to argue ['ɑ:gju:]	**behaupten; erörtern**	I would **argue** that wealth is not as important as health.
employee [ɪm'plɔɪi:]	**Mitarbeiter/-in**	**employee** → employer → to employ → employment

deforestation *(no pl)* [diːˌfɒrɪ'steɪʃn]	Abholzung; Entwaldung	= the act of cutting down or burning the trees in an area
resistant strains of bacteria *(pl)* [rɪ'zɪstənt ˌstreɪnz‿əv bæk'tɪəriə]	resistente Bakterienstämme	= types of bacteria that do not respond to antibiotics
cure [kjʊə]	Heilung	The doctor did her best but she didn't find a **cure** for my illness.
livelihood ['laɪvlihʊd]	Lebensunterhalt	= a way to earn money in order to live
sector ['sektə]	Branche	= a part of a country's economy
to sustain [sə'steɪn]	*hier:* unterhalten; versorgen	After he lost his job he was not able **to sustain** his family and his house.
job loss ['dʒɒb ˌlɒs]	Arbeitsplatzverlust	**Job loss** is a major cause of depression.
blow [bləʊ]	Hieb; Schlag	If sth hits you hard, it gives you a nasty **blow**.
to destroy [dɪ'strɔɪ]	zerstören	**to destroy** → destruction
to do a great deal [duː‿ə ˌgreɪt 'diːl]	eine Menge tun	Young people today are **doing a great deal** to preserve the environment.
to avert [ə'vɜːt]	verhindern; abwenden	**to avert** = to prevent
dire [daɪə]	schlimm; schrecklich	**dire** = terrible; awful
sacrifice ['sækrɪfaɪs]	Opfer	= sth you give up in order to have sth more important
to skip [skɪp]	überspringen; auslassen	Some experts say that it is unhealthy **to skip** breakfast.
scarcity ['skeəsəti]	Mangel; Knappheit	**scarcity** ↔ abundance
for the sake of sth/sb [fə ðə 'seɪk‿əv ˌsʌmθɪŋ/ˌsʌmbədi]	etw/jdm zuliebe; um einer Sache willen	She has put in many hours of volunteer work **for the sake of** poor people in her community.
to concern [kən'sɜːn]	betreffen	I'm sorry, but your problems just don't **concern** me at all.
humanity [hjuː'mænəti]	Menschheit	**humanity** = humankind
reduction [rɪ'dʌkʃn]	Verringerung	**reduction** → to reduce
regulation [ˌregjə'leɪʃn]	Vorschrift; Regeln	**regulation** = rule
defense *(AE)* [ˌdɪ'fens]	Verteidigung	**defense** → to defend
expectation [ˌekspek'teɪʃn]	Erwartung	**expectation** → to expect

Skills workshop 1 - Writing a speech

participant [pɑː'tɪsɪpnt]	Teilnehmer/-in	**participant** → to participate
keynote speech [ˌkiːnəʊt 'spiːtʃ]	Grundsatzrede	= a speech that addresses the main theme of a conference or convention and sets the basic tone of the event
passion [ˌpæʃn]	Leidenschaft	**passion** → passionate
hardly ['hɑːdli]	kaum	I can **hardly** believe it.
to demand [dɪ'mɑːnd]	fordern; verlangen	The teacher **demanded** that Sophie sit down.
everyday ['evrideɪ]	alltäglich; Alltags-	The internet has become part of our **everyday** lives.
literally ['lɪtrli]	wortwörtlich; buchstäblich	**literally** = actually
livestock ['laɪvstɒk]	Nutztiere; Vieh	= animals on a farm
habitat ['hæbɪtæt]	Lebensraum	= the place where a particular type of animal or plant is normally found
to blame sb for sth ['bleɪm fə]	jdn für etw verantwortlich machen; jdn beschuldigen	They **blamed** her **for** spoiling the show.

hook *(fig)* [hʊk]	Haken; Aufhänger	*here:* metaphorical usage: sth that catches the listener's attention, like a hook that is used in fishing catches the fish
appeal [ə'pi:l]	*hier:* Appell	**appeal** → to appeal to

Text workshop B - Facing climate change

severity [sɪ'verəti]	Ernst; Schwere; Gewichtung	**severity** → severe
court ruling [ˌkɔ:t 'ru:lɪŋ]	Gerichtsentscheid; Rechtsprechung	= a judicial decision you have to obey
lawyer ['lɔɪə]	Anwalt/Anwältin; Jurist/-in	**lawyer** → law
fossil-fuel ['fɒsl ˌfju:əl]	fossiler Brennstoff	= a fuel (such as coal, oil or natural gas) formed over millions of years from the remains of animals and plants
to **violate** ['vaɪəleɪt]	verstoßen gegen	= to break (a law, a rule etc.) or act against sth
to **target** ['tɑ:gɪt]	zielen auf; anpeilen	**to target** = to aim at
to **appeal** [ə'pi:l]	Berufung einlegen	They were not happy with the court's ruling and decided to **appeal**.
to **plant** [plɑ:nt]	pflanzen; anpflanzen	Let's **plant** some flowers in the garden.
to **restore** [rɪ'stɔ:]	wiederherstellen; zurückgeben; wieder einsetzen	= to bring sth back to the way it was before
to **offset** [ˌɒf'set]	kompensieren; ausgleichen	**to offset** = to compensate
to **eliminate** [ɪ'lɪmɪneɪt]	beseitigen; ausschließen	**eliminate** → elimination
output ['aʊtpʊt]	Leistung; Ausstoß	The factory's **output** increased by 5 per cent.
verdict ['vɜ:dɪkt]	Urteil	= a decision or ruling by a court of law
subsidiary [səb'sɪdiəri]	Tochterunternehmen	The company was founded in Germany but has **subsidiaries** around the world.
approach [ə'prəʊtʃ]	Herangehensweise; Ansatz	= a method of dealing with a situation or a problem
intervention [ˌɪntə'venʃn]	Eingriff; Intervention	**intervention** → to intervene
opposing [ə'pəʊzɪŋ]	Gegen-; gegnerisch	**Opposing** forces compete or fight against each other.

Grammar workshop - Talking about ability, permission and necessity

permission [pə'mɪʃn]	Erlaubnis; Genehmigung	**permission** → to permit
necessity [nə'sesəti]	Notwendigkeit	**necessity** → necessary
loss [lɒs]	Verlust	**loss** → to lose
shortage ['ʃɔ:tɪdʒ]	Knappheit; Mangel	There is a **shortage** of qualified workers.
irritating ['ɪrɪteɪtɪŋ]	irritierend; ärgerlich	**irritating** = annoying
ought to ['ɔ:t tə]	sollte/-t/-st/-n	**ought to** = should
to **combat** ['kɒmbæt]	bekämpfen	**to combat** = to fight
urgency ['ɜ:dʒnsi]	Dringlichkeit; Eile	**urgency** → urgent
to **prevent** [prɪ'vent]	vorbeugen; verhindern	**to prevent** → prevention

Text workshop C - The blue planet

plastic waste [ˌplæstɪk 'weɪst]	Plastikmüll	Every piece of **plastic waste** that is recycled will not end up polluting the oceans.
sealed [si:ld]	verpackt; dicht	**sealed** = packed (airtight)
disposable [dɪ'spəʊzəbl]	Wegwerf-	**Disposable** packaging produces tons of waste.

garbage *(AE)* **patch** ['gɑ:bɪdʒ ˌpætʃ]	**Müllhalde;** *hier:* **Müllstrudel**	= an accumulation of waste
debris ['debri:]	**Trümmer**	= pieces of rubbish and waste
to **dump** [dʌmp]	**abladen; abkippen; entsorgen**	Although it's illegal, many people just **dump** their waste in the woods.
disgusting [dɪs'gʌstɪŋ]	**ekelhaft; widerlich**	**disgusting** = appalling
garbage *(AE)* ['gɑ:bɪdʒ]	**Müll; Abfall**	**garbage** *(AE)* = rubbish *(BE)*
litter ['lɪtə]	**Müll; Abfall**	**litter** = garbage, rubbish
current ['kʌrnt]	**Strömung**	Don't go swimming here. The strong **currents** can be very dangerous.
to **log** [lɒg]	**erfassen; aufzeichnen**	**to log** = to record
rather ['rɑ:ðə]	**eher; ziemlich**	**rather** = fairly, quite
particles ['pɑ:tɪklz]	**Partikel; Teilchen**	After the fire the air was full of smoke and ash **particles.**
microplastics *(pl)* ['maɪkrəʊˌplæstɪks]	**Mikroplastik(teilchen)**	**Microplastics** are used in cosmetic products.
quantity ['kwɒntəti]	**Menge**	**quantity** = amount
reusable [ˌri:'ju:zəbl]	**wiederverwendbar; Mehrweg-**	= A reusable product can be used more than once.
venture ['ventʃə]	**Projekt; Unternehmen**	= a project or undertaking that is risky or daring
marine [mə'ri:n]	**See-; Meeres-**	Due to pollution **marine** wildlife is in danger.
to **disturb** [dɪ'stɜ:b]	**stören**	Please don't **disturb** Dad. He's trying to sleep.
World Heritage Site [ˌwɜ:ld 'herɪtɪdʒ ˌsaɪt]	**Welterbestätte; Weltkulturerbe**	= a site listed by the UNESCO World Heritage Centre
clean-up ['kli:nʌp]	**Säuberung; Reinigung**	**clean-up** → to clean → cleaner
to **accumulate** [ə'kju:mjəleɪt]	**(an)sammeln**	**to accumulate** = to build up
eventually [ɪ'ventʃuəli]	**schließlich; endlich; irgendwann**	**eventually** = finally

Text workshop D - Water shortage

usage ['ju:sɪdʒ]	**Nutzung; Gebrauch**	**usage** → to use → useful
to **cough** [kɒf]	**husten**	I think I've got a cold. I can't stop **coughing**.
beneath [bɪ'ni:θ]	**unter; unterhalb**	There's a river **beneath** the bridge.
to **sense** [sens]	**spüren; fühlen**	They could **sense** the cold of the night through the wooden walls of their hut.
to **flow** [fləʊ]	**fließen; strömen**	The River Thames **flows** into the North Sea.
drought [draʊt]	**Dürre; Trockenheit**	During a **drought** plants don't grow and animals die due to lack of water.
tap [tæp]	**Wasserhahn**	Most modern wash basins have mixer **taps** that mix hot and cold water.
relief [rɪ'li:f]	**Erleichterung; Unterstützung**	**Relief** efforts in the disaster zone are finally making some progress.
precautionary [prɪ'kɔ:ʃnri]	**vorsorglich**	During the flood, the police closed the bridge as a **precautionary** measure.
occasional [ə'keɪʒnl]	**gelegentlich**	**occasional** ↔ often
earthquake ['ɜ:θkweɪk]	**Erdbeben**	There was an **earthquake** in Christchurch in 2011.
guidance ['gaɪdns]	**Anleitung; Führung**	**guidance** → to guide
validation [ˌvælɪ'deɪʃn]	**Bestätigung**	**validation** = confirmation
to **ease** [i:z]	**erleichtern; vereinfachen**	= to make sth unpleasant (e.g. pain) become less

produce ['prɒdju:s]	landwirtschaftliche Erzeugnisse	You get fresh **produce** at the farmer's market.
preservation [ˌprezə'veɪʃn]	Erhaltung; Bewahrung	**preservation** → to preserve
severe [sɪ'vɪə]	stark; schlimm	**severe** = serious
to **counteract** [ˌkaʊntər'ækt]	entgegenwirken	We need to **counteract** discrimination in all its forms.

Topic project - Sustainable Europe: A film project

to **submit** [səb'mɪt]	einreichen; vorlegen	**to submit** → submission
footage ['fʊtɪdʒ]	Filmmaterial	= filmed material showing a particular event

D23 Vokabellernliste

Topic 2 Science and technology

Getting started

genetic engineering [dʒəˌnetɪk‿endʒɪ'nɪərɪŋ]	Gentechnik	= artificial manipulation, modification and recombination of DNA in order to modify an organism
genetically modified (GM) [dʒəˌnetɪkli 'mɒdɪfaɪd]	gentechnisch verändert	**Genetically modified** wine grapes are illegal in Germany.
scientific [ˌsaɪən'tɪfɪk]	wissenschaftlich; naturwissenschaftlich	**scientific** → science → scientist
ethical ['eθɪkl]	moralisch; ethisch	It's important to consider the **ethical** implications of genetic engineering.
to **arise** [ə'raɪz]	entstehen; aufkommen	A problem has **arisen** with the new smart control panel.
potential [pə'tenʃl]	potenziell; möglich	**potential** = possible; likely
to **be at the forefront** [ˌbi‿ət ðə 'fɔ:frʌnt]	an der Spitze stehen	The university **is at the forefront** of developments in microbiology.
digitalisation [ˌdɪdʒɪtlaɪ'zeɪʃn]	Digitalisierung	= the process of converting information into digital form so that it can be processed by computers
automation [ˌɔ:tə'meɪʃn]	Automatisierung	There are fears that **automation** will produce a lot of unemployment.
to **utilise** ['ju:tɪlaɪz]	nutzen; verwenden	= to use for a particular purpose
artificial intelligence (AI) [ˌɑ:tɪfɪʃl‿ɪn'telɪdʒns (ˌeɪ'aɪ)]	künstliche Intelligenz (KI)	**Artificial intelligence** is going to change the way we work and live very rapidly.
manufacturing [ˌmænjə'fæktʃrɪŋ]	Produktion; Produktionsbetrieb	**manufacturing** → to manufacture
to **elaborate (on sth)** [ɪ'læbreɪt‿ɒn]	(etw) näher ausführen	= to explain sth in detail
facial recognition [ˌfeɪʃl rekəg'nɪʃn]	Gesichtserkennung	Look, I can unlock my phone by fingerprint or facial recognition!
CCTV [ˌsi:si:ti:'vi:]	Videoüberwachung	= Closed Circuit Television
human trafficker [ˌhju:mən 'træfɪkə]	Schlepper	= a criminal who exploits and controls other people with the use of force
to **misuse** [ˌmɪs'ju:z]	missbrauchen	**to misuse** ↔ to use properly
weapon ['wepən]	Waffe	Biological **weapons** involve the use of toxins or infectious agents like viruses, bacteria and fungi.
drone [drəʊn]	Drohne	= an aircraft that is controlled from the ground

poacher ['pəʊtʃə]	Wilderer	The rangers went on patrol to keep **poachers** from shooting elephants.
illegal [ɪ'li:gl]	illegal; unrechtmäßig; rechtswidrig	**illegal** ↔ legal
to hand over [ˌhænd_'əʊvə]	aushändigen; übergeben	**to hand over** = to pass
pedestrian [pə'destriən]	Fußgänger/-in	= sb travelling on foot
to fail [feɪl]	versagen; fehlschlagen	**to fail** = to go wrong
for the sake of sth/sb [fə ðə 'seɪk_əv ˌsʌmθɪŋ/ˌsʌmbədi]	um einer Sache willen; etw/jdm zuliebe	She has put in many hours of volunteer work **for the sake of** poor people in her community.
appliance [ə'plaɪəns]	Gerät	Modern kitchens are full of **appliances** to make cooking easier.
to control remotely [kənˌtrəʊl rɪ'məʊtli]	aus der Ferne bedienen; steuern	Many drones are **controlled remotely** by a human operator.
embedded [ɪm'bedɪd]	eingebettet; *hier:* verlinkt	**embedded** = implanted
to confess [kən'fes]	gestehen; beichten	**to confess** = to admit
virtual reality (VR) [ˌvɜ:tjuəl ri'æləti (ˌvi:'ɑ:)]	virtuelle Realität	= a computer-generated simulation of an environment
augmented reality (AR) [ɔ:gˌmentɪd ri'æləti (ˌeɪ'ɑ:)]	erweiterte Realität	= an environment that is part real and part computer-generated
to enhance [ɪn'hɑ:ns]	verbessern	**to enhance** = to make better; to improve
controversial [ˌkɒntrə'vɜ:ʃl]	umstritten; kontrovers	**controversial** → controversy
crop [krɒp]	Nutzpflanze	We grow a variety of **crops**, including wheat and barley.
to modify ['mɒdɪfaɪ]	verändern	**to modify** → modification

Text workshop A - A smarter world

to access ['ækses]	(auf etw) zugreifen; Zugang erlangen	**to access** = to enter
economy [ɪ'kɒnəmi]	Wirtschaft; Industrie	**economy** → economical
wifi ['waɪfaɪ]	WLAN	Many bars and restaurants try to attract guests with free **wifi**.
to pour [pɔ:]	einschenken; gießen	= to make a substance flow from a container into another container
to unplug [ʌn'plʌg]	abstöpseln; entfernen	**to unplug** ↔ to plug in
to detect [dɪ'tekt]	feststellen; entdecken	**to detect** = to discover
license plate *(AE)* ['laɪsns ˌpleɪt]	Nummernschild	= a plate showing a vehicle's licence number
to be automatically debited [bi_ɔ:təmætɪkli 'debɪtɪd]	automatisch abgebucht werden	**debited** ↔ credited
to notify ['nəʊtɪfaɪ]	benachrichtigen; verständigen	= to officially tell sb about sth
insurance [ɪn'ʃʊərns]	Versicherung	My dad works at an **insurance** company.
in an instant [ɪn_ən_'ɪnstənt]	sofort	**in an instant** = immediately
commute [kə'mju:t]	Strecke zur Arbeit	**commute** → commuter → to commute
mutual ['mju:tʃuəl]	*hier:* gemeinsam	= sth shared by two or more people
database ['deɪtəbeɪs]	Datenbank	= an organised set of data stored on a computer
by default [baɪ dɪ'fɔ:lt]	automatisch; standardmäßig	**by default** = given
to generate ['dʒenreɪt]	erzeugen; generieren	**to generate** → generator

to be projected forward [bi prəˌdʒektɪd 'fɔ:wədz]	(in die Zukunft) projiziert werden; prognostiziert werden	Can your prediction for the next five years **be projected forward**?
instruction [ɪn'strʌkʃn]	Anweisung	If you give people **instructions**, you tell them what to do.
accordingly [ə'kɔ:dɪŋli]	folglich; demgemäß	**accordingly** → in accordance with → according to
air conditioning [ˌeəkən'dɪʃnɪŋ]	Klimaanlage	I'm cold. Please turn off the **air conditioning**.
convenience [kən'vi:niəns]	Komfort; Bequemlichkeit	**convenience** → convenient

Text workshop B - Benefits of innovative technologies

to drive [draɪv]	(an)treiben	**to drive** = to influence; to motivate
prosperity [prɒs'perəti]	Wohlstand	**prosperity** → prosperous
billion ['bɪliən]	Milliarde	= the number 1,000,000,000
to pave [peɪv]	*hier:* Weg bereiten; pflastern	= to make it possible for sth to happen
vision ['vɪʒn]	Vorstellung	= an image or picture that comes into your mind
healthcare ['helθˌkeə]	Gesundheitsversorgung	A good **healthcare** system benefits everyone.
enterprise ['entəpraɪz]	Unternehmen; Vorhaben	**enterprise** → entrepreneur
grant [grɑ:nt]	Zuschuss; Stipendium	**grant** → to take for granted
deficit ['defisɪt]	Mangel; Defizit	**deficit** ↔ surplus
developing country [dɪˌveləpɪŋ 'kʌntri]	Entwicklungsland	= a poor country with low standards in for example education, health or economics
small-scale [ˌsmɔ:l'skeɪl]	in kleinem Maßstab	= involving only a few people or things
agriculture ['ægrɪkʌltʃə]	Landwirtschaft	**agriculture** = farming
revenue ['revnju:]	Ertrag; Einnahmen	Government **revenues** rose by 2% last year because of the higher tax rate.
payment system ['peɪmənt ˌsɪstəm]	Zahlungssystem; Bezahlsystem	Cashless **payment systems** are becoming more and more popular.
to empower sb [ɪm'paʊə]	jdn befähigen; bevollmächtigen	**to empower** → power
loan [ləʊn]	Darlehen; Kredit	= amount of money given for a period of time, for example by a bank
ultimately ['ʌltɪmətli]	letztendlich	**ultimately** = finally
promise ['prɒmɪs]	Versprechen	**promise** → to promise
coding knowledge ['kəʊdɪŋ ˌnɒlɪdʒ]	Programmierkenntnisse	This job ist for computer specialists only. You need **coding knowledge** in Java and C#.
data protection [deɪtə prəˌtekʃn]	Datenschutz	**Data protection** is concerned with questions of data collection and data analysis.
autonomously [ɔ:'tɒnəməsli]	selbstständig; eigenständig	**autonomously** = independently
recreational [ˌrekri'eɪʃnl]	Freizeit-; Erholungs-	= connected not with work but with your free time
to advance [əd'vɑ:ns]	voranschreiten; fortschreiten	When I saw the man **advancing** towards me, I hid behind a car.
aerial ['eəriəl]	Luft-	**aerial** → air
imaging data ['ɪmɪdʒɪŋ ˌdeɪtə]	Bildgebungsdaten	**Imaging data** is used in medicine to compute three-dimensional pictures of tumors.
rescue ['reskju:]	Rettung	Here is a report about a **rescue** in the mountains.
hazardous ['hæzədəs]	gefährlich; riskant	**hazardous** = dangerous; risky
range [reɪndʒ]	*hier:* Reichweite	The electric car has a **range** of 350 km when fully charged.

precise [prɪˈsaɪs]	genau	**precise** = exact; accurate
fertiliser [ˈfɜːtɪlaɪzə]	Dünger	We only use organic **fertiliser** in our garden.
weed [wiːd]	Unkraut	= a plant that grows where it is not wanted
infestation [ˌɪnfesˈteɪʃn]	Befall	= an attack of an organism
to monitor [ˈmɒnɪtə]	überwachen; kontrollieren	= to check on a regular basis
harvest [ˈhɑːvɪst]	Ernte	When the year's crops are ready to be cut or picked, the **harvest** can be brought in.
delivery [dɪˈlɪvri]	Lieferung; Auslieferung; Zustellung	**delivery** → to deliver
retailer [ˈriːteɪlə]	Einzelhändler/-in	= a business that sells goods to customers
conceivable [kənˈsiːvəbl]	vorstellbar; denkbar	**conceivable** = possible
prescription refills [prɪˈskrɪpʃn ˌriːfɪlz]	*hier:* verschreibungspflichtige Medikamente	I should get a **prescription refill** for my pills before going on holidays.
conservation [ˌkɒnsəˈveɪʃn]	Umweltschutz	**conservation** → to conserve
warfare [wɔːˈfeə]	Kriegsführung; Krieg	**warfare** = (armed) conflict
policing [pəˈliːsɪŋ]	Polizeiarbeit	**policing** → police

Grammar workshop - Talking about processes

process [ˈprəʊses]	Vorgang; Verfahren; Prozess	It is a complicated **process** to remember.
mass production [ˌmæs prəˈdʌkʃn]	Massenfertigung	= to produce a large quantity with machines
assembly line [əˈsemblɪ ˌlaɪn]	Fließband	**assembly line** = production line
manual [ˈmænjuəl]	körperlich; manuell	**manual** = by hand
at the dawn of [ət ðə ˈdɔːn‿əv]	am Anfang von	= at the beginning of
artificial intelligence (AI) [ˌɑːtɪfɪʃl‿ɪnˈtelɪdʒns (ˌeɪˈaɪ)]	künstliche Intelligenz (KI)	**Artificial intelligence** is going to change the way we work and live very rapidly.
real-time [ˈrɪəltaɪm]	Echtzeit	**Real-time** data is very useful in navigation and speed control systems.
performance [pəˈfɔːməns]	Leistung	**performance** → to perform
inventory [ˈɪnvntri]	Warenbestand	**inventory** *(AE)* = stock *(BE)*
augmented reality (AR) [ɔːɡˌmentɪd riˈælɪti (ˌeɪˈɑː)]	erweiterte Realität	= an environment that is part real and part computer-generated

Skills workshop - Analysing the structure of a non-fictional text

deliberately [dɪˈlɪbrətli]	bewusst; absichtlich	**deliberately** ↔ by chance
to emphasise [ˈemfəsaɪz]	betonen	= to say strongly or show clearly that a fact, idea etc. is especially important
quote [kwəʊt]	Zitat	To indicate a **quote** you can use "quotation marks" or *italic print*.
credibility [ˌkredəˈbɪləti]	Glaubwürdigkeit	After openly lying about his political motives he lost all his **credibility**.
convenient [kənˈviːniənt]	bequem; angenehm	= If sth is convenient, it is easy and quick to use, or it suits your plans well.
to tighten up [ˈtaɪtn]	verschärfen	**to tighten up** = to toughen; to aggravate
to impose on [ɪmˈpəʊz‿ɒn]	*hier:* eingreifen in	The pandemic has forced the goverment to **impose on** people's personal freedom.
mistrust [mɪsˈtrʌst]	Misstrauen	**mistrust** ↔ trust
shadow [ˈʃædəʊ]	Schatten	His **shadow** is following him everywhere.

Text workshop C - Genetic engineering

defence *(BE)* [dɪˌfens]	Verteidigung	The US spends enormous amounts of time and money on its **defence** systems.
to **be awarded** [bi‿ə'wɔ:dɪd]	bekommen; bekommen	**to be awarded** = to receive
faulty ['fɔ:lti]	fehlerhaft; mangelhaft	**faulty** → fault
to **patch** [pætʃ]	flicken	**to patch** = to fix
inference ['ɪnfrns]	Schlussfolgerung	**inference** → to infer
species *(sg or pl)* ['spi:ʃi:z]	Art; Spezies	There are over 200 **species** of birds in this country.
unpredictable [ˌʌnprɪ'dɪktəbl]	unvorhersehbar	**unpredictable** → to predict
detriment ['detrɪmənt]	Nachteil	**detriment** = disadvantage
gene [dʒi:n]	Gen	**gene** → genetic
basic research [ˌbeɪsɪk rɪ'sɜ:tʃ]	Grundlagenforschung	**Basic research** lies the foundation for applied science and modern technological inventions.
remarkably [rɪ'mɑ:kəbli]	außergewöhnlich; bemerkenswert	**remarkable** = astonishing
urgency ['ɜ:dʒnsi]	Dringlichkeit	**urgency** → urgent
to **submit** [səb'mɪt]	*(hier)* behaupten	**to submit** → submission
inclined [ɪn'klaɪnd]	veranlagt	**to be inclined to** = to be willing to
vaccine ['væksi:n]	Impfstoff	**vaccine** → to vaccinate → vaccination
profound [prə'faʊnd]	umfassend	His words had a **profound** impact on me.
cancer ['kænsə]	Krebs *(Krankheit)*	**Cancer** is one of the most frequent causes of death.
drought-resistant [ˌdraʊt rɪ'zɪstnt]	dürreresistent	= to be able to survive a longer period without water
to **dare** [deə]	wagen; sich trauen	Who **dares** to take part in this experiment?
to **raise** [reɪz]	aufwerfen	This **raises** the question of how they managed to perform so well.
to **be compelled to** [bi kəm'peld tə]	sich genötigt sehen	= to feel forced to do sth
yield [ji:ld]	Ertrag	**yield** = gain
controversy ['kɒntrəvɜ:si]	Auseinandersetzung	**controversy** → controver**sial**
malnutrition [ˌmælnju:'trɪʃn]	Unterernährung	= state of not having had enough food to eat for a long time, resulting in weight loss
starvation [stɑ:'veɪʃn]	Verhungern; Unterernährung	**starvation** → to starve
undernourished [ˌʌndə'nʌrɪʃt]	unterernährt	**undernourished** = starved
to **magnify** ['mægnɪfaɪ]	verstärken	**to magnify** = to intensify
to **put sb/sth at risk** [pʊt‿sʌmbədɪ/sʌmθɪŋ‿ət 'rɪsk]	jdn/etw gefährden	They overloaded the boat and therefore **put everybody at risk** of drowning.
pesticide ['pestɪsaɪd]	Schädlingsbekämpfungsmittel; Pestizid	= chemicals which farmers put on their crops to kill harmful insects
to **have a bearing on sth** [ˌhæv‿ə 'beərɪŋ‿ɒn ˌsʌmθɪŋ]	Auswirkung auf etw haben	Vaccination will **have a bearing on** the number of people who get infected.
deficiency [dɪ'fɪʃnsi]	Mangel; Fehlen	**deficiency** ↔ abundance
harmful ['hɑ:mfl]	schädlich	**harmful** → to harm
soy [sɔɪ]	Soja	Europe is increasing its production of **soy** due to warmer termperatures.
mammal ['mæml]	Säugetier	= any animal that gives birth to live babies, not eggs, and feeds its young on milk
liver ['lɪvə]	Leber	The **liver** is responsible for detoxicating the body.

kidney ['kɪdni]	Niere	A human normally has two **kidneys**.
to interbreed [ˌɪntə'bri:d]	kreuzen	When cultured salmons escape and **interbreed** with wild species it can make the offspring vulnerable to a range of diseases.

Text workshop D - Surveillance and state control

premises *(pl only)* ['premɪsɪz]	Grundstück	**premises** = estate
fictional ['fɪkʃnl]	fiktional; fiktiv; erdichtet	**fictional** → fiction
neither ['naɪðə; 'ni:ðə]	keine/-r/-s (von beiden)	Both rooms have a camera, but **neither** of them works.
anger *(no pl)* ['æŋgə]	Zorn; Wut	**anger** → angry
weariness ['wɪərinəs]	Erschöpfung; Müdigkeit	**weariness** = exhaustion
to contain sth [kən'teɪn]	*hier:* etw zurückhalten	He was so upset that he could not **contain** his disappointment.
fury ['fjʊəri]	Wut	**fury** → furious
quarrel ['kwɒrl]	Streit; Auseinandersetzung	**quarrel** = argument
protection [prə'tekʃn]	Schutz	**protection** → to protect → protective
juvenile crime [ˌdʒu:vnaɪl 'kraɪm]	Jugendkriminalität	**juvenile** = adolescent; young
unemployment [ˌʌnɪm'plɔɪmənt]	Arbeitslosigkeit	The government is trying to reduce **unemployment** by creating new jobs.
pointless ['pɔɪntləs]	sinnlos; zwecklos	Stop trying. It's **pointless**.
selfish ['selfɪʃ]	selbstsüchtig; egoistisch	**selfish** ↔ considerate
welfare ['welfeə]	Wohlergehen	**welfare** = wellbeing
need [ni:d]	Bedürfnis	People with disabilities have special **needs**.
grievance ['gri:vns]	Groll; Kummer	**grievance** → to grieve
lens [lenz]	Linse	= a curved piece of glass or plastic that makes things look larger, smaller or clearer
to penetrate ['penɪtreɪt]	eindringen; durchdringen	**to penetrate** = to access
curiosity [ˌkjʊəri'ɒsəti]	Neugierde	**curiosity** → curious
to grasp [grɑ:sp]	greifen; ergreifen; festhalten	**to grasp** = to grip; to hold
to squeeze [skwi:z]	drücken	**to squeeze** = to press
rigid ['rɪdʒɪd]	starr	**rigid** ↔ relaxed
law enforcement [ˌlɔ:‿ɪn'fɔ:smənt]	Strafverfolgungsbehörde	= usually another term for the police

Topic project - Analysing a film/series about the future

bliss [blɪs]	Seligkeit	**bliss** = joy
various ['veəriəs]	verschieden; verschiedenartig	**Various** authors have written dystopian novels.
famine ['fæmɪn]	Hungersnot	The potato **famine** in Ireland made the Irish immigrate to the US.
oppression [ə'preʃn]	Unterdrückung	**oppression** → to oppress
to be flawed [bi 'flɔ:d]	fehlerhaft sein	The study **was flawed** and therefore of no use to the scientists.
blueprint ['blu:prɪnt]	Plan; Entwurf	= a plan which shows what can be achieved and how it can be achieved
to transcend [træn'send]	übersteigen; übertreffen	**to transcend** = to go beyond
unprecedented [ʌn'presɪdntɪd]	beispiellos; noch nie da gewesen	= having never happened in this way before

to erase [ɪ'reɪz]	löschen	**to erase** = to delete
social distinction [ˌsəʊʃl dɪ'stɪŋkʃn]	Rangunterschied	**distinction** ↔ similarity
to mock sb/sth ['mɒk ˌsəmbədi/sʌmθɪŋ]	etw/jdn lächerlich machen; etw/jdn verhöhnen	**to mock** = to laugh at; to ridicule
totalitarianism *(no pl)* [təʊˌtælɪ'teəriənɪzm]	Totalitarismus	**totalitarianism** = tyranny
to envision sth [ɪn'vɪʒn]	sich etw vorstellen	**to envision** = to imagine
fascism ['fæʃɪzm]	Faschismus	A lot of people volunteered to fight **fascism** in the Spanish Civil War.
epidemic [ˌepɪ'demɪk]	Seuche; Epidemie	The country was hit by a Corona virus **epidemic** last year.
cautionary ['kɔːʃnri]	warnend; abschreckend	When sb tells you a story as a **cautionary** tale it should usually warn you of some kind of danger.
angle ['æŋgl]	Winkel	The **angle** from which you look at sth influences your perspective.

D24 Vokabellernliste

Topic 3 Consumerism

Getting started

consumerism [kən'sjuːmərɪzm]	Konsum; Konsumdenken	**consumerism** → to consume → consumer
notion ['nəʊʃn]	Idee; Vorstellung	Some people have no **notion** of what it means to be poor.
sustainable [sə'steɪnəbl]	nachhaltig; umweltgerecht	**sustainable** → sustainability
to specialise in ['speʃlaɪz‿ɪn]	sich spezialisieren auf	This store **specialises in** wooden furniture.
dozen ['dʌzn]	Dutzend	= twelve of sth
purchase ['pɜːtʃəs]	Kauf; Erwerb	= sth you have bought
item ['aɪtəm]	Gegenstand; Artikel	**item** = object
to access ['ækses]	(auf etw) zugreifen; Zugang erlangen	**to access** = to enter
due to ['djuː tə]	wegen; aufgrund	**due to** = because of
whereas [weə'ræz]	während; wohingegen	In Québec they speak French, **whereas** most people in Canada speak English.
sex [seks]	(biologisches) Geschlecht	She mustn't talk to a member of the other **sex**.
throwaway society [ˌθrəʊəweɪ sə'saɪəti]	Wegwerfgesellschaft	= a society in which people do not keep things for very long
production costs *(pl)* [prə'dʌkʃn ˌkɒsts]	Produktionskosten	Companies want to keep their **production costs** as low as possible.
landfill ['lænfɪl]	Mülldeponie	**landfill** = dump
to accumulate [ə'kjuːmjəleɪt]	(an)sammeln	**to accumulate** = to build up
to entertain [ˌentə'teɪn]	unterhalten	Many Super Bowl commercials are designed to **entertain** the audience.
clothing ['kləʊðɪŋ]	Kleidung	**clothing** = clothes; garments
to underestimate sth [ˌʌndr'estɪmeɪt]	etw unterschätzen	**to underestimate** ↔ to overestimate
raw materials *(pl)* [ˌrɔː mə'tɪəriəlz]	Rohstoffe	= natural materials that have not yet been processed

lifespan ['laɪfspæn]	Lebensdauer; Gebrauchsdauer	Better batteries would increase the **lifespan** of mobile phones.
range [reɪndʒ]	Angebot; Spektrum; Auswahl	**range** = choice; selection
false [fɔ:ls]	falsch	**false** ↔ true
to put a strain on sb/sth [ˌpʊt‿ə 'streɪn‿ɒn ˌsʌmbədi/ˌsʌmθɪŋ]	jdn/etw belasten	**to put a strain on** = to burden
to eliminate [ɪ'lɪmɪneɪt]	beseitigen; ausschließen	**to eliminate** → elimination
on a daily basis [ɒn‿ə ˌdeɪli 'beɪsɪs]	im Alltag; tagtäglich	Have you ever tried to go jogging **on a daily basis**?
temptation [temp'teɪʃn]	Versuchung	**temptation** → to tempt
gruesome ['gru:səm]	grauenhaft	= extremely unpleasant and shocking
to pile up [ˌpaɪl‿'ʌp]	anhäufen	**to pile up** ↔ to get rid of
to inspire [ɪn'spaɪə]	inspirieren; anregen	**to inspire** → inspiration
sensible ['sensɪbl]	vernünftig	**sensible** ↔ stupid
to declutter [ˌdi:'klʌtə]	entrümpeln	**to declutter** = to clear out
peer pressure ['pɪə ˌpreʃə]	sozialer Druck	= acting as expected by the members of the same social group
brand [brænd]	Marke; Handelsmarke	**brand** = trademark

Text workshop A - Shopping addiction

compulsive [kəm'pʌlsɪv]	zwanghaft	He is a **compulsive** shopper. He shops every day.
susceptible [sə'septəbl]	empfänglich	**susceptible** ↔ immune against
confession [kən'feʃn]	Bekenntnis; Geständnis	**confession** → to confess
to overcome [ˌəʊvə'kʌm]	überwinden	**to overcome** ↔ to fail; to lose
response [rɪ'spɒns]	Antwort; Erwiderung; Rückmeldung	**response** → to respond
frequent ['fri:kwənt]	häufig	**frequent** ↔ rare
retail therapy *(coll)* [ˌri:teɪl 'θerəpi]	Frustshoppen *(ugs.)*; Einkaufstherapie	For many of us a bit of **retail therapy** is an essential element of a perfect holiday.
indulgence [ɪn'dʌldʒəns]	Genuss; Schwelgen	**indulgence** = luxury; comfort
excessive [ɪk'sesɪv]	übertrieben; ausschweifend	= greater than what seems reasonable or appropriate
to head ['hed]	fahren; gehen; zusteuern auf	If you **head for** a place, you move towards it.
to evade [ɪ'veɪd]	weichen; entziehen	**to evade** ↔ to confront
craving ['kreɪvɪŋ]	Verlangen	Even tough men have a **craving** for sweets sometimes.
to notify ['nəʊtɪfaɪ]	benachrichtigen; verständigen	= to officially tell sb about sth
thrill [θrɪl]	Aufregung; Nervenkitzel	**thrill** → thriller → thrilling
regardless of sth [rɪ'gɑ:dləs‿əv]	ungeachtet; unabhängig von etw	We are going to launch this product, **regardless of** what market research says.
fortnight ['fɔ:tnaɪt]	vierzehn Tage; zwei Wochen	Two weeks is a **fortnight**.
apparently [ə'pærntli]	anscheinend	**apparently** → to appear
shortcoming ['ʃɔ:tˌkʌmɪŋ]	Schwäche	= a weakness which prevents success or effectiveness
offended [ə'fendɪd]	beleidigt; verletzt	He took the criticism personally and was **offended** by it.
to seek [si:k]	ersuchen; bitten um	**to seek** = to search
to state [steɪt]	darlegen; darstellen	**to state** → statement
self-image [ˌself'ɪmɪdʒ]	Selbstbild	**self-image** = self-perception

instant ['ɪnstənt]	sofortige/-r/-s; sofortig	**instant** = immediate
gratification [ˌgrætɪfɪ'keɪʃn]	Belohnung; Erfüllung	Shopping offers a kind of instant **gratification** which is so desirable in today's world.
to **cope with** ['kəʊp wɪð]	zurechtkommen mit; schaffen	= to be able to deal with sth difficult
urge [ɜ:dʒ]	Drang	**urge** → urgent → urgency
accomplishment [ə'kʌmplɪʃmənt]	Errungenschaft; Leistung	**accomplishment** = achivement
to **cure** [kjʊə]	heilen; kurieren	Some types of cancer can now be **cured**.

Text workshop B - Sustainable consumption

preference ['prefrns]	Vorliebe	**preference** → to prefer → preferable
confusion [kən'fju:ʒn]	Verwirrung	**confusion** = uncertainty
misleading [mɪ'sli:dɪŋ]	irreführend; täuschend	This advertisement is **misleading** because it makes false claims.
ethical ['eθɪkl]	moralisch; ethisch	**ethical** → ethics
proper ['prɒpə]	angemessen; ordentlich; richtig	= in a correct way
to **biodegrade** [ˌbaɪəʊdɪ'greɪd]	(sich) biologisch abbauen	**to biodegrade** → biodegradable
curious ['kjʊəriəs]	neugierig	**curious** → curiosity
cruelty ['kru:əlti]	Grausamkeit	**cruelty** ↔ kindness
animal welfare [ˌænɪml 'welfeə]	Tierwohl	Thomas only buys meat from farmers who care about **animal welfare**.
to **harm** [hɑ:m]	schädigen; schaden	= to cause physical injury deliberately
in regards to [ɪn rɪ'gɑ:dz tə]	in Bezug auf	**in regards to** = concerning
organic [ɔ:'gænɪk]	biologisch; Bio-	Annie prefers **organic** food to conventional food.
fibre ['faɪbə]	Faser	= a thin thread or something that is similar to a thread
toxic ['tɒksɪk]	giftig	**toxic** = poisonous
pesticide ['pestɪsaɪd]	Schädlingsbekämpfungsmittel; Pestizid	= chemicals which farmers put on their crops to kill harmful insects
conscious ['kɒnʃəs]	bewusst	The whole family is very brand-**conscious**.
record ['rekɔ:d]	Dokumentation; Bericht; Aufzeichnung	= information kept about sth that has happened
to **research** [rɪ'sɜ:tʃ]	recherchieren; erforschen; untersuchen	If you **research** sth (or do research on sth), you study the subject in order to discover new information about it.
to **operate** ['ɒpreɪt]	tätig sein	= to work in a certain way
rather than ['rɑ:ðə ðən]	eher als	I would **rather** work in marketing **than** in finance.
support [sə'pɔ:t]	Unterstützung	The team's victory was only possible because of the strong **support** of their fans.
exaggerated [ɪg'zædʒreɪtɪd]	übertrieben	= sth is exaggerated when it seems better or worse than it really is
hazard ['hæzəd]	Gefahr; Risiko	For cleaning purposes, the Smiths use biodegradable products that do not constitute an environmental **hazard**.
to **exploit** [ɪk'splɔɪt]	ausbeuten	**to exploit** → exploitable → exploiter
to **get rid of sth** [get 'rɪd‿əv ˌsʌmθɪŋ]	etw loswerden	Why don't you **get rid of** those old jeans?
to **blow the budget** *(coll)* [ˌbləʊ ðə 'bʌdʒɪt]	das Budget sprengen	= to spend a lot more than you intended to

concise [kən'saɪs]	präzise; kurz; prägnant	= short, to the point
to **fulfil** [fʊl'fɪl]	erfüllen	= to achieve what was hoped for
availability [əˌveɪlə'bɪləti]	Verfügbarkeit	**availability** → available

Text workshop C - Working in advertising

copywriter ['kɒpiˌraɪtə]	Werbetexter/-in	= sb who produces written advertising texts for companies and the media
glass ceiling [ˌglɑ:s 'si:lɪŋ]	Glasdecke; [unsichtbare Barriere, die v.a. Frauen am beruflichen Aufstieg hindert]	Topics such as breaking through the **glass ceiling**, sexual harassment and hate awareness, have been well discussed in all media.
cancer ['kænsə]	Krebs *(Krankheit)*	**Cancer** is one of the most frequent causes of death.
to **comprise** [kəm'praɪz]	umfassen; beinhalten; einschließen	**to comprise** = to include; to contain
occupation [ˌɒkjə'peɪʃn]	Beruf; Beschäftigung	**occupation** = profession; trade
generic [dʒə'nerɪk]	Standard-; gewöhnlich	A love of big things seems to be a **generic** characteristic of Americans.
urban ['ɜ:bn]	städtisch	**urban** ↔ rural
proverbial [prə'vɜ:biəl]	sprichwörtlich	Have you heard of the **proverbial** canary in the coal mine?
recognition [ˌrekəg'nɪʃn]	Anerkennung	**recognition** → to recognise
disclosure [dɪ'skləʊʒə]	Offenlegung; Enthüllung	**disclosure** ↔ cover-up
to **be bound to happen** [bi ˌbaʊnd tə 'hæpn]	sicherlich geschehen werden	Driverless cars as means of transport **are bound to happen.**
cohabitation [ˌkəʊhæbɪ'teɪʃn]	Zusammenwohnen	= to live together
to **brief** [bri:f]	einweisen	**to brief** = to instruct
assignment [ə'saɪnmənt]	Aufgabe; Auftrag	= a piece of work that you must do for school or for a job
hence [hens]	darum; folglich	Siberian tigers are endangered species, **hence** illegal to kill.
to **market** ['mɑ:kɪt]	vermarkten	**to market** → market → marketing
consulting (company) [kən'sʌltɪŋ ˌkʌmpəni]	Unternehmensberatung	**consulting** = advising
passion [ˌpæʃn]	Leidenschaft	**passion** → passionate
to **put sth into practice** [ˌpʊt ˌɪntə 'præktɪs]	etw (in die Praxis) umsetzen	Let's **put** the theory **into practice.**
to **succeed** [sək'si:d]	Erfolg haben	**to succeed** → success
to **compete (with/against)** [kəm'pi:t]	in Wettbewerb treten (mit); konkurrieren (mit); sich messen (mit)	It's fun to **compete with** the other team because we usually win.
technological advance [teknəˌlɒdʒɪkl ˌəd'vɑ:ns]	technischer Fortschritt	The **technological advances** of the last decades have touched nearly every aspect of life.
to **interact** [ˌɪntə'ækt]	interagieren; zusammenspielen	= to talk together, do things together, react to each other
competitor [kəm'petɪtə]	Konkurrent/-in	**competitor** → to compete
USP (unique selling proposition) [ˌju:es'pi: (ju:ˌni:k 'selɪŋ prɒpəˌzɪʃn)]	Alleinstellungsmerkmal	= a feature or characteristic of a product, service, etc. that distinguishes it from others of a similar nature and makes it more appealing
strategy ['strætədʒi]	Strategie	We have to agree on our **strategy** before we start work.

objective [əbˈdʒektɪv]	Zielsetzung; Ziel	**objective** = goal
tonality [təʊˈnæləti]	Tonfall	= what an advert communicates to potential buyers - the feelings it may provoke or the perception it produces
to alienate [ˈeɪlɪəneɪt]	befremden; verprellen	**to alienate** ↔ to unite
authentic [ɔːˈθentɪk]	authentisch; echt; glaubwürdig	Your English sounds **authentic**.
to provoke [prəˈvəʊk]	provozieren	The president's speech **provoked** a lot of protest.
to become extinct [bɪˌkʌm ɪkˈstɪŋkt]	aussterben	**to become extinct** → extinction
unconventional [ˌʌnkənˈvenʃnl]	eigenwillig; unkonventionell	The new phone has an **unconventional** design with its split screen.
to trigger [ˈtrɪgə]	auslösen	**to trigger** = to activate
word-of-mouth [ˌwɜːdəvˈmaʊθ]	mündlich; Mund zu Mund	Giving the customers free coffee leads to plenty **word-of-mouth** advertising.
core concept [ˌkɔː ˈkɒnsept]	Kernkonzept; Kernidee	One of the **core concepts** of sustainability is avoiding waste.
imagery [ˈɪmɪdʒri]	Bildsprache; Metaphorik	= visually descriptive or figurative language, especially in a literary work
to overlook [ˌəʊvəˈlʊk]	übersehen	= to not notice sth
tagline [ˈtæglaɪn]	Werbeslogan	= a word or phrase that draws attention

Skills workshop - Working with advertisements

attention [əˈtenʃn]	Aufmerksamkeit; Beachtung	**attention** → attentive
proof [pruːf]	Beweis; Nachweis	**proof** → to prove
credibility [ˌkredəˈbɪləti]	Glaubwürdigkeit	After openly lying about his political motives he lost all his **credibility**.
textual [ˈtekstʃuəl]	*hier:* schriftlich; in Schriftform	**textual** = written
visual [ˈvɪʒuəl]	visuell; optisch	Pictures or charts are **visual** elements in a presentation.
to intend to [ɪnˈtend tə]	beabsichtigen	**to intend to** → intention
care-free [ˌkeəˈfriː]	sorgenfrei	= to have no troubles or worries
environmentally friendly [ɪnˌvaɪrnˌmentli ˈfrendli]	umweltfreundlich	On their last camping trip they used **environmentally-friendly** soap.
to incorporate [ɪnˈkɔːpreɪt]	integrieren; einbinden	**to incorporate** = to include
previous [ˈpriːviəs]	vorherig; früher	**previous** = before

Text workshop D - Brands with purpose

employee [ɪmˈplɔɪiː]	Mitarbeiter/-in	**employee** → employer → to employ → employment
to stick with sth [ˈstɪk wɪð]	bei etw bleiben	= to hold on to sth
to enable [ɪˈneɪbl]	ermöglichen	**to enable** = to make possible
stand [stænd]	Haltung; Standpunkt	**stand** = point of view
incredibly [ɪnˈkredəbli]	unglaublich	This drink is **incredibly** popular with teenagers.
purpose-driven [ˌpɜpəsˈdrɪvn]	zielgesteuert	**Purpose-driven** marketing takes a brand's cause and makes it available to customers, helping them to connect fully with the brand as a whole.
consistently [kənˈsɪstntli]	gleich bleibend; stetig; konsistent	**consistent** ↔ inconsistent
to embrace [ɪmˈbreɪs]	etw annehmen	*here:* to accept willingly

numerous ['nju:mrəs]	zahlreich; viel	**numerous** = many
enduring [ɪn'djʊərɪŋ]	bleibend; dauerhaft	**enduring** → to endure
well-being [ˌwel'bi:ɪŋ]	Wohlbefinden	= the state of feeling healthy and happy
to **enrich** [ɪn'rɪtʃ]	bereichern	**to enrich** = to enhance; to make better
to **evolve** [ɪ'vɒlv]	entwickeln	**to evolve** = to develop
to **elaborate (on sth)** [ɪ'læbreɪt‿ɒn]	(etw) näher ausführen	= to explain sth in detail
billboard ['bɪlbɔ:d]	Plakatwand	Piccadilly Circus in London features huge digital **billboards**.
prime example [ˌpraɪm‿ɪg'zɑ:mpl]	Musterbeispiel	= a very good example
to **make sense** [ˌmeɪk 'sens]	Sinn ergeben; einleuchten	If sth **makes sense**, you can understand it.
to **arise** [ə'raɪz]	entstehen	A problem has **arisen** with the new product design.
commercial [kə'mɜ:ʃl]	Geschäfts-, geschäftlich; gewerblich	= work related to the selling of products or services
to **label** ['leɪbl]	beschriften; etikettieren	Please **label** the packages.
blurred [blɜ:d]	verschwommen; verwischt	In a **blurred** picture, things are out of focus.
surreptitious [ˌsʌrəp'tɪʃəs]	heimlich	**surreptitious** ↔ obvious, evident, apparent
sinister ['sɪnɪstə]	finster; schlimm	**sinister** = threatening
transparency [træn'spærnsi]	Transparenz	**transparency** → transparent
to **recommend** [ˌrekə'mend]	empfehlen	I'd **recommend** that film. It's a must see.
to **progress** [prə'gres]	fortschreiten	**to progress** = to move forward

Topic project - Creating a marketing campaign

to **proceed** [prə'si:d]	weitermachen	**to proceed** = to carry on
to **sample** ['sɑ:mpl]	(aus)probieren	He **sampled** the soup to see if it was salty enough.
to **show off** [ˌʃəʊ‿'ɒf]	stolz vorzeigen	My brother always **shows off** with his expensive smartphone.

D25 Vokabellernliste

Topic 4 Land of dreams?

Getting started

rooted ['ru:tɪd]	verankert; verwurzelt	**rooted** = firmly fixed
way back [ˌweɪ 'bæk]	vor langer Zeit; lange her	= a long time ago
massive ['mæsɪv]	riesig; massiv	The **massive** rainfalls last week flooded the whole region.
unlimited [ʌn'lɪmɪtɪd]	unbegrenzt	This telephone flat rate gives you **unlimited** free calls within your country.
ancestry ['ænsestri]	Abstammung; Herkunft; Vorfahren	**ancestry** → ancestor
fierce [fɪəs]	heftig; kämpferisch	**fierce** = rough; violent
mistreatment [mis'tri:tmənt]	schlechte Behandlung	= to treat sb badly or abusively
enslaved [ɪn'sleɪvd]	versklavt	**enslaved** → slave → slavery
to **exploit** [ɪk'splɔɪt]	ausbeuten	= to take unfair advantage of sb, e.g. by not paying them enough for their work
foreign policy [ˌfɒrən 'pɒləsi]	Außenpolitik	**foreign policy** ↔ domestic policy

to set out to do sth [set‿aʊt]	**sich vornehmen etw zu tun;** *hier:* **festlegen**	**to set out to do sth** = to intend to do sth
principle ['prɪnsəpl]	**Grundsatz; Prinzip**	You must be true to your own **principles.**
to **hand over** [ˌhænd‿'əʊvə]	**aushändigen; übergeben**	**to hand over** = to pass on
entrepreneurial spirit [ˌɒntrəprəˌnɜ:riəl 'spɪrɪt]	**Unternehmungsgeist**	**entrepreneurial** → entrepreneur → enterprise
enterprise ['entəpraɪz]	**Unternehmen; Vorhaben**	In Sweden, shops selling alcohol are always state **enterprises.**
to **demonstrate** ['demənstreɪt]	**aufzeigen; demonstrieren**	**to demonstrate** = to show

Text workshop A - Shaping the USA

Founding Father [ˌfaʊndɪŋ 'fɑ:ðə]	**Gründungsvater**	In the US, the **Founding Fathers** are the men who signed the Declaration of Independence in 1776.
astonishing [ə'stɒnɪʃɪŋ]	**erstaunlich**	**astonishing** = surprising
plot [plɒt]	**Handlung**	= the series of events that form the story
to **feature** ['fi:tʃə]	**aufweisen; sich auszeichnen durch**	= to have special qualities or characteristics
subtly ['sʌtli]	**dezent; fein**	**subtle** ↔ obvious
distinctive [dɪ'stɪŋktɪv]	**charakteristisch; ausgeprägt**	Some animals produce a **distinctive** smell to scare off their enemies.
incredible [ɪn'kredəbl]	**unglaublich**	**incredible** = unbelievable
social mobility [ˌsəʊʃl mə'bɪləti]	**gesellschaftliche Mobilität**	upward/downward **mobility**
scholar ['skɒlə]	**Gelehrte/-r; Wissenschaftler/-in; Forscher/-in**	= sb who studies a subject in great depth
destiny ['destɪni]	**Bestimmung; Schicksal**	= sth that is supposed to happen to you in the future
to **throw sth off** [ˌθrəʊ sʌmθɪŋ‿'ɒf]	**etw loswerden**	They **threw off** their clothes and jumped into the lake.
mighty ['maɪti]	**gewaltig**	**mighty** = powerful; strong
to **catch sb's eye** ['kætʃ ˌsʌmbədiz‿aɪ]	**jdm auffallen**	= to get sb's attention
boundless ['baʊndləs]	**maßlos**	**boundless** = unrestricted
to **entrust sb with sth** [ɪn'trʌst ˌsʌmbədi wɪð ˌsʌmθɪŋ]	**jdn mit etw betrauen; eine Aufgabe übertragen**	**to entrust** → to trust
to **defeat** [dɪ'fi:t]	**besiegen**	**to defeat** = to beat
to **seek sth** [si:k]	**etw suchen; nach etw streben**	**to seek** = to search
thrill [θrɪl]	**Nervenkitzel**	**thrill** → thrilling
to **be consumed by sth** [bi kən'sju:md baɪ ˌsʌmθɪŋ]	**erfüllt sein von etw**	= to be filled with a strong feeling
selfless ['selfləs]	**uneigennützig; selbstlos**	**selfless** ↔ selfish
disguise [dɪs'gaɪz]	**Verkleidung**	His absence proved to be a blessing in **disguise.**
useless ['ju:sləs]	**sinnlos; zwecklos**	**useless** ↔ useful
envy ['envi]	**Neid**	Paul was full of **envy** towards his sister because he wanted to be as successful as she was.
rage [reɪdʒ]	**Wut; Zorn**	**rage** = anger
obscure [əb'skjʊə]	**unbekannt; unbedeutend**	= not well known or not important
remarkable [rɪ'mɑ:kəbl]	**außergewöhnlich; bemerkenswert**	**remarkable** = astonishing
deliberately [dɪ'lɪbrətli]	**bewusst; absichtlich**	**deliberately** ↔ accidentally
destructive [dɪ'strʌktɪv]	**destruktiv; zerstörerisch**	**destructive** → destruction

virtue ['vɜːtʃuː]	Tugend; Wert	**virtue** ↔ vice
reward [rɪ'wɔːd]	Belohnung	The police are offering a **reward** for any information that will help to solve the case.
lasting ['lɑːstɪŋ]	bleibend; dauerhaft	Too much sugar can have **lasting** negative effects on your health.
fame [feɪm]	Ruhm	**fame** → famous
inability [ˌɪnə'bɪləti]	Unfähigkeit	**inability** ↔ ability
to **outweigh** [ˌaʊt'weɪ]	aufwiegen; wettmachen	The benefits far **outweigh** the drawbacks.
skilful ['skɪlfl]	geschickt	= good at doing sth
conflict ['kɒnflɪkt]	Konflikt; Auseinandersetzung	Everyone should learn how to deal with **conflict**.
loads of ['ləʊdz‿əv]	eine große Menge von	**loads of** = many
scholarship ['skɒləʃɪp]	Stipendium	If you can earn a **scholarship** to a school or college, your parents don't have to pay.
recognition [ˌrekəg'nɪʃn]	Anerkennung	**recognition** → to recognise
to **remind sb of sth/sb** [rɪ'maɪnd]	jdn an etw/jdn erinnern	With his blue eyes and dark hair, he really **reminds me** of his mother.
cast [kɑːst]	Besetzung; Ensemble	If you talk about the **cast** of a play or film, you mean all the people who act in it.
to **dominate** ['dɒmɪneɪt]	dominieren; beherrschen	**to dominate** → dominant
person of color *(AE)* [ˌpɜːsn‿əv 'kʌlə]	nicht-weiße Person	= sb who does not identify as white
overwhelming [ˌəʊvə'welmɪŋ]	überwältigend	**overwhelming** = stunning, great
to **inspire** [ɪn'spaɪə]	inspirieren; anregen	= to give the idea for sth (e.g. a poem or a song)
limitation [ˌlɪmɪ'teɪʃn]	Einschränkung; Begrenzung	**limitation** → to limit
racial ['reɪʃl]	Rassen-	The city-state of Bremen removed the term "race" from its local Constitution and replaced it with "**racial** discrimination."
frontier ['frʌntɪə]	Grenze; Grenzland	**frontier** = borderland

Text workshop B - Dreaming the American Dream

liberty ['lɪbəti]	Freiheit	**liberty** = freedom
pursuit of happiness [pəˌsjuːt‿əv 'hæpɪnəs]	Streben nach Glück	= trying to achieve happiness
to **flee** [fliː]	fliehen	**to flee** = to get away; to escape
civil war [ˌsɪvl 'wɔː]	Bürgerkrieg	= a war between different groups within one country
to **gain entrance** [ˌgeɪn 'entrəns]	Aufnahme erlangen; Eintritt	**to gain** = to obtain
to **bow** [baʊ]	beugen; sich beugen	= to bend the head or body forwards or downwards
to **recite** [rɪ'saɪt]	auswendig aufsagen	**to recite** → recital → citation
payday ['peɪdeɪ]	Zahltag	= the day on which you are paid
humiliating [hjuː'mɪlieɪtɪŋ]	erniedrigend	**humiliating** = embarrassing
to **shrink** [ʃrɪŋk]	schrumpfen	**to shrink** = to get smaller
drunk driving [ˌdrʌŋk 'draɪvɪŋ]	Trunkenheit am Steuer	= driving under the influence of alcohol
none [nʌn]	keine/-r/-s	There were three other people in the room, but **none** of us knew the others.
racist ['reɪsɪst]	rassistisch	**racist** → race → racial
homeless ['həʊmləs]	obdachlos	= to be without permanent residence, home or shelter

filthy ['fɪlθi]	schmutzig; dreckig	**filthy** ↔ clean
fortunately ['fɔːtʃnətli]	zum Glück	**fortunately** = luckily
to **dress up** [ˌdres‿'ʌp]	sich feinmachen; sich herausputzen	= to dress formally
outsider [ˌaʊt'saɪdə]	Außenseiter/-in	= a person who is not accepted as a member of a group
minimum wage [ˌmɪnɪməm 'weɪdʒ]	Mindestlohn	In many jobs people do not earn more than the **minimum wage**.
to **pick** [pɪk]	pflücken	Fruit tastes best when it's freshly **picked**.
produce ['prɒdjuːs]	landwirtschaftliche Erzeugnisse	You get fresh **produce** at the farmer's market.
without notice [wɪˌðaʊt 'nəʊtɪs]	*hier:* ohne Kündigungsfrist	If a contract is illegal you can terminate it **without notice**.
undocumented [ʌn'dɒkjəmentɪd]	nicht dokumentiert; nicht behördlich erfasst; *hier:* illegal	You are **undocumented** when you do not have the documents that allow you to live or work in a foreign country.
citizenship ['sɪtɪznʃɪp]	Staatsangehörigkeit; Staatsbürgerschaft	**citizenship** → citizen
relief [rɪ'liːf]	Unterstützung	**Relief** efforts in the disaster zone are finally making some progress.
conditional residency [kənˌdɪʃnl 'rezɪdnsi]	bedingtes Aufenthaltsrecht	**conditional** ↔ unconditional
to **defer** [dɪ'fɜː]	aufschieben; aussetzen	**to defer** = to postpone; to pause
deportation [ˌdiːpɔː'teɪʃn]	Deportation; Abschiebung	= forcing sb to leave a country
driver's licence *(BE)* ['draɪvəz ˌlaɪsns]	Führerschein	AE: **driver's license** BE: driving licence
work permit ['wɜːk ˌpɜːmɪt]	Arbeitserlaubnis	= an official document to state that a (foreign) person is allowed to work
paralegal *(AE)* [ˌpærə'liːgl]	Anwaltsgehilfe/-gehilfin	= a trained lawyer's assistant
loss [lɒs]	Verlust	**loss** → to lose
to **profit from** ['prɒfɪt frəm]	profitieren von	As sponsors of the team they wanted to **profit from** its fame.
to **make a living** [ˌmeɪk‿ə 'lɪvɪŋ]	Lebensunterhalt bestreiten	= to support oneself
to **fear sth** [fɪə]	fürchten	After hearing all this bad news I truly **fear** the worst.

Skills workshop - Analysing style, tone and register

register ['redʒɪstə]	Sprachebene	It's important to change your **register** to match the situation you're in. That means you should always use the right language for the right situation.
effectively [ɪ'fektɪvli]	effektiv; wirksam	**effectively** = successfully
to **alienate** ['eɪlɪəneɪt]	befremden	**to alienate** → alien
elaborate [ɪ'læbrət]	aufwändig	**elaborate** ↔ plain
witty ['wɪti]	witzig; geistreich	= intelligent and funny
to **weave** [wiːv]	weben	= to produce a cloth by interlacing two threads
patch [pætʃ]	Flicken	**patch** → patchwork
quilt [kwɪlt]	Steppdecke; Quilt	= a blanket made of several layers of cloth with the top layer often displaying a patchwork pattern
equity ['əkwɪti]	Gerechtigkeit	**equity** → equal
welfare ['welfeə]	Sozialhilfe; Fürsorge	= money and/or services you get from the state or an organisation when you are in need

right wing [ˌraɪt'wɪŋ]	rechtsorientiert; Rechts-; rechts stehend	He normally uses regular meetings as a way to express his **right wing** views.
to **despair** [dɪ'speə]	verzweifeln	Mr Higgins **despaired** at the poor level of spelling of his pupils.
common ground [ˌkɒmən 'graʊnd]	eine gemeinsame Basis	The neighbours finally found **common ground** for conversation.

Text workshop C - Space and innovation

space [speɪs]	Weltraum; Weltall	There's endless space in **space**.
to **be reminiscent of sth** [bi ˌremɪ'nɪsnt]	an etw erinnern	**reminiscent of sth** → to remind sb of sth
to **boast sth** [bəʊst]	sich einer Sache rühmen können	India **boasts** one of the best cricket teams in the world.
commercial [kə'mɜːʃl]	gewerblich; kommerziell	= having to do with buying and selling goods or services
edge [edʒ]	Rand; Kante	Don't put that bottle too near the **edge** of the table or it may fall off!
to **be due to do sth** [bi ˌdʒuː tə 'duː sʌmθɪŋ]	etw tun sollen (lt. Planung); bevorstehen, dass jmd etw tut	**due to do sth** = going to do sth
reusable [ˌriː'juːzəbl]	wiederverwendbar; Mehrweg-	Look, I got this great cup with my coffee-to-go this morning. It's **reusable**!
space exploration [ˌspeɪs‿eksplə'reɪʃn]	Weltraumforschung	**exploration** → to explore → explorer
defence [dɪˌfens]	Verteidigung	**defence** → to defend
supremacy [suː'preməsi]	Vorherrschaft; Überlegenheit	**supremacy** = dominance
heir [eə]	Erbe/Erbin	= sb who inherits the property or title of sb who has died
assessment [ə'sesmənt]	Einschätzung; Beurteilung	= a judgement that has been given a lot of thought
competitor [kəm'petɪtə]	Konkurrent/-in	**competitor** → to compete
to **exceed** [ɪk'siːd]	übersteigen; übertreffen	**to exceed** = to surpass; to outperform; to top
capability [ˌkeɪpə'bɪləti]	Fähigkeit	**capability** → capable
like-minded [ˌlaɪk'maɪndɪd]	gleichgesinnt	**to share common interests and background**
faction ['fækʃn]	Interessengruppe; Fraktion	The government could reach an agreement with the opposing **faction**.
leap [liːp]	Sprung; Satz	With a giant **leap** the cat jumped down from the tree.
accusation [ˌækjə'seɪʃn]	Anschuldigung	**accusation** → accuse sb of sth
to **question** ['kwestʃən]	in Frage stellen; hinterfragen	Our trainer always **questions** our motivation.
sensitive ['sensɪtɪv]	empfindlich; sensibel	Talking about politics can be a **sensitive** issue.
to **flourish** ['flʌrɪʃ]	großen Erfolg haben; florieren	Their new business struggled for two years before it really began **to flourish**.
to **allude to sth** [ə'luːd tə]	auf etw anspielen	**to allude to** = to hint at sth

Text workshop D - The USA and the world

alliance [ə'laɪəns]	Bündnis	**alliance** → allies
to **advance** [əd'vɑːns]	voranschreiten; fortschreiten	= to go forward
to **rival** ['raɪvl]	konkurrieren; aufnehmen können mit	**to rival sb** → rivalry
determination [dɪˌtɜːmɪ'neɪʃn]	Entschlossenheit	**determination** → determined → to be determined to do sth
pandemic [ˌpæn'demɪk]	Pandemie	= a worldwide epidemic

to **defend** [dɪ'fend]	verteidigen	**to defend** → defence
dignity *(no pl)* ['dɪgnəti]	Würde	**dignity** → to dignify → dignified
equipped [ɪ'kwɪpt]	ausgestattet	**equipped** → equipment
asset ['æset]	Kapital; Vermögen	**asset** = advantage; resource
adversary ['ædvəsri]	Kontrahent	**adversary** ↔ friend
to **extend** [ɪk'stend]	verlängern; (sich) ausdehnen	**to extend** → extension
to **safeguard** ['seɪfgɑ:d]	schützen	**to safeguard** = to protect
to **renew** [rɪ'nju:]	erneuern	This was my last issue of the "Health Magazine". I need to **renew** my subscription.
to **reclaim** [rɪ'kleɪm]	zurückfordern; zurückgewinnen	**reclaim** = to want sth back; to get sth back
leadership ['li:dəʃɪp]	Führung; Leitung	**leadership** → to lead → leader
objective [əb'dʒektɪv]	Ziel	**objective** = goal
to **elevate** ['elɪveɪt]	anheben; erhöhen	**to elevate** ↔ to lower
resilience [rɪ'zɪliəns]	Belastbarkeit; Stabilität	**resilience** ↔ weakness; helplessness
refugee [ˌrefjʊ'dʒi:]	Flüchtling	= a person who flees to a foreign country
consensus [kən'sensəs]	Übereinstimmung	**consensus** → consent
persecution [ˌpɜ:sɪ'kju:ʃn]	Verfolgung	= harassment of a particular group, usually for their religious or political beliefs
admission [əd'mɪʃn]	Aufnahme	**admission** → to admit sb to sth
unprecedented [ʌn'presɪdntɪd]	beispiellos; noch nie da gewesen	= having never happened in this way before
likelihood ['laɪklihʊd]	Wahrscheinlichkeit	**likelihood** = probability
indigenous [ɪn'dɪdʒɪnəs]	Ureinwohner	Aboriginal and Torres Strait Islander people are the **indigenous** peoples of Australia.
disability [ˌdɪsə'bɪləti]	Behinderung	people with learning/physical/mental **disabilities**
to **abstain** [æb'steɪn]	sich heraushalten; zurückhalten	**to abstain** = to stay away
mutual ['mju:tʃuəl]	gegenseitig	= sth shared by two or more people
to **contradict** [ˌkɒntrə'dɪkt]	widersprechen	**to contradict** → contradiction
war zone ['wɔ: ˌzəʊn]	Kriegsgebiet	A ceasefire was successfully declared for the entire **war zone**.
armed conflict [ˌɑ:md 'kɒnflɪkt]	bewaffneter Konflikt	**armed** → army → armor
military ['mɪlɪtri]	militärisch; Militär-	Soldiers must get used to many **military** routines.
to **undertake** [ˌʌndə'teɪk]	durchführen; auf sich nehmen	**to undertake** = to attempt
liberation [ˌlɪbr'eɪʃn]	Befreiung	In 1863 President Lincoln issued a proclamation that brought the **liberation** of enslaved people.
considerable [kən'sɪdrəbl]	beträchtlich	a **considerable** amount of time = quite a long time
straightforward [ˌstreɪt'fɔ:wəd]	einfach; unkompliziert	**straightforward** = simple; easy
troops *(pl)* [tru:ps]	Truppen	= armed forces
weapon ['wepən]	Waffe	What kind of **weapons** did the Romans fight with?
area of conflict [ˌeəriə‿əv 'kɒnflɪkt]	Konfliktgebiet	Afghanistan has been an **area of conflict** for decades.
to **occur** [ə'kɜ:]	vorkommen; auftreten	**to occur** = to happen
economic system [i:kəˌnɒmɪk 'sɪstəm]	Wirtschaftssystem	**economic** → economy → economical
to **split up** [splɪt]	teilen; trennen	= to divide into two or more parts
to **intervene** [ˌɪntə'vi:n]	eingreifen	**to intervene** → intervention
to **execute sb** ['eksɪkju:t]	jdn exekutieren; hinrichten	**to execute** → execution

to withdraw [wɪð'drɔː]	(sich) zurückziehen	= to formally leave or remove oneself from an organisation, an agreement, or conflict
subsequently ['sʌbsɪkwəntli]	anschließend; folgend	**subsequently** = afterwards

Topic project - The USA seen from abroad – Creating a podcast

contribution [ˌkɒntrɪ'bjuːʃn]	Beitrag; Beteiligung	What's your **contribution** to the party? Food, music?
to quote [kwəʊt]	zitieren	**to quote** → quotation

D26 Vokabellernliste

Topic 5 The UK and its people

Getting started

to be one and the same [bi ˌwʌn‿ən ðə 'seɪm]	ein und dasselbe sein	**to be one and the same** = to be equivalent
to manage (to do sth) ['mænɪdʒ]	schaffen (etw zu tun)	= to succeed in doing sth difficult
to be up *(infml)* [biː 'ʌp]	dran sein	Hold on, I'**m up** next. Please wait until it is your turn.
slightly ['slaɪtli]	ein wenig; etwas	**slightly** = a little
constituency [kən'stɪtjuənsi]	Wahlkreis; Wahlbezirk	= a town or area which is represented by a Member of Parliament
the devolved nations [ðə dɪˌvɒlvd 'neɪʃnz]	die dezentralisierten Länder Großbritanniens: Nordirland, Schottland, Wales	= the devolved nations of the UK: Northern Ireland, Scotland, Wales
reunification [ˌriːjuːnɪfɪ'keɪʃn]	Wiedervereinigung	The official **reunification** of Germany took place in 1990.
connection [kə'nekʃn]	Verbindung	**connection** → to connect
good-natured [ˌgʊd'neɪtʃəd]	gutmütig; freundlich	She is very well liked because of her **good-natured** personality.
with good grace [wɪð ˌgʊd 'greɪs]	mit Humor	**with good grace** = cheerfully
to have sth in common [ˌhæv‿ɪn 'kɒmən]	etw miteinander gemein haben	They **have** a lot **in common**: they both enjoy fantasy films and playing computer games.
parachute ['pærəʃuːt]	Fallschirm	**parachute** → to parachute
to negotiate sth [nɪ'gəʊʃieɪt]	etw aushandeln; etw verhandeln	= to talk about sth in order to reach an agreement
prejudice ['predʒədɪs]	Vorurteil	**prejudice** → to be prejudiced against

Text workshop A - English and its regional varieties

linguistic [lɪŋ'gwɪstɪk]	sprachlich	= relating to language
ingenuity [ˌɪndʒə'njuːəti]	Einfallsreichtum; Genialität	We are looking for people who have both the skills and the **ingenuity** to succeed.
to distract sb (from sth) [dɪ'strækt (frəm)]	jdn (von etw) ablenken	**to distract** ↔ to focus
to announce [ə'naʊns]	bekanntgeben; verkünden	= to give formal information or details about sth
bar [bɑː]	Hemmnis; Hindernis	**bar** → barrier
mobility [mə'bɪləti]	Mobilität	**mobility** → mobile
barn [bɑːn]	Scheune	This big red **barn** houses 75 cows and a large supply of hay.

to delight sb [dɪˈlaɪt]	jdn erfreuen; beglücken	**delight** → delightful → delighted
to remind sb [rɪˈmaɪnd]	jdn erinnern	I almost forgot the meeting. Fortunately, Jane **reminded** me of it.
to figure out [ˌfɪgər‿ˈaʊt]	herausfinden; ergründen	The technicians are still trying to **figure out** a solution to the problem.
properly [ˈprɒpli]	richtig; ordentlich	= in a correct way
reassuring [ˌriːəˈʃʊərɪŋ]	beruhigend	**reassuring** = comforting
upward [ˈʌpwəd]	steigend; aufwärts	= moving or changing from lower to higher
ridiculous [rɪˈdɪkjələs]	lächerlich	**ridiculous** = absurd; laughable
variety [vəˈraɪəti]	Art; Vielfalt	The local vegetable market often has more **variety** than the supermarkets.
to investigate [ɪnˈvestɪgeɪt]	Nachforschungen anstellen; untersuchen	**to investigate** → investigation
to mock sb/sth [ˈmɒk ˌsʌmbədi/ˌsʌmθɪŋ]	etw/jdn lächerlich machen; etw/jdn verhöhnen	**to mock** = to laugh at; to ridicule
connotation [ˌkɒnəˈteɪʃn]	Sinnbezug; Nebenbedeutung	= an implied or indirect meaning of a word or phrase
rather than [ˈrɑːðə ðən]	eher als	I would **rather** work at a hospital **than** in an office.
trustworthy [ˈtrʌstˌwɜːði]	vertrauenswürdig	**trustworthy** = reliable

Text workshop B - National identity

to bake [beɪk]	backen	**to bake** → bakery
savoury [ˈseɪvri]	herzhaft; pikant	Food is often categorised as being either sweet or **savoury**.
enriched [ɪnˈrɪtʃt]	bereichert	**enriched** = enhanced
to roam [rəʊm]	durchstreifen; herumwandern	I imagined a monster **roaming** around outside.
fractured [ˈfræktʃəd]	gespalten; zerbrochen	**fractured** ↔ united
curiosity [ˌkjʊəriˈɒsəti]	Neugierde	**curiosity** → curious
tent [tent]	Zelt	I don't want to sleep in a **tent**. Let's go to a youth hostel.
literally [ˈlɪtrli]	wortwörtlich; buchstäblich	**literally** = actually
to spark [spɑːk]	auslösen; entzünden	A tax rise on petrol **sparked** a lot of demonstrations.
pleasant [ˈpleznt]	angenehm; schön	New York is mild and **pleasant** in spring but often unbearably hot in summer.
exceedingly [ɪkˈsiːdɪŋli]	besonders; in hohem Maße	You have been **exceedingly** quiet all day. Is something wrong?
remnant [ˈremnənt]	Relikt; Überrest	= sth that is left over (*here:* from another time)
sanity [ˈsænəti]	Verstand; Vernunft	**sanity** ↔ insanity
contestant [kənˈtestnt]	Kandidat/-in	**contestant** → contest
coherence [kəʊˈhɪərns]	Zusammenhalt; Geschlossenheit	= to stick together as a unified group
to reject [rɪˈdʒekt]	ablehnen; zurückweisen	**to reject** ↔ to accept
retiree [rɪˌtaɪəˈriː]	Ruheständler/-in	**retiree** → to retire
range [reɪndʒ]	Auswahl; Angebot; Spektrum	**range** = choice; selection
occasional [əˈkeɪʒnl]	gelegentlich	**occasional** ↔ often
valuable [ˈvæljuəbl]	wertvoll	**valuable** → value → valued
venture [ˈventʃə]	Projekt; Unternehmen	**venture** = project; undertaking

flavor *(AE)* ['fleɪvə]	Geschmack; Aroma	Two ice creams, please. – What **flavor**? – One chocolate and one banana.
distinctively [dɪ'stɪŋktɪvli]	charakteristisch; unverwechselbar	**distinctively** → distinct → distinction
treat [tri:t]	Leckerei	= sth good to eat
ingredient [ɪn'gri:diənt]	Zutat	We only use organic **ingredients** in our food.
failure ['feɪljə]	Versagen; Scheitern	**failure** ↔ success
to **mend** [mend]	flicken; reparieren	**to mend** = to repair
charity ['tʃærɪti]	Wohltätigkeit; gute Sache	= the act of giving money to help people, e.g. when they are poor
to **blend in** [ˌblend‿'ɪn]	einfügen; integrieren	**to blend in** ↔ to stick out
shy [ʃaɪ]	schüchtern	**shy** → shyness
fame [feɪm]	Ruhm	**fame** → famous
to **upset** [ʌp'set]	aufregen; stören	= to make sb angry or unhappy

Skills workshop - Working with maps

in a nutshell [ɪn‿ə 'nʌtʃel]	in aller Kürze	**in a nutshell** = briefly; compactly
brief [bri:f]	kurz	We don't have much time, so let me just give you some **brief** instructions.
crop [krɒp]	Nutzpflanze	We grow a variety of **crops**, including wheat and barley.
enslaved [ɪn'sleɪvd]	versklavt	**enslaved** → slave → slavery
raw materials *(pl)* [ˌrɔ: mə'tɪəriəlz]	Rohstoffe	= natural materials that have not yet been processed
to **ship** [ʃɪp]	befördern; verschiffen; versenden	Our oranges are **shipped** fresh every morning to the markets in the north.
scramble ['skræmbl]	Gerangel	There was a **scramble** at the front of the line. Everybody wanted to be first.
to **compete (with/against)** [kəm'pi:t]	in Wettbewerb treten (mit); konkurrieren (mit); sich messen (mit)	It's fun to **compete with** the other team because we usually win.
ethnic ['eθnɪk]	ethnisch; Volks-	What's your **ethnic** background? – I'm half German and half Spanish.
vast [vɑ:st]	gewaltig; riesig	**vast** = massive
to **maintain** [meɪn'teɪn]	unterhalten; unterstützen	**to maintain** → maintenance
to **partition** [pɑ:'tɪʃn]	teilen; spalten	Germany was **partitioned** until 1989.
to **evolve** [ɪ'vɒlv]	entwickeln	**to evolve** = to develop
dominion [də'mɪnjən]	Herrschaftsgebiet; Hoheitsgebiet	= countries of the Commonwealth which had their own government
as time went on [əz ˌtaɪm went‿'ɒn]	im Laufe der Zeit	At first they hated each other, but **as time went on** they became close friends.
relationship [rɪ'leɪʃnʃɪp]	Beziehung	Is the **relationship** between you and your neighbours a good one?
allegiance [ə'li:dʒns]	Ergebenheit; Loyalität	**allegiance** = loyalty
to **issue** ['ɪʃu:; 'ɪsju:]	herausgeben	**to issue** = to release
to **withdraw** [wɪð'drɔ:]	(sich) zurückziehen	= to formally leave or remove oneself from an organisation or an agreement
to **cease** [si:s]	aufhören; beenden	**to cease** = to stop; to terminate
legacy ['legəsi]	Vermächtnis; Erbe	= sth handed down from the past

Text workshop C - History from another perspective

slavery ['sleɪvri]	Sklaverei	**Slavery** in the US ended after the Civil War.
to reverse [rɪ'vɜːs]	umkehren	**to reverse** = to turn around; to turn back
notorious [nə'tɔːriəs]	berüchtigt; berühmt	He is a **notorious** gambler and has lost a lot of money.
decent ['diːsnt]	anständig	= morally correct or acceptable
in spite of oneself [ɪn 'spaɪt‿əv]	unwillkürlich	= although not wanting or expecting (to do sth)
to shove [ʃʌv]	schieben	**to shove** = to push
to vanish ['vænɪʃ]	verschwinden	He saw all his hopes **vanishing**.
to pass out [ˌpɑːs‿'aʊt]	ohnmächtig werden	= to lose consciousness
to put at stake [ˌpʊt‿ət 'steɪk]	aufs Spiel setzen	= to risk sth valuable
to rip [rɪp]	zerreißen; reißen	**to rip** = to tear
to betray [bɪ'treɪ]	verraten	**to betray** → betrayal
large-scale ['lɑːdʒskeɪl]	umfangreich; weitreichend	The university started a **large-scale** research project on sustainable alternatives to mineral oil.
to stick [stɪk]	bleiben; kleben	**to stick** ↔ to remove
greedy ['griːdi]	habgierig; raffsüchtig	**greedy** → greed
seriously ['sɪəriəsli]	ernsthaft; im Ernst	**seriously** → seriousness
memory ['memri]	Erinnerung	We all have great **memories** of our school trip.
to long for sth [lɒŋ]	sich nach etw sehnen; verlangen	**to long for sth** = to wish for sth
drizzle ['drɪzl]	Nieselregen	November weather seems to be **drizzle** every day.
to slap [slæp]	schlagen; einen Klaps geben	= to hit sb or sth with an open hand
captive ['kæptɪv]	Gefangene/-r	**captive** → to capture
imminent ['ɪmɪnənt]	bald; unmittelbar bevorstehend	**imminent** ↔ far off
to bear sth ['beə]	etw tragen	**to bear** = to carry
to erase [ɪ'reɪz]	löschen; ausradieren	**to erase** = to delete

Text workshop D - Food poverty in the UK

plea [pliː]	Bitte; Appell	**plea** → to plead
humanity [hjuː'mænəti]	Menschlichkeit	= the quality of being humane, treating people, animals and things kindly and respectfully
to cancel ['kænsl]	abschaffen	**to cancel** → cancellation
overwhelmed [ˌəʊvə'welmd]	überwältigt	= feeling sth so strongly that you can't think clearly
generosity [ˌdʒen'rɒsəti]	Großzügigkeit	**generosity** → generous
to succeed [sək'siːd]	Erfolg haben	**to succeed** → success
regardless of sth [rɪ'gɑːdləs‿əv]	ungeachtet; unabhängig von etw	We are going to launch this product, **regardless of** what market research says.
alien ['eɪliən]	fremd	**alien** = foreign
closure ['kləʊʒə]	Schließung	**closure** ↔ opening
substitute teacher ['sʌbstɪtʃuːt ˌtiːtʃə]	Vertretungslehrer/-in	The school found a very good **substitute teacher** for the mathematics teacher who had an accident.
figure ['fɪgə]	Ziffer; Zahl	**figure** = number
debit card ['debɪt ˌkɑːd]	Bankkarte	If you use a credit card, you can arrange to pay later; with a **debit card**, the money is taken out of the account immediately.

to **max out** *(infml)* [ˌmæksˈaʊt]	etw ausschöpfen; etw (bis zum Limit) ausreizen	= to use up the full potential
care [keə]	Pflege; Betreuung	**care** → carer
to **fail** sb [feɪl]	jdn hängenlassen; jdn im Stich lassen	**to fail** = to let down
to **cope with** ['kəʊp wɪð]	zurechtkommen mit; schaffen	= to be able to deal with sth difficult
to **be aware of** sth [biˌə'weərˌəv]	sich etw bewusst sein	I'm **aware** of the dangers of driving.
short-term [ˌʃɔ:t'tɜ:m]	kurzfristig	**short-term** ↔ long-term
to **extend** sth to sb [ɪk'stend]	*hier:* jdm etw erweisen; zuteilwerden lassen	**to extend** → extension
persuasive [pə'sweɪsɪv]	überzeugend	**persuasive** = convincing
recollection [rekə'lekʃn]	Erinnerung	**recollection** = memory
to whittle sth down [ˌwɪtl sʌmθɪŋ 'daʊn]	etw reduzieren	**to whittle down** = to reduce
predetermined [ˌpri:dɪ'tɜ:mɪnd]	vorherbestimmt; festgelegt	He believes that his live is **predetermined** by God.
ordinary ['ɔ:dnri]	gewöhnlich; normal	= not unusual or different in any way
to **puncture** ['pʌŋktʃə]	ein Loch machen; durchstechen	The front wheel of the bicycle was **punctured** by a piece of glass.
to **penetrate** ['penɪtreɪt]	eindringen; durchdringen	**to penetrate** = to access
hurdle ['hɜ:dl]	Hürde	**hurdle** = obstacle
barrier ['bæriə]	Barriere; Hindernis	**barrier** → to barricade
meritocratic [ˌmerɪtə'krætɪk]	leistungsorientiert	A **meritocratic** education system implies equal opportunities for all social classes.

Topic project - Staging a talk show

to **stage** [steɪdʒ]	inszenieren; aufführen	How difficult would it be to **stage** something like the moon landing?
life span ['laɪfspæn]	Lebensdauer; Lebenserwartung	Better batteries would increase the **lifespan** of mobile phones.

D27 Vokabellernliste

Topic 6 Diverse identities

Getting started

relationship [rɪ'leɪʃnʃɪp]	Beziehung	Is the **relationship** between you and your neighbours a good one?
to **display** [dɪ'spleɪ]	darstellen; zeigen; sichtbar machen	**to display** → display
aspiration [ˌæspɪ'reɪʃn]	Streben; Sehnsucht	**aspiration** → to aspire
outlook ['aʊtlʊk]	Perspektive; Prognose	= a forecast of the future
to come to mind [ˌkʌm tə 'maɪnd]	in den Sinn kommen; einfallen	The idea of a common lingua franca **comes to mind** when one considers the many languages spoken in Europe.
racial ['reɪʃl]	Rassen-	**racial** → race
to be uncommon [biˌʌn'kɒmən]	ungewöhnlich sein	**uncommon** ↔ common

ethnic ['eθnɪk]	ethnisch; Volks-	What's your **ethnic** background? – I'm half German and half Spanish.
ethnicity [eθ'nɪsəti]	Ethnie; ethnische Zugehörigkeit	Unfortunately, many companies still discriminate based on **ethnicity**.
to reflect [rɪ'flekt]	widerspiegeln	= to give an image of sth/sb
Supreme Court [suːˌpriːm 'kɔːt]	Oberster Gerichtshof *(der USA)*	= highest federal court of law in the US
interracial [ˌɪntə'reɪʃl]	gemischtrassig	= consisting of more than one race
mutual respect [ˌmjuːtuəl rɪ'spekt]	gegenseitiger Respekt	The city wanted to fight discrimination and therefore promoted fairness, cooperation and **mutual respect**.
hate crime ['heɪt ˌkraɪm]	Verbrechen aus Hass; Hasskriminalität	= hostility towards members of certain groups
to embrace [ɪm'breɪs]	*hier:* etw akzeptieren; etw annehmen	*here:* = to accept willingly
to be uncertain [bi ʌn'sɜːtn]	unsicher sein; ungewiss sein	**uncertain** ↔ certain
skin colour ['skɪn ˌkʌlə]	Hautfarbe	Is "yellow" really a **skin colour**?
prejudice ['predʒədɪs]	Vorurteil	**prejudice** → to be prejudiced against
to pass on [ˌpɑːs 'ɒn]	weitergeben	I've got a message for your brother. Could you **pass** it **on**, please?
to recommend [ˌrekə'mend]	empfehlen	I'd **recommend** that film. It's a must-see.
layer (of) ['leɪər əv]	Schicht (aus); Lage (aus)	This cake has three **layers** of chocolate.
employer [ɪm'plɔɪə]	Arbeitgeber/-in	**employer** → employee → employment
to unify ['juːnɪfaɪ]	verbinden; einigen	**to unify** → unification
to make progress [ˌmeɪk 'prəʊgres]	vorankommen	We **made** good **progress** with our renovations.
gender ['dʒendə]	Geschlecht (sozial)	The **gender** of a girl is female. The **gender** of a boy is male.
chairperson ['tʃeəˌpɜːsn]	Vorsitzende/-r; Vorsitz	The committee has 10 members but only one **chairperson**.
outreach group ['aʊtriːtʃ ˌgruːp]	Kontaktgruppe	= bringing information and services to people who would not be able to obtain them in another way
encompassing [ɪn'kʌmpəsɪŋ]	umschließend	**to encompass** = to include
inclusive [ɪn'kluːsɪv]	inklusiv; einschließlich; umfassend	My brother learns more slowly than me. He went to a special school, but now he is in an **inclusive** class at my school.
to represent [ˌreprɪ'zent]	repräsentieren; vertreten	**to represent** → representative
straight [streɪt]	gerade; *hier:* heterosexuell	**straight** = heterosexual
to exclude [ɪks'kluːd]	ausschließen	**to exclude** ↔ to include
origin ['ɒrɪdʒɪn]	Ursprung; Herkunft; Abstammung	= country or race sb/sth comes from
to put sth in perspective [ˌpʊt sʌmθɪŋ ɪn pə'spektɪv]	etw relativieren; etw ins rechte Licht rücken	Having a closer look at last year's figures **puts** the loss of the company **in perspective**.
to prevent [prɪ'vent]	vorbeugen; verhindern	**to prevent** → prevention
to cure [kjʊə]	heilen	**to cure** = to heal
research *(no pl)* [rɪ'sɜːtʃ]	Forschung; Untersuchung	= serious study of a subject to discover new facts
striped [straɪpt]	gestreift	Crosswalks in Germany are **striped** in black and white.
expectation [ˌekspek'teɪʃn]	Erwartung	**expectation** → to expect
to accomplish [ə'kʌmplɪʃ]	erreichen; vollenden	= to successfully complete or achieve sth
initially [ɪ'nɪʃli]	anfangs; zunächst	**initially** = at first

approximately [ə'prɒksɪmətli]	ungefähr; circa	**approximately** ↔ precisely
contaminated [kən'tæmɪneɪtɪd]	verunreinigt; verseucht	**contaminated** → contamination
trait [treɪt]	Eigenschaft; Merkmal	**trait** = feature
supremacy [su:'preməsi]	Vorherrschaft; Überlegenheit	**supremacy** = dominance
below [bɪ'ləʊ]	unten; unterhalb	**below** ↔ above
disability [ˌdɪsə'bɪləti]	Behinderung	**disability** → disabled

Text workshop A - Challenging identities

dissatisfied [dɪs'sætɪsfaɪd]	unzufrieden	= not happy with a situation
mindset ['maɪndset]	Denkweise; Einstellung	**mindset** = attitude
to **vanish** ['vænɪʃ]	verschwinden	He saw all his hopes **vanishing** before his eyes.
to **be set (in)** [bi 'set]	spielen; seinen Schauplatz haben (in)	**to be set** = to take place
identical twins [aɪˌdentɪkl 'twɪnz]	eineiige Zwillinge	My birthday and my brother's birthday are on the same day. We're **twins**.
to **raise** [reɪz]	aufziehen; erziehen	**to raise** = to bring up
delivery [dɪ'lɪvri]	Lieferung; Auslieferung; Zustellung	**delivery** → to deliver
to **figure sth** ['fɪgə]	sich etw vorstellen	I **figured** you'd be here at this time.
flushed [flʌʃt]	errötet	= to be red in the face due to heat or emotion
to **mistake** [mɪ'steɪk]	verwechseln	He **mistook** the salt for sugar and put it in his coffee.
neither ['naɪðə; 'ni:ðə]	keine/-r/-s (von beiden)	Both my parents have bicycles, but **neither** of them cycle to work.
to **pretend** [prɪ'tend]	vorgeben; vortäuschen	= to make others believe you are sb who in reality you are not
boldness ['bəʊldnəs]	Dreistigkeit; Mut	**boldness** = fearlessness; daring
horrified ['hɒrɪfaɪd]	entsetzt	When they returned to their village after the earthquake they were **horrified** by what they saw.
barely ['beəli]	kaum	**barely** = hardly
to **split** [splɪt]	teilen; spalten	= to divide in two
Civil Rights Movement [ˌsɪvl 'raɪts ˌmu:vmənt]	Bürgerrechtsbewegung	Martin Luther King was a leader of the **Civil Rights Movement**.
to **object to sth** [əb'dʒekt]	etw. widersprechen	**to object to sth** ↔ to accept sth; to tolerate sth; to approve of sb/sth
to **be due** [bi 'dʒu:]	fällig sein	The payment **is due** Monday.
mark [mɑ:k]	Note	**mark** *(BE)* = grade *(AE)*
to **type** [taɪp]	tippen; Schreibmaschine schreiben	Where did you learn to **type** so fast?
humiliation [hju:ˌmɪli'eɪʃn]	Demütigung; Erniedrigung	**humiliation** → to humiliate
sample ['sɑ:mpl]	Probe; Muster	= an example of what a product is like
to **tremble** ['trembl]	zittern; beben	People sometimes **tremble** if they feel very frightened or nervous.
to **manage (to do sth)** ['mænɪdʒ]	schaffen (etw zu tun)	= to succeed in doing sth difficult
to **announce** [ə'naʊns]	bekanntgeben; verkünden	= to give formal information or details about sth
relieved [rɪ'li:vd]	erleichtert	**relieved** → relief

no longer [ˌnəʊ 'lɒŋgə]	nicht länger; nicht mehr	**no longer** = not any more
to **linger** ['lɪŋgə]	bleiben; verweilen; lungern	= to stay in one place for some time
truly ['tru:li]	wirklich; wahrhaftig	**truly** → true
to **adopt** [ə'dɒpt]	annehmen; übernehmen	= to formally accept a suggestion or policy
disguise [dɪs'gaɪz]	Verkleidung	She wore a wig and sunglasses as **disguise**.
altogether [ˌɔ:ltə'geðə]	insgesamt; ganz und gar	There are **altogether** 15 students in my group.
to **impact** [ɪm'pækt]	sich auswirken auf	= to have an influence on sth
due to ['dju: tə]	wegen; aufgrund	**due to** = because of
attention [ə'tenʃn]	Aufmerksamkeit; Beachtung	**attention** → attentive
versus ['vɜ:səs]	im Vergleich zu; gegen	**versus** = compared to
to **take sb to be sth** [teɪk ˌsʌmbədi tə 'bi ˌsʌmθɪŋ]	jdn für etw halten	At first glance they **took the young fox to be** a dog.
kin [kɪn]	Verwandtschaft; Familie	**kin** = family; relatives
to **register** ['redʒɪstə]	registrieren	If you want to receive information from us, please **register** here.
fair complected [ˌfeə kəm'plektɪd]	hellhäutig	= to have fair skin and hair
to **be prejudiced against sb** [bi 'predʒədɪst‿əgenst‿sʌmbədi]	voreingenommen sein gegenüber jdm	**prejudiced** ↔ open-minded
elementary school *(AE)* [elɪ'mentri ˌsku:l]	Grundschule	= primary school for children aged of 5–11
to **tan** [tæn]	bräunen (die Haut)	When I go out in the sun I do not **tan**, I simply turn red.
racist ['reɪsɪst]	rassistisch	**racist** → race → racial
to **throw sb off** [ˌθrəʊ sʌmbədi‿'ɒf]	durcheinanderbringen	**to throw sb off** = to distract sb
freckle ['frekl]	Sommersprosse	He looks like a typical red-haired boy with **freckles** on his face.
to **betray** [bɪ'treɪ]	verraten; betrügen	**to betray** → betrayal
to **double-check** [ˌdʌbl'tʃek]	genau nachprüfen	Is the information OK? Let's **double-check** it.

Text workshop B - Diversity in gender

pronoun ['prəʊnaʊn]	Pronomen; Fürwort	'He', 'him' and 'which' are all **pronouns**.
curriculum [kə'rɪkjələm]	Lehrplan	Schools have to follow the national **curriculum** in England.
species *(sg or pl)* ['spi:ʃi:z]	Art; Spezies	There are over 200 **species** of birds in this country.
to **stave off** [ˌsteɪv‿'ɒf]	abwehren; hinausschieben	**to stave off** = to delay
painful ['peɪnfl]	schmerzhaft	**painful** → pain → painless
to **identify** [aɪ'dentɪfaɪ]	identifizieren; erkennen	**to identify** → identification
to **estimate** ['estɪmeɪt]	schätzen	Can you **estimate** how long it will take?
to **enrol** [ɪn'rəʊl]	einschreiben; anmelden	= to sign up for sth
to **fund** [fʌnd]	finanzieren; fördern	After World War II, Britain was no longer able to **fund** its involvement in the colonies.
to **assign** [ə'saɪn]	zuweisen; zuordnen	**to assign** → assignment
immediate [ɪ'mi:diət]	direkt; unmittelbar; spontan	Her **immediate** reaction was happiness.
to **switch** [swɪtʃ]	wechseln; tauschen	We **switched** providers in order to save money.
to **transfer** [træns'fɜ:]	übertragen	**to transfer** → transferable

progressive [prə'gresɪv]	fortschrittlich	**progressive** = modern
social justice [ˌsəʊʃl 'dʒʌstɪs]	soziale Gerechtigkeit	Gender equality, inclusion and non-discrimination are all part of **social justice.**
sibling ['sɪblɪŋ]	Bruder/Schwester; Geschwisterkind	My brother and my sister are my **siblings.**
to **pick** [pɪk]	auswählen; aussuchen	**to pick** = to select
upsetting [ʌp'setɪŋ]	verstörend	**upsetting** ↔ comforting
evident ['evɪdnt]	offensichtlich; erwiesen	From the smell it was **evident** that the food in the oven was burning.
to **recall** [rɪ'kɔ:l]	sich erinnern	**to recall** = to remember
counseling *(AE)* ['kaʊnslɪŋ]	Therapie	**counseling** = therapy
to **make a change** [ˌmeɪk‿ə 'tʃeɪndʒ]	eine Änderung herbeiführen	Taking the train instead of flying will **make a change** in our carbon footprint.
to **file a lawsuit** [ˌfaɪl‿ə 'lɔ:su:t]	eine Klage einreichen	= to bring a case to court
to **violate** ['vaɪəleɪt]	verstoßen gegen	= to break or act against something
to **repeal** [rɪ'pi:l]	widerrufen	= to officially cancel a law
to **be perceived as** [bi pə'si:vd‿əz]	als etw wahrgenommen werden	The refugees **were perceived as** competitors in the labour market.
apprehensive [ˌæprɪ'hensɪv]	besorgt; ängstlich	**apprehensive** ↔ confident
surgery ['sɜ:dʒri]	Operation	He was happy when he could leave the hospital after **surgery.**
compulsion [kəm'pʌlʃn]	Zwang	**compulsion** → compulsory
ignorance ['ɪgnrns]	Ahnungslosigkeit; Unwissenheit	**ignorance** → to ignore
to **integrate** ['ɪntɪgreɪt]	integrieren; sich integrieren	**to integrate** ↔ to exclude
obstacle ['ɒbstəkl]	Hürde; Hindernis	= sth that keeps you from achieving sth

Grammar workshop - Talking about conditions

to **be unlikely** [bi‿ʌn'laɪkli]	unwahrscheinlich sein	The weatherforecast says that rain **is unlikely** today, but who knows?
to **enhance** [ɪn'hɑ:ns]	verbessern	**to enhance** = to make better; to improve

Text workshop C - Two worlds?

priority [praɪ'ɒrəti]	Priorität; Vorrang	= sth that you think is more important than other things and should be dealt with first
potential [pə'tenʃl]	potenziell; möglich	**potential** = possible, likely
hardly ['hɑ:dli]	kaum	I can **hardly** believe it.
to **forge** [fɔ:dʒ]	fälschen	= to make an illegal copy of an official document or money
eventually [ɪ'ventʃuəli]	letztendlich	**eventually** = finally
to **flip through** [ˌflɪp 'θru:]	durchblättern	= to quickly look through a book or a bundle of paper
arranged marriage [əˌreɪndʒd 'mærɪdʒ]	arrangierte Ehe	Theirs was an **arranged marriage**, but they seemed happy nevertheless.
to **go along with sth** [ˌgəʊ‿ə'lɒŋ wɪð ˌsʌmθɪŋ]	etw mitmachen	= to do or accept what other people want
totally ['təʊtli]	völlig; total	My parents are **totally** against the idea.
can't stand sb/sth [ˌkɑ:nt 'stænd ˌsʌmbədi/ˌsʌmθɪŋ]	jdn/etw nicht ausstehen können	**can't stand** ↔ to love

to **get over** sth [ˌget‿ˈəʊvə]	über etw hinwegkommen; mit etw fertigwerden	I was homesick, but I **got over it**.
to **sacrifice** [ˈsækrɪfaɪs]	opfern	= to give sth up in order to have sth more important
lawyer [ˈlɔɪə]	Anwalt/Anwältin; Jurist/-in	**lawyer** → law
to **embarrass** [ɪmˈbærəs]	in Verlegenheit bringen	= to make sb feel uncomfortable
to **make sense** [ˌmeɪk ˈsens]	Sinn ergeben; einleuchten	If sth **makes sense**, you can understand it.
to **figure out** [ˌfɪgər‿ˈaʊt]	herausfinden; ergründen	The technicians are still trying to **figure out** a solution to the problem.
selfish [ˈselfɪʃ]	selbstsüchtig; egoistisch	**selfish** ↔ considerate
astounding [əˈstaʊndɪŋ]	erstaunlich	= so surprising that it is difficult to believe
to **take into consideration** [ˌteɪk‿ɪntə kənˌsɪdrˈeɪʃn]	in Betracht ziehen; berücksichtigen	**to take into consideration** = to consider
significance [sɪgˈnɪfɪkns]	Bedeutung	**significance** = meaning; value
to **maintain** [meɪnˈteɪn]	aufrechterhalten	**to maintain** → maintenance

Text workshop D - Invisible identity?

to **provoke** [prəˈvəʊk]	hervorrufen; provozieren	*hier:* = to bring sth into being
to **discriminate against** [dɪˈskrɪmɪneɪt‿əˌgenst]	diskriminieren; benachteiligen	**to discriminate** ↔ to include
invalid [ɪnˈvælɪd]	ungültig; unzulässig	You cannot travel abroad with an **invalid** passport.
to **burden** sb with sth [ˈbɜːdn ˌsʌmbədi wɪð ˌsʌmθɪŋ]	jdn mit etw belasten; jdn mit etw beladen	**to burden** ↔ to relief
supportive [səˈpɔːtɪv]	unterstützend	**supportive** → to support
to **issue** [ˈɪʃuː; ˈɪsjuː]	verhängen; ausstellen; ausgeben	The judge **issued** an order to search the building.
to **be housebound** [bi ˈhaʊsbaʊnd]	ans Haus gebunden sein	During our quarantine we **were housebound** and not allowed to go out.
to **confide in** sb [kənˈfaɪd‿ɪn]	sich jdm anvertrauen	**to confide** → confidential
to **drop out of** [ˌdrɒp‿ˈaʊt‿əv]	etw abbrechen	Ben **dropped out** of university without getting a degree.
ongoing [ˌɒnˈgəʊɪŋ]	laufend; in Gang befindlich	It is an **ongoing** problem that we can't ignore.
valuable [ˈvæljuəbl]	wertvoll	**valuable** → value → valued
voluntary [ˈvɒləntri]	freiwillig	**voluntary** → volunteer
admission [ədˈmɪʃn]	Aufnahme; Zulassung	**admission** → to admit
to **penalise** [ˈpiːnlaɪz]	bestrafen	**to penalise** = to punish
lapse [læps]	Aussetzer; Fehler	*here:* = an interruption or interval
phased [feɪzd]	stufenweise	= to be realised in planned phases
appointment [əˈpɔɪntmənt]	Termin; Verabredung	= arrangement to meet sb at a particular time and place
empathetic [emˈpæθetɪk]	einfühlsam; empathisch	**empathetic** → emphathy
to **assure** [əˈʃɔː]	versichern; beteuern	I **assure** you that such a mistake will not happen again!
it is thanks to them [ɪt‿ɪz ˌθæŋks tə ˈθem]	ihnen ist es zu verdanken	It **was thanks to** a complaint that the company learned about the faulty delivery.
to **speak up** [ˌspiːk‿ˈʌp]	den Mund aufmachen	= to say what you think clearly and freely
to **dismiss** sth [dɪˈsmɪs]	etw abtun; etw zurückweisen	= to decide that sb/sth is not important
response [rɪˈspɒns]	Antwort; Erwiderung; Rückmeldung	**response** → to respond

reassurance [ˌri:əˈʃɔ:rns]	Beruhigung; Bestätigung	**reassurance** = comfort; sympathy
solely [ˈsəʊlli]	allein; ausschließlich	**solely** = only, exclusively

Topic project - Talking about stereotypes

retirement [rɪˈtaɪəmənt]	Ruhestand	**retirement** → to retire → retiree
pigeon-hole [ˈpɪdʒənhəʊl]	Ablagefach; *hier:* Schublade	Please leave your paper in my **pigeon-hole**. I'll get it in the morning.
outcast [ˈaʊtkɑ:st]	ausgegrenzt; ausgestoßen	As the only person of colour at the party she feels **outcast**.
open-minded [ˌəʊpnˈmaɪndɪd]	aufgeschlossen	= willing to consider other possibilities or ideas

D28 Vokabellernliste

Topic 7 Issues of globalisation

Getting started

globalisation [ˌgləʊblaɪˈzeɪʃn]	Globalisierung	**globalisation** → global
economy [ɪˈkɒnəmi]	Wirtschaft; Industrie	The **economy** of this region is based on services and not industry.
competitive [kəmˈpetɪtɪv]	leistungsorientiert	**competitive** → competition
interaction [ˌɪntəˈrækʃn]	Wechselwirkung; Verflechtung	= action or exchange between two or more people
enhanced [ɪnˈhɑ:nst]	verstärkt; gesteigert	**enhanced** ↔ worsened
to gain momentum [ˌgeɪn məˈmentəm]	an Fahrt gewinnen; Eigendynamik entwickeln	= to become faster or stronger
stock exchange [ˈstɒk‿ɪksˌtʃeɪndʒ]	Börse	= a market in which securities (stocks etc.) are bought and sold
prosperity [prɒsˈperəti]	Wohlstand	**prosperity** → prosperous
for instance [fər‿ˈɪnstəns]	zum Beispiel	If you are looking for details, consider, **for instance**, the technical documentation.
global player [ˌgləʊbl ˈpleɪə]	Weltkonzern	= a large company that operates around the world
corporation [ˌkɔ:prˈeɪʃn]	Konzern; Unternehmen	**corporation** → corporate
to destroy [dɪˈstrɔɪ]	zerstören	**to destroy** → destruction
to bribe sb [ˈbraɪb ˌsʌmbədi]	jdn bestechen	= to give sb money so that they do you a favour
to stimulate [ˈstɪmjəleɪt]	stimulieren; anregen	Increasing prices for fossil fuels **stimulate** the expansion of renewable energies.
world order [ˌwɜ:ld‿ˈɔ:də]	Weltordnung	Globalisation has led to a new **world order**.
to benefit from sth/sb [ˈbenɪfɪt]	von etw/jdm profitieren	**to benefit** ↔ to harm
growth [grəʊθ]	Wachstum	**growth** → to grow
rather [ˈrɑ:ðə]	eher; ziemlich	**rather** = fairly, quite
life expectancy [ˌlaɪf‿ɪkˈspektənsi]	Lebenserwartung	**Life expectancy** for women is higher than it is for men.
child mortality rate [ˌtʃaɪld mɔ:ˈtæləti ˌreɪt]	Kindersterblichkeitsrate	**Infant mortality rate** is the number of infants dying under five years of age.
awareness [əˈweənəs]	Bewusstsein	**awareness** → to be aware of sth
currently [ˈkʌrəntli]	derzeit; zurzeit; momentan	We **currently** have three placements for EU students.

disarmament [dɪ'sɑːməmənt]	**Abrüstung**	= reducing the number of weapons that a country or organisation has
to **acknowledge** [ək'nɒlɪdʒ]	**anerkennen; einräumen**	**to acknowledge** = to recognise
decline [dɪ'klaɪn]	**Rückgang; Verfall**	**decline** ↔ rise
to **insist (on sth)** [ɪn'sɪst‿ɒn]	**(auf etw) bestehen**	The teacher **insisted** that I had failed the oral exam.
inequality [ˌɪnɪ'kwɒləti]	**Ungleichheit; Unterschied**	Unfortunately, there is still too much **inequality** in the world.
disparity [dɪ'spærəti]	**Missverhältnis; Ungleichgewicht**	**disparity** ↔ conformity
trade agreement ['treɪd‿əˌgriːmənt]	**Handelsabkommen**	= an agreement on the trading of goods and services between two countries
to **reject** [rɪ'dʒekt]	**ablehnen; zurückweisen**	**to reject** ↔ to accept
trade association [ˌtreɪd‿əˌsəʊʃi'eɪʃn]	**Handelsverband; Wirtschaftsverband**	= a group that promotes the interests of businesses in a particular industry
tariffs and duties *(pl)* [ˌtærɪfs‿ənd 'djuːtiz]	**Zölle und Abgaben**	The US have imposed **tariffs and duties** on many Chinese products.
to **dismantle** [dɪ'smæntl]	**abbauen; auflösen**	From next year on they will **dismantle** import taxes on luxury goods.
subsidies *(pl)* ['sʌbsɪdiz]	**Subventionen**	**subsidies** → to subsidise
to **strengthen** ['streŋθn]	**stärken**	Her position in the government has **strengthened** over the last few months.
global warming [ˌgləʊbl 'wɔːmɪŋ]	**Erderwärmung**	**Global warming** is already having a negative influence on our environment.
supply chain [sə'plaɪ ˌtʃeɪn]	**Lieferkette**	The ultracold storage of the vaccine makes the **supply chain** so complicated.
to **underestimate sth** [ˌʌndr'estɪmeɪt]	**etw unterschätzen**	**to underestimate** ↔ to overestimate
fragility [frə'dʒɪləti]	**Zerbrechlichkeit**	**fragility** → fragile

Text workshop A - Global work

transmission [trænz'mɪʃn]	**Übermittlung**	**transmission** → to transmit
computer geek [kəmˌpjuːtə 'giːk]	**Computerfreak**	= a person who spends a lot of time with computers and is very good with them
to **be consumed by sth** [bi kən'sjuːmd baɪ ˌsʌmθɪŋ]	**erfüllt sein von etw**	= to be filled with a strong feeling
hesitation [ˌhezɪ'teɪʃn]	**Zögern**	**hesitation** → to hesitate
stationary ['steɪʃnri]	**unbeweglich**	**stationary** = motionless
confusion [kən'fjuːʒn]	**Verwirrung**	**confusion** → confused
obscured [əb'skjʊəd]	**verdeckt**	**obscured** ↔ visible
lens [lenz]	**Brillenglas; Linse**	= a curved piece of glass or plastic that makes things look larger, smaller or clearer
to **startle** ['stɑːtl]	**erschrecken; aufscheuchen**	= to surprise and frighten sb
to **clutch** [klʌtʃ]	**festhalten; umklammern**	= to hold sth tightly
folder ['fəʊldə]	**Ordner; Mappe**	Keep all the handouts from this course in a special **folder**!
to **direct sb to sth** [dɪ'rekt]	**jdm den Weg zu etw zeigen**	**to direct sb to sth** = to give sb directions
to **knock** [nɒk]	**klopfen**	= to hit sth, especially a door, so that sb will let you in
peculiar [pɪ'kjuːliə]	**besonders; eigenartig**	**peculiar** = strange; unusual
clerk [klɑːk; klɜːk]	**Angestellte/-r**	= sb who works in an office or at an information desk

inadequacy [ɪ'nædɪkwəsi]	Unzulänglichkeit	**inadequacy** = inability; incompetence
decay [dɪ'keɪ]	Verfall	= a gradual destruction by natural causes
chest [tʃest]	Brust; Brustkorb	= central part of the body with the heart and the lungs
it's no use [ɪts ˌnəʊ 'ju:s]	es nützt nichts	**It's no use** arguing with him. He never admits he's wrong.
to fake [feɪk]	vortäuschen; fälschen	= to make sth appear better or different than it is
consultant [kən'sʌltnt]	Berater/-in	= a person who gives expert advice on a specific subject
programmer ['prəʊgræmə]	Programmierer/-in	**programmer** → programme → to program
gratitude ['grætɪtju:d]	Dankbarkeit	**gratitude** = thankfulness
outsourcing ['aʊtsɔ:sɪŋ]	Ausgliederung; Fremdbeschaffung	**outsourcing** ↔ insourcing
progress *(no pl)* ['prəʊgres]	Fortschritt	The government published a new report about the **progress** in the use of renewable energy.
to be left out [bi ˌleft ˌ'aʊt]	ausgeschlossen sein	**to be left out** ↔ to be included
low-wage country [ˌləʊweɪdʒ 'kʌntri]	Niedriglohnland	In a globalised world, labour-intensive products are manufactured in **low-wage countries**.
to transfer [træns'fɜ:]	übertragen	**to transfer** → transferable
situated ['sɪtʃueɪtɪd]	gelegen	**situated** = located
bill *(BE)* [bɪl]	Rechnung	We'd like to pay. Can you bring us the **bill**, please?
internally [ɪn'tɜ:nli]	intern	**internally** ↔ externally
to trace back [ˌtreɪs 'bæk]	zurückverfolgen	I can **trace** my family **back** to the 16th century.
to manufacture [ˌmænjə'fæktʃə]	fertigen; herstellen; produzieren	= to produce goods by machinery or by hand
labour ['leɪbə]	Arbeit; Arbeitskraft	**labour** → laborious → labourer
emerging country [ɪˌmɜ:dʒɪŋ 'kʌntri]	Schwellenland	Bangladesh is one of the leading **emerging countries** in the world today.
numerous ['nju:mrəs]	zahlreich; viel	**numerous** = many
exploitation [ˌeksplɔɪ'teɪʃn]	Ausbeutung	**exploitation** → to exploit
cause [kɔ:z]	Sache; Angelegenheit	One **cause** I feel strongly about is the environment.
to handle ['hændl]	umgehen mit; handhaben	**to handle** = to deal with
wastewater ['weɪstˌwɔ:tə]	Abwasser; Schmutzwasser	**wastewater** = sewage
to discharge [dɪs'tʃɑ:dʒ]	ableiten; freisetzen	**to discharge** = to dispose of
toxic ['tɒksɪk]	giftig	**toxic** = poisonous
protection [prə'tekʃn]	Schutz	**protection** → to protect → protective

Skills workshop - Writing a blog post

consulting (company) [kən'sʌltɪŋ ˌkʌmpəni]	Unternehmensberatung	**consulting** = advising
to await [ə'weɪt]	erwarten	After two years of absence they were **awaiting** his return.
overwhelmed [ˌəʊvə'welmd]	überwältigt	= feeling sth so strongly that you can't think clearly
multitude ['mʌltɪtʃu:d]	Vielzahl; Menge	The **multitude** of different nationalities and cultures makes the USA very attractive.
to pound [paʊnd]	klopfen	**to pound** = to beat
wavering ['weɪvrɪŋ]	schwankend; unschlüssig	In this election, the opposition won a great number of **wavering** voters.

to come in handy [ˌkʌm ˌɪn ˈhændi]	gelegen kommen	Oh great, your visit **comes in handy**! You can help me to move this box.
evident [ˈevɪdnt]	offensichtlich; erwiesen	**evident** = apparent

Text workshop B - Working across cultures

collaboration [kəˌlæbˈreɪʃn]	Zusammenarbeit	**collaboration** → to collaborate → labour
currently [ˈkʌrəntli]	derzeit; zurzeit; momentan	We **currently** have three placements for EU students.
readily [ˈredli]	unmittelbar; leicht	**readily** = easily
to accompany [əˈkʌmpəni]	begleiten	If you **accompany** a person, you go somewhere with them.
obstacle [ˈɒbstəkl]	Hürde; Hindernis	= sth that keeps you from achieving sth
to impact [ɪmˈpækt]	sich auswirken auf	= to have an influence on sth
flow [fləʊ]	Strom; Fluss	= the steady and continuous movement of sth
efficiency [ɪˈfɪʃnsi]	Leistungsfähigkeit; Effizienz	**efficiency** → efficient
to tag [tæg]	markieren	Is it ok to **tag** other people on social media?
related [rɪˈleɪtɪd]	ähnlich; zusammengehörig	**related** → relation → relative
to equate to [ɪˈkweɪt tə]	gleichsetzen mit	**to equate** ↔ to contrast
sensitive [ˈsensɪtɪv]	verständnisvoll; sensibel	A **sensitive** person notices other people's feelings.
disruption [dɪsˈrʌpʃn]	Unterbrechung; Störung	**disruption** ↔ continuity
to clarify [ˈklærɪfaɪ]	verdeutlichen; darlegen	= to make sth clear
counterpart [ˈkaʊntəpɑːt]	Gegenüber; Gegenpart	The creative director called her **counterpart** in the other company.
straightforward [ˌstreɪtˈfɔːwəd]	einfach; unkompliziert	He asked me a **straightforward** question.
expression [ɪkˈspreʃn]	Ausdruck	**expression** → to express
to overcome [ˌəʊvəˈkʌm]	überwinden	He **overcame** all difficulties.
beneficial [ˌbenɪˈfɪʃl]	nützlich	**beneficial** → benefit
otherwise [ˈʌðəwaɪz]	sonst	Hurry up, **otherwise** we'll be late.
to allot [əˈlɒt]	zuweisen; vergeben	How come there is no extra time **alloted** for exam preparation?
to negotiate sth [nɪˈgəʊʃieɪt]	etw aushandeln; etw verhandeln	= to talk about sth in order to reach an agreement
to attribute sth to sb/sth [əˈtrɪbjuːt]	etw auf etw zurückführen; zuschreiben	The poor harvest was **attributed to** the bad weather.
manners *(pl)* [ˈmænəz]	Manieren; Benehmen	= polite behaviour

Text workshop C - Global trade

to interact [ˌɪntəˈækt]	interagieren; zusammenspielen	= to talk together, do things together, react to each other
shipping [ˈʃɪpɪŋ]	Versand; Transport *(von Gütern)*	**Shipping** costs to Germany range from $5 to $13, depending on the number of purchases.
virtually [ˈvɜːtʃuəli]	nahezu; praktisch	**virtually** = nearly
to load [ləʊd]	(be)laden	**Load** the dishwasher please.
ultimately [ˈʌltɪmətli]	letztendlich	**ultimately** = finally
gadget [ˈgædʒɪt]	Gerät; technische Spielerei	Smartphones and play stations are **gadgets**.
appliance [əˈplaɪəns]	Gerät	Modern kitchens are full of **appliances** to make cooking easier.

commodity [kə'mɒdəti]	Artikel	= an object that can be sold or traded
grain [greɪn]	Getreide	Bread is usually made from **grain**.
to pour [pɔ:]	schütten; gießen	= to make a substance flow from a container into another container
fabric ['fæbrɪk]	Stoff; Gewebe	The clothing company sells many beautiful **fabrics**.
storage container ['stɔ:rɪdʒ kən,teɪnə]	Lagerbehälter; Vorratsbehälter	Our ceramic **storage containers** for coffee, tea and cocoa all have the same size and fit perfectly into the cupboard.
advanced [əd'vɑ:nst]	fortschrittlich; fortgeschritten	This English course is for **advanced** learners, not beginners.
shape [ʃeɪp]	Gestalt; Form	**shape** = figure; form
partially ['pɑ:ʃli]	teilweise	**partially** → part
to soar [sɔ:]	sprunghaft steigen; in die Höhe schnellen	**to soar** = to rise a lot
surge [sɜ:dʒ]	(plötzlicher) Anstieg	= sudden increase
to be capable of doing sth [bi ˌkeɪpəbl‿əv]	in der Lage sein, etw zu tun	Modern smartphones **are capable of** storing large amounts of data.
bank [bæŋk]	Ufer	A river has two **banks**.
either ['aɪðə; 'i:ðə]	beide(s)	There are trees on **either** side of the entrance.
vessel ['vesl]	Schiff	Only oceangoing **vessels** should make this trip.
praise [preɪz]	Lob	= the fact that you tell sb he did a very good job
frequently [ˌfri:kwəntli]	häufig	**frequently** = often
charge [tʃɑ:dʒ]	Gebühr	In the US you need to add a service **charge** to your restaurant bill.
to tax [tæks]	besteuern	**to tax** → taxation
to be at risk [ˌbi‿ət 'rɪsk]	gefährdet sein	**at risk** = endangered
to impose sth on sb [ɪm'pəʊz ˌsʌmθɪŋ‿ən ˌsʌmbədi]	jdm etw auferlegen	**to impose** = to force sth on sb
to plummet ['plʌmɪt]	stark absinken	= to fall or drop suddenly
to avert [ə'vɜ:t]	verhindern; abwenden	**avert** = prevent
severely [sɪ'vɪəli]	stark; schlimm	**severely** = seriously
domestic [də'mestɪk]	Inlands-; inländisch	**domestic** ↔ foreign
to start from scratch [ˌstɑ:t frəm 'skrætʃ]	ganz neu anfangen	The snowman melted in the sun and we had **to start from scratch** building a new one.
to fall by the wayside [ˌfɔ:l baɪ ðə 'weɪsaɪd]	auf der Strecke bleiben	= to have done sth in vain

Text workshop D - Global economy?

supply and demand [səˌplaɪ‿ən dɪ'mɑ:nd]	Angebot und Nachfrage	The price of goods depends on the relation between **supply and demand**.
surplus ['sɜ:pləs]	Überschuss	= more than is needed
foundation [faʊn'deɪʃn]	Grundlage; Fundament	**foundation** = basis
ecological [ˌi:kə'lɒdʒɪkl]	ökologisch	My **ecological** conscience tells me that I should walk to the shop and not take the car.
to meet the needs [ˌmi:t ðə 'ni:dz]	den Bedarf decken	= to fulfil the requirements
notion ['nəʊʃn]	Idee; Vorstellung	**notion** = concept

degradation *(no pl)* [ˌdegrəˈdeɪʃn]	Verschlechterung; Schädigung	**degradation** → to degrade → degrading
habitable [ˌhæbɪtəbl]	bewohnbar	= suitable for living
thread [θred]	Faden; *hier:* Themenstrang	There are several different **threads** in the novel and all of them are resolved in the end.
broad [brɔːd]	breit angelegt; weit	**broad** = wide; large
folks *(infml) (pl)* [fəʊks]	Leute	Hi **folks**, what's going on?
to **take the lead** [ˌteɪk ðə ˈliːd]	die Führung übernehmen	My mum always **takes the lead** when we go hiking.
will [wɪl]	Wille	Where there is a **will** there is a way.
manure [məˈnjʊə]	Mist; Dung	**manure** = dung
to **deplete** [dɪˈpliːt]	verringern; abbauen	**deplete** ↔ build up

Topic project - A survey on English as a company language

branch [brɑːnʃ]	Niederlassung	The bank has closed all of its **branches** in the small towns.
general [ˈdʒenrl]	allgemein; Haupt-	**general** ↔ specific
questionnaire [ˌkwestʃəˈneə]	Fragebogen	= a form with questions used to collect information from different people

D29 Vokabellernliste

Topic 8 The world of work

Getting started

manual [ˈmænjuəl]	körperlich; manuell	**manual** = by hand
gender pay gap [ˌdʒendə ˈpeɪ ˌgæp]	Lohngefälle zwischen Männern und Frauen	= the difference in the pay for men and women who do the same work
barrier [ˈbæriə]	Barriere; Hindernis	**barrier** → to barricade
participant [pɑːˈtɪsɪpnt]	Teilnehmer/-in	**participant** → to participate
virtual [ˈvɜːtʃuəl]	virtuell	= by means of computers and the internet
contradiction [ˌkɒntrəˈdɪkʃn]	Widerspruch; Widersprüchlichkeit	= a situation that is contrary to or very different from the normal situation
to **collaborate** [kəˈlæbreɪt]	zusammenarbeiten	**to collaborate** → collaboration
fundamental [ˌfʌndəˈmentl]	wesentlich; grundlegend	**fundamental** = essential
gross [ˈgrəʊs]	Brutto-	= the total amount of money before tax
deduction [dɪˈdʌkʃn]	Abzug; Kürzung	**deduction** ↔ addition
tax [tæks]	Steuer	= money that is paid to the state from the citizens' incomes, from sales etc., to be used by the state for public services
invisible [ɪnˈvɪzəbl]	unsichtbar	If something becomes **invisible**, you can't see it anymore.
above [əˈbʌv]	oberhalb; oben	**above** ↔ below
hierarchy [ˈhaɪrɑːki]	Rangordnung; Hierarchie	**hierarchy** → hierarchical
occupation [ˌɒkjəˈpeɪʃn]	Beruf; Beschäftigung	**occupation** = profession; trade
care [keə]	Pflege; Betreuung	Nurses and doctors have jobs in health **care**.
retail *(no pl)* [ˈriːteɪl]	Einzelhandel	= selling goods to consumers in small quantities

to widen ['waɪdn]	erweitern; ausdehnehn	**to widen** ↔ to narrow
food bank ['fu:d ˌbæŋk]	Lebensmittelausgabe; "Tafel"	= charity organisation that collects and distributes food
unemployment [ˌʌnɪm'plɔɪmənt]	Arbeitslosigkeit	The government is trying to reduce **unemployment** by creating new jobs.
factor ['fæktə]	Faktor; Umstand	**factor** = component
automation [ˌɔ:tə'meɪʃn]	Automatisierung	There are fears that **automation** will result in a lot of unemployment.
to operate ['ɒpreɪt]	bedienen; steuern	If you **operate** a machine, you make it do its work.
intervention [ˌɪntə'venʃn]	Eingriff; Intervention	**intervention** → to intervene
similar ['sɪmɪlə]	ähnlich	= when one thing is very much like another
subtle ['sʌtl]	fein; hier: klein	There is a **subtle** difference between the two twins.
preference ['prefrns]	Vorliebe	**preference** → to prefer → preferable
vast [vɑ:st]	gewaltig; riesig	**vast** = massive
freelance ['fri:lɑ:ns]	freiberuflich	To work **freelance** means not to be employed regularly by a company but to sell your services independently.
workload ['wɜ:kləʊd]	Arbeitsbelastung	= the amount of work that a person or organisation has to do
to intimidate [ɪn'tɪmɪdeɪt]	einschüchtern	Jim **was intimidated** by all the new technologies.
works council ['wɜ:ks ˌkaʊnsl]	Betriebsrat	= a form of employee representation
teleworking ['telɪˌwɜ:kɪŋ]	Telearbeit	**teleworking** → teleworker
to acquire [ə'kwaɪə]	bekommen; erwerben	**to acquire** = to purchase; to gain

Text workshop A - Why do we work?

critic ['krɪtɪk]	Kritiker/-in	**critic** → to criticise → criticism
demand [dɪ'mɑ:nd]	Bedarf	= a request or need for sth
leisure ['leʒə]	Freizeit	**leisure** = free time
proportionately with sth [prə'pɔ:ʃnətli wɪð ˌsʌmθɪŋ]	proportional zu etw; entsprechend etw	**proportionately** → proportion → portion
income ['ɪnkʌm]	Einkommen	**income** = earnings
forecast ['fɔ:kɑ:st]	Vorhersage	The weather **forecast** for tomorrow is not good.
work ethic ['wɜ:k‿eθɪk]	Arbeitsmoral	= willingness to work hard at one's job
relative ['relətɪv]	relativ; vergleichsweise; verhältnismäßig	= compared to or depending on sth else
to fuel ['fju:əl]	anheizen	= to make sth stronger, to increase sth
to exacerbate [ɪg'zæsəbeɪt]	verschärfen; verschlimmern	His clumsy excuse only **exacerbated** the situation.
pursuit [pə'sju:t]	Streben	= the act of following or trying to find sth
detrimental [ˌdetrɪ'mentl]	nachteilig; schädlich	**detrimental** ↔ beneficial
misunderstanding [ˌmɪsʌndə'stændɪŋ]	Missverständnis	Excuse me, there must be some **misunderstanding**. I ordered a salad and not a pizza.
essentially [ɪ'senʃli]	im Wesentlichen; im Großen und Ganzen	**essentially** → essential → essence
accumulation [əˌkju:mjə'leɪʃn]	Ansammlung; Häufung	**accumulation** → to accumulate → accumulated
in relation to [ɪn rɪ'leɪʃn tə]	im Verhältnis zu	**in relation to** → to relate → relative
basic ['beɪsɪk]	grundlegend; Grund-	**basic** = essential
to possess [pə'zes]	besitzen	**to possess** → possession

quantity ['kwɒntəti]	Menge	Prices may vary according to the available **quantity** of products.
deprived [dɪ'praɪvd]	sozial benachteiligt; verarmt	**deprived** → deprivation
to **pretend** [prɪ'tend]	vorgeben; vortäuschen	= to make others believe you are sb who in reality you are not
conception [kən'sepʃn]	Auffassung	Our **conception** of the world changes as we grow older.
regulation [ˌregjə'leɪʃn]	Regelung; Vorschrift	**regulation** = control
unconditional basic income [ˌʌnkən'dɪʃnl ˌbeɪsɪk‿'ɪnkʌm]	bedingungsloses Grundeinkommen	**unconditional basic income** = citizens' income
to **motivate** ['məʊtɪveɪt]	motivieren	**to motivate** → motivation
distracted [dɪ'stræktɪd]	abgelenkt	They were **distracted** by the conversation at the next table.
to **drag on** [ˌdræg‿'ɒn]	sich dahinschleppen	**to drag on** = to go on and on
carbon footprint [ˌkɑ:bn 'fʊtprɪnt]	Kohlendioxid-Bilanz	You should reduce your **carbon footprint** by buying local products.
disposable [dɪ'spəʊzəbl]	Wegwerf-	**Disposable** packaging produces tons of waste.
spontaneity [ˌspɒntə'neɪəti]	Spontanität	**spontaneity** → spontaneous
unreliable [ˌʌnrɪ'laɪəbl]	unzuverlässig	**unreliable** ↔ reliable

Text workshop B - The future of money

urge [ɜ:dʒ]	Drang	**to urge** → urgent → urgency
to **hoard** [hɔ:d]	(an)sammeln; horten	**to hoard** → hoarder
to **gather** ['gæðə]	sammeln; zusammentragen	**to gather** = to collect
shameful ['ʃeɪmfl]	beschämend	This has been a **shameful** episode.
hardly ['hɑ:dli]	kaum	I can **hardly** believe it.
monthly wage [ˌmʌnθli 'weɪdʒ]	Monatslohn	Instead of being paid by the hour they got a **monthly wage**.
to **retire** [rɪ'taɪə]	in Rente gehen; sich zur Ruhe setzen	My grandpa **retired** from work when he was 65.
to **demolish** [dɪ'mɒlɪʃ]	vernichten	**to demolish** = to destroy
to **differ** ['dɪfə]	sich unterscheiden	**to differ** → difference
to **eradicate** [ɪ'rædɪkeɪt]	auslöschen	**to eradicate** = to eliminate
couple ['kʌpl]	Paar	A **couple** consists of two people or things.
barely ['beəli]	kaum	She could **barely** breathe because she was so scared.
to **nod** [nɒd]	nicken	If you agree, just **nod** your head.
to **divorce** [dɪ'vɔ:s]	sich scheiden lassen	**to divorce** ↔ to marry
to **seize** [ˌsi:z]	beschlagnahmen	**to seize** → seizure
to **inherit sth** [ɪn'herɪt]	etw erben	= to receive sth after sb has died
addict ['ædɪkt]	Süchtige/-r; Abhängige/-r	**addict** → addiction → addicted (to)
smoothly ['smu:ðli]	glatt; reibungslos	**smooth** ↔ rough
shelter ['ʃeltə]	Schutz; Obdach	When the rain started we found **shelter** under a roof.
universal basic income (UBI) [ˌju:nɪ'vɜ:sl ˌbeɪsɪk‿'ɪnkʌm]	allgemeines Grundeinkommen	One of the ideas to get rid of poverty is a **universal basic income**.
to **get by** [ˌget‿'baɪ]	zurechtkommen; durchkommen	**to get by** = to cope
motivation [ˌməʊtɪ'veɪʃn]	Motivation; Beweggründe	**motivation** → to motivate

to oversimplify [ˌəʊvə'sɪmplɪfaɪ]	zu stark vereinfachen	**to (over)simplify** ↔ to complexify
altogether [ˌɔːltə'geðə]	insgesamt; ganz und gar	There are **altogether** 15 students in my group.
to hand out [ˌhænd‿'aʊt]	austeilen	= to give sth to other people, usually for free
hopeless ['həʊpləs]	hoffnungslos	**hopeless** ↔ hopeful
to be work in progress [bi ˌwɜːk‿ɪn 'prəʊgres]	in Arbeit sein	**work in progress** ↔ finished
domestic abuse [dəˌmestɪk‿ə'bjuːs]	häusliche Gewalt	= mistreatment or harm by sb who shares the victim's living quarters
exploitation [ˌeksplɔɪ'teɪʃn]	Ausbeutung	**exploitation** → to exploit
to subsidise ['sʌbsɪdaɪz]	subventionieren; bezuschussen	The council **subsidised** the students' tickets.

Grammar workshop - Talking about likes and dislikes

core [kɔː]	Kern; Zentrum	Nobody understands the **core** of the problem.
to go on strike [ˌgəʊ‿ɒn 'straɪk]	streiken	Oh no, the train workers are **going on strike** tomorrow! How will I get to work?

Text workshop C - Inequality at work

labour market ['leɪbə ˌmɑːkɪt]	Arbeitsmarkt	= the number of people who are available for work in relation to the number of jobs available
figure ['fɪgə]	Ziffer; Zahl	**figure** = number
to advocate ['ædvəkeɪt]	eintreten für; befürworten; verteidigen	**to advocate** = to support
to be locked out [bi ˌlɒkt‿'aʊt]	ausgeschlossen sein; sich ausgeschlossen fühlen	**locked out** = excluded
suspended [sə'spendɪd]	außer Kraft gesetzt; gesperrt sein	One of my classmates **was suspended** for two weeks for skipping class so often.
to reinstate [ˌriːɪn'steɪt]	wiedereinsetzen	The company fired him and then **reinstated** him in his old job 4 weeks later. I wonder why?
progression [prə'greʃn]	Weiterentwicklung	**progression** = development
regulator ['regjəleɪtə]	Regulierungsbehörde	**regulator** → regulation → to regulate
bias ['baɪəs]	Voreingenommenheit; Vorurteil	This newspaper is known for its conservative **bias**.
to be awarded [bi‿ə'wɔːdɪd]	bekommen; zuerkannt werden	**to be awarded** = to receive
overall [ˌəʊvr'ɔːl]	insgesamt	**Overall**, I think it's a great idea, but I have one small issue with it.
median ['miːdiən]	mittlere/-r/-s; Mittel-	**median** = average
suggestion [sə'dʒestʃn]	Vorschlag; Anregung	**suggestion** → to suggest
entry-level [ˌentri'levl]	Anfänger-; Einsteiger-	The **entry-level** pay for beginners has been raised recently.
various ['veəriəs]	verschieden; verschiedenartig	This shop sells glasses in **various** shapes and sizes.
head [hed]	Leiter/-in; Chef/-in	= the person in charge
to distinguish [dɪ'stɪŋgwɪʃ]	unterscheiden; klar erkennen	Colourblind people cannot **distinguish** between certain colours, such as red and green.
legal entitlement [ˌliːgl‿ɪn'taɪtlmənt]	Rechtsanspruch	**legal entitlement** = legitimate claim
to boast [bəʊst]	prahlen; angeben	**to boast** = to show off
previous ['priːviəs]	vorherig; früher	**previous** ↔ following

Text workshop D - Workforce of the future

nursing home ['nɜ:sɪŋ ˌhəʊm]	Pflegeheim	**nursing** → nurse → to nurse
ageing ['eɪdʒɪŋ]	älterwerdend	Many cities around the world are seeing a rise in **ageing** populations.
unremarkable [ˌʌnrɪ'mɑ:kəbl]	nicht außergewöhnlich; nicht bemerkenswert; unauffällig	**unremarkable** ↔ remarkable
to **warn** [wɔ:n]	warnen	Experts have repeatedly **warned** of a shortage of skilled staff in healthcare.
to **argue** ['ɑ:gju:]	behaupten; erörtern	I would **argue** that wealth is not as important as health.
to **complement** ['kɒmplɪmənt]	ergänzen	**to complement** → complementary
entity ['entɪti]	Einheit	= a single and complete unit
selling point ['selɪŋ ˌpɔɪnt]	Verkaufsargument	Energy saving is the main **selling point** for a new fridge.
dozen ['dʌzn]	Dutzend	= twelve of sth
waist [weɪst]	Bauch; Taille	These trousers are too small, or my **waist** is too big!
lower back [ˌləʊə 'bæk]	Kreuz (Rücken)	Many desk workers have pain in their **lower back**.
to **ease** [i:z]	erleichtern; vereinfachen	**to ease** → easy
severe [sɪ'vɪə]	stark; schlimm	**severe** = serious
fertility rate [fə'tɪləti ˌreɪt]	Geburtenrate	= the average number of children born to a woman over her lifetime
healthcare ['helθˌkeə]	Gesundheitsversorgung	A good **healthcare** system benefits everyone.
deployment [dɪ'plɔɪmənt]	Verwendung; Einsatz	**deployment** = usage
widespread ['waɪdspred]	weit verbreitet	**widespread** = common
relatively ['relətɪvli]	vergleichsweise; verhältnismäßig	If you know French, then languages in the same family like Italian or Spanish are **relatively** easy to learn.
alongside [əˌlɒŋ'saɪd]	neben; daneben	The city built a number of big apartment houses **alongside** the waterfront.
to **fear sth** [fɪə]	fürchten	After hearing all this bad news I truly **fear** the worst.
professional sector [prəˌfeʃnl 'sektə]	beruflicher Bereich	**professional sector** = area of work
to **dread** [dred]	etw fürchten	**to dread** = to fear
purpose ['pɜ:pəs]	Ziel; Absicht; Zweck	= the reason why sth is done, the motive behind sth
to **head** ['hed]	zusteuern auf	If you **head for** a place, you move towards it.
adjutant ['adʒətnt]	Gehilfe; Adjutant	**adjutant** = aide
medieval serf [ˌmedii:vl 'sɜ:f]	mittelalterliche/-r Leibeigene/-r	**medieval** = during the Middle Ages **serf** → servant
insatiable [ɪn'seɪʃəbl]	unersättlich	**insatiable** ↔ satifiable
to **upend** [ˌʌp'end]	umkrempeln	**to upend** = to turn around; to disrupt
to **charge** [tʃɑ:dʒ]	berechnen; verlangen	= to ask for a certain amount to be paid for goods or services
slog [slɒg]	Schinderei	Cleaning the whole house in one day was a real **slog**.
to **be on the dole** *(BE)* [[bi‿ɒn ðə 'dəʊl]	Arbeitslosenunterstützung bekommen	= to receive benefits
to **get rid of sth** [get 'rɪd‿əv ˌsʌmθɪŋ]	etw loswerden	**fervour** ↔ passion
fervour ['fɜ:və]	Leidenschaft; Eifer	**fervour** = compassion

welfare ['welfeə]	Sozialhilfe	= money and/or services you get from the state or an organisation when you are in need
relegation [ˌrelɪ'geɪʃn]	Abstieg; Verbannung	**relegation** = assignment (usually to a lower position)
to **discriminate against** [dɪ'skrɪmɪneɪt‿əˌgenst]	diskriminieren; benachteiligen	**to discriminate** ↔ to include
to **intend to** [ɪn'tend tə]	beabsichtigen	**to intend to** → intention
to **monitor** ['mɒnɪtə]	überwachen; kontrollieren	= to check on a regular basis
Tube *(BE)* [tju:b]	U-Bahn	Another name for the London Underground is the **Tube**.
dependence [dɪ'pendəns]	Abhängigkeit	**dependence** → to depend

Topic project - Designing a social media job advert

shortage ['ʃɔ:tɪdʒ]	Knappheit; Mangel	**shortage** ↔ abundance
to **combat** ['kɒmbæt]	bekämpfen	**to combat** = to fight
knowledge *(no pl)* ['nɒlɪdʒ]	Wissen; Kenntnisse	**knowledge** → to know

D30 Vokabellernliste
D31 Classroom phrases

be, was/were, been	sein
beat, beat, beaten	schlagen
bear, bore, borne	tragen
become, became, become	werden
begin, began, begun	anfangen
blow, blew, blown	blasen
break, broke, broken	(zer)brechen
breed, bred, bred	züchten, erzeugen
bring, brought, brought	(mit)bringen
build, built, built	bauen
buy, bought, bought	kaufen
catch, caught, caught	fangen
choose, chose, chosen	wählen
come, came, come	kommen
cost, cost, cost	kosten
cut, cut, cut	schneiden
do, did, done	tun, machen
draw, drew, drawn	zeichnen
drink, drank, drunk	trinken
drive, drove, driven	fahren
eat, ate, eaten	essen
fall, fell, fallen	fallen
feel, felt, felt	(sich) fühlen
fight, fought, fought	(be)kämpfen
find, found, found	finden
flee, fled, fled	fliehen, flüchten
fly, flew, flown	fliegen
forbid, forbade, forbidden	verbieten
forget, forgot, forgotten	vergessen
freeze, froze, frozen	frieren
get, got, got	bekommen
give, gave, given	geben
go, went, gone	gehen, fahren
grow, grew, grown	wachsen
hang, hung, hung	hängen
have, had, had	haben
hear, heard, heard	hören
hide, hid, hidden	(sich) verstecken
hit, hit, hit	schlagen
hold, held, held	(fest)halten
hurt, hurt, hurt	(sich) wehtun
keep, kept, kept	aufbewahren
know, knew, known	wissen; kennen
lead, led, led	führen
leave, left, left	(ver)lassen
lend, lent, lent	(ver)leihen

lie, lay, lain	liegen
lose, lost, lost	verlieren
make, made, made	machen
mean, meant, meant	meinen, bedeuten
meet, met, met	treffen
pay, paid, paid	bezahlen
read, read, read	lesen
ride, rode, ridden	reiten, fahren
ring, rang, rung	klingeln
rise, rose, risen	steigen
run, ran, run	laufen
say, said, said	sagen
see, saw, seen	sehen
seek, sought, sought	suchen
sell, sold, sold	verkaufen
send, sent, sent	senden
set, set, set	setzen; aufstellen
shine, shone, shone	scheinen
shoot, shot, shot	(er)schießen
show, showed, shown	zeigen
shrink, shrank, shrunk	schrumpfen
shut, shut, shut	schließen
sing, sang, sung	singen
sink, sank, sunk	sinken
sit, sat, sat	sitzen
sleep, slept, slept	schlafen
speak, spoke, spoken	sprechen
spend, spent, spent	ausgeben; verbringen
split, split, split	teilen, trennen
spread, spread, spread	ausbreiten
stand, stood, stood	stehen
steal, stole, stolen	stehlen
strike, struck, struck	schlagen; betreffen
strive, strove, striven	anstreben, sich bemühen
swim, swam, swum	schwimmen
take, took, taken	nehmen
teach, taught, taught	unterrichten
tear, tore, torn	zerreißen
tell, told, told	sagen; erzählen
think, thought, thought	denken
throw, threw, thrown	werfen
understand, understood, understood	verstehen
wake, woke, woken	aufwachen
wear, wore, worn	tragen
win, won, won	gewinnen
write, wrote, written	schreiben

Quellennachweis

10 plainpicture GmbH & Co. KG, Hamburg (Cavan Images/Cavan Social); **12.1** ShutterStock.com RF, New York (Brum); **12.2** Getty Images Plus, München (iStock / BoraYetimoglu); **12.3** ShutterStock.com RF, New York (Photographee.eu); **12.4** ShutterStock.com RF, New York (franco lucato); **13** stock.adobe.com, Dublin (Marco Birn); **14.1** ShutterStock.com RF, New York (Alexander Prokopenko); **14.2** graphitecture book & edition, Bernau am Chiemsee, Nach: Joseph Poore & Thomas Nemecek, Science, 2018; **16** stock.adobe.com, Dublin (Jukov studio); **17** Alamy stock photo, Abingdon (Peter Alvey); **18** ShutterStock.com RF, New York (fizkes); **20.1** ShutterStock.com RF, New York (Nicole Glass Photography); **22** stock.adobe.com, Dublin (HollyHarry); **23** graphitecture book & edition, Bernau am Chiemsee. Nach: Department for Business, Energy & Industrial Strategy, 2020. www.gov.uk; **24** ShutterStock.com RF, New York (dies-irae); **25** Getty Images Plus/Microstock, München (iStock / ipeggas); **27** Ben Lecomte; **28.1** Alamy stock photo, Abingdon (Paulo Oliveira); **28.2** Stuff Limited; **29.1** ShutterStock.com RF, New York (Thomas Dutour); **31** CartoonStock Ltd, Bath (Madden, Chris); **32.1** ShutterStock.com RF, New York (Monkey Business Images); **32.2** Getty Images, München (Moment / Halfpoint Images); **32.3** ShutterStock.com RF, New York (mustbeyou); **33.1** akg-images, Berlin (Album / Atlantic Productions); **33.3** graphitecture book & edition, Bernau am Chiemsee ; ShutterStock.com RF, New York (Liudmila Klymenko); (Ikons Bio Diversität EPS); Text: 6 biggest threats to biodiversity, 2018, https://www.bioexplorer.net/threats-to-biodiversity.html/; **34** ShutterStock.com RF, New York (DreamHack); **37.1** graphitecture book & edition, Bernau am Chiemsee, nach: Eurostat, 2019; **37.2** CartoonStock Ltd, Bath (Benjamin Schwartz); **38.1** ShutterStock.com RF, New York (Gorodenkoff); **38.2** Getty Images Plus, München (iStock / kynny); **38.3** ShutterStock.com RF, New York (vchal); **38.4** ShutterStock.com RF, New York (ducu59us); **38.5** ShutterStock.com RF, New York (ImageFlow); **41** CartoonStock Ltd, Bath (Dator, Joe); **42.1** © 2020 Guardian News & Media Ltd., London; **42.2** graphitecture book & edition, Bernau am Chiemsee. Source: Cinch Home Services, 2021; **43.1** ShutterStock.com RF, New York (CECIL BO DZWOWA); **43.2** Alamy stock photo, Abingdon (RZAF_Images); **43.3** Picture-Alliance, Frankfurt/M. (REUTERS/Noor Khamis); **45** Nach: wearesocial.com 2018.; **46** CartoonStock Ltd, Bath (Royston Robertson); **47** ShutterStock.com RF, New York (Trueffelpix); **49** ShutterStock.com RF, New York (metamorworks); **50.1** ShutterStock.com RF, New York (TotallyMJ); **50.2** ShutterStock.com RF, New York (Visual Generation); **53.1** CartoonStock Ltd, Bath (Steve Greenberg); **53.2** graphitecture book & edition, Bernau am Chiemsee. Source: International Science Survey 2019-2020. Q20. „Science and Sceintists Held in High Esteem Across Global Publics"; **54.1** ShutterStock.com RF, New York (MemoryMan); **57** https://creativecommons.org/licenses/by-nd/4.0/, Mountain View ; CC-BY-ND-4.0 Lizenzbestimmungen: https://creativecommons.org/licenses/by-nd/4.0/legalcode. Source: Pew Research Center, siehe *2; **58.1** Boclips/TED-Ed Animations; **58.2** Getty Images Plus, München (Ahmed Muntasir); **59.1** ShutterStock.com RF, New York (PopTika); **59.2** ShutterStock.com RF, New York (Gorodenkoff); **59.3** ShutterStock.com RF, New York; **59.4** ShutterStock.com RF, New York (Gorodenkoff); **59.5** ShutterStock.com RF, New York (Zapp2Photo); **59.6** ShutterStock.com RF, New York (TarikVision); **60** ShutterStock.com RF, New York (ChickenDoodleDesigns); **64.1** Alamy stock photo, Abingdon (Jochen Tack); **64.2** Getty Images Plus, München (E+ / johnnyscriv); **64.3** Getty Images Plus, München (DigitalVision / Tony Anderson); **64.4** ShutterStock.com RF, New York (HollyHarry); **64.5** Kranenberg, Hendrik, Drolshagen; **66.1** Getty Images Plus, München (E+ / Eva-Katalin); **68** stock.adobe.com, Dublin (alfa27); **69.1** Polyp cartoons - Paul Fitzgerald, Manchester M15 5RF; **69.2** CartoonStock Ltd, Bath (Maria Scrivan); **70.1** Stephen Cunningsworth Photography, London; **73.1** ShutterStock.com RF, New York (Jacob Lund); **75** www.CartoonStock.com, Bath (Morris, John); **77** ShutterStock.com RF, New York (Mirage_studio); **80** Getty Images, München (MediaNews Group/Bay Area News via Getty Images); **81** ShutterStock.com RF, New York (Rawpixel.com); **82** Alamy Ltd., Abingdon (M&N); **83** graphitecture book & edition, Bernau am Chiemsee, nach: Epsilon, 2019; **85** CartoonStock Ltd, Bath (Joseph Farris); **87.1** graphitecture book & edition, Bernau am Chiemsee; **87.3** www.CartoonStock.com, Bath (Royston Robertson); **88.1** Picture-Alliance, Frankfurt/M. (John Bazemore / AP Photo); **88.2** ShutterStock.com RF, New York (lev radin); **88.3** Getty Images Plus, München (DigitalVision / Matteo Colombo); **88.4** ShutterStock.com RF, New York (Everett Historical); **88.5** ShutterStock.com RF, New York (anderm); **89** 2021, BoClips / Canadian Broadcasting Corporation; **90.1** Picture-Alliance, Frankfurt/M. (AP / Invision / Evan Agostini); **93** akg-images, Berlin; **94.1** Getty Images, München (Portland Press Herald); **96** Bernhard, Julia - Illustratorin, Mainz; **97** Bernhard, Julia - Illustratorin, Mainz; **98.1** ullstein bild, Berlin (dpa, Deutsche Presseagentur / EP); **99.1** Getty Images, München (Bettmann); **101.1** ShutterStock.com RF, New York (Paopano); **101.2** graphitecture book & edition, Bernau am Chiemsee, nach: Berlesmann Stiftung; **102.1** stock.adobe.com, Dublin (warloka79); **104** Alamy stock photo, Abingdon (Daniren); **106** ShutterStock.com RF, New York (DW labs Incorporated); **107** Media Office GmbH, Kornwestheim/nach: Max Galka, Metrocosm, 2016; **108** Mauritius Images, Mittenwald (Shawshots / Alamy); **109** graphitecture book & edition, Bernau am Chiemsee ; © Statista 2021. Source: United States; BEA; US Department of Commerce; 2020; (Percentage added to the Gross Domestic Product (GDP) of the United States of America in 2020, by industry); **112.1** Mauritius Images, Mittenwald (Robert Melen); **112.2** Alamy stock photo, Abingdon (Edward Simons); **112.3** Mauritius Images, Mittenwald (John Potter); **112.4** Getty Images, München (Westend61); **113** CartoonStock Ltd, Bath (Marian Kamensky); **114.1** Alamy stock photo, Abingdon (Britain); **116** graphitecture book & edition, Bernau am Chiemsee, nach: ITV/ComRes; **117.1** ShutterStock.com RF, New York (CKP1001); **119** Getty Images Plus, München (iStock / shironosov); **120.2** Alamy stock photo, Abingdon; **121** Zwick, Joachim, Gießen; **122** Schaar, Wolfgang, Grafing; **123.1** Alamy stock photo, Abingdon (Matt Crossick); **126.1** Schobel, Ingrid, Hannover; nach ©2021 Guardian News & Media Ltd.; (Sixty-nine tributes to slave traders, colonialists and racists have been removed across the UK); **126.2** Alamy stock photo, Abingdon (PA Images); **127.1** ddp media GmbH, Hamburg (Graeme Robertson); **129** Getty Images, München (TF-Images / DeFodi Images); **130.1** From Class system in the UK. Video supplied by BBC Worldwide Learning; **130.2** CartoonStock Ltd, Bath (Marty Bucella); **131.1** ShutterStock.com RF, New York (Ron Adar); **131.2** Getty Images, München (NurPhoto); **131.3** Alamy stock photo, Abingdon (WENN Rights Ltd); **131.4** Alamy stock photo, Abingdon (GARY DOAK); **133** ShutterStock.com RF, New York (Ivan Marc); **136.1** Getty Images Plus, München (DigitalVision / Stephen Zeigler); **136.2** ShutterStock.com RF, New York (AlessandroBiascioli); **136.3** Getty Images Plus, München (E+ / SrdjanPav); **136.4** Getty Images Plus, München (E+ / SolStock); **136.5** ShutterStock.com RF, New York (Durch Rawpixel.com); **138.1** ddp media GmbH, Hamburg (Leonardo Cendamo/opale.photo/lai); **141.1** stock.adobe.com, Dublin (Hurca!); **141.2** Tom Silverstone, Francisco Navas, 25th July 2019 Copyright Guardian News & Media Ltd 2020; **142.1** laif, Köln (Cassidy Araiza/The Guardian); **144** © BBC Motion Gallery — British Broadcasting Corporation — Media Centre, London; **145** iStockphoto, Calgary, Alberta (SnowWhiteimages); **146.1** imago images/Everett Collection. Film Poster: The Big Sick, written by Emily V. Gordon & Kumail Nanjiani, directed by Michael Showalter.; **149.1** ShutterStock.com RF, New York (Rawpixel.com); **149.2** ShutterStock.com RF, New York (Sea Wave); **149.3** Getty Images Plus, München (iStock / Deklofenak); **149.4** Alamy stock photo, Abingdon (Todd Bannor); **150.1** ShutterStock.com RF, New York (Mary Long); **153.2** CartoonStock Ltd, Bath (Fran); **154.1** ShutterStock.com RF, New York (minnebaevpro); **154.2** ShutterStock.com RF, New York (Kzenon); **154.3** ShutterStock.com RF, New York (Africa Studio); **154.4** ShutterStock.com RF, New York (BrAt82); **154.5** Getty Images, München (Felisandro Pasana / EyeEm); **154.6** ShutterStock.com RF, New York; **155.1** Interfoto, München (Glasshouse Images); **155.2** ShutterStock.com RF, New York (Kathy Hutchins); **160.1** ShutterStock.com RF, New York (nexus 7); **160.2** Getty Images Plus, München (iStock / AvigatorPhotographer); **160.3** Getty Images Plus, München (iStock / gorodenkoff); **161.1** Getty Images Plus, München (E+ / pixelfusion3d); **164** Alamy stock photo, Abingdon (SCPhotos / Rob Crandall); **165** ShutterStock.com RF, New York (fizkes); **166.1** ShutterStock.com RF, New York (aleknext); **166.2** ShutterStock.com RF, New York (fizkes); **166.3** ShutterStock.com RF, New York (fizkes); **166.4** ShutterStock.com RF, New York (Jat306); **167.1** ShutterStock.com RF, New York (Enkel); **169** CartoonStock Ltd, Bath (Mike Mosedale); **170.1** ShutterStock.com RF, New York (Stuart Jenner); **170.2** ShutterStock.com RF, New York (Cookie Studio); **170.3** Getty Images Plus, München (E+ / LordHenriVoton); **170.4** ShutterStock.com RF, New York (stockfour); **170.5** ShutterStock.com RF, New York (Annette Shaff); **171.1** ShutterStock.com RF, New York (Albert Stephen Julius); **173** Getty Images, München

(Anadolu Agency); **174** 2020, BoClips / Newsy; **175.1** ShutterStock.com RF, New York (desdemona72); **177** Kate Raworth and Christian Guthier. CC-BY-SA 4.0 https://creativecommons.org/licenses/by-sa/4.0/deed.de, Mountain View ; CC-BY-SA-4.0 Lizenzbestimmungen: https://creativecommons.org/licenses/by-sa/4.0/legalcode, siehe *3; **178** graphitecture book & edition, Bernau am Chiemsee. Nach: Joseph Poore & Thomas Nemecek, Science (2018) und MarketWatch reporting, 2019; **179** Getty Images Plus, München (iStock / nito100); **180.1** ShutterStock.com RF, New York (Nomad1988); **180.3** graphitecture book & edition, Bernau am Chiemsee, nach: Ethnologue; **181** Mauritius Images, Mittenwald (Image Press Agency); **183** CartoonStock Ltd, Bath (Tim Mellish); **185.1** Tony Biddle, Perfect World Design, Toronto, ON; **186.1** ShutterStock.com RF, New York (Vadym Pastukh); **186.2** ShutterStock.com RF, New York (Matt Gibson); **186.3** Mauritius Images, Mittenwald (mexb5m); **186.4** stock.adobe.com, Dublin (ixelbliss); **187** Oser, Liliane, Hamburg; **187** graphitecture book & edition, Bernau am Chiemsee; **188.1** stock.adobe.com, Dublin (magele-picture); **190** ShutterStock.com RF, New York (Khakimullin Aleksandr); **191.1** ShutterStock.com RF, New York (microcosmos); **194** ShutterStock.com RF, New York (1000 Words); **195.1** stock.adobe.com, Dublin (Andrey Popov); **196** ShutterStock.com RF, New York (Syda Productions); **197** https://www.statista.com/chart/3958/gender-pay-gap-by-ethnicity/ - statista - Quellle: National Women's Law Centre, AAUW
https://creativecommons.org/licenses/by-sa/4.0/deed.de, Mountain View ; CC-BY-SA-4.0 Lizenzbestimmungen: https://creativecommons.org/licenses/by-sa/4.0/legalcode, siehe *3; **198** CartoonStock Ltd, Bath (Barry Deutsch); **199.1** Getty Images Plus, München (iStock / miriam-doerr); **200** Getty Images Plus, München (iStock / miriam-doerr); **201** Alamy Ltd., Abingdon (Ihor Svetiukha); **202.2** © BBC Motion Gallery — British Broadcasting Corporation — Media Centre, London; **203** ShutterStock.com RF, New York (metamorworks); **204.1** ShutterStock.com RF, New York (Stokkete); **204.2** graphitecture book & edition, Bernau am Chiemsee, nach: OECD; **205.1** ShutterStock.com RF, New York (Monkey Business Images); **205.2** graphitecture book & edition, Bernau am Chiemsee, nach: ILO; **208.2** CartoonStock Ltd, Bath (Roz Chast); **209** Statista GmbH, Hamburg, May 2021 Sources: Alight Solutions; National Business Group on Health; **212.1** Alamy stock photo, Abingdon (Keith Ramsey); **238** stock.adobe.com, Dublin (Igor Mojzes); **240** Thinkstock, München (iStock / gpointstudio); **241** iStockphoto, Calgary, Alberta (R-J-Seymour); **242** ShutterStock.com RF, New York (Jacob Lund); **246** iStockphoto, Calgary, Alberta (Steve Debenport); **248** Getty Images Plus, München (iStock / Rawpixel); **248** ShutterStock.com RF, New York (Diego Cervo); **250** stock.adobe.com, Dublin (kaipong); **252.1** Romo, Virginia, Stuttgart; **252.2** Romo, Virginia, Stuttgart; **252.3** Romo, Virginia, Stuttgart; **253.1** Bananastock, Watlington / Oxon; **253.2** MEV Verlag GmbH, Augsburg; **253.3** Thinkstock, München (iStockphoto); **253.4** Avenue Images GmbH, Hamburg (Stockbyte RF, George Doyle); **257** Getty Images Plus, München (swissmediavision/E+); **258** stock.adobe.com, Dublin (Photographee.eu); **260.1** Getty Images Plus, München (Anna_Om/iStock); **260.2** Getty Images Plus, München (tobiasjo/iStock); **260.3** Getty Images Plus, München (tobiasjo/iStock); **260.4** Getty Images Plus, München (javarman3/iStock); **260.5** Getty Images Plus, München (Pilipavicius/iStock); **260.6** Getty Images Plus, München (nikpal/iStock); **262.1** Ernst Klett Verlag GmbH, Stuttgart; **262.2** Ernst Klett Verlag GmbH, Stuttgart; **262.3** Ernst Klett Verlag GmbH, Stuttgart; **263** Romo, Virginia, Stuttgart; **268** iStockphoto, Calgary, Alberta (clu); **269** Alamy stock photo, Abingdon; **270** Getty Images Plus, München (PeopleImages); **273.1** imago images, Berlin (imago stock&people); **273.2** imago images, Berlin (imago stock&people); **274** www.panthermedia.net, München (keerati); **275** plainpicture GmbH & Co. KG, Hamburg (plainpicture); **277.2** Romo, Virginia, Stuttgart; **343** Ernst Klett Verlag GmbH, Stuttgart; **346** Ernst Klett Verlag GmbH, Stuttgart; KOMA AMOK ®, Stuttgart; KOMA AMOK ®, Stuttgart; KOMA AMOK ®, Stuttgart; KOMA AMOK ®, Stuttgart; KOMA AMOK ®, Stuttgart; KOMA AMOK ®, Stuttgart; KOMA AMOK ®, Stuttgart; **Umschlag** Getty Images RF, München (Hero Images)

*3 Lizenzbestimmungen zu CC-BY-SA-4.0 siehe: http://creativecommons.org/licenses/by-sa/4.0/legalcode
*2 Lizenzbestimmungen zu CC-BY-ND-4.0 siehe: http://creativecommons.org/licenses/by-nd/4.0/legalcode

Text:

15 Sarah Marsh ©2021 Guardian News & Media Ltd.; **20.2** Diederik Baazil and Laura Millan Lombrana, 04.06.2021, www.bloomberg.com; **26** by Hilary Brueck, https://www.businessinsider.de, 13th August 2019; **29.2** Dry by Neal Shusterman and Jarrod Shusterman, Simon & Schuster Inc., 2018, p. 3-8; **33.2** Attributed to David Attenborough; **35** Keynote speech delivered by HRH The Prince of Wales at the World Economic Forum in Davos, Switzerland, 22.01.2020, https://www.princeofwales.gov.uk/; **37.3** Attributed to David Attenborough; **40** Andreas Weigend, Data for the people: How to make our post-privacy economy work for you; Publisher: Basic Books, New York, 2017; **43.4** Revolutionary technologies will drive African prosperity – this is why, Cathy Smith, World Economic Forum, 2019; **51** Dan Rather, ©2019 Guardian News & Media Ltd.; **54.2** Colin Neville, Inversion; from Momaya Short Story Review 2017 Utopia Dystopia, Momaya Press, p. 29-33; **61** Sarah Baxter, ©2020, Guardian News&Media Ltd.; **66.2** Dev Sarkar, MENSXP, 2018; **70.2** Aja Barber ©2019 Guardian News & Media Ltd.; **73.2** From: Copygirl, Anna Mitchael & Michelle Sassa, Berkley Books, New York, an imprint of Penguin Random House LLC, 2015; **78** The power of purpose: How taking a stand helps brands to win customer's hearts (and business), Ash Read, Buffer.com, 2019; **84** ©2021 Jennifer Bailey, tinybuddha.com; **87.2** Attributed to Margaret Cho; **90.2** Jason Opal, https://theconversation.com; **94.2** Abdi Nor Iftin, Call Me American; Alfred A. Knopf, Random House, 2018, S. 274-276; **98.2** July 19, 1988, The Reverend Jesse Louis Jackson; **99.2** Luke Harding ©2021 Guardian News & Media Ltd.; **102.2** Joe Biden, 4th February 2021, www.whitehouse.gov; **110** © 2021 CBS Interactive Inc.; **114.2** Katy Guest © 2019 Guardian News & Media Ltd.; **117.2** Virginia Postrel, 2019 https://www.bloombergquint.com; **120.1** Rebecca Nicholson ©2021 Guardian News & Media Ltd.; **123.2** From Blonde Roots ©2009 Bernardine Evaristo; **127.2** Marcus Rashford ©2020 Guardian News & Media Ltd.; **134** Akram Khan ©2019 Guardian News & Media Ltd.; **138.2** From The Vanishing Half ©2020 Brit Bennett; **140.1** From The Vanishing Half ©2020 Brit Bennett; **140.2** From The Vanishing Half ©2020 Brit Bennett; **142.2** © 2019 Guardian News & Media Ltd.; **146.2** The Big Sick © 2017 Emily V. Gordon & Kumail Nanjiani; **150.2** ©2020, Newport Academy, www.newportacademy.com; **150.3** https://www.time-to-change.org.uk; **153.1** ©2020, Newport Academy, www.newportacademy.com; **156** 30.03.2020 Marie Beecham auf Twitter; **157** 2014. Tayler B Ulmer, www.matadornetwork.com; **161.2** 2016, Barack Obama; **161.3** Kofi Annan, Address to World Economic Forum in Davos, 31st January 1999; **161.4** 2001, Jack Welch; **161.5** from: Doughnut Economics: Seven Ways to Think Like a 21st-Century Economist , ©2018 Kate Raworth; **162** From: Transmission, © 2004 Hari Kunzru; **167.2** Angela Ng, 2019 https://www.userinterviews.com; **171.2** Anna Nagurney, 05.04.2021, www.theconversation.com; **175.2** Robert Raymond, 26.01.2021, www.shareable.net; **180.2** attributed to René Girard; **182** 12.02.2021, Ulrike Schneeweiß, https://www.helmholtz.de; **185.2** Kofi Annan, Address to Harvard University, September 17, 1998; **188.2** Robert Skidelsky and Edward Skidelsky, How much is enough? Other Press, 2013, pp. ix-xii.; **191.2** Rosalyn Kelly, One wage; from Momaya Short Story Review 2017 Utopia Dystopia, Momaya Press, S. 103-112; **195.2** Richard Adams ©2020 Guardian News & Media Ltd.; **199.2** 2020, Bryan Lufkin, British Broadcasting Corporation; **202.1** Capucine Yeomans, 2018, https://www.linkedin.com; **206** Hazel Davis © 2017, Guardian News & Media Ltd.; **207** 2019, Greta Thunberg; **208.1** Attributed to Tyler Perry, https://www.positivityblog.com/quotes-for-work/, 2022; **210** Frauke Schobelt; 2018, Werben & Verkaufen, www.wuv.de; **212.2** Jr Harper, 2020 www.dw.com; **214** Liz Mohn, Bertelsmann Stiftung, 2008; **277.1** From: The White Tiger ©2008, Aravind Adiga;

International Boundary
Internal Boundary
LONDON National Capital
Belfast Administrative Unit Capital
LONDON over 1 000 000 inhabitants
LEEDS 500 000 – 1 000 000 inhabitants
Oxford 100 000 – 500 000 inhabitants
Cambridge under 100 000 inhabitants
Urban Area
Railway
Tunnel
Car Ferry
Motorway
Road
International Airport
Coastline
River
Lake
Canal
0 50 100 150 km
ATLANTIC OCEAN
UNITED KINGDOM
North Sea
Irish Sea
English Channel
SCOTLAND
ENGLAND
WALES
NORTHERN IRELAND
IRELAND
NETHERLANDS
BELGIUM
FRANCE
ISLE OF MAN
GUERNSEY
JERSEY
Shetland Islands
Orkney Islands
Outer Hebrides
Inner Hebrides
Unst
Yell
Mainland
Lerwick
Foula
Fair Isle
Westray
Sanday
Kirkwall
Hoy
Pentland Firth
Rona
Wick
Flannan Is.
Stornoway
Lewis
North Minch
Little Minch
St. Kilda
North Uist
South Uist
Barra
Skye
Rhum
Coll
Mull
Jura
Islay
Arran
Loch Shin
Moray Firth
Inverness
Loch Ness
Spey
Dee
Aberdeen
Fort William
Tay
Dundee
Firth of Tay
Firth of Lorn
Sea of the Hebrides
Loch Lomond
Firth of Forth
Edinburgh
GLASGOW
Clyde
Tweed
Kilmarnock
Firth of Clyde
North Channel
Stranraer
Larne
Londonderry
Lough Foyle
L. Neagh
L. Erne
Belfast
Donegal Bay
Sligo
Achill I.
Dundalk
L. Mask
L. Ree
L. Corrib
Galway
Galway Bay
Aran Is.
Shannon
Tullamore
DUBLIN
(BAILE ÁTHA CLIATH)
Lough Derg
Limerick
Kilkenny
Barrow
Suir
Tralee
Blackwater
Waterford
Rosslare Harbour
Cork
St. George's Channel
Newcastle upon Tyne
Tyne
Sunderland
Carlisle
Eden
Solway Firth
Middlesbrough
Douglas
Lancaster
York
Blackpool
Bradford
LEEDS
Kingston upon Hull
Bolton
Huddersfield
Trent
Humber
Grimsby
Anglesey
Liverpool
Birkenhead
Manchester
Holyhead
Stockport
SHEFFIELD
The Wash
Stoke-on-Trent
Derby
Nottingham
Cardigan Bay
Norwich
Great Yarmouth
Walsall
Leicester
Ouse
Wolverhampton
BIRMINGHAM
Peterborough
Coventry
Northampton
Severn
Cambridge
Fishguard
Wye
Stratford-upon-Avon
Ipswich
Gloucester
Luton
Harwich
Milford Haven
Oxford
Rhondda
Newport
Thames
LONDON
Southend on Sea
Swansea
Bristol
Greenwich
Cardiff
Bath
Reading
Canterbury
Bristol Channel
Dover
Lundy
Salisbury
Strait of Dover
Calais
Hastings
Southampton
Brighton
Exeter
Portsmouth
Newhaven
Bournemouth
Isle of Wight
Torbay
Weymouth
Penzance
Plymouth
Isles of Scilly
Cherbourg
Seine Bay
St. Peter Port
St. Helier
Le Havre
Rouen
Seine
Beauvais
Oise
Amiens
Somme
St-Quentin
Aisne
Reims
Dunkerque
Lille
Ostend
Brugge (Brugge)
Ghent
Antwerp
BRUSSELS
ROTTERDAM
The Hague
Haarlem
Alkmaar
Texel
60
58
56
54
52
50
12
10
8
6
4
2
0